LIBRARY OF HEBREW BIBLE/
OLD TESTAMENT STUDIES

577

Formerly Journal for the Study of the Old Testament Supplement Series

PROPHECY AND POWER

Jeremiah in Feminist and Postcolonial Perspective

Edited by

Christl M. Maier

and

Carolyn J. Sharp

Bloomsbury T&T Clark
An imprint of Bloomsbury Publishing Plc

B L O O M S B U R Y
LONDON · NEW DELHI · NEW YORK · SYDNEY

Bloomsbury T&T Clark

An imprint of Bloomsbury Publishing Plc

Imprint previously known as T&T Clark

50 Bedford Square	1385 Broadway
London	New York
WC1B 3DP	NY 10018
UK	USA

www.bloomsbury.com

BLOOMSBURY, T&T CLARK and the Diana logo are trademarks of Bloomsbury Publishing Plc

First published 2013
Paperback edition first published 2015

British Library Cataloguing-in-Publication Data
A catalogue record for this book is available from the British Library.

ISBN: HB: 978-0-5671-8211-1
PB: 978-0-5676-6305-4
ePDF: 978-0-5670-2865-5

Library of Congress Cataloging-in-Publication Data
A catalog record for this book is available from the Library of Congress.

Series: The Library of Hebrew Bible/Old Testament Studies

Typeset by Forthcoming Publications Ltd (www.forthpub.com)

CONTENTS

"LIKE A WOMAN IN LABOR":
GENDER, POSTCOLONIAL, QUEER, AND TRAUMA PERSPECTIVES
ON THE BOOK OF JEREMIAH

ACKNOWLEDGMENTS

This volume would not have been possible without the generous support of the Alexander von Humboldt Foundation, which underwrote our collaboration on this project and the related Jeremiah commentary via a TransCoop grant. We are deeply grateful to Harold W. Attridge, recent former dean of Yale Divinity School, who provided matching funds that have been crucial for continuing support of our collaborative work in New Haven and Marburg. We were inspired by the intellectual vision of scholars who participated in the Jeremiah consultation at Yale Divinity School in September 2010: Mark Brummitt, Mary Chilton Callaway, Steed V. Davidson, Wilda C. Gafney, and Judith E. McKinlay. We found equally energizing the intellectual engagements offered by colleagues who participated in the consultation on Jeremiah and commentary writing at Philipps-Universität Marburg in May 2011: Ulrike Bail, Gerlinde Baumann, Irmtraud Fischer, Michaela Geiger, Alexandra Grund, Else K. Holt, Ruth Poser, Ulrike Sals, and Ingrun Weiß.

We are grateful to the Writing/Reading Jeremiah group of the Society of Biblical Literature for sponsoring a panel entitled "Feminist and Postcolonial Perspectives on Jeremiah" related to this book at the 2011 SBL Annual Meeting in San Francisco. We owe a debt of gratitude to our research assistants on both sides of the Atlantic: Heather V. Vermeulen, Spencer Kasko, Mareike Schmied, Josephine Haas, Tabea Kraaz, and Sebastian Plötzgen. We offer our thanks to Claudia V. Camp for accepting this volume in the Library of Hebrew Bible/Old Testament Studies series, and to the excellent staff at Bloomsbury T&T Clark, especially Anna Turton and Caitlin Flynn. Finally, we thank our copy-editor, Duncan Burns, for his work on the manuscript.

We have learned much from this project. It is our hope that these essays will catalyze continuing feminist and postcolonial engagement with the tumultuous and haunting book of Jeremiah.

Christl M. Maier and Carolyn J. Sharp
15 February 2013

ABBREVIATIONS

AB	Anchor Bible
ABD	*The Anchor Bible Dictionary.* Edited by David Noel Freedman. 6 vols. New York: Doubleday, 1992
AGJU	Arbeiten zur Geschichte des antiken Judentums und des Urchristentums
AOTC	Abingdon Old Testament Commentaries
ASV	American Standard Version
ATD	Das Alte Testament Deutsch
ATR	*Anglican Theological Review*
ATSAT	Arbeiten zu Text und Sprache im Alten Testament
BBB	Bonner Biblische Beiträge
Bib	*Biblica*
BibInt	*Biblical Interpretation: A Journal of Contemporary Approaches*
BIS	Biblical Interpretation Series
BKAT	Biblischer Kommentar: Altes Testament
BZ	*Biblische Zeitschrift*
BZAW	Beihefte zur Zeitschrift für die alttestamentliche Wissenschaft
CBQ	*Catholic Biblical Quarterly*
CBR	*Currents in Biblical Research*
CEV	Contemporary English Version
ConBNT	Coniectanea biblica, New Testament
CRBS	*Currents in Research: Biblical Studies*
ExpTim	*Expository Times*
Exuz	Exegese in unserer Zeit
FAT	Forschungen zum Alten Testament
FCB	Feminist Companion to the Bible
FOTL	Forms of the Old Testament Literature
FRLANT	Forschungen zur Religion und Literatur des Alten und Neuen Testaments
HAR	*Hebrew Annual Review*
HALOT	Koehler, L., W. Baumgartner, and J. J. Stamm, *The Hebrew and Aramaic Lexicon of the Old Testament.* Translated and edited under the supervision of M. E. J. Richardson. 4 vols. Leiden, 1994–1999
HAT	Handbuch zum Alten Testament
HBS	Herders Biblische Studien
HSM	Harvard Semitic Monographs
HTKAT	Herders Theologischer Kommentar zum Alten Testament

HTR	*Harvard Theological Review*
IBC	Interpretation: A Bible Commentary for Teaching and Preaching
ICC	International Critical Commentary
IECOT	International Exegetical Commentary on the Old Testament
JBL	*Journal of Biblical Literature*
JFSR	*Journal of Feminist Studies in Religion*
JR	*Journal of Religion*
JSem	*Journal of Semitics*
JSJ	*Journal for the Study of Judaism in the Persian, Hellenistic and Roman Period*
JSOT	*Journal for the Study of the Old Testament*
JSOTSup	Journal for the Study of the Old Testament: Supplement Series
JSP	*Journal for the Study of the Pseudepigrapha*
KHC	Kurzer Hand-Commentar zum Alten Testament
KJV	King James Version
LHBOTS	Library of the Hebrew Bible/Old Testament Studies
LXX	Septuagint
MT	Masoretic Text
NASB	New American Standard Bible
NEchtB	Neue Echter Bibel
NICOT	New International Commentary on the Old Testament
NIV	New International Version
NJPS	*Tanakh*, produced by the Jewish Publication Society
NRSV	New Revised Standard Version
NSKAT	Neuer Stuttgarter Kommentar: Altes Testament
OBO	Orbis Biblicus et Orientalis
OBT	Overtures to Biblical Theology
OTL	Old Testament Library
OTS	Old Testament Studies
RBL	*Review of Biblical Literature*
SBLSS	Society of Biblical Literature Semeia Studies
SBLSymS	Society of Biblical Literature Symposium Series
SJOT	*Scandinavian Journal of the Old Testament*
TDOT	*Theological Dictionary of the Old Testament*. Edited by G. J. Botterweck and H. Ringgren. Translated by J. T. Willis. 14 vols. Grand Rapids: Eerdmans, 1974–93
VT	*Vetus Testamentum*
VTSup	Supplements to Vetus Testamentum
WBC	Word Biblical Commentary
WiBiLex	*Das wissenschaftliche Bibellexikon im Internet (www.wibilex.de)*
WMANT	Wissenschaftliche Monographien zum Alten und Neuen Testament
WW	*Word and World*
ZAW	*Zeitschrift für die alttestamentliche Wissenschaft*
ZBKAT	Zürcher Bibelkommentar Altes Testament

LIST OF CONTRIBUTORS

Walter Brueggemann, Professor Emeritus of Old Testament, Columbia Theological Seminary, Decatur, Georgia, USA

L. Juliana Claassens, Associate Professor of Old Testament, Stellenbosch University, South Africa

Steed Vernyl Davidson, Assistant Professor of Old Testament, Pacific Lutheran Theological School and the Graduate Theological Union, Berkeley, California, USA

Irmtraud Fischer, Professor for Old Testament, University of Graz, Austria

James E. Harding, Senior Lecturer in Hebrew Bible/Old Testament Studies, University of Otago, New Zealand

Else K. Holt, Associate Professor of Old Testament Studies, Aarhus University, Denmark

Christl M. Maier, Professor of Old Testament, Philipps-Universität Marburg, Germany

Stuart Macwilliam, Honorary Research Fellow, University of Exeter, England

Judith E. McKinlay, Senior Lecturer in Biblical Studies (ret.), University of Otago, Dunedin, New Zealand.

Carolyn J. Sharp, Professor of Hebrew Scriptures, Yale Divinity School, New Haven, Connecticut, USA

Louis Stulman, Professor of Religious Studies, University of Findlay, Findlay, Ohio, USA

no longer take methodological issues for granted, and that is an excellent thing. Thus, while one still encounters articles and books that represent the author's (usually implicit) methodological approach as if it were a transparently "natural" way to approach the text and suggest that the author's research findings should be self-evident to any intelligent reader, such methodological naïveté is, thankfully, far less the norm than it once was in Western biblical scholarship.

This flourishing of a spectacular variety of methods, combined with increasing attentiveness to methodological commitments, has been salutary for feminist biblical criticism and postcolonial biblical interpretation. Each complex set of approaches and commitments—feminist and postcolonial—places a high premium on the sophisticated analysis of power relations, within texts and in the history of interpretation.

Recognizing the power relations implicated in and promoted by biblical interpretations is something that matters a great deal to the feminist and postcolonial scholars who have contributed to this volume. One editor, Christl M. Maier, is a native of Germany, a country that was among the European colonizing nations, albeit as a late-comer and dominating less territory than its neighbors. Having experienced strong democratic and economic progress after World War II and the non-violent regime change of Eastern Germany in 1989, the country now prides itself on being an important democracy and key economy in Europe. Despite very restrictive immigration laws and striving to avoid becoming a society of immigrants, Germany has attracted many workers from other European countries as well as refugees from abroad and now has a substantial population of migrants and practitioners of Muslim faith. Being still influenced by the mother-ideology of the Nazi regime and living in rural areas, many Germans, especially in the Southern and Western parts of the country, disapprove of feminist ideas such as equal pay and a fair distribution of responsibilities in family and society among men and women. While many of these more conservative circles still seek guidance in the Bible, especially within Protestant churches, the country's eastern states and urban areas face a strong secularism that challenges biblical interpretation as outdated. Within this blend of uneven societal changes, academic education has become a key issue for the country's economic strength and progress in integrating people of different ethnicities and religious affiliations.

The other editor, Carolyn J. Sharp, comes from the United States of America. Feminist inquiry and praxis have flourished there since the 1970s, but a great deal of work remains to be done regarding the reconfiguration of stubbornly androcentric educational, medical, and judicial paradigms and prejudices at every level of society. Many communities within the United States cherish a mythology that celebrates the pursuit of freedom of religion as foundational for the identity of those who came to this continent from Europe to settle. Those descended from European colonizers are often called "Americans" without regard for the other North Americans and South Americans in the Western hemisphere who do not live in the United States, as if there were only one "America," understood to be naturally or inevitably based on the mythos of the independent, freedom-loving (White) maverick. This ideological construction of "American" identity continually collides with other political and cultural realities not yet fully explored or adequately acknowledged within dominant-culture media of the United States. Such realities include the history of robust efforts of European colonizers to displace, constrain, and exterminate the indigenous peoples already living there; the history of White individuals' and White-led institutions' uncritical embrace of the chattel slavery that held generations of Africans in bondage there; the country's severe restriction of the formal civil rights of darker-skinned peoples well into the twentieth century; practices of racial injustice that continue unimpeded, from the national level of racially biased incarceration patterns to the local level of daily microaggressions, in many communities to this day; and the ongoing failure of many in political, educational, and social leadership positions adequately to address sexism and racism, to destabilize androcentric cultural norms, and to interrogate White privilege.

In what follows, we chart our work on Jeremiah among current approaches that have emerged from shifts of hermeneutical paradigms.

Feminist Biblical Criticism

The feminist interpretive paradigm emerged with the rise of the second wave of the women's movement in the 1960s, challenging the categories and definitions that male scholars and artists had set forth, and in particular the ways in which they had defined and constrained women's speech, women's bodies, and women's roles. Feminist interpreters laid bare the androcentric bias of biblical texts for readers who may have never before questioned the ways in which authority and truth had been shaped in ancient patriarchal contexts. Feminist biblical scholars declined the ways, implicit and overt, in which their colleagues had constructed male experience, narrowly defined, as the norm for identity and for political and clerical authority. Feminist analysis refused to take as normative and natural the phallocentric assumptions that implicitly and explicitly guided biblical scholarship in the European and North American guild. Feminist challenges created social change both in the secular academy and in other contexts in which biblical interpretation was important, such as theological schools, churches, and synagogues.[1] Introducing the category of gender as a social construct in contrast to sex, which most scholars up to the 1980s perceived as a biological given, feminist theory critically assessed societal norms and values in Western societies as androcentric and patriarchal. While in the United States gender had become accepted as a category of analysis in the 1970s, it took about 20 years longer for it to win scholarly approval in Germany due to the different systems of higher education, women's share in teaching positions, and the fact that the German language has only one word, "Geschlecht," for sex and gender. With regard to this uneven development of theories, Edward W. Said's concept of "traveling theory"[2] proved helpful for critics who explore the asymmetrical distribution of knowledge and "knowledge divides" in discourses, for example in the discourse on race, class, and gender.[3] While French feminist theory had been known in Germany since Simone de Beauvoir's book *The Second Sex* (published in 1949; translated into German in 1951 and into English in 1953), the U.S. gender discourse was abruptly introduced to Germany with Judith Butler's book *Gender Trouble*, which was among the first to be translated into German (1991).[4] The book's discursive context was hardly known in Germany, and the studies of Teresa De Lauretis, Sandra Harding, Nancy Fraser, and Donna J. Haraway had not yet been translated into German.[5] Hence Butler's deconstruction of gendered identity and

    1.   For an articulate history of proto-feminist and feminist biblical scholarship, see Susanne Scholz, *Introducing the Women's Hebrew Bible* (New York: T&T Clark International, 2007), 12–56.
    2.   Edward W. Said, "Traveling Theory," in *The World, the Text, and the Critic* (Cambridge, Mass.: Harvard University Press, 1983), 226–47.
    3.   See Gudrun-Axeli Knapp, "Race, Class, Gender: Reclaiming Baggage in Fast Travelling Theories," *European Journal of Women's Studies* 12 (2005): 249–65.
    4.   Simone de Beauvoir, *The Second Sex* (trans. and ed. H. M. Parshley; New York: Knopf, 1953; French original 1949; German trans. 1951); Judith Butler, *Gender Trouble: Feminism and the Subversion of Identity* (New York: Routledge, 1990; German trans. 1991).
    5.   See Teresa De Lauretis, *Alice Doesn't: Feminism, Semiotics, Cinema* (Bloomington: Indiana University Press, 1984); eadem, *Technologies of Gender: Essays on Theory, Film, and Fiction* (Bloomington: Indiana University Press, 1987); eadem, *Practice of Love: Lesbian Sexuality and Perverse Desire* (Bloomington: Indiana University Press, 1994; German trans. 1996); Sandra Harding, *Whose Science? Whose Knowledge? Thinking from Women's Lives* (Ithaca: Cornell University Press, 1991; German trans. 1994); Nancy Fraser, *Unruly Practices: Power, Discourse, and Gender in Contemporary Social Theory* (Minneapolis: University of Minnesota

her thesis that sexuality, too, is a social and cultural construct met with refusal and protest.[6] The controversy between gender equality and gender difference as contrasting definitions and models of political agency was more persistent in Western Europe, since their proponents came from different philosophical traditions, German and French.[7] Since the mid-1980s, however, feminist discourses on both sides of the Atlantic came to acknowledge the concept of intersectionality introduced by Kimberlé Crenshaw, who theorizes race, class, and gender as a trilogy of discrimination and challenges identity politics along gender lines.[8] From that time on, the concept of intersectionality has been elaborated in different directions, either standing for an analytical programmatic in policy concepts or representing a more general theoretical programmatic that seeks to relate large-scale societal structures of dominance, mid-level institutional arrangements, interactions between individuals and groups, and individual experiences.[9] Essentialism has since the mid-1990s been roundly rejected in many arenas of feminist thought, especially as regards essentialist constructions of gendered experiences of embodiment. For example, Elizabeth Grosz calls for resistance to "biologistic or essentialist accounts of the body. The body must be regarded as a site of social, political, cultural, and geographical inscriptions, production, or constitution. The body is not opposed to culture, a resistant throwback to a natural past; it is itself a cultural, *the* cultural, product."[10]

It must be stated that the adoption of multi-voiced feminist discourse in biblical interpretation specifically has lagged behind, especially since feminist deconstructive approaches and postmodern challenges to what

Press, 1989; German trans. 1994); Donna J. Haraway, *Primate Visions: Gender, Race, and Nature in the World of Modern Science* (New York: Routledge, 1989), and eadem, *Simians, Cyborgs, and Women: The Reinvention of Nature* (London: Free Association, 1991; German trans. 1995).

6. See Inge Stephan, "Gender, Geschlecht und Theorie," in *Gender Studien: Eine Einführung* (ed. C. von Braun and I. Stephan; 2d ed.; Stuttgart: Metzler, 2006), 52–90 (57–63).

7. See Seyla Benhabib, Judith Butler, Drucilla Cornell, and Nancy Fraser, *Der Streit um Differenz: Feminismus und Postmoderne in der Gegenwart* (Frankfurt: Fischer, 1993); Hadumod Bußmann and Renate Hof, eds., *Genus: Zur Geschlechterdifferenz in den Kulturwissenschaften* (Stuttgart: Kröner, 1995).

8. Kimberlé Crenshaw, "Mapping the Margins: Intersectionality, Identity Politics, and Violence Against Women of Color," *Stanford Law Review* 43 (1991): 1241–99.

9. Knapp, "Race, Class, Gender," 255.

10. Elizabeth A. Grosz, *Volatile Bodies: Toward a Corporeal Feminism* (St. Leonards: Allen & Unwin, 1994), 23.

have been termed "master narratives" have been highly contested in a discipline that has tended to seek "universal truth" and has relied on a rather outdated positivist concept of history. Again, the interactions between feminist theory and biblical interpretation in the United States and in Germany were uneven and not synchronous. Elisabeth Schüssler Fiorenza, who was trained in Germany but has taught in the United States since 1970, was the first to publish a feminist hermeneutics of biblical interpretation.[11] She introduced important hermeneutical steps, among them her famous "hermeneutics of suspicion," which are intended to help interpreters untangle androcentric biblical texts and critically evaluate the even more androcentric translations and interpretations that have arisen in the history of interpretation. Schüssler Fiorenza emphasized a theology of liberation and reconstructed the early movement around Jesus as a discipleship of equals. From the beginning, Schüssler Fiorenza argued against an essentialist appropriation of female biblical characters, insisting on a strategic and politically subversive practice of interpretation. Her model of feminist biblical interpretation was flexible enough to accommodate the critical objections of womanist and Latina theologians who challenged the Eurocentrism and exclusivism of white middle-class feminist theology.[12] Schüssler Fiorenza's hermeneutical model is also valid for Hebrew Bible texts, although those texts' socio-historical settings are more difficult to explore due to the scarcity of parallel textual and archaeological sources.[13] Other feminist theologians, among them Letty M. Russell and Margaret A. Farley, demonstrated that a reevaluation of the biblical tradition ought to be complemented by a critical feminist revision of Christian theology and ethics, a revision that would necessarily include the perspectives of feminist theologians from so-called Third World countries.[14] Given this hermeneutical re-orientation

---

11. Elisabeth Schüssler Fiorenza, *In Memory of Her: A Feminist Reconstruction of Christian Origins* (New York: Crossroad, 1983; German trans. 1988).

12. See Elisabeth Schüssler Fiorenza, *Wisdom Ways: Introducing Feminist Biblical Interpretation* (Maryknoll: Orbis, 2001; German trans. 2005), 77–101.

13. Cf. Luise Schottroff, Silvia Schroer, and Marie-Theres Wacker, *Feministische Exegese: Forschungserträge zur Bibel aus der Perspektive von Frauen* (Darmstadt: Wissenschaftliche Buchgesellschaft, 1995; English trans. 1998), 100–143.

14. See Letty M. Russell, *Human Liberation in a Feminist Perspective: A Theology* (Philadelphia: Westminster, 1974); eadem, *Household of Freedom: Authority in Feminist Theology* (Philadelphia: Westminster, 1987); eadem et al., eds., *Inheriting Our Mothers' Gardens: Feminist Theology in Third World Perspective* (Philadelphia: Westminster, 1988); and eadem, *Church in the Round: Feminist Interpretation of the Church* (Louisville: Westminster John Knox, 1993); Margaret

in the last three decades, feminist biblical interpretation "makes no pretense to objectivity; it challenges the notion of universals; it is more interested in relevance than in so-called absolute truth."[15]

Feminist Bible scholars employ a wide variety of methodological approaches, often placing heavy emphasis on literary criticism, which developed parallel to feminist criticism and integrated methodologies from literature and cultural studies, for example narrative criticism, deconstructive criticism, and reader-response criticism.

Narrative criticism in feminist circles has been influenced by the work of the Dutch cultural critic Mieke Bal, whose work borrows from semiotics, psychoanalysis, and anthropology. She transformed the concept of point of view, well-known to literary critics, into a feminist reading strategy called "focalization." By exploring who sees and who is seen in a narrative, Bal discloses the gendered concept and perception of characters as well as the power relations in the text.[16]

Deconstructive criticism "involves both discovering the incompleteness of the text and finding a fresh, if transient, insight made possible by the 'free play' or indeterminacy of the text."[17] Jacques Derrida, who established deconstruction as a reading strategy, regards all communication as "text," a configuration interwoven with previous communications. Deconstruction sets out to resist what Derrida has called "logocentrism," a commitment to the principle that there is some metaphysical thread that connects words and their referents, signifiers and signified.[18] Thus, deconstruction displaces the *logos* from its position of authority.[19] Derrida's emphasis on undecidability—the irreducibly plural meaning of texts—aims at challenging the traditional reading and the dominant

A. Farley, *Compassionate Respect: A Feminist Approach to Medical Ethics* (New York: Paulist, 2002); and eadem, *Just Love: A Framework for Christian Sexual Ethics* (New York: Continuum, 2006).

15. Danna N. Fewell, "Reading the Bible Ideologically: Feminist Criticism," in *To Each Its Own Meaning: An Introduction to Biblical Criticisms and Their Application* (ed. S. L. McKenzie and S. R. Haynes; rev. and exp. ed.; Louisville: Westminster John Knox, 1999), 268–82 (269).

16. See Mieke Bal, *Narratology: Introduction to the Theory of Narrative* (2d ed.; Toronto: University of Toronto Press, 1997), 144–60.

17. William A. Beardslee, "Poststructuralist Criticism," in McKenzie and Haynes, eds., *To Each Its Own Meaning*, 253–67 (253).

18. Jacques Derrida, *Of Grammatology* (trans. G. C. Spivak; Baltimore: The Johns Hopkins University Press, 1976), 3.

19. Andrew K. M. Adam, *What Is Postmodern Biblical Criticism?* (Minneapolis: Fortress, 1995), 28.

social groups that control this tradition of reading. Deconstruction, therefore, is highly critical of traditional theology and its history of interpretation.

Reader-response criticism has been influenced by the work of Jacques Derrida, Stanley E. Fish, and Roland Barthes. Derrida's deconstructive reader seeks to discover distinctions between what the author of a text commands and what the language of a text offers in order to break the domination of the conventional reading.[20] Fish posits that the reader is the one who "makes" literature; yet Fish situates the reader in an interpretive community that would select specific readings and contain the number of possible readings.[21] Barthes sees a text as dynamic and involving the reader in a process of analysis without a final synthesis and end.[22] Thus, reader-response criticism approaches the biblical text as literature not of an unknown past but of relevance for contemporary readers who seriously interact with the text in light of their own context, linguistic expertise, and literary competence. Reader-response criticism does not exclude the reading of "informed" readers who know the ancient context of the biblical writings. Yet, this approach challenges the historical-critical framing of the Bible as a historical "source" that can be interpreted only by experts and only by a specific set of methods that privilege historical data. Used with a feminist perspective, reader-response criticism challenges the traditional androcentric way of reading and generates a heightened sensibility for hierarchical relations and gender-specific metaphors. In sum, reader-response criticism is not a unified method of textual analysis. Rather, it is a collection of critical attitudes applied in order to read the biblical texts in ways responsive to local contextual needs, according to interpretive norms and priorities set by the reader or reading community.

Although most feminist biblical scholars use literary methods and read the texts synchronically, some feminist exegetes combine literary methods with an analysis of the assumed socio-historical context of the text in order to explicate biblical metaphors,[23] to trace the development

20. Derrida, *Of Grammatology*, 158.

21. See Stanley E. Fish, *Is There a Text in This Class? The Authority of Interpretive Communities* (Cambridge, Mass.: Harvard University Press, 1980), 340–45.

22. See Roland Barthes, *S/Z* (trans. R. Miller; Oxford: Blackwell, 1992).

23. See, e.g., Gerlinde Baumann, *Love and Violence: Marriage as Metaphor for the Relationship Between YHWH and Israel in the Prophetic Books* (trans. L. M. Maloney; Collegeville: Liturgical, 2003; German original 2000), and Sharon Moughtin-Mumby, *Sexual and Marital Metaphors in Hosea, Jeremiah, Isaiah, and Ezekiel* (Oxford: Oxford University Press, 2008).

of a theological concept,[24] or to evaluate implicit social norms that motivate textual constructions of power, identity, and agency. These objectives are congruent with Schüssler Fiorenza's goal to reconstruct the ancient history from a feminist perspective in order to level long-held male-centered evaluations of the past. Historical inquiry in the twenty-first century can no longer be naïve, of course, about the values and biases that interpreters bring to their readings. But it remains essential to analyze critically the ways in which texts as cultural productions both reflect and respond to the historical circumstances of their composition and editing.

Over the past several decades, feminist biblical criticism has laid groundwork that has been crucially important for the flourishing of new ways of reading, including three of the youngest subdisciplines in biblical interpretation: womanist criticism, queer criticism, and disability studies. Womanist biblical scholars, still few in number in the guild, are committed to praxes of social justice that promote the flourishing of African, African-American, and all women and men (some would include genderqueer persons as well). Some womanist scholars, such as Wilda C. Gafney, are alert to the risks of heteronormativity and homophobia within the intersectional matrix of oppressions constraining those who cannot claim dominant-culture subjectivity.[25] Queer biblical interpretations have emerged in the Western academy only in the past two decades or so.[26] Essays and books that promote a queer hermeneutic are most often expressly reader-centered; they tend to draw on ideological criticism and deconstructive and poststructuralist reading strategies in service

24. See, e.g., Christl M. Maier, *Daughter Zion, Mother Zion: Gender, Space, and the Sacred in Ancient Israel* (Minneapolis: Fortress, 2008).

25. See, e.g., Kelly B. Douglas, "Marginalized People, Liberating Perspectives: A Womanist Approach to Biblical Interpretation," *ATR* 83 (2001): 41–47; Wilda C. Gafney, "A Black Feminist Approach to Biblical Studies," *Encounter* 67 (2006): 391–403; Nyasha Junior, "Womanist Biblical Interpretation," in *Engaging the Bible in a Gendered World: An Introduction to Feminist Biblical Interpretation in Honor of Katharine Doob Sakenfeld* (ed. L. Day and C. Pressler; Louisville: Westminster John Knox, 2006), 37–46.

26. Important works in queer biblical interpretation include: Robert E. Goss and Mona West, eds., *Take Back the Word: A Queer Reading of the Bible* (Cleveland: Pilgrim, 2000); Ken Stone, ed., *Queer Commentary and the Hebrew Bible* (Sheffield: Sheffield Academic, 2001); Deryn Guest et al., eds., *The Queer Bible Commentary* (London: SCM, 2006); Teresa J. Hornsby and Ken Stone, eds., *Bible Trouble: Queer Reading at the Boundaries of Biblical Scholarship* (Atlanta: Society of Biblical Literature, 2011); and Stuart Macwilliam, *Queer Theory and the Prophetic Marriage Metaphor in the Hebrew Bible* (BibleWorld; Sheffield: Equinox, 2011).

of political resistance to textual and interpretive norms that deny or
distort the full humanity of lesbian, gay, queer, and other sexual- and
gender-minority readers. Queer criticism still goes unengaged in many
theological schools; articles and books that promote queer reading
strategies do not yet enjoy wide deployment on syllabi in undergraduate
and graduate-level biblical studies classes. Nevertheless, queer scholarship continues to flourish and promises to have an enduring impact on
the submerged norms and implicit master narratives that undergird many
interpretive paradigms, including that of second-wave feminist biblical
interpretation. Disability studies presses further the interrogation of
normative categories presumed within biblical traditions and (implicitly
or overtly) within the history of interpretation regarding cultural constructions of bodily wellness, injury, sickness, purity, and impurity, as
well as understandings of physical and cognitive difference as impair-
ment and reconfigurations or refusals of such understandings.[27] Scholars
in this subfield are regularly alert to the ways in which gender and power
are deeply implicated in construals of able-bodiedness and disability.

Postcolonial Biblical Interpretation

Since the late 1970s, the ever-expanding field of postcolonial theory
influences a range of scholarly disciplines, among them political science,
sociology, and cultural and literary studies. Edward W. Said's book
Orientalism, published in 1978, was among the first to question the
leading perspectives in Western Europe and North America as highly
particular viewpoints. Said defined orientalism as "a Western style for
dominating, restructuring, and having authority over the Orient,"[28] based
on the actual discovery of archaeological sites and ancient texts, but also
on Western fantasies, myths, and obsessions. Said's thesis that Western
academic knowledge about the Orient is imperialistic and associated with

---

27. Works of biblical scholarship in disability studies include: Jeremy Schipper,
Disability Studies and the Hebrew Bible: Figuring Mephibosheth in the David Story
(LHBOTS 441; New York: T&T Clark International, 2006); idem, *Disability and
Isaiah's Suffering Servant* (Oxford: Oxford University Press, 2011); Hector Avalos,
Sarah J. Melcher, and Jeremy Schipper, eds., *This Abled Body: Rethinking Disabili-
ties in Biblical Studies* (Atlanta: Society of Biblical Literature, 2007); Saul M.
Olyan, *Disability in the Hebrew Bible: Interpreting Mental and Physical Differences*
(Cambridge: Cambridge University Press, 2008); and Jeremy Schipper and Candida
Moss, eds., *Disability Studies and Biblical Literature* (New York: Palgrave Mac-
millan, 2011).

28. Edward W. Said, *Orientalism* (New York: Vintage, 1978), 3.

practices of power has been criticized as ideologically constricted, essentialist, and undifferentiated.[29] Yet his thesis provided decisive impulses for postcolonial studies as well as for a critical self-perception of religious studies, a field that evolved in a period of European colonialism.[30]

Homi K. Bhabha, one of the pioneers of the postcolonial paradigm, sees these new perspectives emerge from the colonial testimony of Third World countries and the discourse of "minorities" within the geopolitical division of East and West, North and South. They intervene in all ideological discourses of modernity that attempt to give a hegemonic "normality" to the uneven development and the differential, often disadvantaged, histories of nations, races, communities, and peoples.[31] In this regard, postcolonial perspectives, like feminist approaches, have a liberationist agenda and a political tenet, namely to have the voices from the margin, the colonized, and minorities speak their own mind and gain agency in their struggle against political, social, and economic domination.

Gayatri Chakravorty Spivak, another influential postcolonial thinker, however, raised the question whether the subaltern can truly speak.[32] Spivak holds that already the concept of a subaltern self-consciousness is positivistic because, in her view, a subaltern voice cannot be separated from the dominant discourse that provides the language and the conceptual categories with which the subaltern voice speaks.[33] The bondage of both the colonized and the colonizer in the same discourse is addressed by Bhabha's concept of mimicry, which describes the ambivalent relationship between the two as camouflage: the colonized are forced to adopt the language, cultural habits, assumptions, and values of the colonizer, yet their mimicry is not a simple reproduction of those traits but a "blurred copy" that can be threatening to the colonizer because it oscillates between imitating and mocking the colonial authority.[34]

---

29. See, e.g., John R. Irwin, *The Lust of Knowledge: The Orientalists and Their Enemies* (London: Penguin, 2006), 299–304.

30. Ulrike Brunotte, "Religion und Kolonialismus," in *Europäische Religionsgeschichte: Ein mehrfacher Pluralismus*, vol. 1 (ed. H. G. Kippenberg et al.; Göttingen: Vandenhoeck & Ruprecht, 2009), 339–69.

31. Homi K. Bhabha, *The Location of Culture* (London: Routledge, 1994), 245.

32. Gayatri C. Spivak, "Can the Subaltern Speak?," in *Marxism and the Interpretation of Culture* (ed. C. Nelson and L. Grossberg; Urbana: University of Illinois Press, 1988), 271–313.

33. See *The Spivak-Reader: Selected Works of Gayatri Chakravorty Spivak* (ed. D. Landry and G. MacLean; New York: Routledge, 1996), 203–5.

34. Bhabha, *Location of Culture*, 122–29.

foster a conversation among the different approaches, with the result that
the intersections and mutual interrogations of these methodologies are
both theorized and illustrated.

Judith E. McKinlay's essay, "Challenges and Opportunities for
Feminist and Postcolonial Biblical Criticism," frames hermeneutical
questions for feminist and postcolonial biblical interpretation via an
exploration of the author's history as a feminist *Pakeha* New Zealander.
McKinlay highlights the complexity of postcolonial questions involving
center and periphery in ancient Judah and relations of domination and
subordination within the book of Jeremiah. She problematizes the contemporary endeavor to hear a subaltern voice speaking in Jeremiah,
noting that the prophetic book constitutes a multi-layered discourse and
suggesting that postcolonial readings must resist simplistic construals
of agency and voicing there. Important for future work on Jeremiah is
McKinlay's cautionary note about the risks of reductionism whenever
binary analytical categories are deployed and her alertness to ways in
which critical methodologies may yet be pressed into service of dynamics
of domination by those who enjoy the privileges of academic training.

Carolyn J. Sharp's piece, "Mapping Jeremiah as/in a Feminist Landscape: Negotiating Ancient and Contemporary Terrains," names the
challenge of ongoing androcentrism in biblical studies and offers a
reading of Jer 30:5–22 that seeks to open up new interpretive spaces for
feminist and queer commentary. Sharp identifies as goals of feminist
critique the countering of ideologies of subjugation, the deconstruction
of essentialist notions, and the promotion of *shalom*. For the feminist
exegetical project, she finds in Jer 30:5–22 a poetics of absence, shaming
of the masculine subject, the positioning of YHWH over against imperialism, micro-semantic poetic moves that underline the message of salvation, and a poetics of reversal that makes visible the future possibility of
freedom from domination.

Louis Stulman's "Commentary as Memoir? Reflections on Writing/
Reading War and Hegemony in Jeremiah and in Contemporary U.S.
Foreign Policy," probes the ways in which memoir and commentary
writing are inevitably implicated in one another. Resisting conventional
academic expectations regarding the genre of commentary, Stulman
positions his reading of Jeremiah at the interstices between the writing of
self and the writing of history, arguing for an indissoluble fusion of
personal, communal, and historical horizons in the art of interpretation.
Jeremiah as disaster literature, as survival literature, as protest literature:
these frameworks of meaning are vital for the commentator who seeks to
understand how the book of Jeremiah names Judah's woundedness and
struggles toward healing in a purposeful chaos of performative grief.

Stulman frames an interdisciplinary space in which trauma studies, feminist criticism, and postcolonial inquiry can encounter, provoke, and enrich one another.

Christl M. Maier's essay, "After the 'One-Man Show': Multi-Authored and Multi-Voiced Commentary Writing," engages the question of how to construct the authority of the biblical commentator in a postmodern age in which metanarratological pronouncements are no longer tenable. The commentator's control of all voicing must yield to a new elucidation of multivocality, that is understood within the biblical text and in subsequent interpretation. Responding to key contributions from Continental literary theory, Latin American liberation theology, and ideological criticism, Maier argues that the feminist commentary in the twenty-first century must decline to participate in hierarchical dynamics of power, instead attending to textual polyphony and engaging multiple perspectives from reception history. To illustrate this hermeneutic, she offers a reading of Jer 7:16–20 that interweaves literary observations, ancient Near Eastern comparative work, and feminist analysis. Maier declines to revoice the polemical dominant position of the text as if it were the only viable perspective, inviting the reader to consider the ethics of reading from multiple perspectives in every act of interpretation.

Yosefa Raz's piece, "Jeremiah 'Before the Womb': On Fathers, Sons, and the Telos of Redaction in Jeremiah 1," offers a cultural analysis of ways in which scholarly study of the prophets has been shaped by the Romantic preoccupation with origins and a related anxiety about derivative authority and the uncertainties of transmission. Raz examines the biblical figuring of Jeremiah in prophetic and royal terms by scribes responding to the breach in traditions of Mosaic lineage and monarchical stability, reading these scribal moves as instantiations of patriarchy's age-old fantasy of paternal and dynastic continuity. Situating the call of Jeremiah with regard to Deuteronomy and Kings, Raz argues that the traditio-historical lineage of Jeremiah is depicted in terms both conventional and innovative, for the prophet must represent divine authority in ways that are intelligible to normative Israelite social expectations while also envisioning a new kind of agency given that the old infrastructures had decisively failed.

Else K. Holt's "'The Stain of Your Guilt Is Still Before Me' (Jeremiah 2:22): (Feminist) Approaches to Jeremiah 2 and the Problem of Normativity" surveys a variety of scholarly positions taken up in response to the patriarchal theology and cultural anthropology on view in Jer 2, especially as regards the portrayal of God's violent use of power and the offensive gendered depiction of Israel within the covenant metaphor. Analyzing strengths and vulnerabilities of treatments within feminist analysis, ideological criticism, and trauma studies, Holt argues that readers should not forget the deliberateness of the offense given in the Jeremiah text, which employs rhetorical strategies characterized by misandry as well as misogyny. She urges that contemporary readers not reject Jeremiah outright but, instead, make use of sociohistorical analysis, intratextual dynamics of contestation within the polyphony of Jeremiah, and other critical resources in order to remain engaged productively with this prophetic text. Holt finds it to be an ethical mandate for critically trained readers to continue to shape the history of reception of these and other troubling biblical texts.

L. Juliana Claassens's essay, "'Like a Woman in Labor': Gender, Postcolonial, Queer, and Trauma Perspectives on the Book of Jeremiah," frames her reading of Jeremiah's use of the metaphor of a woman in labor within the intersectionality of gender, postcolonial, queer, and trauma-studies perspectives. Advocating a multidimensional approach, Claassens seeks to negotiate a new space for critical interrogations of gender, sexuality, and power in the metaphorization of Jeremiah. Thus she argues that culturally disruptive gender reversals in Jeremiah, whereby the implicit male subject is constructed as female, may be exploited as a resource for queer readings. Likewise, postcolonial attentiveness to the development of "counter-language" in the face of imperial threat may be useful for feminist and other modes of resistant reading in service of justice and cultural transformation.

Maier's "God's Cruelty and Jeremiah's Treason: Jeremiah 21:1–10 in Postcolonial Perspective" works at the intersection of redaction criticism and postcolonial analysis, arguing for the significance of the exilic context for the final form of Jer 21:1–10. Tensions within this redacted passage reveal a shift in perspective from the depiction of God's power in an ambiguous way in Jer 2–6 to the portrayal in later Jeremiah traditions of a harshly punitive deity who wields power expressly to discipline Judah. Drawing on the work of Homi Bhabha, Maier finds that the theology of divine retributive justice in the Deutero-Jeremianic material "narrates" the experience of the Judean subjects in a way that helps to diminish Babylonian imperial power over the Judean cultural imagination. Emphasizing the diversity of social groups within the Judeans subjugated by Babylon, Maier argues that the counsel of submission to Babylon serves the interests of the Judean elite, who "speak for" the Judean subalterns in a way that illustrates the ambivalence of the authority of the colonized. Survival, in this multivocal ancient text, has required the strategic deployment of ambiguity and ambivalence in the elites' "narration" of God, the prophet, and Judah as a subjugated people.

the postcolonial optic, and that is lasting.[8] The paradox is perhaps best summed up by Laura Donaldson's pithy heading: "Post-colonialism Is Dead; Long Live Postcolonialism."[9]

A further question is whether the concern is colonialism or empire. Segovia himself suggests "a more comprehensive" term, "Imperial-Colonial Studies or imperial-colonial discourse," while admitting, "the relationship between the two concepts "is far from clear."[10] Certainly, both terms seem to be used almost interchangeably, yet the terms themselves would seem to imply a significant difference. Most discussions follow Edward Said: "imperialism means the practice, the theory, and the attitudes of a dominating metropolitan center ruling a distant territory; 'colonialism,' which is almost always a consequence of imperialism, is the implanting of settlements on distant territory."[11]

Segovia, in summarizing four different uses of the term postcolonialism, prefers that employed by Ania Loomba, seeing the difference in terms of "source and impact: while imperialism refers to whatever has to do with the originating and dominating center, colonialism points to whatever has to do with the receiving and subordinate periphery."[12] The complication comes, as Said further comments, in the fact that imperialism "lingers where it always has been, in a kind of general cultural sphere as well as in specific, ideological, economic, and social practices."[13]

What this issue does highlight is that there is a choice to be made. Where to focus? Will it be on the originating center as it exerts its power, or on the periphery, as it either succumbs or finds coping strategies? Will it be primarily on the ways in which the center imposes itself or will it be on the effects, whether immediate or long term, this has on the dominated or colonized? Or is it to be both? What makes the book of Jeremiah particularly interesting is that it records Judah's move from one category to another.

---

8. Fernando F. Segovia, "Mapping the Postcolonial Optic in Biblical Criticism: Meaning and Scope," in *Postcolonial Biblical Criticism: Interdisciplinary Intersections* (ed. S. D. Moore and F. F. Segovia; London: T&T Clark International, 2005), 23–78 (65).

9. Laura E. Donaldson, "Postcolonialism and Biblical Reading: An Introduction," *Semeia* 75 (1996): 1–14 (3).

10. Segovia, "Mapping the Postcolonial Optic," 65–66.

11. Edward W. Said, *Culture and Imperialism* (London: Chatto & Windsor, 1993), 9.

12. Segovia, "Mapping the Postcolonial Optic," 66.

13. Ibid.

As Louis Stulman notes of ch. 25, "the text presents the word coming to the prophet...at the end of one epoch—the crumbling of the state with its established domain assumptions—and at the beginning of another, in which Judah is now a displaced or dislocated community within the great neo-Babylonian empire."[14]

If the focus is mostly directed on those who suffer both under and after the center's intrusion, then the question follows: How do they suffer? Is the focus to be on the material consequences or the ideological and psychological? Postcolonialism, however, has an equal interest in how dominant powers maintain their dominance. I have frequently quoted the New Zealand scholar Jane Kelsey commenting on the "durability" of colonialists: "colonial leopards do not change their spots; they just stalk their prey in different ways."[15] So the task here, to quote Musa Dube and Jeffrey Staley, is "to examine how the colonizer constructs and justifies domination of the other in various places and periods of history."[16] The critical question is, how does Empire work? Judah is crumbling, but is there a sense of Babylon's strategies as the late sixth-century drama unfolds? And what of the ongoing processes of domination? And is the empire in question always Babylon or, if some sections are post-exilic, does Persia take its place? And where do Jeremiah's sympathies lie? Is the Jeremiah voice resistant or compliant? Economic, military, social, and ideological forces all become part of the task, as the Marxist roots of postcolonial theory serve to remind us.[17]

In Jeremiah, of course, this is undergirded by a theology. As ch. 25 expresses it, if the people turn from their ways, they will get to stay in

14. Louis Stulman, "The Prose Sermons as Hermeneutical Guide to Jeremiah 1–25: The Deconstruction of Judah's Symbolic World," in *Troubling Jeremiah* (ed. A. R. P. Diamond et al.; JSOTSup 260; Sheffield: Sheffield Academic, 1999), 34–63 (46).

15. Jane Kelsey, "From Flagpoles to Pine Trees: Tino Rangatiratanga and Treaty Policy Today," in *Racism and Ethnic Relations in Aotearoa/New Zealand* (ed. P. Spoonley et al.; Palmerston North: Dunmore, 1996), 177–201 (178).

16. Musa W. Dube and Jeffrey L. Staley, "Descending from and Ascending into Heaven: A Postcolonial Analysis of Travel, Space and Power in John," in *John and Postcolonialism: Travel, Space and Power* (ed. M. W. Dube and J. L. Staley; London: Sheffield Academic, 2002), 1–10 (3), adding "how the colonized collaborate, resist and assert their rights to be free in various places and periods of history; and how both parties travel and cross boundaries."

17. See Jon L. Berquist, "Postcolonialism and Imperial Motives for Canonization," *Semeia* 75 (1996): 15–35 (23), and Roland Boer and David Jobling's contributions to Moore and Segovia, eds., *Postcolonial Biblical Criticism*.

the land that "Yʜᴡʜ has given to you and your ancestors from of old and forever" (25:5). If they do not, they will be enslaved by the king of Babylon for seventy years (25:11). In considerable portions of Jeremiah, there is no question: All that happens is because of the people's short-comings in the faith, cause and effect, God and the politics, neatly and disturbingly tied together. Sugirtharajah's insistence that "the Bible itself is part of the conundrum rather than a panacea for all the ills of the postmodern/postcolonial world," that "it continues to be an unsafe and problematic text," is ringing loudly for those of us who belong to faith communities,[18] especially as Jeremiah has long been a key prophetic work, as the editors intended, for this is the prophet like Moses, par excellence. Another opportunity arises here: to explore the reception history through a postcolonial lens.

The complicating factor in all of this is that the book of Jeremiah is a collection of material, a patchwork of pieces from differing experiences of political power.[19] This will both unsettle and enrich the postcolonial readings, for whose voice do we hear? Is it the prophet Jeremiah's or the voices of many later writers and editors?

And is there a class distinction to be noted, in that it was the élite that were drafted off to Babylon? Do the various writers share the same or similar views? For a feature of colonized countries, such as New Zealand, is that even in the early days of colonization "not all colonial writers felt the same way about empire and race." Perhaps, considering the political shifts and uncertainties, it is not surprising that these early colonial writers were not consistent, that they "display conflicting and contradictory stances, often within a single text."[20] Carolyn Sharp's persuasive thesis of two voices held in tension in the Deutero-Jeremianic prose passages points to the complexities, as does Mary Chilton Callaway's recognition of these in ch. 37, both detecting a pro-*golah* and a Judah-based group, each with its own ideological and theological reading of the situation.[21]

18. Sugirtharajah, *Postcolonial Criticism and Biblical Interpretation*, 100.

19. See William McKane, *A Critical and Exegetical Commentary on Jeremiah, Volume 1: I–XXV* (ICC; Edinburgh: T. & T. Clark, 1986), xlviii, describing "a complicated, untidy accumulation of material, extending over a very long period to which many people have contributed."

20. Jane Stafford and Mark Williams, *Maoriland: New Zealand Literature 1872–1914* (Wellington: Victoria University Press, 2006), 15.

21. Carolyn J. Sharp, *Prophecy and Ideology in Jeremiah: Struggles for Authority in the Deutero-Jeremianic Prose* (London: T. & T. Clark, 2003); Mary Chilton Callaway, "Black Fire on White Fire: Historical Context and Literary Subtext in Jeremiah 37–38," in Diamond et al., eds., *Troubling Jeremiah*, 171–78.

What, too, of the poetic texts, in particular, the confessional laments? Are these Jeremiah's personal cries, "acutely sensitive to the pain and failure of his community"? Or is it the voice of "a jeopardized Israel" either overcome or about to be overcome by the imperial power of Babylon?[22] The further question here is how does this voice voice it? How do poetry, metaphor, and imagery act as political response? Is lament solely pathos or a strategic ploy of political resistance?

The flip side is, of course, whose voice do we not hear? Said may write, "In reading a text, one must open it out both to what went into it, and to what its author excluded," but finding what is excluded is not so easy.[23] The Queen of Heaven passage in Jer 44 might appear to offer a brief hearing to a sector whose worship practices were definitely not those of the writer. Or does it? Is this, rather, a clever rhetorical device deliberately introduced to provide a dramatic platform for the writer's own opposing views? To quote Gareth Griffiths, "[e]ven when the subaltern appears to 'speak' there is a real concern as to whether what we are listening to is really a subaltern voice or whether the subaltern is being spoken by the subject position they occupy within the larger discursive economy."[24] A significant feature of Maoriland writing, the term "used to describe late colonial and early Dominion New Zealand," is that the past and the present are seen as the *Pakeha* writers wished to present it: "Maori exist...only as the assumed and artificial voice deployed by the Pakeha author." As the researchers comment, "for that literature to acknowledge the existence of actual present-day Maori would jeopardize Pakeha ownership of the Maori past."[25] One needs constantly to remember Sugirtharajah's description of the postcolonial lens as "an interventionist instrument which refuses to take the dominant reading as an uncomplicated representation of the past."[26]

---

22. Bruce C. Birch et al., *A Theological Introduction to the Old Testament* (Nashville: Abingdon, 1999), 328, 334.

23. Said, *Culture and Imperialism*, 67.

24. Gareth Griffiths, "The Myth of Authenticity: Representation, Discourse and Social Practice," in *De-Scribing Empire: Post-Colonialism and Textuality* (ed. C. Tiffin and A. Lawson; London: Routledge, 1994), 70–85 (75), quoted by Berquist, "Postcolonialism and Imperial Motives," 27. This, of course, echoes Gayatri Chakravorty Spivak's question explored in "Can the Subaltern Speak?," in *Marxism and the Interpretation of Culture* (ed. C. Nelson and L. Grossberg; Urbana: University of Illinois Press, 1988), 271–313.

25. Stafford and Williams, *Maoriland*, 11, 74.

26. R. S. Sugirtharajah, *The Bible as Empire: Postcolonial Explorations* (Cambridge: Cambridge University Press, 2005), 3.

So far, I have been using the language of colonizers and colonized, center and periphery—simplistic binary language, which today spills over into talk of First vs. Third World, North vs. South, and so on. While all too easy to use, these dualistic categories are reductionist, locking people into identities that reify both dominance and marginalization. As the study of colonialist New Zealand literature noted of its period, "the centre-periphery model of empire needs to be modified to accommodate the complex cross-affiliations and influences of the period."[27] Carolyn Sharp has noted the difficulties with the Jeremiah material, both in that Jeremiah's own position is ambiguous, and that the 597 B.C.E. deportations changed the political landscape to such a degree that the terms are difficult to apply.[28]

For how does one categorize the voice of Judah in Babylon? Are we hearing the first whispers of a diasporic voice "attempt[ing] to preserve what they had left behind and to keep those ideas alive in order to make sense of their transplanted lives in an environment that was at times hostile and apathetic"? That is Sugirtharajah's description of early diasporic writing.[29] Is there a hint of this in ch. 29? Although the obligation to pray for the welfare of Babylon complicates this. The *Realpolitik* here may, of course, be quite different, and the chapter a window onto another ploy of empire: contact allowed but with the exiles now held as hostages, the counsel has to be, as Fretheim writes, "do not make waves" for those of us still here in Jerusalem.[30]

---

27. Stafford and Williams, *Maoriland*, 16. See Cheryl B. Anderson, "Round-table Discussion: Feminist Biblical Studies: Transatlantic Reflections: Contesting the Margins and Transgressing Boundaries in the Age of Aids," *JFSR* 25, no. 2 (2009): 103–7; also Warren Carter, *John and Empire: Initial Explorations* (New York: T&T Clark International, 2008), 78, "Such simplicity is deficient not only because imperial control is experienced in different ways by groups of differing societal status and interests...but also because imperial control is effected not only through force, intimidation, and spin, but also through complex and disguised means.... These strategies often benefited the subordinated in some ways, thereby mixing gift with obligation, benefits with dependency, accommodation with dissent."

28. Sharp, *Prophecy and Ideology in Jeremiah*, 52–53.

29. Sugirtharajah in D. N. Premnath, "Margins and Mainstream: An Interview with R. S. Sugirtharajah," in *Border Crossings: Cross-Cultural Hermeneutics* (ed. D. N. Premnath; Maryknoll: Orbis, 2007), 153–65 (158). See, too, his discussion in *Postcolonial Criticism and Biblical Interpretation*, 183–86.

30. Terence E. Fretheim, *Jeremiah* (Smith & Helwys Bible Commentary; Macon: Smyth & Helwys, 2002), 400.

Or, if some of Jeremiah is postexilic, is it the more recent settler theory that provides the critical key, seeing the "settler subject...(as) colonized at the same time as it is colonizing,"[31] recognizing that the exiles were returning both as outsider settlers and as people under a Persian imperial rule? Or, if one follows the work of Homi Bhabha, is this postexilic speaking subject now a hybrid character, a product both of Babylon and Judah, settled in an unfamiliar Yehud that would be home?

So many questions! Perhaps the most challenging is this: How does one gauge what is going on in these texts? If one looks to the leaders in the biblical field, they do not give exact answers—no comfort here of a precise blueprint. For, as Sugirtharajah describes it, postcolonial criticism is "a reading posture," rather than a methodology.[32] Elsewhere he talks of "its theoretical and intellectual catholicism," in that it "is attracted to all kinds of tools and disciplinary fields."[33]

31. Alan Lawson, "Comparative Studies, Post-Colonial 'Settler' Cultures," *Australian and Canadian Studies* 10, no. 2 (1992): 153–59 (157), quoted by Edward Watts, "Settler Postcolonialism as a Reading Strategy," *American Literary History* 22, no. 2 (2010): 459–70 (462). See further Alan Lawson, "Postcolonial Theory and the 'Settler' Subject," in *Unhomely States: Theorizing English-Canadian Postcolonialism* (ed. C. Sugars; Peterborough: Broadview, 2004), 151–64 (158–59), quoted by Watts (467), that settler writing is "both postimperial and postcolonial...it must speak of and against both its own oppressiveness and its own oppression.... The address of the settler is toward both the absent(ee) cultural authority of the imperium and the effaced, recessive cultural authority of the Indigene." Here, too, there is a stress "on keeping the homeland as much like the old one in terms of its language, literature and...cultural practices," as Leonard Tannenhouse notes in *The Importance of Feeling English: American Literature and the British Diaspora, 1750–1850* (Princeton: Princeton University Press, 2007), 2, quoted by Watts (463).

32. R. S. Sugirtharajah, "A Postcolonial Exploration of Collusion and Construction in Biblical Interpretation," in *The Postcolonial Bible* (ed. R. S. Sugirtharajah; Sheffield: Sheffield Academic, 1998), 91–116 (93), allowing the reader to see and recognize the "lopsidedness and inadequacies" of "the dominant system of thought." See, too, Segovia's answers, in his 2005 review of the literature in "Mapping the Postcolonial Optic," 64 to his two questions: "What is the operative definition of postcolonial analysis at work—its object? What is the proposed range contemplated for such analysis—its parameters?" What he found was a "highly diverse and conflicted" field with "quite disparate and discordant" frameworks and approaches.

33. Sugirtharajah, *Postcolonial Criticism and Biblical Interpretation*, 100. Re: the matter of "its theoretical and intellectual catholicism," Russell Jacoby's question, in his trenchant article, "Marginal Returns," *Lingua Franca* 6 (September/October, 1995): 30–37 (32), should, perhaps, be considered, "Are they serious students of colonial history and culture or do they just pepper their writings with references to Gramsci and hegemony?"

So, what tools? Historical-critical? What then of the charge that, with its claimed objectivity and assumption of universal meaning, this is itself an imperial tool?[34] The other side of the matter is, as Marie-Theres Wacker insists, "we need historical perspectives and methods to do justice to these texts which are like guests in our world."[35] On a literary level, the task is uncovering and revealing the devices employed by these ancient writers in their persuasive ideological rhetoric. Athalya Brenner, in her response to the volume *Her Master's Tools?*, talks of "a re-molding through a judicious utilization coupled with departure," for "when the gaze shifts, previously dark realms can come to light…texts can be read anew…and new programs can be sought."[36] This is surely one of the aims of postcolonial criticism: to identify the hidden realms of human power plays, and yes, the choice of tools lies open. We may take what we want and hone them in new ways.

This leads to some significant decisions for the postcolonial writer: will the work be a purely text-based reading, whether historical or literary, or a more personalized text/reader dialogue? Will you stay behind the study, steering it almost anonymously, or will you be a player out in front? This, in turn, leads to the challenging matter of who is the postcolonial reader. For particularly within countries with histories of colonial or imperial intrusion or domination, there will be readers occupying very different subject positions. You may also need to consider the charge of Aijaz Ahmad that postcolonial studies has become the domain

34. See, as examples, Fernando F. Segovia, "'And They Began to Speak in Other Tongues': Competing Modes of Discourse in Contemporary Biblical Criticism," in *Reading from This Place*, vol. 1. (ed. F. F. Segovia and Mary Ann Tolbert; Minneapolis: Fortress, 1995), 1–32 and Sugirtharajah's comment in Premnath, "Margins and Mainstream," 158, that "'[s]cholarly' is also code for taking seriously only the Enlightenment and modernity, namely, the historical-critical method." As Alice Keefe, "Rapes of Women/Wars of Men," *Semeia* 61 (1993): 79–97 (79–80) reminds us, "the relation between literary texts and social reality is too complex and elusive" for drawing positivist historical conclusions.

35. Marie-Theres Wacker, "Roundtable Discussion: Feminist Biblical Studies: Challenges and Opportunities in Feminist Theology and Biblical Studies in Europe," *JFSR* 25, no. 2 (2009): 117–21 (120). See also Bradley L. Crowell, "Postcolonial Studies and the Hebrew Bible," *CBR* 7, no. 2 (2009): 217–44 (233), who, while agreeing that "historical criticism…does expose the historical and material matrix in which the biblical text was composed," also notes the pitfalls.

36. Athalya Brenner, "Epilogue: Babies and Bathwater on the Road," in *Her Master's Tools? Feminist and Postcolonial Engagements with Historical-Critical Discourse* (ed. C. Vander Stichele and T. Penner; Atlanta: Society of Biblical Literature, 2005), 333–38 (334–35).

of a First World educated élite, although he is referring here to those whom he accuses of using Third World material for their own academic advantage.[37]

This does, however, lead to the further question: How appropriate is it for someone from the dominant culture to work in this field? I, of course, have to answer this for myself. As I have said, I am the descendent of settlers—rather than colonizers, in that they were part of the next wave, buying their land directly from the Crown. Were they aware of the questionable land deals that in all probability lay behind the purchase? I don't know, although my grandfather writes, "if Sir George Grey had remained in New Zealand he would have expedited the purchase, for he had great influence with the Maoris."[38] Much, I suspect, hangs on that word "influence." Do I mention that these were Scottish highlanders, driven off their lands by the highland clearances? Or is that special pleading? Then, again, what am I pleading? For as a person of the dominant culture am I not complicit in the ways in which my postcolonial society lives and orders its life? We all make our own choices. As Sugirtharajah writes, postcolonial criticism "is a product of the contentious reciprocation between…colonizing countries and the colonized."[39] I am quite clear in my goal: to attempt to write as a *Pakeha*, owning our history and not assuming a cultural heritage which is not mine. On some occasions I have gone close to the boundary line, and afterwards felt uncomfortable, but too late. Once published, what is written has gone. I worked at one time with a Maori elder who taught me much; one of his frequent sayings was, "you make your decisions and you live with them." So it is.

Reader/text dialogues inevitably lead to multi-layered discourses, where contexts too may become reading partners. If you go down this path, how will you present your own postcolonial history? How do you understand it? Have you met it?

In the preface of *Reframing Her* I wrote about being confronted with exactly this.[40] Near the end of my time with the Refuge, a group of Maori women recognized the need for a separate safe house for Maori/Pacific

---

37. See the discussion of Aijaz Ahmad, *In Theory: Classes, Nations, Literatures* (London: Verso, 1992); Stephen D. Moore, "Questions of Biblical Ambivalence and Authority Under a Tree Outside Delhi, or, the Postcolonial and the Postmodern," in Moore and Segovia, eds., *Postcolonial Biblical Criticism*, 79–96 (82).

38. N. R. McKenzie, *The Gael Fares Forth* (2d ed.; Wellington: Whitcombe & Tombs, 1942), 57.

39. Sugirtharajah, *Postcolonial Criticism and Biblical Interpretation*, 23.

40. Judith E. McKinlay, *Reframing Her: Biblical Women in Postcolonial Focus* (Sheffield: Phoenix, 2004), ix–x.

women. The crux was money: Was what we had—which was always too little and hard won—to be halved and shared? Feelings ran high. A group of us met with the Maori women and were immediately challenged on our understanding of the Treaty of Waitangi, New Zealand's foundational document, signed in 1840 by the Crown and a significant number of Maori chiefs. One by one, we were to state our understanding of the key term *te tino rangatiratanga.* It was a knee-shaking moment. Did I really understand it? Did I appreciate its full significance?

Again the complications of history: The Treaty was circulated in two languages, English and Maori, with significant differences. According to the first article of the English version, the chiefs ceded to the Crown "absolutely and without reservation all the rights and powers of Sovereignty," which, in Maori, would imply *te tino rangatiratanga.* Yet in the translation into Maori the term used was *kawanatanga,* meaning governorship, that is, not full sovereignty. Consequently what the Maori signatories thought they were granting was not that at all. Not surprisingly, it is the English version that "successive governments have relied on to this day for their legitimacy or their own unilateral proclamation of sovereignty."[41] The challenge to us was: Did we understand our complicity in the ways of the dominant culture to which most of us belonged? It was their recognition of the strategy noted by Homi Bhabha, that "forgetting...constitutes the *beginning* of the nation's narrative,"[42] or "the need to get history wrong to get nation right," as Patrick Evans, writing of New Zealand, describes it: the "process by which the white settler culture managed and continues to manage its sense of belonging."[43]

I note similar statements of the United States: Michael Warner writes that "[n]ational culture began with a moment of sweeping amnesia about colonialism. Americans learned to think of themselves as living in an immemorial nation, rather than in a colonial interaction of cultures."[44]

---

41. Quoted from the document *Tino Rangatiratanga,* produced by the Joint Methodist Presbyterian Public Questions Committee [n.p., cited 21 May 2010]. Online: http://twm.co.nz/Maori_tino.htm# Meaning. For the treaty versions see online: www.teara.govt.nz/en/government-and-nation/1/2.

42. Homi K. Bhabha, *The Location of Culture* (London: Routledge, 1994), 160 (original emphasis).

43. Patrick Evans, *The Long Forgetting: Post-colonial Literary Culture in New Zealand* (Christchurch: Canterbury University Press, 2007), 40–41.

44. Michael Warner, "What's Colonial About Colonial America?," in *Possible Pasts: Becoming Colonial in Early America* (ed. R. Blair St. George; Ithaca: Cornell University Press, 2000), 49–71 (63), quoted by Watts, "Settler Postcolonialism as a Reading Strategy," 460.

Then there is the matter of how to set up a reader/context dialogue. Edward Said used the term "contrapuntal" for a reading where music's theme and counter-theme become ideology and counter-ideology, colonized's and colonizer's narratives woven in and over each other, disrupting the colonialist hegemony.[45] It is a biblical postcolonial counterpoint that Musa Dube advocates, "reading sacred and secular texts, ancient and contemporary texts…side by side, to highlight 'imperializing or decolonizing' ideologies."[46] I have been attempting to do this, sometimes with settlers' letters, sometimes with works of historical fiction, most recently with a mixture of historical resources.

This in turn raises yet another question: For whom are we writing? If what we write tends to be published in international journals and presented at international conferences, why are we making these connections? This is very much an issue for us "down under" in Aotearoa New Zealand. What is true for all of us is that our readership and audience is other biblical scholars. Is this a problem? If postcolonial studies is, at heart, political, should we be reaching out beyond this? Stephen Moore writes trenchantly, summarizing Ahmad, of Third World material being "turned into refined or luxury products for a privileged intelligentsia…all direct engagement with the extra-academic world… being foreclosed almost as a matter of course."[47]

The issue has a personal edge for me: In the review of *Reframing Her*, Sugirtharajah wrote "those without any special training in biblical studies will find it hard to get into the meat of the book, a blemish which has dogged mainstream scholarship, and which those of us involved in postcolonial criticism should avoid."[48] He talks elsewhere of scholars' use of "an insider writing style that involves complicated phrases and syntax" that exclude the outsider.[49] Is this a concern? It worries me, but I have not got beyond the worry. Those engaged in a roundtable discussion on feminist biblical interpretation at the 2008 SBL meeting raised the same

---

45. Said, *Culture and Imperialism*, 51, for a rereading of the cultural archive "with a simultaneous awareness both of the metropolitan history that is narrated and of those other histories against which (and together with which) the dominating discourse acts."

46. Dube, *Postcolonial Feminist Interpretation of the Bible*, 199–200.

47. Moore, "Questions of Biblical Ambivalence and Authority," 82.

48. R. S. Sugirtharajah, "Book Review: Decolonizing Biblical Narratives," *ExpTim* 118 (2007): 201.

49. Sugirtharajah in Premnath, "Margins and Mainstream," 157.

issue, including the matter of pricing, so many academic studies being priced out of reach of the interested reader.[50]

But where is the feminist in all this, and what is meant by that? I have long been reading and using Mary Chilton Callaway's and Angela Bauer's work, and more recently, Carolyn Sharp's, and I have heard Wilda Gafney presenting at SBL—so know that feminist biblical scholars working in the area of Jeremiah are well aware of the problem.

At the same time, to quote Amy Kalmanofsky, "the very definition of feminism remains a contested question among scholars and activists,"[51] and as Stephen Moore describes it, feminist biblical criticism is "a radically eclectic enterprise."[52] This year as I was rereading material for a course on biblical criticisms, I noted that The Bible and Culture Collective ended their 1995 discussion on feminist and womanist criticisms with a quote from Elizabeth Weed, written in 1989:

> The critical advantage of the feminist project has been that when one area of feminism has settled on a truth, another has emerged to disrupt that truth, to keep at bay truths too easily produced by cultural and political

---

50. Anderson, "Roundtable Discussion," 105. See Susanne Scholz, *Introducing the Women's Hebrew Bible* (London: T&T Clark International, 2007), 56: "Today, some of us feel almost compelled to devise marketing strategies to explain why it still makes sense to spend considerable resources on the study of the Bible. The dominant economic ideology of free-market capitalism does not support intellectual endeavors that do not advance immediate profit and power. Biblical studies, feminist or androcentric, do not speak to mainstream audiences that favor a celebrity culture, shallow diversion from everyday concerns, and spiritual fast-foods."

51. Amy Kalmanofsky, "Roundtable Discussion: Feminist Biblical Studies: Outside Insiders and the Future of Feminist Biblical Studies," *JFSR* 25, no. 2 (2009): 129–33 (131).

52. Stephen D. Moore, "A Modest Manifesto for New Testament Literary Criticism: How to Interface with a Literary Studies Field That Is Post-Literary, Post-Theoretical, and Post-Methodological," *BibInt* 15 (2007): 1–25 (23), adding that "what feminist scholars share in common…is a critical sensibility, an encompassing angle of vision that, in a more fundamental fashion than a methodological framework, brings previously unperceived or disavowed data into focus." See also J. Cheryl Exum, "Developing Strategies of Feminist Criticism/Developing Strategies for Commentating The Song of Songs," in *Auguries: The Jubilee Volume of the Sheffield Department of Biblical Studies* (ed. D. J. A. Clines and S. D. Moore; Sheffield: Sheffield Academic, 1998), 206–49 (207), "Feminist biblical criticism is neither a discipline nor a method, but more a variety of approaches, informed…by the interests and concerns of feminism as a world view and political enterprise. Pluralism and interdisciplinarity are two of its most important features."

formations…. As long as feminism remains a process of coming to terms
but never arriving, always interrogating the very terms it constitutes and
never mastering them, it will continue to be a challenging mode of inquiry.[53]

I suggest the postcolonial turn is one such challenging mode. There have
been many voices issuing this challenge, since the 1999 SBL session
chaired by Kwok Pui-lan,[54] but its full force came with Musa Dube's
2000 *Postcolonial Feminist Interpretation of the Bible.* In 2002 Laura
Donaldson and Kwok Pui-lan wrote urging us to take the interactions
between colonialism, gender, and religion as the focus of study in that
together they "constitute some of the most significant and contradictory
forces influencing our world today."[55] Dora Mbuwayesango in the 2008
roundtable discussion talked of the need "to correlate gender issues with
the persistent issue of imperialism. It is not a matter of prioritizing one
over another but of recognizing the interlocking of imperialism, race,
class, and gender."[56] It is, as Kwok Pui-lan describes it, the "exploration
of the interstices of different forms of oppression under the shadow of
the empire" that "constitutes the exciting postcolonial feminist project."[57]
    The connections are there in Jeremiah as early as ch. 2: Jerusalem
sprawling promiscuously under every green tree (v. 20), and Jeremiah so
keen to turn his audience from a religious practice he opposes, he uses
female sexuality, shamefully. I find sharp connections here with concerns for religious orthodoxy with New Zealand. The ancestors of Maori
tradition known as *atua* continue to play a vital role in Maori spirituality
as significant life forces. For Maori Christians there is no faith conflict.
In *Reframing Her* I recounted the incident of a student accosting the
Maori lecturer, an ordained Presbyterian, with the charge of syncretism.[58]
Said's lingering voice of empire!

    53. Quoted by The Bible and Culture Collective, *The Postmodern Bible* (New
Haven: Yale University Press, 1995), 270, from Elizabeth Weed, ed., *Coming to
Terms: Feminism/Theory/Politics* (New York: Routledge, 1989), xxxi.
    54. Under the title New Testament Studies and Postcolonial Studies.
    55. Laura E. Donaldson and Kwok Pui-lan, "Introduction," in *Postcolonialism,
Feminism, and Religious Discourse* (ed. L. E. Donaldson and Kwok P.-l.; New
York: Routledge, 2002), 1–38 (1).
    56. Dora Mbuwayesango and Susanne Scholz, "Roundtable Discussion: Feminist
Biblical Studies: Dialogical Beginnings: A Conversation on the Future of Feminist
Biblical Studies," *JFSR* 25, no. 2 (2009): 93–103 (95).
    57. Kwok Pui-lan, "Making the Connections: Postcolonial Studies and Feminist
Biblical Interpretation," reprinted in *The Postcolonial Biblical Reader* (ed. R. S.
Sugirtharajah; Oxford: Blackwell, 2006), 45–63 (48).
    58. McKinlay, *Reframing Her*, 36.

Male writing and the female body, female sexuality: so complex, so worrying, so ever present, Jeremiah's animalized imagery of ch. 2 a disturbing example.[59] Its use as a marker "of national, racial, religious and ethnic communities in dominant discourses of identity," to quote Irene Gedalof, has been well recognized across the disciplines. So, too, its use in representing "place" in the sense of the pure space of "home."[60] So mother Rachel in that poignantly utopian homecoming of ch. 31. But, as Alice Keefe and others remind us, "woman's violated body" is also used biblically "as a metonym for social disruption and warfare": Jerusalem, the loveliest, must not only be destroyed (6:3–8), but, most disturbingly, raped by YHWH himself (13:20–27).[61] So, too, the feminizing of Babylon and others in the Oracles against the Nations. Again the complexities: Jeremiah's use of the adultery metaphor is clearly both sexual in its language and political in its purpose, and, if Carolyn Sharp is right, both parties, the pro-*golah* and the Judahite group, used it differently for their own purposes.[62] The Jeremiah writers knew well the power of female imagery, and used it to full disturbing effect. Angela Bauer's question of the "shifting layers of competing sounds and echoes, who have been the audiences…and whose voices have they heard?" once again highlights the difficulties in teasing out the full postcolonial implications.[63] Whose male discourse is it, that employs such gendered images and to what end?[64]

59. See Athalya Brenner, "On Prophetic Propaganda and the Politics of 'Love': The Case of Jeremiah," in *A Feminist Companion to the Latter Prophets* (ed. A. Brenner; FCB 8; Sheffield: Sheffield Academic, 1995), 256–74 (262–63).

60. Irene Gedalof, "Taking (a) Place: Female Embodiment and the Re-grounding of Community," in *Uprootings/Regroundings: Questions of Home and Migration* (ed. S. Ahmed et al.; Oxford: Berg, 2003), 91–112 (91).

61. Keefe, "Rapes of Women/Wars of Men," 81, noting, 89, that it is "the sacrality of woman's body as the source and matrix of the life of Israel which undergirds the power of rape as a rhetorical device in these narratives." See Pamela Gordon and Harold C. Washington, "Rape as a Military Metaphor in the Hebrew Bible," in Brenner, ed., *A Feminist Companion to the Latter Prophets*, 308–25; Christl M. Maier, *Daughter Zion, Mother Zion: Gender, Space, and the Sacred in Ancient Israel* (Minneapolis: Fortress, 2008), 108–9; Julia M. O'Brien, *Challenging Prophetic Metaphor: Theology and Ideology in the Prophets* (Louisville: Westminster John Knox, 2008), 109–10.

62. Sharp, *Prophecy and Ideology in Jeremiah*, 116–18.

63. Angela Bauer, "Dressed to Be Killed: Jeremiah 4.29–31 as an Example for the Functions of Female Imagery in Jeremiah," in Diamond et al., eds., *Troubling Jeremiah*, 293–305 (303). See also, among others, Bauer, *Gender in the Book of*

Those of us who are feminist scholars need to ask ourselves the same question of our own work: to what end? Susanne Scholz sets the over-arching goal as "the socio-political, economic, and religious understanding and transformation of androcentric and hierarchical structures in our postcolonial world."[65] Over twenty years ago Patrocinio Schweickart wrote that "the point is not merely to interpret literature in various ways; the point is to *change the world*," reminding us that "[f]eminist criticism...is a mode of *praxis*."[66] It is inherently political because it recognizes the connection between what we read and how we act. A challenge indeed, but can we really bear its weight?

Five years ago, Athalya Brenner asked the question *"Quo vadis, feminist biblical scholarship?... Is the Master's House still the house you long to possess, only that you would like to become its legitimate(d) masters and mistresses instead of marginal(ized) lodgers?... Should we not simply demolish the house?"*[67]

So what do we do? I am still pondering, although I also keep asking myself whether there is a particularly feminist or women's way of writing. Recently I have been tentatively toying with Schüssler Fiorenza's

---

Jeremiah: A Feminist-literary Reading (New York: Lang, 1999); Maier, *Daughter Zion, Mother Zion*; O'Brien, *Challenging Prophetic Metaphor*; Kathleen M. O'Connor, "Jeremiah," in *The Women's Bible Commentary* (ed. C. A. Newsom and S. H. Ringe; London: SPCK, 1992), 169–77.

64. Brenner, "On Prophetic Propaganda," 261, asks the same question. See Robert Carroll's response, Robert P. Carroll, "Desire Under the Terebinths: On Pornographic Representation in the Prophets—A Response," in Brenner, ed., *A Feminist Companion to the Latter Prophets*, 275–307 (289).

65. Scholz, *Introducing the Women's Hebrew Bible*, 125. See also Mbuwaye-sango and Scholz, "Roundtable Discussion," 98–99: "[d]oes our work endorse scientific positivism, a presumably 'disinterested' attitude or does it assume an epistemological-ethical stance that fosters multiplicity of meanings, reader centeredness, and sociopolitical explorations...?"

66. Patrocinio P. Schweickart, "Reading Ourselves: Toward a Feminist Theory of Reading," in *Gender and Reading: Essays on Readers, Texts and Contexts* (ed. E. A. Flynn and P. P. Schweickart; Baltimore: Johns Hopkins University Press, 1986), 31–62 (39): "We cannot afford to ignore the activity of reading, for it is here that literature is realized as *praxis*. Literature acts on the world by acting on its readers."

67. Brenner, "Epilogue: Babies and Bathwater on the Road," 338. Sugirtharajah in Premnath, "Margins and Mainstream," 160, referring to the position of scholars from outside the West, but now resident and working in Western academic institutions, issues a similar warning of postcolonialism "being co-opted by the mainstream" with the loss of its "radical potency."

hermeneutic of imagination.[68] In a recent paper on Achsah (Judg 1:12–15; Josh 15:15–19) I write,

> Don't you realize, I say to her, how you're being used? You may be a clever opportunist but don't you realize how you're being used here, as a pawn of Judean politics?… This is no innocent text nor is your place in it…
>
> I decide to confront her again, reminding her of the question which all settler peoples have to answer: "By what authority and on what grounds can they justify to themselves either their own moves or those of their parents, grandparents or great-grandparents to gain and preserve authority over land and the people of the land."[69]
>
> Answering this is one of the functions of settler master narratives, I tell her, and you are a significant figure in just such a narrative. She, however, remains silent.
>
> Oh yes, I say, I know about silences too. There are notable silences in our histories; what is well remembered in Maori oral tradition frequently remains a silence for those of us who are Pakeha, just as you have a voice but not those Canaanites enslaved as forced labour (Judg 1:28, 30, 33, 35).[70]

But, leaving Achsah and returning to the paper, can I claim this as womanly, when Jeremiah may have been doing much the same in ch. 44? If I were a poet I might attempt to write a woman's poetry as the counter voice, as Julie Kelso does in her Irigarayan reading of Chronicles, although it seems the writer of Jer 4:19–21 has done this already.[71]

So, finally, what are we all doing as postcolonial writers? Sugirtharajah describes postcolonialism as "an undertaking of social and political commitment";[72] Jon Berquist talks of a "moral act of commitment," of postcolonialism "provid[ing] a space in which to choose voices to

68. Elisabeth Schüssler Fiorenza, *But She Said: Feminist Practices of Biblical Interpretation* (Boston: Beacon, 1992), 53, 73–76.

69. Augie Fleras and Paul Spoonley, *Recalling Aotearoa: Indigenous Politics and Ethnic Relations in New Zealand* (Auckland: Oxford University Press, 1999), 14.

70. Judith E. McKinlay, "Meeting Achsah on Achsah's Land," *The Bible and Critical Theory* 5, no. 3 (2009): 39.1–39.11 (39.5, 8).

71. Julie Kelso, *O Mother, Where Art Thou? An Irigarayan Reading of the Book of Chronicles* (London: Equinox, 2007). See Barbara B. Kaiser, "Poet as 'Female Impersonator': The Image of Daughter Zion as Speaker in Biblical Poems of Suffering," *JR* 67 (1987): 164–82; Angela Bauer, "Jeremiah as Female Impersonator: Roles of Difference in Gender Perception and Gender Perceptivity," in *Escaping Eden: New Feminist Perspectives on the Bible* (ed. H. C. Washington et al.; The Biblical Seminar 65; Sheffield: Sheffield Academic, 1998), 199–207 (199–203); Maier, *Daughter Zion, Mother Zion*, 89.

72. Sugirtharajah, *Postcolonial Criticism*, 14.

construct interpretations that may have decolonizing effects in the contemporary world."[73] For Sugirtharajah the critical tools are of use only "as long as they probe injustices, produce new knowledge which problematizes well-entrenched positions, and enhances the lives of the marginalized."[74] Current race relations in Aotearoa New Zealand bear the marks of colonization all too clearly: Health, education, prison statistics stand as clear witness, and most recently the rise of Maori unemployment to 16.4%.[75] If, as a reader of the dominant culture, I am complicit in the ways in which this postcolonial society orders its life, do I have an ethical responsibility to take this into account? As Daniel Patte wrote some time ago,

> the question "Why did we choose this interpretation rather than another one?" can no longer be avoided by pretending that it was demanded by the text and that we had no choice…assuming responsibility for our critical studies is not simply a matter of…making sure that our studies are truly scholarly, but also a moral obligation toward all those believers and unbelievers who are affected by our critical studies.[76]

One aspect of postcolonial work that I have personally found challenging is uncovering disturbing facets in a text I have always valued positively. For me, that difficulty first came with the book of Ruth. Accepting the tension that remains between the heart-warming and the discomforting is not easy, just as there is always that risk that we will convince ourselves we have the right readings, the right analysis, and the right answers, forgetting that we always read subjectively.

The reminder of Gordon Collier needs to be taken to heart:

> So long as postcolonial analysts remain aware of the fact that they themselves are engaged in fruitful processes of mistranslations, mistranscription and misidentification not dissimilar to those they would expose, then the project's health will be safeguarded by its own antibodies.[77]

---

73. Berquist, "Postcolonialism and Imperial Motives," 32, 29.
74. Sugirtharajah, *Postcolonial Criticism*, 100.
75. See New Zealand Labour Party Press Release, 5 August 2010, quoting Parekura Horomia, Labour Maori Affairs spokesperson, "While unemployment nationally has jumped from 6 percent to a staggering 6.8 percent, the Maori rate has climbed from 14.2 percent to 16.4 percent," n.p. [cited 9 August 2010]. Online: www.labour.org.nz/news/unemployment-impact-particularly-savage-maori.
76. Daniel Patte, "Critical Biblical Studies from a Semiotics Perspective," *Semeia* 81 (1998): 3–26 (22).
77. Gordon Collier, "Introduction," in *Us/Them: Translation, Transcription and Identity in Post-Colonial Literary Cultures* (ed. G. Collier; Atlanta: Rodopi, 1992),

The last word goes to Tat-siong Benny Liew: viewing through a post-colonial lens means reading the text by way of a detour "that takes one in and through a different land(scape).... By the time one (re)turns to the biblical text, what and how one sees will...have become different because of all the differences that one has encountered along the way."[78] I wish you well as you take the detour.

xii–xv (xv), quoted by Berquist, "Postcolonialism and Imperial Motives," 26. So, too, Sugirtharajah's reminder, *Postcolonial Criticism and Biblical Interpretation*, 14, that it "is always open to its own contradictions and shortcomings."

78. Tat-siong Benny Liew, "Margins and (Cutting-)Edges: On the (Il)Legitimacy and Intersections of Race, Ethnicity, and (Post)Colonialism," in Moore and Segovia, eds., *Postcolonial Biblical Criticism*, 114–65 (146).

Mapping Jeremiah as/in a Feminist Landscape: Negotiating Ancient and Contemporary Terrains

Carolyn J. Sharp

In the winter of 2003, I found myself in Scottsdale, Arizona, hiking up Camelback Mountain with a group of educators from across the country who had gathered to reflect on theological teaching and learning.[1] One Christian Education colleague, an experienced hiker, raced ahead, shouting words of encouragement to the rest of us. I was eager to join him, but the trail was more demanding than I had realized. It quickly became a steep climb over boulders and loose shale, requiring constant focus so as not to lose one's footing. Finally I came to a place where I had to clutch a guide rope and clamber up the daunting pitch of a giant boulder blocking the trail. This required some strategizing. I looked up and saw that I was in trouble: huge rocks everywhere, no visible trail, a cliff on the left with just a rickety chain-link fence between us and a 200-foot drop-off, and nothing but a rope to hold onto. It finally came home to me: I had moved into a harsh and dangerous landscape. I had come far, but now I felt trapped: I could neither go forward nor easily go back. There were stunning views of the Arizona desert, to be sure, but the risk was too great. With some shame, I painstakingly made my way back down and appreciated the view from another vantage point far below, where I found community with two other women who had not attempted the summit. I learned only later just how dangerous that trail is. Every year hikers die on Camelback Mountain. A week earlier, there had been a fatality only a few dozen yards from where we were.[2]

1.   I am grateful to the Wabash Center for Teaching and Learning in Theology and Religion for its important work in support of the professional development of theological educators. The Scottsdale gathering was a component of the Workshop for Theological School Faculty program that the Wabash Center regularly hosts.
    2.   I cannot now verify what I had been told verbally at the time, viz., that a hiker died in early 2003 on Camelback Mountain. One can verify the more recent tragic

This is not a story of how perseverance and training can help one make it to the top of a huge mountain. It is a story about looking up and recognizing only late that one has been moving deeper and deeper into a harsh landscape, at significant risk to one's well-being.

I began scholarly work on Jeremiah in the early 1990s because I was fascinated by the tradition of God's "servants the prophets" in the Jeremianic prose. The prophetic function of warning the people was a motif that I wanted to study more deeply because it appealed to my idealistic desire for reformation of faith communities, the academy, and society. I was aware, of course, that women come up seldom in the book of Jeremiah. There is the metaphorization of Israel as unfaithful wife and as Daughter Zion, the stirring image in ch. 31 of Rachel weeping for her children, ch. 44's pejorative characterization of Judean women's leadership of the cult of the Queen of Heaven, and gendered shaming of foreign nations in the oracles against the nations. But apart from those texts, Jeremiah shows little interest in women's bodies, women's cultural or social roles, and women's spiritual experience. This did not trouble me because, as a feminist, I have always rejected the notion that a text can be meaningful for me only if it talks about "women's issues." I claim as my own the tradition of Jeremiah as preacher because I too am a preacher. I claim as my own the lamentations of Jeremiah because I too lament the agonies of our broken world. I claim as my own the political struggles visible in the Deutero-Jeremianic prose, because I too struggle with conflict in my own communities of conviction.

So the androcentrism of Jeremiah did not surprise me, nor did it stop me from exploring the book with intellectual eagerness. But as I pursued my work, the androcentrism of *biblical studies* did shock me. The major commentaries on Jeremiah were all written by men[3]—wonderfully

fatalities through news reports: a 50-year-old man died on the mountain in December 2008, a 20-year-old woman died in February 2009, and a 63-year-old man died in March 2011.

3.   The major commentaries in English were by John Bright, William Holladay, Robert Carroll, and William McKane. Other important male scholars working on Jeremiah in English at that time included Walter Brueggemann, R. E. Clements, Philip King, Jack Lundbom, J. G. McConville, and Louis Stulman. In German scholarship, important full-length studies had been done by Georg Fischer, Karl-Friedrich Pohlmann, Konrad Schmid, Hermann-Josef Stipp, and Winfried Thiel. See Georg Fischer, *Trostbüchlein: Text, Komposition und Theologie von Jer 30–31* (Stuttgart: Katholisches Bibelwerk, 1993), as well as his more recent books, *Jeremia* (2 vols.; Freiburg: Herder, 2005), *Jeremia—der Stand der theologischen Diskussion* (Darmstadt: Wissenschaftliche Buchgesellschaft, 2007), and *Der Prophet wie*

learned scholars, of course, but not a female commentary-writer among them. The only woman I found whose work undertook to offer a wide-ranging explanation for textual issues throughout the book of Jeremiah was Helga Weippert.[4] Angela Bauer's *Gender in the Book of Jeremiah* would not be published until 1999, Christl Maier's *Jeremia als Lehrer der Tora* would not come out until 2002, and Maria Häusl's *Bilder der Not: Weiblichkeits- und Geschlechtermetaphorik im Buch Jeremia* would not be published until 2003.[5] Further, with the exception of Robert Carroll's work, the commentaries by male authors did not engage the gendering of metaphors in Jeremiah, the construction of Judah as a normative masculine subject, or the sexism of biblical reception history. My biblical studies professors at Yale did not comment often on issues of gender in the ancient world, nor did they reflect on the rampant andro-centrism in contemporary biblical scholarship and the implications of it for our acts of interpretation.

To find a life-giving moment of feminist possibility that could sustain me, I had to look back to my college years, to a seminar in Religious Studies taught by Ron Cameron at Wesleyan University when I was 21 years old. Our class had been discussing Elisabeth Schüssler Fiorenza's new book, *Bread Not Stone*.[6] One student could not understand how Schüssler Fiorenza could identify as a Roman Catholic when her strong feminist views about the harmful effects of kyriarchy seemed to situate

Mose: Studien zum Jeremiabuch (Wiesbaden: Harrassowitz, 2011); Karl-Friedrich Pohlmann, *Studien zum Jeremiabuch: Ein Beitrag zur Frage nach der Entstehung des Jeremiabuches* (FRLANT 118; Göttingen: Vandenhoeck & Ruprecht, 1978); Konrad Schmid, *Buchgestalten des Jeremiabuches: Untersuchungen zur Redaktions- und Rezeptionsgeschichte von Jer 30–33 im Kontext des Buches* (WMANT 72; Neukirchen–Vluyn: Neukirchener, 1996); Winfried Thiel, *Die deuteronomistische Redaktion von Jeremia 1–25* (WMANT 41; Neukirchen–Vluyn: Neukirchener, 1973), and *Die deuteronomistische Redaktion von Jeremia 26–45* (WMANT 52; Neukirchen–Vluyn: Neukirchener, 1981).

4. Helga Weippert, *Die Prosareden des Jeremiabuches* (BZAW 132; Berlin: de Gruyter, 1973).

5. Angela Bauer, *Gender in the Book of Jeremiah: A Feminist-Literary Reading* (New York: Lang, 1999); Christl Maier, *Jeremia als Lehrer der Tora: Soziale Gebote des Deuteronomiums in Fortschreibungen des Jeremiabuches* (FRLANT 196; Göttingen: Vandenhoeck & Ruprecht, 2002); Maria Häusl, *Bilder der Not: Weiblichkeits- und Geschlechtermetaphorik im Buch Jeremia* (HBS 37; Freiburg: Herder, 2003).

6. Elisabeth Schüssler Fiorenza, *Bread Not Stone: The Challenge of Feminist Biblical Interpretation* (Boston: Beacon, 1995; originally published 1985).

her so far outside of traditional Roman Catholic theology and ecclesiology. "How can she call herself a Catholic?" the student asked, visibly impatient. Dr. Cameron paused and then said quietly, "She declines to see herself on the margins. She claims the center." I was astonished to hear that she could claim the center when others were trying to assign her to the margins, and I marveled at Schüssler Fiorenza's courage.

With that single transformative moment to sustain me as a feminist in the biblical studies classroom, I worked hard for many years in the terrain of androcentric historical-critical biblical scholarship. My joy in exploring the historical, literary, and theological riches of biblical text energized me and continues to catalyze my engagements with Scripture. It is only in recent years that I have looked up and recognized just how harsh and inhospitable is this landscape, how strewn the path with giant boulders, how steep and dangerous the drop-offs on every side. Even today, although we now have excellent monographs on aspects of religious practice and cultic thought pertaining to women in ancient Israel, the need for a thoroughgoing feminist commentary on Jeremiah remains,[7] and the need for ongoing feminist dialogue about biblical studies remains urgent.

Prolegomena on Method and the Writing of Commentaries

In our collaborative Jeremiah commentary,[8] Christl Maier and I are making use of late-modern and postmodern methods of interpretation—chiefly literary, feminist, and postcolonial criticism—while also honoring historical-critical scholarship on Jeremiah. It is a daunting task, not least because the book of Jeremiah is characterized by a rich polyphony in both diachronic and synchronic dimensions. Texts in Jeremiah reflect diverse historical settings from the 620s B.C.E. through the decline of the Assyrian empire and the rise of Babylonia in the last decade of the seventh century, through Babylon's deportation of leading Judean priests and officials in 597 to the fall of Jerusalem in 586; some material in Jeremiah reflects knowledge of the rise of Persia in the mid-sixth

---

7. See Kathleen M. O'Connor's *Jeremiah: Pain and Promise* (Minneapolis: Fortress, 2011), which does address much of the book of Jeremiah but is not a verse-by-verse commentary.

8. This collaborative Jeremiah commentary is a work in progress under contract with Kohlhammer Verlag. Maier's *Jeremia 1–25* and my *Jeremiah 26–52* are slated to appear simultaneously in the series International Exegetical Commentary on the Old Testament (IECOT)/Internationaler Exegetischer Kommentar zum Alten Testament (IEKAT).

century, and the Masoretic tradition of Jeremiah unquestionably underwent expansion even after that time. Some Jeremiah traditions seem to
have focused on promotion of the political authority of the Judeans in
diaspora in Babylon, whereas other traditions do not do so and may
reflect settings back in Judah or in Egypt, hence we will contend also
with geographical diversity in the ancient contexts.[9] Literarily, Jeremiah
presents many genres: chilling oracles of doom and luminous oracles
of salvation; short prose comments on poetic oracles, and lengthy biographical narratives that include paraenesis and sign-acts. And the
ideological-critical elements that beg for analysis are too many to list.
This essay will explore only the beginnings of several ideological-critical
issues that arise in just 18 verses of text.

A feminist commentary must read wisely all of the historical, literary,
and ideological dimensions of this text. Historical analysis is urgently
needed because it is in the embodied, lived experience of culture and
relationships that feminism works to create conditions of justice, for
women and for all who have been marginalized, silenced, or oppressed.[10]

---

9. See my *Prophecy and Ideology in Jeremiah: Struggles for Authority in the
Deutero-Jeremianic Prose* (New York: T. & T. Clark, 2003).

10. This is one response to the challenge issued by Dora Mbuwayesango and
Susanne Scholz in their piece entitled "Dialogical Beginnings: A Conversation on
the Future of Feminist Biblical Studies," *JFSR* 25, no. 2 (2009): 93–143. They write,
"We need to challenge those among us who use, for instance, historical criticism in
their feminist interpretations, to delineate more explicitly how feminist goals are met
through such methodologies. Among the questions we could ask are: How does this
or that method make a reading 'feminist,' and how does it 'matter' and relate to the
world today? Also crucial is that there is enough space for those whose ways of
interpretation are classified as 'other.' Dora thinks that methods are often used to set
boundaries, to define who is 'inside' and who is 'outside' assumed norms. In short,
the use of methodologies needs to be linked to feminist purposes and goals that need
to be articulated more thoroughly. We find the following three questions helpful in
this process: How does one method serve a clearly identified and articulated feminist
goal and not another? Do our various intellectual and academic traditions and
settings limit our openness to certain methods, and how do we account for such
limitations? Both Susanne and Dora propose that the choice of method should be
correlated with the established reading goals. In other words, feminist biblical
hermeneutics should always consider the question: So what? Dora also affirms that
an interpretation needs to challenge oppressive ideas embedded in biblical texts so
that feminist interpretations contribute to the liberation of oppressed segments in
society. Hence, we suggest that a use of methods that endorses androcentric perspectives and agendas does not lead to liberative goals in feminist interpretation of
the Bible or in the world" (pp. 96–97).

Literary and ideological-critical analysis are equally crucial because it is by means of "texts" writ in the broadest sense—from scrolls to coins to other painted, sculpted, and otherwise inscribed cultural artifacts, ancient and contemporary—that ideologies of domination and ideologies of liberation are communicated in the most enduring ways within and across cultures. Sophisticated feminist analysis must deal with the history of the generation of the text and its representations of history; with its literary artistry and rhetoric; with reception history and *Wirkungs-geschichte*; and with political and social dimensions of performances of power within reading communities that claim Jeremiah as sacred or as culturally significant.

Goals of Feminist Critique
Dr. Maier and I are considering the goals of feminist cultural critique more generally as foundational for our work on Jeremiah. In this essay, I propose three driving concerns of feminist critique as I understand them and then offer a reading of Jer 30:5–22 with these goals framing my interpretive questions. Because feminist work is collaborative and honors many voices, I offer these only as an opening of conversation, not an authoritative pronouncement.

First: feminism interrogates and seeks to destabilize ideologies of subjugation and the oppressive practices to which those ideologies give rise, wherever those may be discerned. As regards lived experience, discourse, and cultural representations of every kind, feminists seek to identify and expose deforming misuses of power and to destabilize them in whatever ways are possible to us. Feminist biblical interpreters should offer sustained critique of androcentric and patriarchal ideologies performed by or assumed in ancient sacred texts, and further, should reveal the limitations and oppressive biases of contemporary Western biblical analysis, listening to those who identify as non-Western or not vested in a particular aspect of dominant culture. Most important, feminist biblical interpreters must dare to read resistantly, creatively, and constructively with and for communities of readers who privilege the voices and experiences of the marginalized. That is to say, feminist interpreters engage in advocacy.

A second important goal of feminist critique is to assist cultural systems in moving beyond essentialism, an epistemological perspective that assigns necessary and "natural" ontological characteristics related to gender, race, or other dimensions of human living. Essentialism has been rampant not only in patriarchal constructions of hermeneutics and the social contexts of scholarship but also within feminist thought itself until the pioneering work of Judith Butler[11] and other "Third Wave" feminists, some of whom would identify more as gender theorists than feminist thinkers. Essentialism is a crucial component in many ideologies of oppression and must be addressed vigorously, for it allows oppressors, colonizers, and antagonists to limit and dehumanize those against whom they are working.

A third goal of feminist analysis, in critique and in constructive thought alike, *is to facilitate work for justice and shalom*. Feminism is not "disinterested" or neutral; it has seen through the artificial mask of scientific objectivity that is a chief disguise of patriarchal interests. Feminists know that all human viewpoints and cultural productions are driven by vested interests and ideologies, whether their proponents recognize that or not. Feminists claim positions of advocacy for justice and *shalom* as urgently needed in a world that is fractured and distorted by ideologies of subjugation. It follows that feminist analysis must continually inquire into its own motivations, commitments, and ideological positions, so as to challenge its own distortions and misuses of power. This is why feminist work is so often collaborative and dialogical: because we cannot easily see our own distortions and mistakes, feminists recognize the need for ongoing lively critique and dialogue as the most effective mode in which to seek to challenge all ideologies of subjugation, including our own. It is a basic tenet of feminism that, while telling one's own story is vital, it is equally vital to take seriously the stories of others (including those vested in dominant cultures), to seek to hear what is at stake for the Other. Only in a dialogical and collaborative way can feminists dismantle what needs to be dismantled without producing new dynamics of silencing and oppression.

As regards biblical scholarship on the book of Jeremiah, then, the dominance of historical-critical modes of inquiry has traditionally brought with it many artificial assumptions about who and what mattered in ancient Judah and ancient Near Eastern geopolitical and local landscapes. Historical critics have tended to focus fetishistically on wars, kings, monumental buildings, and international politics as if those subjects were the only viable topics for investigation. Male power was privileged and assumed to be appropriate in the ancient texts themselves, in synagogue and church contexts within which biblical interpretation

---

11. See Judith Butler, *Gender Trouble: Feminism and the Subversion of Identity* (New York: Routledge, 1990), and *Bodies That Matter: On the Discursive Limits of "Sex"* (New York: Routledge, 1993).

took place for many centuries, and in the guild of contemporary biblical scholarship as well. It should be transparently clear that women's bodies, domestic practices, constructions of masculinity, and so on are also important topics of historical inquiry; but the androcentrism of biblical interpretation was so thoroughgoing—and in many contexts is still so pervasive—that the lives, ideas, bodies, and social and political constructions of women and non-normative men have been treated as if they were "special topics." And so feminist inquiry into Jeremiah must continue to interrogate ideologies of subjugation in the text and in its reception history, decline the ways in which gender, economic class, sexuality, ethnic identity, and able-bodiedness may be essentialized within the text and in scholarship, and provide readings of the text—critical and constructive—that further the work of justice and *shalom*.

Postcolonial and Queer Dimensions of the Feminist Project
I pause to articulate postcolonial and queer dimensions of the feminist interpretive project as I understand them, with the caveat that of course postcolonialism and queer theory cannot be wholly subsumed under feminist analysis. Postcolonial criticism refuses the claims, overt predations, and oppressive gestures of empire: namely, cultural discourses and pragmatic actions (military, social, political) that seek to establish the "naturalness" and beneficence of imperial rule over against the supposed primitive, immoral, benighted, or ineffective character of indigenous colonized persons and native cultures. Under pressure of colonialism, colonized subjects—subalterns—deploy a variety of strategies to survive, that is, to resist the colonizing distortions, commodifications, and threatened erasure of their indigenous culture and the deformation of their own subjectivity and agency. Those surviving under colonialism use tactics of assimilation, mimicry, parody, and strategic silence as well as outright resistance. Postcolonial biblical criticism aims to support the flourishing of the resistant subaltern, especially by critiquing imperialist ideologies within texts and in interpretive practices, whether in the scholarly guild, in missional work by the Church, or in any other cultural venue. Feminists and other allies of colonized persons listen for the voice of the subaltern and its distortions,[12] and they engage in practices of reading that seek to destabilize Western and other intellectual claims of empire. I would note that the rejection of essentialism is crucially

12. See, e.g., Gayatri Chakravorty Spivak, "Can the Subaltern Speak?," in *Marxism and the Interpretation of Culture* (ed. C. Nelson and L. Grossberg; Urbana: University of Illinois Press, 1988), 271–313.

important for postcolonial work, which honors the subjectivity of the subaltern as fluid, strategic, and hybrid. Because feminist analysis is opposed to all misuses of power from the interpersonal to the global, ideologies of empire writ domestically, regionally, nationally, and internationally fall under the purview of feminism.

Queer theory inquires into ways in which social constructions reinforce certain ideas of what is normative or "natural," including but not limited to notions of sexuality, sexual identity, and gender identity. Phallocentrism, misogyny, and heterosexist constructions of subjectivity and relationship are unmasked as fearful cultural productions that harm queer (and other) persons and that are inexcusably false to the rich variety of sexual and gender expressions existing in the world. Queer theory opens up new spaces for the authentic performance of sexual and social identity in creative, hybrid ways that resist the attempts of patriarchy to keep alternative identities on the margins of psycho-sexual space. Queer biblical hermeneutics deploy a variety of reading strategies in service of queer creativity and queer resistance, honoring the irreducible queerness of ancient lived witness to the holy. Queer theologian Marcella Althaus-Reid has said, "The unique characteristic of revelation in history lies in its queerness, that non-normalising, subversive discourse which resists identity's claims to finality and fixity."[13] Queer engagements of biblical prophetic witness, then, participate in (re)interpreting the ways in which the ancient prophets such as Jeremiah offered subversive discourse in order to decline false fixities and destabilize unjust norms.

As a White, Western, well-educated, upper-middle-class, straight married person, I myself cannot claim the status of subaltern in my social context. But I do claim the truth of my lived, embodied experience as a woman under patriarchal systems of many kinds as having important resonances with the experiences of colonized peoples, as I have heard those experiences described. In the academy and in the Church, my body, my spiritual and intellectual energy, and my political imagination have been repeatedly shamed, silenced, rewarded for not rebelling, and in other ways colonized by the androcentrism, phallic heterosexism, and misogyny on which patriarchy feeds. The distorting imperial ideologies of patriarchy go far beyond any particular culture. These ideologies have harmed female, male, transgender, and genderqueer subjects for millennia. As a feminist, I absolutely do claim that they have harmed me and harmed those whom I love. So I am deeply grateful for postcolonial and queer theory, and I stand ready, as an ally, to learn from and support

---

13. Marcella Althaus-Reid, *The Queer God* (London: Routledge, 2003), 156.

the practitioners of these critical interventions. Allowing postcolonial and queer modes of analysis to interrogate the cultural categories of Jeremiah—and of contemporary biblical scholarship—sheds light on the anxieties that lie behind constructions of subjectivity in Jeremiah and in contemporary biblical interpretation. A feminist theoretical position informed by postcolonial and queer criticism will be better equipped to see beyond the terrible rigidities and failures of imagination that constitute patriarchy.

Exegetical Journey Through Jeremiah 30:5–22

We may now turn our attention to Jer 30:5–22, a key text within the so-called "Book of Consolation" of Jer 30–31. It is a fascinating text that both illustrates and challenges feminist hermeneutical convictions. A rich and beautiful landscape lies before us, but it is also challenging terrain: there are grave risks for the feminist who would map this androcentric text. I will argue that five dimensions of the rhetoric and poetic artistry of this passage are directly relevant for the feminist interpretive endeavor.

Poetics of Absence

First, we may discern in vv. 5–17 a structuring poetics of absence. In vv. 5–7, the prophet[14] names the agony of his people under siege: "a cry of panic, of terror, and no peace." The reader hears the tumult and screams of a people under attack: Jerusalem is being assaulted by the invading Babylonian army. No peace: this is a true prophetic word within the discourse of Jeremiah and also true of Jeremiah as landscape for feminist travelers. It is the false prophets who cry "*shalom*" when there is no *shalom* (שלום שלום ואין שלום).[15] The true prophet, as sentinel, compels the people to face the spiritual and moral failures of their community through history (the persistence of sin through past generations is important in Jeremiah) and in the present moment of the text. Naming sin and brokenness is essential if God's covenant people are to live. This אין שלום inaugurates a brilliant poetics of absence that structures the next 12 verses. We see the predication of absence with אין over and over: אין מחריד in v. 10; אין־דן דינך למזור and רפאות תעלה אין לך in v. 13; and דרש אין לה in v. 17.

---

14. Some have argued that YHWH is the speaker in v. 5.
15. Jer 6:14; 8:11; cf. Jer 4:10; 5:12–13; 23:16–17; 28:8–9.

Restoration moves from the naming of terror—אין שלום—to the
reversal of diaspora ("I am going to save you from far away, and your
offspring from the land of their captivity") and the establishment of a
new social reality in which no one shall make Jacob afraid: אין מחריד
(v. 10). But the people must understand how deep is their sinfulness, so
vv. 12 and 13 return to the woundedness of this people as a punishment
leveled by God against them: "Your hurt is incurable, your wound is
grievous." Again a poetics of absence: "there is no medicine for your
wound, no healing [flesh] for you." It is only God who can heal: "I have
done these things to you," God says (v. 15, עשיתי אלה לך), and "your
wounds I will heal" (v. 17, ממכותיך ארפאך). Where enemies and allies
alike are absent, God alone stands with Israel, powerful to punish and
powerful to heal.

The last signifier of absence in our passage is beautifully and ironically polyvalent. It manages to gesture toward the absence of all human
help while implicitly underscoring the unseen but mighty presence of
God: the end of v. 17: God will heal, "because they have called you an
outcast: 'It is Zion; no one cares for her!'," or more literally, "Zion, for
whom no one bothers to search": ציון היא דרש אין לה. This quoted
speech of an antagonistic commentator invites Zion to understand that
her forsaken status has indeed been observed. Yet, as is always the case
with irony, what has been said here is not the deepest or most important
truth.[16] It may seem that Zion has been forsaken, but God does take
account of Zion and will care for her.[17] Feminists may choose to read this
meta-textually as the promise of divine reversal of all oppression.[18]

Shaming of the Masculine Subject
A second dimension of the rhetoric of this passage begins with the
shaming of the normative masculine subject in v. 6. The Judahite male
subject is derisively likened to a woman in labor, in a move rightly called
"ironisch-provozierend"[19] that is used in the prophetic books to shame

16. On the theorizing of irony in biblical texts, see my *Irony and Meaning in the
Hebrew Bible* (Bloomington: Indiana University Press, 2009), and the literature cited
in Chapter 1 there.

17. Jack Lundbom (*Jeremiah 21–36* [AB 21B; New York: Doubleday, 2004],
372) translates the last phrase of v. 17 as "The Zion Whom No One Cares About."

18. Further elaboration of the pattern of אין as a marker of absence in Jeremiah
shows a broad poetics of absence that is deployed throughout the book, with אין
formulations occurring also at Jer 4:4, 23, 29; 5:21; 6:14; 7:33; 8:11, 13, 15; 9:21;
13:19; 14:16, 19; 21:12; 30:5, 10; 44:2; 46:23, 27; 49:5; and 50:32.

19. Fischer, *Jeremia 26–52*, 125.

enemy warriors: those in defeat become, as it were, "like girls," which is highly insulting to a male subject conditioned in a patriarchal world-view. To liken the male to the feminine or the female body, especially in a sexuality-related or impurity-related context as with childbirth, is shame-inducing for the male subject in an androcentric cultural paradigm such as that of ancient Israel.[20] Childbirth is metaphorized as a source of terror and anguish, rather than life-giving, creative, or powerful; women's experience here is refracted through the gaze of the horrified and repulsed male subject. The feminist critic may choose to read this misogynistic metaphor resistantly, as opening the door to the transgendering of the ostensibly male subject in Jeremiah. This childbirth metaphor gestures toward a feminized male body and thus creates a fracture in the androcentrism of Jeremiah—a fracture deepened by notable gender fluidity throughout the rest of our passage, as the addressee/subject changes from Jacob (masculine singular, vv. 8–11) to Zion (feminine singular, vv. 12–17), back to Jacob (v. 18), and then to a communal plural subject (vv. 19–22).[21]

Feminists may theorize this gender fluidity as inviting the construction of a queer freedom for the subjectivity of all who listen for God's prophetic word. That is, this pattern of switching from masculine to feminine addressees betrays the constructed nature of sexual and social identity (entirely apart from the ancient authors having intended this, of course) and thus may constitute a helpful tactical resource for moving beyond both misogyny and essentialism writ more broadly. Jacob, the eponymous ancestor and normative male subject of ancient Israel, is transmuted into Zion, the vulnerable and powerful mother who is metonymic for Jerusalem as the sacred "place" that forms and re-forms the covenant people and who may signal the motherhood of YHWH as well.[22]

---

20. For the theorizing of gender as it relates to the figure of the warrior in the ancient Near East, see Gale A. Yee, "By the Hand of a Woman: The Metaphor of the Woman Warrior in Judges 4," *Semeia* 61 (1993): 99–132; Claudia D. Bergmann, "We Have Seen the Enemy, and He Is Only a 'She': The Portrayal of Warriors as Women," in *Writing and Reading War: Rhetoric, Gender, and Ethics in Biblical and Modern Contexts* (ed. B. E. Kelle and F. R. Ames; SBLSymS 42; Atlanta: Society of Biblical Literature, 2008), 129–42. The masculine singular participle יֹלֵד is quite rare in Biblical Hebrew, coming up only elsewhere in Prov 17:21 in the metaphorical phrase "the one who begets a fool gets trouble."

21. This *Geschlechterwechsel* is regular and systematic in the Book of Consolation, as Georg Fischer and others have noted; see Fischer, *Jeremia 26–52*, 121.

22. See Christl M. Maier, *Daughter Zion, Mother Zion: Gender, Space, and the Sacred in Ancient Israel* (Minneapolis: Fortress, 2008), esp. 201–4.

Once Zion becomes Jacob, her feminized agency can never be erased from the metaphorically male "body" of Jacob. Thus, Jeremiah's rhetoric of gender fluidity marks the body of "Israel" as hybrid and genderqueer, and Jer 30 becomes a place of queer freedom within the dominant gender discourse of a brutal honor- and shame-based society. Here a breach has been made—an incurable wound, we may say—in the androcentrism of the book of Jeremiah.

YHWH Against Imperialism

Third, the feminist reader may notice that vv. 8–9 set YHWH against imperialism. In v. 8, God signals the divine intention to break the colonial yoke from Jacob's neck. Liberation theology claims that God is on the side of the oppressed; Jon Sobrino characterizes the poor as a "crucified people" without whom salvation is impossible.[23] If that is so, then God is on the side of the colonized and the redemption of creation cannot be comprehended apart from God's healing of the colonized, these to include not only ancient Judeans who underwent forced migration to Babylon but economic migrants and refugees in every age, as well as those whose imaginations have been colonized by patriarchal *Bibelwissenschaft* and androcentric preaching. With God as ally, the position of the subaltern can become a position of strength. Womanist theologian Kelly Brown Douglas has argued that choosing subalternity— choosing agency that signifies from the margins—can mean locating oneself in a site of epistemological authority because the marginalized can see "the fragility of dominating power."[24]

The choice of subalternity, of course, can be dangerous when one romanticizes or essentializes marginalization. Our Jeremiah text is dangerous as well, for God remains a sovereign power whom Jacob must serve; more difficult still, the text locates imperial power positively in the Davidic king, and thus v. 9 keeps a monarchical model in place. I need not remark the androcentrism of many—although not all—monarchies in the history of the world, nor the regular exploitation of rural and urban-poor workers to supply the insatiable needs and fantasies of

---

23. I encountered this bold formulation first in the book of Jon Sobrino, *No Salvation Outside the Poor: Prophetic-Utopian Essays* (Maryknoll: Orbis, 2008), 3 and *passim*, who in turn was building on a 1977 monograph by Ignacio Ellacuría, "The Crucified People: An Essay in Historical Soteriology," reprinted in *Mysterium Liberationis* (trans. P. Berryman; ed. R. R. Barr; Maryknoll: Orbis, 1993), 580–603.

24. Kelly Brown Douglas, "Marginalized People, Liberating Perspectives: A Womanist Approach to Biblical Interpretation," *ATR* 83 (2001): 41–47 (43).

machines of empire, nor the threat of military expansionism that has accompanied the establishment of so many empires due to their inexorable drive to swallow territory and resources, as well as to press their own subjects into compliance rather than rebellion. Pro-monarchy statements in the Bible of any kind, including metaphors for God as king, are in need of feminist and postcolonial critique. Such critique may draw on resources from within the Bible, among them the idealistic construction of sovereignty in Deut 17 and biblical reflections of the ancient Near Eastern view of the king as one who defends the cause of the poor, delivers the needy, and crushes the oppressor (as seen, for example, in Ps 72).[25] In any case, the resistant reader can see in Jer 30:8–9 that YHWH is positioned against all other claims of dominance.

The Semantics of Salvation

Fourth, the reader attentive to the semantics of salvation may discern many beautiful poetic techniques, of which I will briefly mention two. First is an intense clustering of phrases of נאם יהוה in moments of reassurance to Jacob (vv. 3, 10, 11, 17, and 21). These are not just formulaic markers of oracle boundaries: where they are positioned, they function to emphasize the reliability of the divine promise to heal. Second, the repeated *shin* sounds in v. 10 are beautiful: ושב יעקב ושקט ושאנן (the aural effect of which is lost in translation: "Jacob shall return and have quiet and ease"). The repetition of *shin* has a soothing effect aurally. Further, it harkens back to הנני מושיעך ("I am going to save you") earlier in the verse, underlining the coherence of Jacob's return and quiet and rest with God as being-about-to-redeem or being-redeemer. Use of the participle in מושיעך is a stroke of poetic genius: its syntactical ambiguity allows a claim for the identity of God as always Israel's redeemer—the nominal force of the participle—while also evoking the incipient verbal sense, "I am about to redeem you," that is foundational for the utopian promise of this passage.

Liminality and Reversal

Last, we may explore a larger poetics of reversal in this passage. In v. 10 the audience enjoys utopian imagery of tranquility and *shalom*, but v. 11 returns the audience to their present moment of unresolved fear. Verse 11 creates a liminal moment in which the audience is suspended between hope and horror. (The intentional placement of these verses is clear:

---

25. E.g. Ps 72:4; this representation of the duties of the king is widespread throughout the ancient Near East.

vv. 10–11 are a doublet of 46:27–28 and have been added here secondarily, as they are not present in the LXX.) First, hope: God will destroy the nations but not Israel: "I will make an end of all the nations among which I scattered you, but of you I will not make an end." Following is brilliant ambiguity with ויסרתיך למשפט: God will…discipline Israel? Correct Israel? Yes, but יסר Piel may also have the sense of "to guide or train,"[26] and למשפט may underline both the appropriateness of Judah's punishment (*nach dem Recht* or *mit Maß*, per Georg Fischer)[27] and the justice, the recompense against enemies, for which Judah hopes. This crucial ambiguity is key to the entire passage. Here is a liminal moment that encompasses present domination and future freedom. It is precisely this ambiguity that allows Jeremiah to remain both a true prophet of the harsh present moment (אין שלום) and a visionary who sees God's redemptive purposes on the horizon.

The prophet names Judah's manifold sins and woundedness (vv. 12–15), and more reversals unfold in a semantics of recompense for enemy predations: "all who devour you shall be devoured…those who plunder you shall be plundered, and all who prey on you I will make a prey" (v. 16). Writ even larger are reversals that govern all of Jer 30. The sound of terror and fear in v. 5 will be turned into thanksgiving and the sound of merrymakers קול חרדה [וקול] פחד (the *nomen regens* is implicitly carried over to the second clause) yields to תודה וקול משחקים in v. 19. Verse 6's image of childbirth as alarming—not fruitful but unnatural and death-dealing—is reversed in v. 20 with the hope for offspring as in the days of old (והיו בניו כקדם). The most profound reversal for this community under siege[28] is the theological reversal that claims healing from the same God who had sent the *Plagentrias* of pestilence, famine, and sword stalking through the terrified community of Judah.

Cartography in the Borderlands

I have sought to show that there are resources within the text of Jeremiah for feminist cartographers, and so Jeremiah may be mapped as a feminist landscape. Yet there remain significant obstacles and threats for

26. It is fascinating that the doublet of this passage in 46:27–28 follows the oracle against hated enemy Egypt but also, in 46:26b, most immediately follows a brief word of promise to Egypt.
27. Fischer, *Jeremia 26–52*, 118.
28. "Under siege" metaphorically; this is no claim for a dating of Jer 30 to the period before the fall of Jerusalem.

feminists who would travel through the Jeremiah traditions. We must look up, recognize the dangers, and discern how we can safely traverse this landscape. In closing, I will briefly sketch two pathways along which feminist biblical scholars may journey as we continue to interrogate ideologies of subjugation, move beyond essentialism, and promote justice and *shalom*.

Decolonizing Covenant

First, I propose that feminist Hebrew Scripture scholars set about the hermeneutical work of "decolonizing" representations of Israel's covenant with YHWH. How might this be possible, when historically it is clear that Israel's covenant forms show influence from Hittite and Neo-Assyrian vassal treaties (vassalage being a classic institution of colonization), and further, when Israel's conception of the monarchy so deeply infuses Israel's notion of the divine? יהוה מלך—the LORD is king; God rules over the heavens and the earth; God sits enthroned on the flood and in the heavens and in the Temple.[29] In Deuteronomistic theology, Israel is the weaker party in a conditional covenant with God; in the Zion theology, Jerusalem is the impregnable seat of divine kingship, and the Davidic line is the eternal dynastic expression of God's love for Israel. Empire is at the heart of covenant, it would seem. But there are powerful resources within the Hebrew Scriptures for resisting the brutality with which humans have inscribed domination into our understandings of truth and holiness. I submit that the death-dealing ways of imperialism are refused, over and over again, by the God of the Hebrew Scriptures. Consider Hos 11:9: "I am God and no mortal, the Holy One in your midst, and I will not come in wrath." Consider the brutal ironizing of Israel's chosenness effected by the rhetoric of Amos. Consider Isa 19:24–25: "On that day Israel will be the third with Egypt and Assyria, a blessing in the midst of the earth, whom the LORD of Hosts has blessed, saying, 'Blessed be Egypt my people, and Assyria the work of my hands, and Israel my heritage'." Those who read Scripture for justice can deploy such biblical texts in our sacred work of "opening the Bible from the closures of previous readings."[30] Those who reject the predations of patriarchal power and the deformations of colonialism may ground our resistant readings in these sacred texts and many others, including some that might seem to be unlikely resources for feminist, postcolonial, and

29. See e.g. Pss 2 and 29; Isa 6, 37, and 40.
30. Althaus-Reid, *The Queer God*, 110.

queer advocacy.[31] Where the human imagination turns inevitably to domination, dissenters may claim Isa 55:8: "My thoughts are not your thoughts, nor are your ways my ways, says the LORD."

Further, the servants of YHWH may choose "subaltern" status as a site of creative resistance to oppression. This choice declines to acknowledge the "naturalness" of colonial power, and indeed ironizes scriptural claims that God wielded enemies as weapons to harm God's people. We may deploy Jer 30:9a—serving *only* YHWH—in a contestatory dialogue[32] with difficult texts, for example to fund our resistance to the claim that Assyria was ever a club wielded by a furious God (Isa 10:5) or that Nebuchadrezzar could possibly have been acting as "God's servant" (Jer 25:9; 27:6) when he slaughtered Judeans in the streets of Jerusalem.

The choice of subaltern status is something that must be done with great care, of course. We must be clear that this is not submission to worldly forms of domination but precisely the opposite: a refusal of the terms in which patriarchal power is configured. This choice, a feminist embrace of power Otherwise,[33] will reconfigure everything in the web of covenant relationships, for when one party within a system changes, all the others change too, as any pastoral-care practitioner knows. This decolonizing of covenant means a destabilizing of the power of empire and a claiming of the power of grace, something seen already in the Suffering Servant songs in Isaiah. The Christian feminist may cite also Phil 2:5–11, Rom 6, and 2 Cor 12 (where Paul says, "I will boast all the

---

31. On February 7, 2013 in Marquand Chapel at Yale Divinity School, I heard a powerful sermon by South African liberation theologian Allan Boesak on the notice of the burial of Abraham in Gen 25:9a, "His sons Isaac and Ishmael buried him." I would never have guessed that such a simple clause could be mustered in a paradigm-shifting argument for racial reconciliation and justice for sexual minorities.

32. See the work of Walter Brueggemann on dynamics of contestation within Scripture, for example in his *Texts Under Negotiation: The Bible and Postmodern Imagination* (Minneapolis: Fortress, 1993), and his *Theology of the Old Testament: Testimony, Dispute, Advocacy* (Minneapolis: Fortress, 1997). One may consider also the work of biblical scholars who have appropriated insights of Mikhail Bakhtin, such as Carol A. Newsom, *The Book of Job: A Contest of Moral Imaginations* (Oxford: Oxford University Press, 2003), and Barbara Green, "Mikhail Bakhtin and Biblical Studies," *Perspectives in Religious Studies* 32 (2005): 241–48, as well as Green's earlier work, *Mikhail Bakhtin and Biblical Scholarship: An Introduction* (Atlanta: Society of Biblical Literature, 2000).

33. Here I acknowledge the influence of John S. McClure's *Other-wise Preaching: A Postmodern Ethic for Homiletics* (St. Louis: Chalice, 2001).

more gladly of my weaknesses, so that the power of Christ may dwell in me"). Decolonizing covenant leaves the beloved servant renamed, recreated, through the grace of God. This is one of the deepest meanings of יהוה מלך.

Queering "Israel"

A second pathway that may be productive for feminist readers is to work toward queering "Israel." Those who study the Hebrew Scriptures know that Otherness already lies at the heart of Israelite identity. We know that Rahab the Canaanite "has lived in the midst of Israel to this day" (Josh 6:25). We know that King David had a potentially Canaanite ancestor (Tamar) and Moabite ancestor (Ruth), yet despite the prohibition in Deut 23:3 on Ammonites or Moabites entering the assembly,[34] this ethnically hybrid king is acclaimed (in some streams of Israelite tradition) as the paradigmatic leader of Israel's golden age and the spiritual "author" of the worshipping congregation. There is ample warrant within Scripture for queering Israel—queering the beloved subject, welcoming counter-voices, honoring infinitely diverse performances of faithfulness in community. Gender warriors, sexually marginalized believers, political prisoners, and refugees from the life-deforming prejudices of the Church: all these and more must dare to claim their subjectivity as beloved Jacob, as cherished Zion. Indeed, the broken and disempowered Jeremiah of the confessions may be a powerful model here.[35] שירו ליהוה שיר חדש:[36] we must sing fierce new songs to the LORD, we must shout with Deutero-Isaiah that God is doing a new thing.[37] Every feminist and postcolonial and queer interpreter can boldly claim the rewriting of tradition in Jer 36: the deconstruction, reconstruction, and expansion of sacred texts as an ongoing practice of witness in community, seen

---

34. "To the tenth generation" was likely not intended to be understood as a precise calculation but as a signifier of perpetuity.

35. There are many possibilities that have not yet been explored by feminist biblical criticism. One that has received attention: gender warriors may claim the mysterious Jer 31:22. For another example, we may work with the brutal deconstructive rhetoric of Hosea—dangerous though it be—to destroy the idols created by human exploitation and subjugation. See my "Hewn By the Prophet: An Analysis of Violence and Sexual Transgression in Hosea with Reference to the Homiletical Aesthetic of Jeremiah Wright," in *Aesthetics of Violence in the Prophets* (ed. C. Franke and J. M. O'Brien; LHBOTS 517; New York: T&T Clark International, 2010), 50–71.

36. Isa 42:10; Pss 96:1; 98:1; 149:1.

37. Isa 43:19.

historically in the divergence of the Old Greek and Masoretic text traditions of Jeremiah and to be seen in new ways in the utopian future. Queering Israel will be a complex issue for halakhically observant Jewish feminists who are not Reconstructionist, given the gender-essentialist underpinnings of traditional ritual practices required by the Law; but some kind of resistant posture is surely still possible there. For Christians, Otherness is already grafted into our notions of "Israel" via Rom 11, and we have recourse to Gal 3:28 as well ("There is no longer Jew or Greek, there is no longer slave or free, there is no longer male and female; for all of you are one in Christ Jesus").

With its "many dangers, toils, and snares"[38] for feminist travelers, the landscape of Jeremiah can be neither fully diaspora nor fully home. Jeremiah is a borderland sited between judgment and redemption. Like Jacob, readers of this text (feminist, queer, and Others) must sojourn in liminal places as we map this borderland territory. But if we dare to look with our own gaze—not the androcentric gaze, not the imperial gaze, but our own—we may see that these borderlands are breathtakingly beautiful. There are shadows and deep crevices, to be sure. As a commentator, I am destabilized by the thunderous silence of this prophet concerning female subjectivity, and I live in dread of the political viciousness of the Deutero-Jeremianic prose. But as we journey, we may glimpse rich textures of clay and rock, mysterious hidden grottos, and meadows lush with odd grasses and strange flowers. For Jeremiah is finally a queer landscape—and there is room for all of us to wander, together.

---

38. The phrase is taken from the hymn "Amazing Grace," lyrics by Anglican priest John Newton (1725–1807).

Commentary as Memoir?
Reflections on Writing/Reading War and Hegemony in Jeremiah and in Contemporary U.S. Foreign Policy

Louis Stulman

Introduction

I have been asked to reflect on my 2005 Abingdon commentary on Jeremiah[1] as a specific way to respond to the question, "How Do Feminist and Postcolonial Perspectives Change the Genre 'Scholarly Commentary'?" I hesitate to revisit my work in the present context because it is not exemplary in either interpretive perspective. Furthermore, I am painfully aware of the myriad pitfalls of commentary writing, foremost of which in my mind is the projection of finality. Once language and thought come to expression in written form, especially in scholarly discourse, a certain authority is afforded and certitude is expected, even if the work is envisioned as provisional in character and artistic in effort. This is a circuitous way of saying that as I think about the commentary today, there are a number of things I would do differently. And I confess that this tinge of regret began early on.

Several months after the commentary appeared, I was in New York with a friend whose neighbor was an editor at a major publishing house. When introducing me, she mentioned that my book had just been published, to which her editor neighbor responded without missing a beat, "Oh, a memoir?" "No," I said rather sheepishly, "a book on Jeremiah...the biblical prophet." I felt I needed to clarify that point since not everyone is as well informed as those reading this piece...and she looked rather puzzled by my explanation!

But the more I thought about her response, the more exasperated I became. Why the cultural fascination with memoir? Why this preoccupation with the private lives of others, this almost voyeuristic anxiety?

---

1. Louis Stulman, *Jeremiah* (AOTC; Nashville: Abingdon, 2005).

Memoir explores the symbolic terrain of *self*, but we biblical scholars analyze the discursive space of *others*, in fact, a constellation of meanings extant in ancient Near Eastern texts.

That's what I *really* wanted to say: "I write scholarly stuff, not memoirs!" Of course I am entirely aware that her question was little more than an innocuous greeting and my own musings were rather hypersensitive! But her comment set my mind spinning. What do we *really* do when we write so-called scholarly commentaries? Perhaps we engage in work that is more self-referential than we would like to admit. And I am referring not only to the sections we conveniently label, "Reflections" (New Interpreter's Bible), "Connections" (Smyth & Helwys), "Theological and Ethical Analysis" (Abingdon Old Testament Commentaries), or that unfortunate generic banner "Relevance."

Commentary Writing

Not unlike the *Introduction to the Hebrew Bible/Old Testament—Einleitung in das Alte Testament*—biblical commentary is its own distinctive genre. Regardless of editorial policy, target audience, or governing methodology, the scholarly commentary on the Bible seeks to clarify authorial or textual meanings, or more accurately reservoirs of meaning. As stated in the prospectus and foreword of the Abingdon Old Testament Commentary, for instance, writers "provoke a deeper understanding of the Bible in all its many facets."[2] The original editorial board of the Hermeneia series put it this way: "It is expected that authors will struggle to lay bare the ancient meaning of a biblical work or pericope"[3] (i.e., I suppose, without confessional constraints).[4]

While such outcomes are straightforward enough, few today would argue that commentary writing is ever innocent or non-contested. Our postmodern sensitivities call for self-awareness, theological candor, as

---

2. See Patrick D. Miller, "Foreword" of the series, in Stulman, *Jeremiah*, xiii.

3. See Frank Moore Cross and Helmut Koester, "Foreword" of the series, in William L. Holladay, *Jeremiah 1: A Commentary on the Book of the Prophet Jeremiah: Chapters 1–25* (Hermeneia; Philadelphia: Fortress, 1986), ix.

4. Of course AOTC and Hermeneia, which are representative of the vast majority of modern scholarly commentaries, especially in the Protestant tradition, privilege the ancient socio-cultural contexts. The only exception that comes to mind is the Blackwell Bible Commentary, which by editorial design focuses on the reception history (*Nachleben*) of the Bible.

Robert Carroll argued,[5] ideological candor, as Walter Brueggemann responded,[6] and parochial transparency, as A. R. Pete Diamond summed up.[7] In his incisive piece on the Jeremiah guild in the twenty-first century, Diamond invites contemporary writers/readers of Jeremiah to be transparent regarding their communal identity, which is "a complex, layered, yet fragmented, [and] oft-contested reality."[8] Moreover, he urges us "to become more sophisticated in self-evaluation, as readers standing *within* the…reception history of Jeremiah, and not just as critics standing *outside* the creative process."[9]

Yet that is exactly where most of us think we stand: *outside of history* and beyond its constraints. We envision ourselves transcending our own particular cultural horizon and seeing things and writing things as *they really are.* I was reminded of this not long ago when a colleague delivered a fine critique of Bernhard Duhm's early twentieth-century work on Jeremiah.[10] He argued skillfully how and why Duhm got it wrong, but at the same time he was certain that we get it right today. In many respects, we all think we get it right; it seems self-evident and is difficult to imagine it otherwise.

In his own recent memoir, *In the Valley of the Shadow,*[11] a quite remarkable work, James Kugel suggests that we are wired to think that we will defy the ultimate history marker, our own mortality. If this is the case—and I have good reason not to doubt it—of course we would imagine ourselves transcending our own particular cultural horizons, thus "standing outside the creative process."[12] But as Kugel so eloquently reminds us, there are far too many brutal reminders that history holds all of us captive.

---

5. Robert Carroll, "Century's End: Jeremiah Studies at the Beginning of the Third Millennium," in *Recent Research on the Major Prophets* (ed. A. J. Hauser; Recent Research in Biblical Studies 1; Sheffield: Sheffield Phoenix, 2008), 217–31.

6. Walter Brueggemann, "Sometime Wave, Sometime Particle," *CBR* 8 (2010): 376–85.

7. A. R. Pete Diamond, "The Jeremiah Guild in the Twenty-First Century," in Hauser, ed., *Recent Research on the Major Prophets*, 232–48.

8. Ibid., 242.

9. Ibid. (italics mine).

10. Bernhard Duhm, *Das Buch Jeremia* (KHC 11; Tübingen: J. C. B. Mohr, 1901).

11. James Kugel, *In the Valley of the Shadow: On the Foundations of Religious Belief* (New York: Free Press, 2011).

12. Diamond, "The Jeremiah Guild," 242.

My point here is that memoir and commentary writing may not be as irreconcilable as we think. When we write Jeremiah, we are in some sense writing ourselves, albeit through an interpretive veil. Regardless of where we place or "displace" the book—whether in an ancient socio-cultural context that we deem original or in some subsequent setting in its *Nachleben*—we can hardly circumvent our own autobiographical print and cultural particularities.

Such an argument is by no means novel, but no one has made it as persuasively in recent years as Mary Chilton Callaway. Her two essays in *Jeremiah (Dis)Placed: New Directions in Writing/Reading Jeremiah* reflect such surgical precision and artistic force that they dispel any illusion of writing Jeremiah outside of history.[13] The fusion of interpretive horizons across time and space is as much an exegetical fact on the ground as the problematic character of "claiming ours as the true meaning, whether historical or theological, of this unfathomable book."[14] Callaway's first contribution moves beyond Hans-Georg Gadamer's groundbreaking work of a half-century ago,[15] as she chips away at the *reception history* of Jeremiah. Her second essay peers inside this *Nachleben*, particularly the world of early modern England, as a way to relativize what is for contemporary readers of Jeremiah perhaps the most "self-evident" characteristic of the book: namely, Jeremiah's supposed interior life and personal religious experience.

Despite our rich interpretive arsenal and methodological sophistication, drawn largely from the Enlightenment, no one peers inside Jeremiah from outside its reception history; no one writes a commentary divorced from a local, community identity with its own distinctive network of interests. There are no innocent interpreters of Jeremiah, Ezekiel, Isaiah, or any textual tradition, ancient or contemporary.

Some would of course dispute this claim, but the burden of proof, I think, rests on modernity. And if this is the case, then "the reader"

---

13. Mary Chilton Callaway, "Reading Jeremiah with Some Help from Gadamer," in *Jeremiah (Dis)Placed: New Directions in Writing/Reading Jeremiah* (ed. A. R. P. Diamond and L. Stulman; LHBOTS 529; New York: T&T Clark International, 2011), 266–78, and "Peering Inside Jeremiah: How Early Modern English Culture Still Influences our Reading of the Prophet," in Diamond and Stulman, eds., *Jeremiah (Dis)Placed*, 279–89.

14. Callaway, "Peering Inside Jeremiah," 289.

15. Hans-Georg Gadamer, *Wahrheit und Methode* (Tübingen: Mohr, 1960), translated into English as *Truth and Method* (2d ed.; trans. J. Weinsheimer and D. G. Marshall; New York: Continuum, 1998).

(commentator) of Jeremiah may now take a seat at the table alongside "author and text." And if *author, text, and reader* enjoy center stage, then feminist and postcolonial perspectives—along with other reader- or praxis-oriented approaches—must surely accompany them, especially in light of the pervasive presence of the disempowered within the social world of the Jeremiah tradition and beyond its confines. I would suggest that the recent *Jeremiah (Dis)Placed* goes a long way toward making this point, especially as it calls for careful scrutiny of "writing/reading" Jeremiah across time and space.[16] *Jeremiah (Dis)Placed* de-centers the old normative author/text strategies, such as source, form, redaction, and historical critical criticism, for a new repertoire of approaches as broad in scope as aesthetics and as pragmatic as postcolonial, feminist, and trauma criticism.

Distant Horizon: Distinctive Indices of AOTC Jeremiah

Because I can no longer avoid my specific assignment, let me say a few words about my Abingdon commentary on Jeremiah and its own con- crete history-specific location. I wrote much of it during the years of 2001–2004 under the editorial direction of Kathleen M. O'Connor and the general editorship of Patrick D. Miller. And again I concede that I did not write the commentary from a postcolonial or feminist perspec- tive. Carolyn Sharp was surely correct that "missing in [my] work is any sustained attention to issues of gender and sexuality in Jeremiah...[and that] a closer engagement with postcolonial analysis would likely yield theological interpretations of Jeremiah rather different from those [I reached]."[17]

What I did attempt to do in the commentary, however, was to pay attention to the text's range of responses to gratuitous suffering— especially in the form of war and forced relocation. With this in mind, I broached Jeremiah as *disaster literature*, that is, as a "penetrating response to the multifaceted configurations of evil."[18] I asked how a fragmented war-torn community could survive "a past that is gone and a

---

16. See A. R. Pete Diamond and Louis Stulman, "Analytical Introduction: Writ- ing and Reading Jeremiah," in Diamond and Stulman, eds., *Jeremiah (Dis)Placed*, 1–32.

17. Carolyn Sharp, review of L. Stulman, *Jeremiah*, *RBL* (2005), n.p. Online: http://www.bookreviews.org/pdf/4643_4778.pdf.

18. Stulman, *Jeremiah*, 1.

future…yet inscribed"?[19] How do victims of war and forced migration come to grips with massive cultural and symbolic disjunction? And what type of literature does a refugee community employ to map out a future when none seems possible? As Albert Hourani put it: "Defeat goes deeper into the human soul than victory. To be in someone else's power is a conscious experience which induces doubts about the ordering of the universe, while those who have power can forget it, or can assume that it is part of the natural order of things and invent…ideas which justify their possession of it." The book of Jeremiah "re-presents" a world in which enormous loss and geo-military subjugation have undoubtedly induced "doubts about the ordering of the universe."[20]

In effect, Jeremiah, I argued, is a complex and contested communal meditation on the horror of war. It is a literary reenactment of a cultural and symbolic universe on the brink of annihilation. Accordingly, its performance is deeply fractured and pulsates with unspeakable pain. Every word, every metaphor, every social and cultural construction, every theological claim is rooted in and tied to the collapse of meaning. It makes perfect sense to me, for instance, that the Deuteronomistic prose sermons would problematize the community's core social and symbolic worlds: temple (Jer 7:1–15), covenant (11:1–17), election (18:1–12), capital city and dynasty (21:1–10), and national autonomy (25:1–14). All are under siege by geo-political forces far beyond little Judah's control. The prose tradition is intent on refocusing understandings of power and pain within a context of meaning.

At the same time, the book's painful voices—even its most disturbing gender and sexual images and cacophonous constructions of the empire—are in the service of communal survival. These arrangements dare to break the silence that often debilitates victims of violence, individually and as nations.[21] They reenact the horror of war in a way that makes grief manageable. They participate in a contested communal dialogue over the meaning of the wreckage, and perhaps most remarkably they imagine a world beyond it. And so Jeremiah is as much *survival literature* as it is *disaster literature*: by the end of the prophetic performance, the prophet survives, as a deeply wounded refugee; his companion Baruch survives,

---

19.   Ibid., 6.

20.   Albert Hourani, *A History of the Arab Peoples* (New York: Warner, 1991), 300–301.

21.   See, e.g., Winfried G. Sebald, *On the Natural History of Destruction* (New York: Random House, 2003).

although on the margins and without the "great things" for which he so longs (45:1–5); YHWH survives, as grief-stricken, conflicted, and livid; and the implied writing/reading community survives, although competing groups admittedly "disappear" from the literary horizon.

All participate in a frightful narrative about a world riddled with loss and near extinction. No one escapes this world unscathed. No one eludes the massive assault and the cities in ruin. Yet some survive, if only as victims of war.

This prophetic performance of Jeremiah dares to imagine a nation's most excruciating moment. In one frightful instant, it would seem, Judah's sense of equilibrium, longstanding institutions, and belief systems suffer a massive assault. Its time-honored images and well-tested social workings crumble in plain view. For some it felt as if the world were ending; for others it had. For this community at war and under siege, the year 587 B.C.E. represented an all-too palpable historical moment—a sacred temple burned to the ground, a city in ruins, the dead and deported numbering in the thousands, a whole universe long associated with God's blessings now gone. As strikingly, this haunting moment, 587, symbolized the forfeiture of hope, cosmic crumbling, the end of life as it had long been lived.

Given the scale of the wreckage and the intensity of the despair, the poets were summoned. Who else could speak for a suffering community without words?[22]

> I looked at the earth,
> and it was without shape or form;
> at the heavens
> and there was no light.
> I looked at the mountains
> and they were quaking;
> all the hills were rocking back and forth.
> I looked and there was no one left;
> every bird in the sky had taken flight.
> I looked and the fertile land was a desert;
> all its towns were in ruins
> before the LORD,
> before his fury. (Jer 4:23–26)[23]

22. Note that the book of Jeremiah's multiplicity of voices includes noticeably few from the Judean populace itself.

23. Translations are from the Common English Bible unless otherwise noted.

The horrors of war, armed occupation, and forced migration are imagined as the collapse of the order of creation, a moment when all is reduced to rubble.

To envision the empire's dreadful military machine, the poets speak of a mythic foe from the north:

> Announce in Judah,
> in Jerusalem proclaim,
> sound the alarm throughout the land,
> cry out and say,
> "Gather together!
> Let's flee to the fortified towns!"
> Set up a flag to Zion;
> take cover, don't just stand there!
> I'm bringing disaster from the north,
> massive devastation.
> A lion bursts out of the thicket;
> a destroyer of nations advances.
> He's gone forth from his place
> to ravage your land,
> to wipe out your towns,
> until no one is left.
> So put on funeral clothing.
> Weep and wail,
> for the LORD's fierce anger
> hasn't turned away from us.
> At that time, this people and Jerusalem
> will be told:
> A blistering wind from the bare heights;
> it rages in the desert toward my people,
> not merely to winnow or cleanse.
> This wind is too devastating for that.
> Now I, even I, will pronounce
> my sentence against them.
> Look! He approaches like the clouds;
> his chariots advance like a tempest,
> his horses swifter than eagles.
> How horrible! We're doomed! (Jer 4:5–8, 11–13)

Such speech dares to imagine the terrifying military exercise of the empire as a haunting expression of divine judgment. Although the dreaded forces no doubt evoke terror, they are at least dispatched by "the LORD of heavenly forces"; consequently, they do not intrude upon the world without moral constraints but are harnessed, so to speak, to the divine chariot.

To shatter all forms of denial, professional mourners are called upon:

> The LORD of heavenly forces proclaims:
> Pay attention!
> Summon the women who mourn,
> let them come;
> send for those best trained,
> let them come.
> Hurry!
> Let them weep for us
> so that our eyes fill up with tears
> and water streams down.
> The sound of sobbing
> is heard from Zion:
> "We're devastated!
> We're so ashamed!
> We have to leave the land
> and abandon our homes!"
> Women, hear the LORD's word.
> Listen closely to the word
> from his mouth:
> teach your daughters to mourn;
> teach each other to grieve.
> Death has climbed
> through our windows;
> it has entered our fortresses
> to eliminate children from the streets,
> the youth from the squares. (Jer 9:17–21)

Those skilled in grief lead a community that is anesthetized and debilitated by violence. These mourning women implore the nation to "acknowledge its wounded condition and work through its grief. Such liturgical expressions of sorrow facilitate healing…. The liturgy of the dirge…eventually makes new life possible."[24]

Notwithstanding the compelling force of this language, one still wonders how anyone could live through the collapse of their world. How could a community make sense of this avalanche of grief? Given its debilitating character, competing interpretations of the disaster emerge in Jeremiah: some argue for coherent networks of meaning and deploy blame as a means of imposing some degree of symbolic symmetry: "it's our fault" or more often "it's your fault." Jeremiah's accusation that the nation has broken its covenant obligations is a case in point:

---

24. Stulman, *Jeremiah*, 104.

Jeremiah received the LORD's word:

Listen to the terms of this covenant and proclaim them to the people of Judah and the citizens of Jerusalem. Say to them: This is what the LORD, the God of Israel, says: Cursed are those who don't heed the terms of this covenant that I commanded your ancestors when I brought them out of the land of Egypt, that iron crucible, saying, Obey me and observe all that I instruct you…

The LORD said to me: Announce all these words in the towns of Judah and on the streets of Jerusalem: Obey the terms of this covenant and perform them. I repeatedly and tirelessly warned your ancestors when I brought them out of the land of Egypt to this very day, saying, Obey me. But they didn't listen or pay attention; they followed their own willful ambitions. So I brought upon them all the punishments I prescribed for violating this covenant—for refusing to obey…

Therefore, the LORD proclaims: I will bring upon them a disaster from which they won't be able to escape. They will cry out to me, but I won't listen to them. Then the people of Judah and those living in Jerusalem will call upon the gods they worship, but they won't save them when disaster strikes. You have as many gods as you have towns, Judah, and you have as many shameful altars for worshipping Baal as you have streets in Jerusalem. (Jer 11:1–4, 6–8, 11–13)

While this conventional language blames the victim, the text's surplus of guilt, here and elsewhere in the book, serves to exonerate God of injustice and make seemingly gratuitous suffering intellectually manageable.[25] Better to imagine a moral structure with meaning—even if it wages war against you—than an arbitrary moral universe in which raw power is ultimate power!

Other Jeremianic voices are less certain and as a result give expression to a morally ambiguous world in which even innocent prophets suffer great misfortune. The so-called "confessions of Jeremiah" question the moral order in the universe and above all God's covenantal loyalty.

If I took you to court, LORD,
you would win.
But I still have questions
about your justice.
Why do guilty persons enjoy success?
Why are evildoers so happy?
You plant them, and they take root;
they flourish and bear fruit.

---

25. See Daniel L. Smith-Christopher, *A Biblical Theology of Exile* (OBT; Minneapolis: Fortress, 2002).

You are always on their lips
but far from their hearts.
Yet you, LORD, you know me.
You see me.
You can tell that I love you.
So drag them away
and butcher them like sheep.
Prepare them for the slaughterhouse.
How long will the land mourn
and the grass in the fields dry up?
The animals and birds are swept away
due to the evil of those in the land.
The people say,
"God doesn't see what we're up to!" (Jer 12:1–4)

The Jeremiah of these probing poems not only questions God's justice and due diligence in the world, but challenges the symmetrical categories of the prose tradition. And eventually the embattled *bios* or physicality of Jeremiah wages an ideological war on the prophetic tradition itself, inasmuch as it represents the *innocent suffering* of a myriad of tormented people.

Still other voices in Jeremiah speak of the wreckage without God or God's spokesperson, perhaps to extricate both from the horror of brutality.[26] The story of Gedaliah and his post-587 provisional government is told without reference to God or Jeremiah (40:7–41:18), even though the broader literary context does not lend itself well to such absence: Nebuzaradan had entrusted Jeremiah into Gedaliah's care in the previous vignette (40:1–6) and the prophet and his God re-emerge in the subsequent scene to take center stage (42:1–22). Yet their absence, that is, the "missing voice," makes sense if only, as Kathleen M. O'Connor suggests in her reading of Lamentations,

[to] prevent us from sliding prematurely over suffering toward happy endings. It gives the book daring power because it honors human speech. God's absence forces us to attend to voices of grief and despair, and it can reflect…our own experiences of a silent God…. If God spoke, God's words would diminish the voices of pain, wash over them, and crowd them out. Even one word from God would take up too much space in the book.[27]

26. Stulman, *Jeremiah*, 321–29.
27. Kathleen M. O'Connor, *Lamentations and the Tears of the World* (Maryknoll: Orbis, 2002), 86.

Remarkably, these contested voices and silences in Jeremiah participate in a mythic tale that trades in candor, values complexity, and refuses to flatten the world into static and monolithic categories. This concentrate of trouble, eventually preserved in two major text traditions, is frayed almost beyond recognition. No wonder traditionalists attempt to tame it and bring a degree of symbolic order to it. Despite their efforts, however, the rich cacophony prevails, as does the disjointed character of the witness.

John Bright, of course, nailed it many years ago when he described all this as "a hopeless hodgepodge."[28] But at the same time he completely missed the mark: Jeremiah's literary chaos is neither gratuitous nor a mere nuisance to modern readers, but rather it is a literary performance of a community's profound grief. And so the text's structure, or lack of structure, is the key to the meaning of the book. The chaos *is* the message; the structure or its absence *is* the meaning. Through it, Judah's finest poets create a dark and somber space to remember massive loss, to mourn it, interpret it, and survive it.[29]

Near Cultural Horizon (2001–2004)

Does this narrative sound familiar? I should remind you that I wrote the major part of the commentary between the years of 2001 and 2004. Was I writing myself or Jeremiah, preparing a memoir or commentary, doing art or historical reconstruction, excavating memories from a distant past, 587 B.C.E., or reliving the searing images of a recent past, the collective trauma of 9/11 and the disastrous preemptive U.S. invasion of Iraq?

When I was writing and reading Jeremiah, the world that enveloped us was in disarray. On 9/11 the dominant symbols of U.S. economic stability and political power were dealt a crushing blow. As Clyde Prestowitz observed, "part of the shock of September 11 was the shattering of the myth that bad things happen only to other people. It was the shock of joining the world...recogniz[ing] that others' problems are our problems too and that we don't have all the answers."[30] This defining moment

---

28. John Bright, *Jeremiah: Introduction, Translation, and Notes* (AB 21; Garden City: Doubleday, 1965), lvi.

29. See Walter Brueggemann, "Meditation Upon the Abyss: The Book of Jeremiah," *WW* 22, no. 4 (2002): 340–50.

30. Clyde Prestowitz, *Rogue Nation: American Unilateralism and the Failure of Good Intentions* (New York: Basic, 2003), 284.

shattered illusions of national invincibility on a grand scale and, as Serene Jones suggests, "drew the nation as a whole into the *trauma drama of its violence*."[31]

We all have our haunting stories associated with this event. I will mention only one, which I noted some time ago in another context.[32] On 9/13 I received an email from Professor John Hill who expressed his deep sympathy and wrote that 80 Australians were either dead or missing. He said something quite extraordinary in that email that I still ponder more than ten years later: "we continue to pray here for strength, healing and restraint, because the political pressure to go out and attack someone will be almost irresistible."

I am not sure whether John was consciously thinking about traumatology when he made that comment. But PTSD studies have long shown that victims of traumatic violence—whether as individuals or groups—often replay their violent scenarios on themselves and/or others.

And that is precisely what happened on May 19, 2003. Less than two years later, despite a huge public outcry, the U.S. invaded Iraq, bombed its major cities, disposed of its leader, and occupied its land. In the course of several years, hundreds of thousands of Iraqis were displaced and tens of thousands died. And any semblance of international morality was squandered away. This geo-military maneuver is now a well known example of American exceptionalism, one of the principal tenets of neoconservative ideology. But as Serene Jones has put it, the U.S. shock and awe campaign was also a frightful demonstration of *a superpower reenacting scenes of violence*.[33]

And if superpowers reenact their scenes of violence, how much more so do the historical losers, whose cities are leveled, whose lives are shattered, and who must thereafter manage in "someone else's power." Their reenactment often deploys the only weapons in their arsenal: the words of the poets, or, as Oscar Romero noted from his own terrible context, the "violence of love."[34]

---

31. Serene Jones, *Trauma and Grace: Theology in a Ruptured World* (Louisville: Westminster John Knox, 2009), 28 (italics mine).

32. Louis Stulman, "Conflicting Paths of Hope in Jeremiah," in *Shaking Heaven and Earth: Essays in Honor of Walter Brueggemann and Charles B. Cousar* (ed. C. R. Yoder et al.; Louisville: Westminster John Knox, 2005), 43–57 (44).

33. Jones, *Trauma and Grace*, 23–42.

34. Oscar Romero, *The Violence of Love* (comp. and trans. J. R. Brockman; Rifton; Plough, e-book publication, 2011).

By the time I had completed the commentary, I was convinced that the book of Jeremiah is not only literature of disaster and survival but *literature of the losers*. Its "language of violence" is a daring artistic expression of protest, rage, pain, and horror. As was the case in the months and years after 9/11, Judah's disaster of 587 triggered an artistic deluge.[35] Traumatic violence requires speech. "Deep calleth unto deep" (Ps 42:7 KJV). As Walter Brueggemann notes with respect to 587 and 9/11: "everyone had to speak. Every poet, every pastor, every prophet, every public figure was summoned in dread to voice something."[36] Perhaps the only thing to combat despair, especially among the powerless, is speech—often in artistic expression. Perhaps the only thing to survive the violence of the empire is the violence of poetry, testimony, and liturgy.[37]

Conclusion

In this brief reflection, I have suggested that memoir and commentary are closer relatives than we readily imagine. These distinct-though-related genres, in the first place, speak to Gadamer's fusion of cultural horizons. We never write or read outside of history. We never write or read as disinterested parties. This confluence of worlds, however, is no mere causality of writing and reading texts in space and time. On the contrary, the lively interface of the ancient and contemporary defines the aesthetic practice of commentary writing.

---

35. See Louis Stulman and Hyun Chul Paul Kim, *You Are My People: An Introduction to Prophetic Literature* (Nashville: Abingdon, 2010).

36. Walter Brueggemann, *Disruptive Grace: Reflections on God, Scripture, and the Church* (ed. and intro. C. J. Sharp; Minneapolis: Fortress, 2011), 113.

37. Despite the strong resonances in these worlds of violence—then and now— as well as the astonishing fusion of cultural horizons, one cannot ignore the profound dissonances, not only in time and space but also in power arrangements: I was writing/reading Jeremiah from the social location of the winners, albeit vulnerable and wounded, yet still with all the rights and privileges of a geo-political superpower. The ancient text of Jeremiah represents the painful testimony of victims of hegemonic exploits and so is in some respects a mirror image of my own social location. Can the well-positioned in fact decipher the texts of the losers? Do the disparities in power arrangements create an insurmountable interpretive chasm? See Stulman, "Here Comes the Reader," in Diamond and Stulman, eds., *Jeremiah (Dis)Placed*, 99–103.

When reading/writing Jeremiah in the initial years of the twenty-first century, we encounter *dissonant* and *resonant* worlds that bristle with pain, horrific violence, and palpable despair. And so I would put forward that traumatology may be a most appropriate interpretive lens through which to imagine the fractured world of old and the fractured world we now inhabit. Kathleen O'Connor has broached this imaginative space in her important book, *Jeremiah: Pain and Promise*.[38] As O'Connor's work demonstrates, virtually everything in Jeremiah assumes new rhetorical and theological force in light of trauma studies. Trauma studies demand a reassessment of Jeremiah's atonal quality and grief-stricken character, its surplus of blame and ambivalence about empire, and even its violent symbolic outbursts and disconcerting sexual language.

And this reassessment is especially *consonant* with feminist and postcolonial readings. In fact, the integration of trauma, postcolonial, and feminist perspectives—with their focus on pain, power, and the periphery respectively—might present a promising interdisciplinary matrix for Jeremiah commentary writing in the next decade. This kind of inter-disciplinary engagement would no doubt demand an intense collaborative effort; indeed, as Dr. Maier has argued, "a multi-authored and multi-voiced" undertaking.[39]

---

38. Kathleen M. O'Connor, *Jeremiah: Pain and Promise* (Minneapolis: Fortress, 2011).

39. See Christl M. Maier, "After the 'One-Man Show': Multi-authored and Multi-voiced Commentary Writing," in this volume.

AFTER THE "ONE-MAN SHOW": MULTI-AUTHORED AND MULTI-VOICED COMMENTARY WRITING

Christl M. Maier

With regard to the huge number of published Jeremiah commentaries, the question arises as to why the world would need another one. From the publisher's perspective, one could argue that each publishing house aims at establishing its own commentary series. From the readers' perspective, there are certainly many different scholarly interests and also needs concerning length, previous knowledge, depth, applicability, and so on among diverse groups of recipients. However, for a scholar who has to recognize what has been done in the field and therefore work through many previous commentaries, the endeavor sometimes seems futile. First, there is the task of adequately analyzing an enormous amount of biblical and commentary text. Second, one has to find one's own overall assessment of the given biblical writing as well as search for something new to say. When Carolyn Sharp and I accepted the invitation to collaborate in writing a new commentary on the book of Jeremiah in Kohlhammer's new IECOT series,[1] we were both aware of the enormous task ahead and confident about including new interpretative perspectives developed by feminist and postcolonial approaches to the Bible. There are, however, certain obstacles on our way, among them the essential question about our role as commentators, especially since we are well aware that the time of the "master narrative" as an ingenious re-reading of ancient texts has ended.[2]

---

1. For an introduction to the series, its goals, and its anticipated audience, see below.

2. A thorough critique of the master narrative or metanarrative was introduced by Jean-François Lyotard, *The Postmodern Condition: A Report on Knowledge* (trans. G. Bennington and B. Massumi; Minneapolis: University of Minnesota Press, 1984), esp. 31–41. See also Gina Hens-Piazza, "Lyotard," in *Handbook of Postmodern Biblical Interpretation* (ed. A. K. M. Adam; St. Louis: Chalice, 2000), 160–66.

While in this essay I can speak only for myself, I am grateful for many lively discussions with my esteemed colleague Carolyn Sharp as well as with Jeremiah scholars who participated in two consultations.[3] Essential to my argument in this essay is a definition of "voice," which I use for two levels of discourse. Following the designation of Athalya Brenner and Fokkelien van-Dijk-Hemmes in their book *On Gendering Texts*, a textual voice is:

> the sum of speech acts assigned to a fictive person or the narrator within a text. By implication, a voice's fictive owner has a privileged position of power in the literary discourse within which it features…. When all or most of the affirmative answers to the questions, Who speaks? Who focalizes the action? Whose viewpoint is dominant?—[*sic*] converge on one and the same textual figure, then that figure embodies the dominant voice of a passage, be it prose narrative or poetic.[4]

Everybody who is familiar with the book of Jeremiah may obviously detect many different and even conflicting textual voices within the text. In a commentary, there is a second level of discourse since the commentator engages these different textual voices in his or her writing while offering his or her interpretation as the dominant voice. In short: the commentator becomes the new narrator, the all-knowing controller and focalizer of textual voices. He or she may stress a certain position while diminishing another one. A multi-voiced commentary may thus be one that elaborates the different textual voices in the text's discourse and/or one that engages different interpretive perspectives on any given text and thus multiplies the commenting voices. Yet, the most important issue is how such multi-vocality may be practically achieved.

So far, most commentaries on Jeremiah appear to be rather univocal, that is, they present the one authoritative voice of a (usually male) commentator who would explain how any given passage should be interpreted with regard to the historical setting, theological evaluation, or the concerns of postmodern readers. Contrary to this tradition, I hold that the twenty-first century requires a new and multi-voiced way of commentary writing, for at least two reasons. First, the hermeneutical paradigm of biblical interpretation as an academic discipline has shifted considerably. Second, due to shifts in the Continental philosophical tradition and the *Zeitgeist* in the Western academic guild, many postmodern readers, for

---

3. For the settings of our joint research on Jeremiah, see the acknowledgments.

4. Athalya Brenner and Fokkelien van Dijk-Hemmes, *On Gendering Texts: Female and Male Voices in the Hebrew Bible* (BIS 1; Leiden: Brill, 1993), 7.

example many of my students, are no longer willing to accept just one authoritative voice that tells them what they should think of a certain text. Within the history of biblical interpretation, each epoch has so far developed its own hermeneutics.[5] In my view, the current state of Jeremiah studies is ripe for a new paradigm of interpretation.

In the following, I will try to explain what I mean by the transformation of hermeneutics, point to similar interpretive projects, and illustrate my reflections on multivocality with an example from the book of Jeremiah.

Transformations of Hermeneutics That Change the Task of Commentary Writing

Since the 1970s, Jeremiah studies in Germany have shifted from source-criticism, which was interested primarily in the *ipsissima vox* of Jeremiah, to redaction-critical analyses that highlight the contribution of later book editors. Among English-speaking Jeremiah scholars the focus of interest has shifted to synchronic readings, with rhetorical and ideology criticism taking the lead. Through critical assessment of the texts' ideologies, scholars such as Robert Carroll, Walter Brueggemann, Louis Stulman, Pete Diamond, Carolyn Sharp, Mark Leuchter, and Kathleen O'Connor as well as feminist scholars Angela Bauer, Gerlinde Baumann, and Mary Shields either find competing voices in the text or deconstruct the authoritative textual voice.[6] Their studies witness to a shift of the

5. For an overview see, e.g., Henning Graf Reventlow, *History of Biblical Interpretation* (trans. L. G. Perdue; 4 vols.; Atlanta: Society of Biblical Literature, 2010). Volume 4 covers the time from the Enlightenment to the early twentieth century, ending with Karl Barth's and Rudolf Bultmann's hermeneutics. *The Oxford Handbook of the Reception History of the Bible* (ed. M. Lieb, E. Mason, and J. Roberts; Oxford: Oxford University Press, 2011) offers 12 articles of different authors on selected biblical books (Genesis, Job, Psalms, Isaiah, Ezekiel, Daniel, Judges, John, Romans, 1 Corinthians, Galatians, and Revelation) and 32 articles on a broad and eclectic range of topics; these cover the reception of certain biblical texts in literature, art, and music as well as in specific areas or among ethnic or religious groups around the world. Concerning feminist or other liberationist approaches, there is one article on "Elizabeth Cady Stanton's *The Woman's Bible*" and one article entitled "Exodus in Latin America." In sum, the more recent approaches have not yet been covered in adequate measure.

6. See Robert P. Carroll, *Jeremiah: A Commentary* (OTL; London: SCM, 1986); Walter Brueggemann, *A Commentary on Jeremiah: Exile and Homecoming* (Grand Rapids: Eerdmans, 1998); Louis Stulman, *Order Amid Chaos: Jeremiah as Symbolic*

interpretative paradigm from a historical-critical model, which aims at reconstructing a historical situation or audience of a given text, to a rhetorical-ideological model, which analyzes the interests of ancient authors and postmodern readers. This shift surfaced under the influence of literary theory, under the guidance of Roland Barthes and Umberto Eco, among other key Continental figures.[7] Starting in the 1960s, Latin American liberation theology has challenged the hegemony of academic bible interpretations by presenting the farmers of Solentiname as interpreters.[8] Since the 1970s feminist, womanist, and *mujerista* scholars have begun to criticize biblical texts and traditional interpretations as androcentric and oriented to a male pedagogical model.[9] Scholars adept in

---

Tapestry (Sheffield: Sheffield Academic, 1998); idem, *Jeremiah* (AOTC; Nashville: Abingdon, 2005). A. R. Pete Diamond et al., eds., *Troubling Jeremiah* (Sheffield: Sheffield Academic, 1999); Carolyn J. Sharp, *Prophecy and Ideology in Jeremiah: Struggles for Authority in the Deutero-Jeremianic Prose* (London: T. & T. Clark, 2003); Mark Leuchter, *The Polemics of Exile in Jeremiah 26–45* (Cambridge: Cambridge University Press, 2008); A. R. Pete Diamond and Louis Stulman, eds., *Jeremiah (Dis)placed: New Directions in Writing/Reading Jeremiah* (LHBOTS 529; New York: T&T Clark International, 2011); Kathleen M. O'Connor, *Jeremiah: Pain and Promise* (Minneapolis: Fortress, 2011); Angela Bauer, G*ender in the Book of Jeremiah: A Feminist-Literary Reading* (New York: Lang, 1999); Gerlinde Baumann, *Love and Violence: Marriage as Metaphor for the Relationship Between YHWH and Israel in the Prophetic Books* (trans. L. M. Maloney; Collegeville: Liturgical, 2003), esp. 105–34; Mary E. Shields, *Circumscribing the Prostitute: The Rhetorics of Intertextuality, Metaphor, and Gender in Jeremiah 3.1–4.4* (JSOTSup 387; New York: T&T Clark International, 2004), esp. 166–67.

7. See Roland Barthes et al., *Structural Analysis and Biblical Exegesis: Interpretational Essays* (trans. A. M. Johnson, Jr.; Pittsburgh: Pickwick, 1974); idem, *The Pleasure of the Text* (trans. R. Miller; New York: Hill & Wang, 1975); Umberto Eco, *A Theory of Semiotics* (Bloomington: Indiana University Press, 1976).

8. See Ernesto Cardenal, *The Gospel in Solentiname* (trans. D. D. Walsh; 4 vols.; Maryknoll: Orbis, 1976–82).

9. To name only a few milestones of feminist and womanist approaches, see Elisabeth Schüssler Fiorenza, *In Memory of Her: A Feminist Theological Reconstruction of Christian Origins* (New York: Crossroad, 1985); Luise Schottroff et al., *Feministische Exegese* (Darmstadt: Wissenschaftliche Buchgesellschaft, 1995), English version: *Feminist Interpretation: The Bible in Women's Perspective* (trans. M. and B. Rumscheidt; Minneapolis: Fortress, 1998); Luise Schottroff and Marie-Theres Wacker, eds., *Kompendium Feministische Bibelauslegung* (2d ed.; Gütersloh: Gütersloher, 1999); English version: *Feminist Biblical Interpretation: A Compendium of Critical Commentary on the Books of the Bible and Related Literature* (Grand Rapids: Eerdmans, 2012); Phyllis Bird, ed., *Reading the Bible as Women: Perspectives from Africa, Asia, and Latin America* (Atlanta: Scholars Press, 1997).

Marxist theory pointed to issues of class struggle and hierarchies of economic power in the biblical texts.[10] Since the 1980s, these newly emerging inquiries have inspired academics in Africa and Asia to challenge the interpretations of European missionaries and scholars. The emergence of postcolonial analyses in the field of cultural studies[11] has influenced academics from formerly colonized countries to offer readings of biblical texts from such a perspective.[12] Different communities of lay readers in Africa and Asia are now reading the Bible with regard to their own cultural and sociological contexts.[13]

This shift in the interpretive paradigm demonstrates a "process of conscientization," which Elisabeth Schüssler Fiorenza claims as one of the characteristics of both liberation theology and feminist biblical interpretation.[14] As David Clines argued years ago, writers and readers of biblical texts are "interested parties," the biblical text is an "ideological production," and "the interpreter is reading the text from within a particular ideological formation."[15] Interpreting the Bible critically with regard to the rhetoric and ideology of both text and reader reveals relations of power both in ancient and postmodern contexts. In my view, such relations of power, hierarchies, or dichotomist evaluations do not exist

10. See Roland Boer, *Marxist Criticism of the Bible* (London: Sheffield Academic, 2003); Roland Boer and Jorunn Økland, eds., *Marxist Feminist Criticism of the Bible* (Sheffield: Sheffield Phoenix, 2008); Randall W. Reed, *A Clash of Ideologies: Marxism, Liberation Theology and Apocalypticism in New Testament Studies* (Eugene: Pickwick, 2010).

11. See, e.g., Edward W. Said, *Orientalism* (New York: Vintage, 1978); idem, *Culture and Imperialism* (London: Chatto & Windus, 1993); Gayatri Chakravorty Spivak, *The Spivak-Reader: Selected Works of Gayatri Chakravorty Spivak* (ed. D. Landry and G. MacLean; New York: Routledge, 1996); Homi K. Bhabha, *The Location of Culture* (London: Routledge, 1994).

12. See, e.g., R. S. Sugirtharajah, *Postcolonial Criticism and Biblical Interpretation* (Oxford: Oxford University Press, 2001); Laura E. Donaldson and Kwok Pui-lan, eds., *Postcolonialism, Feminism, and Religious Discourse* (New York: Routledge, 2002); Tat-siong Benny Liew, ed., *Postcolonial Interventions: Essays in Honor of R. S. Sugirtharajah* (Sheffield: Sheffield Phoenix, 2009).

13. Gerald O. West, ed., *Reading Other-Wise: Socially Engaged Biblical Scholars Reading with Their Local Communities* (Atlanta: Society of Biblical Literature, 2007); Hugh R. Page Jr., ed., *The Africana Bible: Reading Israel's Scriptures from Africa and the African Diaspora* (Minneapolis: Fortress, 2010).

14. Elisabeth Schüssler Fiorenza, *Wisdom Ways: Introducing Feminist Biblical Interpretation* (Maryknoll: Orbis, 2001), 93–95 (93).

15. David J. A. Clines, *Interested Parties: The Ideology of Writers and Readers of the Hebrew Bible* (JSOTSup 205; Sheffield: Sheffield Academic, 1995), 19.

along lines of gender or culture but across such differentiation or, more precisely, at the very place where distinctions of gender, race, class, religion, and so on intersect. Thus, interpreters of biblical texts, be they scholars or lay readers, should be conscious of their own assumptions and agenda, which may have been shaped not only by their current socio-political situation but also by the reception history of certain texts. As an example of the latter, Mary Callaway has convincingly demonstrated that the idea of Jeremiah's inner self is based less on the Hebrew text than on the English translation of the Hebrew terms לב, קרב, and נפש and the understanding of those terms in sixteenth- and seventeenth-century English culture.[16]

In arguing that each epoch exerts its own paradigm of interpretation, I posit that the time has come to abstain from master narratives and one-voice commentaries. Therefore, the task for a contemporary author and commentator would be to accept the various voices in the biblical book as an opportunity to provide a multi-voiced commentary that offers differing readings of any given passage. In support of my thesis, I will point to some new formats of biblical interpretation, several of which claim to be commentaries for the twenty-first century.

Commentaries for the Twenty-first Century

Commentaries That Focus on Reception History
Currently, there are at least three new commentary series that emphasize reception history and thus incorporate multiple voices and perspectives on the biblical text from many contexts and periods. The *Blackwell Bible Commentary* takes historical-critical exegesis as part of the reception history of a biblical book and "emphasizes the influence of the Bible on literature, art, music, and film, its role in the evolution of religious beliefs and practices, and its impact on social and political developments."[17] While exhaustive treatment of any passage is not possible, "all those

---

16. See Mary Chilton Callaway, "Peering Inside Jeremiah: How Early Modern English Culture Still Influences Our Reading of the Prophet," in Diamond and Stulman, eds., *Jeremiah (Dis)placed*, 179–89. Callaway is currently working on a Jeremiah commentary in the *Blackwell Bible Commentary* series that focuses on the book's reception history; cf. the description of this series below.

17. Series editors' preface in Richard Coggins and Jin H. Han, *Six Minor Prophets Through the Centuries: Nahum, Habakkuk, Zephaniah, Haggai, Zechariah, and Malachi* (Blackwell Bible Commentaries 29; Malden: Wiley-Blackwell, 2011), xii.

interested in the influence of the Bible on western culture...should be given a representative sampling of material from different ages, with emphasis on interpretations that have been especially influential or historically significant."[18] The main series editors are John Sawyer, Judith Kovacs, Christopher Rowland, and David M. Gunn. Since 2007, ten volumes have been published, among them Exodus, Judges, Psalms, Esther, Ecclesiastes, and Six Minor Prophets. The commentary to each biblical book proceeds chapter by chapter, breaking these into passages or even verses that have had a significant reception. While the commentator's voice still analyzes the sources listed as influential reception, the presentation is more descriptive than evaluative. Thus, the commentator's major role is to choose convincing examples and to attain a certain balance between epochs and areas of reception. These published volumes are a treasure trove of literary and iconographic sources; they offer exciting insights into time- and culture-specific readings of biblical passages.

The *Smyth & Helwys Bible Commentary* claims to be "a visually stimulating and user-friendly series that is as close to multimedia in print as possible...for a visual generation of believers."[19] Each printed volume includes an additional CD-Rom in which the commentary's text and other sources, such as images, photographs, and maps, are searchable and indexed. In the print-version, the multi-voiced character of the commentary is marked by a series of insets, so-called "sidebars" or "special interest boxes," to cite other authors, highlight extra-biblical connections, present religious art or archaeological finds, and other interesting details. The target audience is students and Christian lay readers of the Bible. The biblical text is divided into longer paragraphs or chapters, each of which is treated in two sections named "commentary" and "connections." The former discusses traditional elements of literary and historical-critical exegesis. The latter presents potential applications relevant for preaching, instruction, or spiritual guidance, and includes references to the reception history. The general editors are R. Scott Nash, Samuel E. Balentine, and R. Alan Culpepper. So far, twelve volumes relating to the Hebrew Bible have been published, among them a commentary on Jeremiah by Terence Fretheim. Due to Fretheim's expertise in the field, this volume offers basic and well-balanced information for each passage of the book of Jeremiah, yet the debate with other scholars is

18. Ibid., xii–xiii.
19. Series preface in Terence E. Fretheim, *Jeremiah* (Smith & Helwys Bible Commentary; Macon: Smith & Helwys, 2002), xiv.

significantly reduced. While some alternative voices are cited in the special interest boxes, they mainly add to or accentuate Fretheim's voice and do not propose controversial issues.

Lastly, there is the brand-new *Eerdmans Illuminations* series. The first volume on Job 1–21, authored by Choon-Leong Seow, is to be released on March 1, 2013.[20] The series offers a literary interpretation that engages the biblical text as theological literature, including instances of reception by Jewish and Christian writers, literature, the visual arts, and music. This series, too, will address a wider audience of interested Bible readers.[21]

texts@contexts

The new book series *texts@contexts*, edited by Athalya Brenner and Nicole Wilkinson Duran with Fortress Press, is not a commentary series *per se*. Aiming at "de-centering the predominant first-world orientation of past biblical scholarship," authors of the series are encouraged to foreground their perspectives and commitments as well as issues of identity, ethnicity, gender, class, location, and power, offered for a diverse and increasingly globalized world.[22] The word "contexts" is presented as a blanket term with many components: "For some, their geographical context is uppermost; for others, the dominant factor may be gender, faith, membership in a certain community, class, and so forth. The balance is personal and not always conscious; it does, however, dictate choices of interpretations."[23]

The first volume on Genesis was published in 2010 by Athalya Brenner, Archie Chi Chung Lee, and Gale A. Yee.[24] Its seventeen essays are authored by scholars from Nigeria, South Africa, Zambia, Israel, Finland, Hong Kong, and the United States.[25] While the strength of this

---

20. Publisher's website [cited November 8, 2012]. Online: http://www.eerdmans. com /Products/4895 /job-121.aspx.

21. These are parts of the project description sent to invited authors, among them Carolyn Sharp, who kindly passed this information to me.

22. Athalya Brenner et al., eds., *Genesis* (texts@contexts; Minneapolis: Fortress, 2010), xv.

23. Ibid., xvi.

24. The next volumes cover Mark (2010) and Exodus and Deuteronomy (2012). The website of Fortress Press announces volumes on Leviticus and Numbers, Joshua and Judges, Matthew, and 1 & 2 Corinthians that are scheduled for publication in 2013. Online: http://store.fortresspress.com/store/productfamily/118/Text-Contexts-series [cited November 8, 2012].

25. Cf. the list of contributors in Brenner et al., *Genesis*, 327–31.

volume is to offer fresh readings of over-interpreted biblical texts, the selection of biblical texts is somewhat imbalanced, with eight essays focusing on Gen 1–3 and four on the Joseph story, which gives the impression of incoherence and random selection. Multi-vocality is achieved with single interpretations often contradicting each other. Contrary to the stated goals of the series, however, not all interpreters reflect upon their context so that the connections between the biblical text and the scholar's context are fairly loose or not clear at all.[26] Therefore, this new series does not replace a commentary, since the latter has to treat all texts of a certain biblical book.

Wisdom Commentary Series
Under the title *Wisdom Commentary* Liturgical Press is currently planning a sixty-volume biblical commentary series written entirely by feminist scholars, male and female. General editor Barbara E. Reid is assisted by an editorial board of eleven leading feminist scholars, most of whom live and teach in the United States.[27] Quoting from the guidelines of contributors,

> The aim of this commentary series is to provide feminist interpretation of every book of the Bible, in serious, scholarly engagement with the whole text from a feminist perspective, not only those texts that explicitly mention women.... The commentary will address not only issues of gender..., but also those of power, authority, ethnicity, racism, and classism, which all intersect.[28]

In order to present diverse voices, the series' ideal is to include in each volume contributions from a number of authors from other countries and contexts. As well, a number of the volumes have co-lead authors, demonstrating the collaborative nature of feminist biblical interpretation. The first volumes are expected to be published in 2014.

---

26. Cf. the similar critique of John E. Anderson, review of A. Brenner, A. C. Chung Lee, and G. A. Yee, eds., *Genesis*, *RBL* 2010: 1–13 (12) [cited November 10, 2011]. Online: http://www.bookreviews.org. See also Philipp M. Sherman, review of A. Brenner, A. C. Chung Lee, and G. A. Yee, eds., *Genesis*, *RBL* 2011: 1–11 (11) [cited November 10, 2011]. Online: http://www.bookreviews.org. Both reviews provide helpful summaries of the volume's goals and of single essays.

27. Mary Ann Beavis, Athalya Brenner, Linda Day, Carol Dempsey, Mignon Jacobs, Amy-Jill Levine, Linda Maloney, Ahida Pilarski, Elisabeth Schüssler Fiorenza, Sarah Tanzer, and Seung Ai Yang.

28. Guidelines for contributors, revised August 8, 2012, sent to me by the general editor Barbara E. Reid.

The International Exegetical Commentary on the Old Testament (IECOT)
This new commentary series is designed to be international, ecumenical, and contemporary. The two main editors, David Carr and Walter Dietrich, work with a board of ten exegetes from Europe and the United States, among them Protestant, Roman Catholic, and Jewish scholars.[29] The main feature of the commentary is a synthesis of both synchronic and diachronic perspectives in the analysis of the biblical text, which includes aspects of contextualization, reception history, hermeneutical considerations, and theological perspectives:

> The goal is to achieve a multi-voiced commentary…larger books are to be treated…by small teams. The aim is to generate as intensive and multi-faceted a combination of the methodological perspectives as possible…. The collaboration within the teams is to be cooperative and complementary in the form of a dialogue.[30]

The first volume on *Zechariah 9–14*, authored by Paul Redditt was published in the fall of 2012.[31]

Since this outline sounded promising to us, Carolyn Sharp and I agreed to write the commentary on the book of Jeremiah in this series. In our endeavor, we hope to bridge the gap between the German and the English scholarship on Jeremiah. Yet, in working out the details of our collaboration, we are encountering a range of obstacles to our hope for a fully collaborative commentary model. For example, the book of Jeremiah is so long that time constraints have forced us to divide up the chapters of the book of Jeremiah: I will write on Jer 1–25 and Dr. Sharp will write on Jer 26–52. In the following, I will present some of my preliminary deliberations on our common task.

Towards a New Commentary on the Book of Jeremiah

Given the definition of "voice" cited above, it is obvious that my voice as author of the commentary on Jer 1–25 will be dominant. My aim to offer a multi-voiced commentary thus would entail that I mark out different voices in the biblical text and honestly include other interpreters'

---

29. Board members are: Adele Berlin, Erhard Blum, Beate Ego, Irmtraud Fischer, Shimon Gesundheit, Walter Groß, Gary Knoppers, Bernard M. Levinson, Ed Noort, and Helmut Utzschneider.

30. Project description of IECOT, September 16 (2005): 2. Cited November 9, 2012. Online: http://www.iekat.de/appEN/nav_category.php?category=DIE_KONZEPTION.

31. Paul Redditt, *Zechariah 9–14* (IECOT; Stuttgart: Kohlhammer, 2012).

voices without evaluating them in a way that would give me the definite final word. I imagine some sort of weaving together of other voices while refraining from conducting the chorus too strictly. As it is hard to formulate this theoretically, I will illustrate my intention with regard to Jer 7:16–20.

As part of the temple sermon this passage is first introduced as a private communication of God with the prophet (vv. 16–17), but then shifts to an accusation of the people (vv. 18–19) and to an oracle of doom (v. 20). The dominant divine voice accuses Judean families of jointly venerating a goddess named "Queen of Heaven," a practice that is judged as apostasy and shameful behavior. Such veneration has a parallel in the narrative of Jer 44, in which Jeremiah accuses the Judeans who fled to Egypt of the same practice while the addressees are defending themselves.

> As for you, do not pray for this people, do not raise a cry or prayer on their behalf, and do not intercede with me, for I will not hear you. Do you not see what they are doing in the towns of Judah and in the streets of Jerusalem? The children gather wood, the fathers kindle fire, and the women knead dough, to make cakes for the queen of heaven; and they pour out drink offerings to other gods, to provoke me to anger. Is it I whom they provoke? says the LORD. Is it not themselves, to their own hurt? Therefore thus says the Lord GOD: "My anger and my wrath shall be poured out on this place, on human beings and animals, on the trees of the field and the fruit of the ground; it will burn and not be quenched." (Jer 7:16–20 NRSV)

Since Jer 7:16–20 stands in tension with the overall communicative structure of the temple sermon, scholars debate whether the passage originally belonged to the sermon or was inserted later. An argument for the latter position is that the prohibition of intercession occurs in 11:14 and 14:11 in relation to other accusations. The description of the cult for the Queen of Heaven mentions children, fathers, and women as worshippers and situates the practice "in the towns of Judah and in the streets of Jerusalem" (7:17). Because this situation is corroborated by the setting of Jer 44, the cult is most plausibly a local family cult in pre-exilic Judah and not part of the national temple worship.[32] Although the Queen of Heaven cannot be clearly identified with one of the leading ancient Near

---

32. See Christl Maier, *Jeremia als Lehrer der Tora: Soziale Gebote des Deuteronomiums in Fortschreibungen des Jeremiabuches* (FRLANT 196; Göttingen: Vandenhoeck & Ruprecht, 2002), 92–95 and 100–105.

Eastern goddesses Ishtar, Anat, Astarte, or Asherah, her title and the burning of incense provide her with astral connotations and thus liken her to the Neo-Assyrian worship of the host of heaven.[33] The act of baking bread over charcoal with her symbol or in her shape (so 44:19 MT+) is clearly attested as a cultic praxis in Mari and in Neo-Assyrian rituals; the *kawwanim-cakes* (7:18; 44:19) are a loanword from Assyrian *kamānu*-cakes mentioned in relation to Ishtar. Women seem to play an important role in this cult, as they speak in 44:15–19, in which they correlate the devastating harm Judah has experienced with a cessation of the cult for this goddess.[34] In both texts, Jeremiah and the people obviously disagree about the salutary effect of such worship. The dominant textual voice in Jer 7 and 44 completely dismisses this cult as one of the causes for the destruction of Jerusalem.

Most male commentators side with the God of Israel and his prophet in their assessment of the Queen of Heaven. Jack Lundbom writes, "[T]he reason for the ban on intercessory prayer is clear. Yahweh is provoked by Queen of Heaven worship that had ceased, thanks to Josiah's reform, but is now flourishing again. Whole families are doing it, and it is going on everywhere."[35] Ronald E. Clements offers a different dating but affirms that

> this type of worship had continued long after the time of Jeremiah's original temple sermon. Most probably the destruction of the temple in 587 B.C. had encouraged a revival in this popular and seductive form of religion. All the greater importance, therefore, was attached to emphasizing Jeremiah's outright condemnation of it.[36]

Feminist scholars, however, often interpret the veneration of the Queen of Heaven as a positive example of women's contribution to cult and religion. In her dissertation on Jer 44, Renate Jost argues that the Queen of Heaven had national significance, being worshipped by both men and women not only in the family but in local cults, and that the group of women mentioned in Jer 7 and 44 may have even had an official cultic

---

33. See Christl M. Maier, "Himmelskönigin," *WiBiLex*, n.p. [cited November 9, 2012]. Online: http://www.bibelwissenschaft.de/nc/wibilex.

34. Since the women are the sole addressees of the indictment in Jer 44:25 according to the Old Greek, the reference to the men has most probably been added in Jer 44:15. See Maier, *Jeremia als Lehrer der Tora*, 100–101.

35. Jack R. Lundbom, *Jeremiah 1–20* (AB 21A; New York: Doubleday, 1999), 478.

36. Ronald E. Clements, *Jeremiah* (IBC; Atlanta: John Knox, 1988), 47.

role as bakers in the temple of Jerusalem.[37] According to Susan Ackerman, Jer 7 and 44 point to a conflict between Jeremiah (along with his Deuteronomistic editors) and the people of Judah about the cult for this goddess, in which women in particular play an important role.[38] Based on a literary reading of Jer 44, James Harding argues that the goddess is silenced and her devotees marginalized by the dominant discursive strand that genders truthful divine speech as male and construes prophetic masculinity in Jeremiah.[39]

In order to honor the textual voices and their divergent scholarly interpretations, I as commentator must choose not to side with the dominant voice. Since both descriptions of the cult in Jer 7 and 44 are heavily loaded with irony, the biblical texts witness to a debate over the weal and woe of worship for the Queen of Heaven. While this cult probably existed in pre-exilic Judah, I think that its negative portrayal was inserted in the temple sermon after the city's destruction in order to support the prophet's exoneration.[40] Given the prejudices concerning women and their attachment to superstition and magic that we see in traditional commentaries, I would try to describe this cult without any polemic on the basis of all available biblical and extra-biblical sources. I would also draw on Carolyn Sharp's assessment that the competing ideologies in Jer 44, a Judean traditionalist perspective and a pro-Golah stance that sarcastically calls those who fled to Egypt to continue in their ideology, destabilize the text, and preclude a clear statement of who is right and who is wrong.[41] As a commentator concerned about discrimination at the intersection of gender, class, ethnicity, and religion, I cannot perpetuate the polemic against this cult and any overt or hidden critique of women's idolatrous behavior. Instead, I would try to mark clearly the interests of both conflicting parties. For instance, I would argue against the oracle of doom in Jer 44:12–14 that many Judeans actually survived in Egypt and that in the Persian Period the Egyptian goddess Isis was venerated as a motherly deity with astral connotations around the Mediterranean Sea. In the end, I would be less confident about the message of Jeremiah in

---

37. See Renate Jost, *Frauen, Männer und die Himmelskönigin: Exegetische Studien* (Gütersloh: Gütersloher, 1995), 214–20.

38. See Susan E. Ackerman, *Under Every Green Tree: Popular Religion in Sixth-Century Judah* (HSM 46; Atlanta: Scholars Press, 1992), 5–35.

39. See James E. Harding, "The Silent Goddess and the Gendering of Divine Speech in Jeremiah 44," in this volume.

40. Following Ackerman, *Under Every Green Tree*, 6.

41. See Sharp, *Prophecy and Ideology in Jeremiah*, 69–80.

his time and more inclined to demonstrate the divergent voices that discuss the fate of Judeans after the Babylonian conquest until the late postexilic period. I suggest being less confident with dating and more audacious to capture the theological assumptions that emerged in retrospect after the trauma of Jerusalem's fall and the people's dispersion.

In sum, I seek to propose a commentary on Jeremiah that analyzes the debate and power relations within the text and includes feminist, postcolonial, and other literary readings beside traditional historical-critical ones. In offering various interpretations of any given passage, I aim at stimulating readers to reflect upon their own context, to see their own limitations and discriminatory perceptions, and to appropriate the biblical text for their own situation. Seeking to deconstruct discriminatory speech and hidden assumptions of hierarchies, my interpretation aims at promoting an ethical awareness of the detrimental effects of othering. As all readers and interpreters are "interested parties," it is only fair to state my interests and to discern the interests behind other voices. What I do *not* want to suggest is a one-woman or even two-women show after the one-man show, but a discourse of voices, which demonstrates that any interpretation is contextual and by all means related to the knowledge, worldview, and skills of the interpreters, be they single persons or a team of scholars. Such a multi-voiced reading of the book of Jeremiah seems the best way to engage in biblical interpretation that will honor the multiplicity of readers in community in accordance with the precepts of feminist and postcolonial criticism.

Jeremiah "Before the Womb": On Fathers, Sons, and the Telos of Redaction in Jeremiah 1

Yosefa Raz

Critical discourse about prophets and prophetic texts is often organized around an essentially Romantic dichotomy between primary and secondary figures, original material and inauthentic additions. Consider, for example, Hermann Gunkel's influential distinction between "actual" prophetic speech, which was oral, and the "contrived speech" of later prophetic texts.[1] Julius Wellhausen goes a step further in his dismissal of "late" prophets such as Ezekiel: "the water which in old times rose from a spring, the Epigoni stored up in cisterns."[2] Wellhausen's image implies that Ezekiel's prophetic power does not flow from the font of inspiration, but is dependent on the inspiration of the past, which flowed more freely. For Wellhausen, the earlier prophetic texts, which seem to record the *ipsissima verba* of the charismatic oral prophet, are valued over the baroque creations of later epigones. Along the same lines, the task of redaction criticism has often been formulated as an attempt to retrieve an authentic prophetic kernel from within the additions made by prophetic schools and traditions and from the obscurations of scribal mistakes and glosses.[3]

---

1. Hermann Gunkel, *Water for a Thirsty Land: Israelite Literature and Religion* (ed. K. C. Hanson: Minneapolis: Fortress, 2001), 87.

2. Julius Wellhausen, *Prolegomena to the History of Ancient Israel* (New York: Meridian, 1957), 410.

3. For example, though William McKane slightly qualifies the search for a core in interpreting Jeremiah, his approach is still formed by the dichotomy between primary and secondary: "my treatment of 'kernel' is not necessarily connected to the recovery of the *ipsissima verba* of the prophet Jeremiah, but is directed towards the identification of a core, whether or not it is a Jeremianic core. It is an attempt to discern how additional material has been aggregated and organized in relation to that core." William McKane, *A Critical and Exegetical Commentary on Jeremiah, Volume 1: I–XXV* (ICC; Edinburgh: T. & T. Clark, 1986), liii.

In fact, many scholarly models, from those of biblical exegetes to literary critics who are concerned with the Bible's literary reception, still evoke a golden age of prophecy that is followed by a diminished or weakened prophetic practice or "voice." Though these models appear to be describing a historical phenomenon, they are often implicitly based on a Romantic teleology of origins, which values the authentic, original, and primary text over the redacted and secondary copy. Thus, a kind of scholarly melancholia is introduced into our reading of the prophetic texts. Though we observe that the prophetic texts seem to grow in complexity, from short, homespun oracles to longer and more sophisticated texts, this literary development is often imagined as a loss; the rise of prophetic sophistication is linked to a decline in moral value and power, or a corruption in literary style. The righteous rage of the prophet is co-opted by a powerful establishment, or as Gerald Bruns, who follows in the footsteps of Wellhausen, has it, there is "a fundamental opposition between Hebrew prophets and those who produced and canonized the sacred texts."[4] We construct a similar telos about the shift from specific historical prophecies to more totalizing apocalyptic visions. This shift is imagined as almost inevitable, but at the same time it has been described as "prophecy among the scribes,"[5] implying the loss of the classic or authentic "prophetic" element in its reinterpretation and expansion into an apocalyptic vision.

The evocation of Moses in the book of Jeremiah encourages this kind of Romantic reading. The text seems to fashion Jeremiah as secondary or diminished in relation to great ancestors. For example, Jer 15:1 names Moses and Samuel as prophetic predecessors who belong to a kind of golden age of prophecy in which YHWH had been responsive to prophetic intercession:

ויאמר יהוה אלי אם יעמד משה ושמואל לפני אין נפשי אל העם הזה שלח
מעל־פני ויצאו

And YHWH said to me, even if Moses and Samuel stood before me, I am not inclined to this people; send them out from upon me and let them go.[6]

---

4. Gerald Bruns, "Canon and Power in the Hebrew Scriptures," *Critical Inquiry* 10 (1984): 462–80.

5. Lars Hartman, *Prophecy Interpreted: The Formation of Some Jewish Apocalyptic Texts and of the Eschatological Discourse of Mark 13 Par* (ConBNT 1; Lund: Gleerup, 1966), as quoted in Ronald E. Clements, *Old Testament Prophecy: From Oracles to Canon* (Louisville: Westminster John Knox, 1996), 182.

6. All biblical translations are mine unless otherwise indicated.

At first glance, if we read the text autobiographically, Jeremiah could be a Romantic poet caught in the throes of Bloomian "anxiety of influence,"[7] concerned and even doubtful about measuring up to the great prophets that came before him. William Holladay reads this verse, as well as other parallels to Moses, as evidence that Jeremiah's self-understanding was shaped by the figure of Moses, as depicted in the book of Deuteronomy, and by the "conviction that he was the 'prophet like Moses' (Deut 18:18)."[8] "It was in the light of the figure of Moses that Jeremiah lived out his own ministry, and that the figure of Samuel and the words of Ps 22 also played a part in his self-understanding."[9] In a later article, Holladay claims that the poetry of Moses functioned as a literary model for Jeremiah's compositions, as Deut 32 "was known to Jeremiah as a song sung by Moses and...thus became a model for Jeremiah's own poetic diction."[10] As opposed to Holladay's optimistic reading of the influence of Moses on Jeremiah, Luis Alonso Schökel claims that "Jeremiah is presented in the book as an anti-Moses"[11] because "he goes through an itinerary that is the opposite of Moses." Schökel is less interested in the biographical details of the prophet's life; rather, his interpretation is based on an attention to literary forms. In Schökel's view, Jeremiah's failure to live up to the example of Moses enacts the failure and destruction of the old covenant of the law, giving way to a new covenant announced in Jer 30–33.

However, reading Jeremiah as simply the diminished literary heir of the great poet-prophet Moses misses the way in which the Masoretic Text of Jeremiah, a product of extensive redactions, is anxiously constructing a prophetic tradition. In fact, the figure of Moses in the Jeremianic text may precede parts of Deuteronomy, such as Deut 18. As opposed to the

---

7. "Poetic influence is a variety of melancholy or an anxiety principle.... Poetic influence...is the study of the life-cycle of the poet-as-poet. When such a study considers the context in which that life-cycle is enacted, it will be compelled to examine simultaneously the relations between poets as cases akin to what Freud calls the family romance." So Harold Bloom, *The Anxiety of Influence: A Theory of Poetry* (2d ed.; New York: Oxford University Press, 1997), 7–8.

8. William L. Holladay, "Jeremiah and Moses: Further Observations," *JBL* 85 (1966): 17–27 (17).

9. William L. Holladay, "The Background of Jeremiah's Self-Understanding: Moses, Samuel, and Psalm 22," *JBL* 83 (1964): 153–64 (153).

10. Holladay, "Jeremiah and Moses," 19.

11. Luis Alonso Schökel, *The Literary Language of the Bible: The Collected Essays of Luis Alonso Schökel* (ed. T. Holm; trans. H. Spencer; North Richland Hills, Tex.: D&F Scott, 2001), 27.

linear progression of the Romantic model, the texts of Exodus, Deuter-onomy, and Jeremiah were composed in many stages and may have influenced each other at various compositional points.

In my discussion of the figure of Moses as imagined in the text of Jer 1, I propose to look critically "at the way Romantic idioms and inter-ests stick in prophetic studies,"[12] to paraphrase Yvonne Sherwood. After Sherwood, I propose to invert the Romantic model of reading the proph-ets, which privileges authenticity and originality over secondary and derivative redaction. Rather than overvaluing the authentic kernel of prophetic texts and at the same time positing a lost golden age of proph-ecy, I suggest that we examine the unique productive capacities and possibilities generated by secondary figures and secondary additions. This kind of analysis reveals the anxieties that later additions are attempt-ing to cover over, especially in relation to beginnings, origins, and trans-mission. This analysis exposes the fictionality of the opposition between primary and secondary, both in relation to the figures of prophets and in relation to prophetic texts on which the Romantic narrative of prophecy is based.

One of the most important chapters for considering Jeremiah's posi-tion, in relation to both prophetic lineage and historical narrative, is ch. 1. While the chapter establishes Jeremiah's unique authority, it also fash-ions Jeremiah as a prophet in the shadow of Mosaic and Deuteronomistic leaders. The chapter thematizes beginnings: it frames the entire book and narrates Jeremiah's initial call to prophecy. At the same time, it provides an image for the beginning of "the evil," (1:14), which culminated in the "exile of Jerusalem in the fifth month" (1:3). In fact, there is a constant interplay in this chapter, as in the book as a whole, between the destiny of the prophet and the destiny of the nation. Thus, the complex relation-ship between what is primary and secondary in the chapter in regards to lineage and the chronology of Jeremiah's life also thematizes an anxiety over the causes and effects of national history.

---

12. Sherwood primarily critiques the subjects on which biblical scholars tend to focus when they read the prophetic texts. According to Sherwood, reading the prophets as proto-Romantic poets obscures the more violent and revolting aspects of the prophetic imagination. Furthermore, by focusing on the "prophetic soul," critics "strip it of secondary accretions, or its editorial 'body,' in order to get at the book's vital pumping heart, the words of the original inspired [prophet], stifled with layers of secondary additions." Thus, the distinction between primary and secondary texts is often mapped unto metaphors of the body. See Yvonne M. Sherwood, "Prophetic Scatology: Prophecy and the Art of Sensation," *Semeia* 82 (2000): 183–224 (186).

While ch. 1 thematizes beginnings and origins, it is not a text that is easily dated. It does not seem to have a kernel of authentic material that can be traced back to the poetic "A" layer of Jeremianic prophecy; rather, the overview it presents of Jeremiah's life and mission seems to have been composed in an attempt to frame an already existent corpus. Thus, we cannot rely here on an interpretive strategy that separates the text into the classic strata named by Duhm and Mowinckel, viz., layers A, B, and C.[13] In a sense, all of the text of ch. 1 is secondary. The chapter seems to contain a patchwork of introductory material that reflects different stages of composition; the superscription in vv. 1–3 was probably intended as a heading for an earlier iteration of the book containing chs. 1–25,[14] while Jeremiah's commission, which contains a mission to "the nations," reflects a longer collection of Jeremianic prophecies, which in all probability included the oracles against the nations appearing in chs. 46–51. Because of the appeal to "the nations," Robert Carroll, like William McKane, dates the commission as exilic or post-exilic: "in the light of the catastrophe of 587, any introduction to the book of Jeremiah would need to appeal to those who suffered the most at the fall of Jerusalem and in order to do that must address itself to the contemporary context of such social groups."[15] The prophecy of the boiling-over pot in vv. 13–16 is also ambiguous as to the enemy from the North. It may have originally been addressed to the enemies of Judah,[16] but was certainly expanded to refer to the Judeans themselves, who are castigated as idolaters in v. 16b. Both Carroll and McKane remark on the atypical nature of the chapter: McKane points to a stylistic "unevenness" in the call narrative that stems from a "concern to do justice to the contents of the

---

13. Since the groundbreaking work of Duhm and Mowinckel in the early part of the twentieth century, biblical scholars have posited a complex compositional process for the book of Jeremiah. Duhm and Mowinckel hypothesized that the poetic oracles of the book, primarily in chs. 1–25, were composed earlier than the prose. This "A" layer, containing what many claim to be the poetry of the original prophet, was expanded by the addition of a biographical prose narrative, which they called a "B" layer, and a Deuteronomic expansion and redaction of the poetic oracles, dubbed layer "C."

14. According to Carroll, who follows Thiel, "the form here provides closure with 25.1–3 and may be regarded as a post-Deuteronomistic editorial introduction to the book of Jeremiah"; see Robert P. Carroll, *Jeremiah* (London: T&T Clark International, 2004), 90.

15. Ibid., 96.

16. See ibid., 106.

Book of Jeremiah."[17] With some frustration, Carroll asserts that "remarkably little of the tradition is reflected in the prologue."[18] Rather than searching for the kernel or core of the chapter, it is better to read it as a pastiche of prophetic vocabulary and conventions. Though the superscription and the commission seem to originate in different ideologies and aesthetical approaches, when juxtaposed, they reveal an anxiety about time, transmission, and lineage in a time of catastrophe.

The superscription in vv. 1–3 attempts to impose order on chaos. It depicts Jeremiah's career in relation to a line of Judean kings that establishes him within normative Judean history and structures of monarchial authority. However, a close reading of the superscription reveals the instabilities and gaps this narration must cover over.

The notion of lineage, which includes the transmission of wisdom and authority from father to son, is an important feature of Deuteronomic ideology. Moshe Weinfeld calls attention to "the constant emphasis on the educational role of the father"[19] as characteristic of the pedagogical address of the book of Deuteronomy. This didactic transmission of tradition, imagined as going from father to son, is a recurring image in Deuteronomy, from the injunction to discipline a rebellious son (Deut 21:18–22) to the "pedagogical expression with which the instructor or preacher generally begins his address."[20] Perhaps the notion of continuity and patriarchal tradition is not a reflection of a shared reality but rather a fantasy of social relations, similar to the fiction of Moses' address to the people of Israel before entering the land. The interlocking metaphorical systems of primary and secondary, father and son, cause and effect often implicitly map onto each other in the Deuteronomistic rhetoric. The didactic tone of the father-teacher, which appears in Deuteronomy, is a mirror image of the attempt to order history under the sign of the father in the Deuteronomistic History. Each event in the past time of the fathers leads into the catastrophe of the sons, in an unbroken chain of causative lineage.

The superscription begins with Jeremiah's own lineage: his father's name, as well as his lineage "from the priests at Anathoth" and the tribal affiliation with Benjamin. At the same time, Jeremiah's life as prophet is

---

17. McKane, *Jeremiah 1*, 24.

18. Carroll, *Jeremiah*, 111.

19. Moshe Weinfeld, *Deuteronomy and the Deuteronomic School* (Oxford: Clarendon, 1972), 305.

20. Ibid.

represented alongside a line of kings: Josiah son of Amon, Jehoiakim, Josiah's son, and Zedekiah, also son of Josiah. These dual lines of lineage suggest the continuity of father to son. The inherited roles of priest and king connote a continuous social fabric of inherited patriarchal traditions, knowledge, and power.[21]

Generally, prophetic superscriptions mark the peculiar genre of the prophetic narratives and oracles: the strange and fabulous is firmly anchored in history, often dated by the calendars of kings.[22] Yet the superscription of Jeremiah is noticeably long in comparison to the superscriptions of other prophetic books, perhaps because it both does the regular work of the prophetic superscription and is the record of a problem. With exile on the near horizon, fixing events "in history" becomes more problematic as the calendar itself becomes unmoored. Thus, the end of Jeremiah's ministry is marked by dual calendars: time is counted by the old system, the lineage of Judean kings, but it is also marked by the catastrophic historical event of the exile of Jerusalem. The doubling of the preposition, עַד, "until," in v. 3 reveals a kind of stutter in the text in bridging the distance between these two calendars. Hence, the conventional superscription sets up a tension between "normal," linear, historical time, counted by the succession of monarchs, and disrupted time—between inherited roles and the complete disruption and transformation of social roles due to catastrophe and exile.

Though the superscription seems at first glance to convey a continuity of priests and kings, a closer look at the history behind the dry facts reveals the fissures in continuity. Despite the seeming authority Jeremiah gains from being from a line of priests at Anathoth, the allusion to Anathoth also anticipates the upcoming national exile, as Abiathar the priest was banished to Anathoth from Shiloh by Solomon after he aided the rebellion of his older brother, Adonijah, against the king.[23] According to Deuteronomistic historiography, Abiathar's banishment is a part of the

21. "The association of the speaker named in the titular introduction with the reigns of specific kings is conventional, and reflects the Deuteronomistic presentation of prophecy and monarchy as twin institutions in the history of Israel"; see Carroll, *Jeremiah*, 92.

22. "The way in which the prophets give the exact time at which they received certain revelations, dating them by events in the historical and political world, and thereby emphasising their character as real historical events, has no parallel in any other religion"; see Gerhard von Rad, *Old Testament Theology*, Vol. 2, *The Theology of Israel's Prophetic Traditions* (trans. D. M. G. Stalker; New York: Harper, 1962), 363.

23. See 1 Kgs 2:26–27.

fulfillment of the word of YHWH, who promised dynastic punishment for the sons of Eli.[24] In addition to exile and banishment, then, this back-story alludes to an interrupted lineage, as the sons of Eli are replaced in the tabernacle work by Samuel.

The superscription reveals a tension between the messy and terrible events of history and the attempt to frame history and use it to create structures of authority. Thus, while listing the last kings of Judah as the backdrop to Jeremiah's ministry, the superscription also erases two of the kings recorded in the book of Kings, smoothing out a more complicated history. The superscription of Jeremiah lists Josiah as king, and his sons Jehoiakim and Zedekiah, who succeeded him. It does not list two other kings listed in the book of Kings: Jehoahaz, the first of Josiah's sons to ascend to the throne, or Jehoiachin, son of Jehoiakim, both of whom ruled for only three months. According to the book of Kings, the last kings of Judah come to power in a series of violent breaks in lineage; as opposed to a Deuteronomistic ideal of an orderly succession of fathers and obedient sons, the sons of Judean kings tend dramatically to reverse their fathers' projects. For example, Josiah, who is the ultimate positive role model for Judean kingship in Deuteronomistic ideology, stands in contrast to his father, Amon, who was killed in a slave rebellion after reigning for a mere two years. After Josiah, the institution of kingship became destabilized as various powers attempted to seize control of the throne. Rather than a smooth line of inheritance that goes from father to son, the kingship moves horizontally, between the sons of Josiah, and back from Josiah's grandson, Jehoiachin, to Zedekiah, his uncle. Perhaps the most final symbolic rupture of the line of fathers and sons is the slaughter of Zedekiah's sons before Zedekiah by the Babylonians (2 Kgs 25:7).

The superscription presents a somewhat tidied-up version of the lineage of kings, upon which depends the stability of the kingdom. The commission that follows the superscription uses a different strategy for creating authority for the figure of Jeremiah. Rather than linking his position to the lineage of Judean monarchs, who, as we have seen, are presented in a crisis of authority in the book of Kings, the commission constructs a prophetic lineage that can supersede the father–son transmission and the hierarchical structures of pre-exilic Judean society. The commission suggests that in addition to monarchial and priestly lineage, there is a prophetic lineage that exists alongside kings and priests, or

24. See 1 Kgs 2:27.

perhaps supersedes them.[25] As I will show, the hyperbole of the chapter attempts to bolster Jeremiah's authority, while at the same time revealing the instability of the prophetic position in the time of exile. Though Moses is not mentioned by name, there are a number of elements that hint at his phantom presence as Jeremiah's prophetic "ancestor," suggesting a prophetic lineage to replace the lost stability of the line of Judean monarchs.

Before reiterating how the text echoes the conventions of call narratives, I want to consider the literary effect of this particular text within the chapter as a whole, especially in comparison to the genealogical lines of the superscription. As opposed to the lines of fathers and sons of vv. 1–3, the parallel verses of the commission set up a chronological paradox. How can a prophet be commissioned before being "formed"? If prophetic calls are meant to be answered, Jeremiah's call to prophecy is impossible—he could not answer it because he did not yet exist. He could not be "consecrated" or set apart because he was still completely united with and dependent on his mother's body.

Jeremiah's commission in vv. 4–10 is given to him when he is a "youth," but it seems to echo a previous divine act that occurred before Jeremiah's birth, making this call only a repetition of an earlier call. The text creates an echo effect; we could call it prophetic déjà-vu. At the time in which Jeremiah receives his call to prophecy, he is not answering a call. He has been here before. This echo is constructed around a gap, a previous commission scene, some missing knowledge.

This commission, then, even as it establishes Jeremiah's authority, disrupts the historical temporality of cause and effect, of gestation and birth. It functions according to a temporality different from that of the linearity of fathers and sons. YHWH's call disrupts linear time, lineage time. Lineage supposes initiation: fathers are supposed to teach their sons at the right time. But here, the "initiation" occurs before birth; YHWH reaches into and beyond a pregnant woman's belly to create it. The knowledge of YHWH is not the traditional knowledge taught by father to son, as in Deuteronomy; knowledge of YHWH, this text suggests,

---

25. Carroll (*Jeremiah*, 98) acknowledges the possibility of the supersession of the institution of kingship by prophecy, though he claims, perhaps because prophecy too was fated to end, that "it is a moot point whether in the absence of the monarchy after 587 the commissioning of Jeremiah to be a prophet to the nations is a replacement of kingship with prophecy." See also Baltzer, who notes a basic competition between the office of prophet and king, and a tendency to diminish the human king in the classical prophets. See Klaus Baltzer, "Considerations Regarding the Office and Calling of the Prophet," *HTR* 61 (1968): 567–81.

supersedes tradition. It is not taught through methods of repetition, dictation, or memorization; rather, it is almost erotically inserted into Jeremiah's mouth. In the words of Geoffrey Hartman, "the word that knew him before he was conceived has displaced father and mother as begetter."[26]

On the one hand, this divine intervention seems to reinforce patriarchal structures of power, positing YHWH as the greatest of father figures, whose initiation miraculously supersedes gestation and birth from the female body. On the other hand, by disrupting linear chronology, the initiation suggests a traumatic rupture in the patriarchal transmission of knowledge, power, and tradition. In the same way, the allusions to powerful predecessors such as Moses bolster prophetic authority, while at the same time the almost baroque hyperbole of the rhetoric bares the anxieties that motivate its composition.

Jeremiah's commission scene seems to suggest a previous moment of initiation for Jeremiah, but its language also recalls other call narratives, positioning Jeremiah in a line of transmission. In fact, as Norman Habel points out, Jeremiah's commission functions within the conventions of call narratives, similar to the Elohist version of Moses' call in Exod 3 and the call of charismatic leaders, such as Gideon in Judg 6:11b–17.[27] Habel concludes that the parallels between the call narratives point to a possibly pre-literary form, with "associated traditions."[28] The particular similarity between Exod 3–4, Judg 6, Jer 1, and Deut 18, however, can also point to similar literary influence by Deuteronomistic editing. Rather than an autobiographical reminiscence, "the call form is designed to be preached or read."[29] In the same vein, Baltzer also points out that call narratives are meant to vindicate and legitimize a prophet in office.[30]

To summarize Habel's concise argument, conventional call narratives include divine confrontation, introductory word, commission, objection, reassurance, and a sign that further motivates and inspires the prophet. Thus, Jeremiah's objection to the commission in v. 6 is formulaic, and echoes both Gideon's and Moses' objections:

26. Harold Bloom and Geoffrey Hartman, "The Poetics of Prophecy: Jeremiah," in *The Bible: Edited with an Introduction by Harold Bloom* (New York: Chelsea House, 2000), 205–23 (218).

27. Norman Habel, "The Form and Significance of the Call Narratives," *ZAW* 77 (1965): 297–323.

28. Ibid., 305.

29. Ibid., 306.

30. Baltzer, "Considerations Regarding the Office and Calling of the Prophet," 568.

ואמר אהה אדני יהוה הנה לא ידעתי דבר כי נער אנכי

Ah, Y<small>HWH</small> Elohim, behold, I do not know how to speak, for I am a youth.

Moses' commission in Exod 4:10 also contains a statement of refusal, based on an inability to speak:

לא איש דברים אנכי גם מתמול גם משלשם גם מאז דברך אל עבדך

I have never been a man of speaking, not in the past and not since you have spoken to your servant.

Both Jeremiah's and Moses' problem with language can be read as a Deuteronomistic ideal. As Helen Kenik points out, "for the prophet to be an effective spokesman for Yahweh, he must be utterly dependent and trusting; he must speak the word that is given to him and not his own thoughts."[31]

By characterizing Jeremiah as a נער, a youth, the text evokes another prophet called as a נער: Samuel, an ideal prophet who unites political and religious power in the Deuteronomic history, already mentioned as part of Jeremiah's prophetic lineage in 15:1. The word נער is a kind of *Leitmotif* of Samuel's commission, described in 1 Sam 2–3. Samuel is called by Y<small>HWH</small> when he is a נער serving Eli, and this youthful commission seems to guarantee his innocent loyalty to Y<small>HWH</small>. He grows up under the supervision of Y<small>HWH</small> (1 Sam 3:19), and "all of Israel from Dan to Be'er Sheva knew that Samuel was a trustworthy prophet of Y<small>HWH</small>." In the same way, though being young may negatively affect Jeremiah's rhetorical power, it also establishes a kind of authority for his prophetic office, as he comes to prophecy unsullied.[32]

After the formulaic objection, according to Habel, comes a formulaic reassurance such as Jer 1:9:

הנה נתתי דברי בפיך

Behold, I have set my words in your mouth.

The language here seems to be directly patterned after Exod 4:12, when Y<small>HWH</small> says to Moses:

ואנכי אהיה עם פיך

And I will be with your mouth.

---

31. Helen A. Kenik, *Design for Kingship: The Deuteronomistic Narrative Techniques in 1 Kings 3:4–15* (Chico: Scholars Press, 1983), 105.
32. See Kenik's point about the motif of the "little child" (ibid., 104–9).

Both prophets claim to have difficulty with speech, and both prophets are reassured that divine inspiration is to be located in their mouth.

There is a further intertextuality between Jer 1, Exod 3–4, and Deut 18, as many exegetes have pointed out. YHWH promises to raise up a prophet like Moses, "from among [the Israelites'] brothers" (18:18) and to put YHWH's words in his mouth. The language is similar to the language in both Exodus and Jeremiah—ונתתי דברי בפיו, "and I put my words in his mouth." However, as opposed to Holladay's supposition that the man Jeremiah knew Deut 18 and supposed he might be the prophet that the text predicted,[33] we need to posit a more complex relation between the texts, especially considering that Jer 1:4–10 is probably a late composition. In fact, it may well be that the text of Deut 18 was composed in reaction to the Jeremianic tradition.[34]

The conventional language of Jeremiah's commission links him to idealized Deuteronomistic prophets such as Moses and Samuel, as well as charismatic military leaders such as Gideon. In addition to establishing Jeremiah's commission within the conventions of prophetic call narratives, the text also alludes to conventions for the commission of kings. Solomon is also commissioned as a נער protesting his monarchic role;[35] the hyperbolic nature of the chapter imagines Jeremiah not only as the greatest of prophets, on par with or even superseding Moses, but also on par with the kings of Judah and Israel. While the superscription suggests that monarchic power and prophetic power function side by side, as two parallel and complementary lines of succession and social continuity, in the commission scene Jeremiah himself replaces Judean kings as the subject of lineage and succession.

The uterine commission is also a convention of Mesopotamian and Egyptian royal ideologies, at times coming to stabilize monarchal authority in cases of broken lineage. For example, the Assyrian Assurbanipal (668–627) and Pianchi, a Nubian king who conquered Egypt and founded the 25th dynasty in the eighth century, describe themselves as having been commissioned from the womb. The god Amun addresses King Pianchi: "It was in the belly of your mother that I said concerning you

---

33. Holladay, "The Background of Jeremiah's Self-Understanding," 160.

34. Dating the composition of Deut 18 is a vexed problem. Carroll and Rofé, for example, both hypothesize that the Jeremianic tradition could have influenced a late insertion into Deuteronomy. See Carroll, *Jeremiah*, 99; Alexander Rofé, "The Strata of the Law About Centralization of Worship in Deuteronomy and the History of the Deuteronomic Movement," in *IOSOT Congress Volume Uppsala 1971* (VTSup 22; Leiden: Brill, 1972), 221–26 (225).

35. See 1 Kgs 3:7.

that you were to be ruler of Egypt; it was as seed and while you were in the egg that I knew you."[36] Yet Assurbanipal's succession to the throne was contested as he was the younger brother, while the Nubian Pianchi founded a new Pharaonic dynasty—in both cases the overblown hyperbole may be coming to compensate for an anxiety regarding interruption in lineage.

The idea of a figure that combines both divine and civil authority comes to cover over the break in the Judean monarchic succession, or more broadly, in the dissolution of Judean monarchy. This Near Eastern convention for royal authority during an interrupted line of succession is now utilized to cover up and create continuity in a more large-scale "irregular succession"—national succession that has been interrupted by historical upheaval.

By composing a text that is a pastiche of a variety of conventions of prophecy *and* civic leadership, the Deuteronomic or post-Deuteronomic authors hope to establish Jeremiah's authority at a time of competing prophetic claims. While creating a link between Jeremiah and Moses, and even offering Moses as an ancestor or model for Jeremiah, thus creating a sense of continuity and authority to the prophetic office and oracles, the redactors of the passage, who put the commission with the superscription, actually reveal the disjunctive nature of this lineage. Moses, as prophetic father, is in some ways only possible as a mirage, as this particular echo of the prophetic figure of a man who combined absolute and exclusive divine inspiration, civic leadership and heroism, and a quasi-monarchic power is probably manifested for the first time in the Jeremianic corpus. Through these comparisons, Jeremiah becomes a figure who is both greater and weaker than the prophets and leaders he resembles. By combining echoes of all these various figures, the Jeremiah text actually evokes a man who never was, a strong prophet, a melancholic object constituted only by the threatened and weakened text.

At the same time that the chapter functions as a prologue to the life of Jeremiah, it also is made to serve as the prologue for national catastrophe. The second sign YHWH provides to Jeremiah is a סִיר נָפוּחַ, usually translated as "boiling-over pot" (Jer 1:13). YHWH interprets the image or vision for Jeremiah as "evil will be opened from the North on all the dwellers of the land" (1:14). The "dwellers of the land" could conceivably refer to the enemies of Judah, but vv. 16–19, perhaps later additions, gloss the message of disaster as addressed to "the kings of Judah, to its ministers, its priests, and to the people of the land" (1:18). This oracle

36. M. Gilula, "An Egyptian Parallel to Jeremiah I 4-5," *VT* 17 (1967): 114.

answers questions about the direction of danger: Where is the enemy coming from? How will this evil be "opened" or be born?

The question of physical direction signals also an over-determined "quest" for the origin of "the evil."[37] In Deuteronomistic ideology, the behavior of empires, Judah's external enemies, is described in the language of Yahwistic crime and punishment. Thus the evil is to come about on account of leaving YHWH, worshipping other gods, and bowing down to man-made idols (1:16). But the Deuteronomistic History, as well as the book of Jeremiah, seem to reflect a preoccupation with the origin of "the evil." When did YHWH first turn against his chosen nation? At times the destruction is blamed on dynastic retribution, traced specifically to King Manasseh's idolatry (see Jer 15:4 and 2 Kgs 23) and by implication, to the problematic institution of monarchy itself. Elsewhere, though, the nation is found guilty from the era of the conquest, or even further back "from the day that your fathers departed from the land of Egypt until this day" (Jer 7:25). Sometimes the punishment is attributed to false prophets; at other times the prophets are considered real, only the problem is that nobody listened to them.

In "Différance," Derrida links the question of authority to questions of origins, and to a quest for a "principal responsibility." For Derrida, writing itself entails a complex set of problems relating to authority and origin. In writing down a text, "what is put into question is precisely the quest for a rightful beginning, an absolute point of departure, a principal responsibility."[38] The quest for Jeremiah's beginning, both the concern with his birth and call to prophecy, as well as the sources of his prophetic lineage, mirrors the over-determined allocation of blame and responsibility in the book of Jeremiah, especially in its Deuteronomistic redactions.

The chapter posits two possible ways of thinking about temporality and history. The first is a historiography of cause and effects. By going back to the beginning of catastrophe, one can understand its causes. Though the post-exilic position can be one of political powerlessness, the fantasy of first causes is a fantasy about divine and human power in history—to know, to understand, and to influence great events, even if only retrospectively. This fantasy is also one of continuity—the same divine ruler and rules occur before and after exile; YHWH is unchanged despite the destruction of his temple.

37. The exegetical wild goose chase for the "Scythians" is motivated by this rhetoric in the text.

38. Jacques Derrida, *Margins of Philosophy* (trans. with additional notes by A. Bass; Chicago: University of Chicago Press, 1982), 6.

However, the first chapter of Jeremiah also contains a traumatic perception of history, in which the catastrophe has no cause, no beginning, and no reason; this stance threatens to break through the Deuteronomistic ordering process, through disjunctive and incoherent connections, or to topple its rhetorical structures through its over-reaching hyperbole. It infects the way in which the narrative of Jeremiah's life and calling can be ordered. If the catastrophe has no principal responsibility, or is wildly over-determined, how is it possible to envision an orderly narrative for Jeremiah, the prophet presiding over the fall of Jerusalem? The way in which the chapter presents Jeremiah's life and times reveals the strain of the attempt to provide a normative call narrative that would make sense of the years leading up to the catastrophe as well as the disjunctive oracles that the redactors inherited from that time period. On the one hand, Jeremiah is made to conform to the patriarchal structures of power—fathers and sons, monarchical lineage, and even a (Mosaic) prophetic lineage. On the other hand, the divine call is presented as an interruption of tradition and knowledge transmitted from father to son— an alternative, impossible temporality in which Jeremiah could be called before he existed, in which effect and cause are scrambled, when it is impossible to have true knowledge about prophetic beginnings, or by extension, historical causes.

The juxtaposition of this orderly historiography and an underlying chaos reveals the fragility of the father–son transmission. As opposed to the Deuteronomistic fantasy of culture and tradition, in which fathers create and teach their children, this chapter seems to suggest a melancholic alternative, in which sons must constitute themselves in a lineage of phantasmagorical fathers. After the catastrophe, the "fathers" of the chapter, both as historical causes (of catastrophe) and as prophetic ancestors, must be imagined and created by their sons. Perhaps the backwards construction of this prophetic lineage of the chapter can function as a new image for considering textual transmission and redaction of prophetic sources, making the *ipsissima verba* of the prophet an unattainable melancholic object.

"THE STAIN OF YOUR GUILT IS STILL BEFORE ME" (JEREMIAH 2:22): (FEMINIST) APPROACHES TO JEREMIAH 2 AND THE PROBLEM OF NORMATIVITY

Else K. Holt

It is no secret that some—even large parts—of the language of the book of Jeremiah are unpleasant, abusive, violent, sexist, and (on the verge of) pornographic. And not only is the language abusive and violent, the message is also abhorrent: the fate of the Judeans and Jerusalemites of the sixth century B.C.E.—the siege, hunger, and diseases, the destruction of the capital and temple, the deportation of the upper levels of society, life in a foreign country—all these miseries had one, and only one cause, the sins of the Judeans and Jerusalemites themselves. In the book of Jeremiah God is an angry father who beats up his children; God is a cuckolded husband, abusing and threatening his wife; God's justice is retributive; his "educational strategy" is violent and merciless; and the way to salvation goes through submission and the acknowledgment of his superiority. This theology is a given with which readers of the book of Jeremiah have to deal, one way or another.

One easy way out of this horridness is total negligence—another is furious condemnation of the message. Neither way, however, should be viable for the academic reader; nevertheless, both ways are found within scholarly literature on the book of Jeremiah.

The Landscape

One of the most unpleasant texts in the book of Jeremiah is Jer 2:1–3:4, which is part of a larger poetic unit, 2:1–4:4, labeled "The Metaphor of a Broken Family" by Kathleen O'Connor.[1] In the introduction, 2:1–3, God speaks about the original, harmonious relationship between himself and

---

1. Kathleen M. O'Connor, *Jeremiah: Pain and Promise* (Minneapolis: Fortress, 2011), 35.

young Israel, personified as his fiancée (fem.) and as his most precious belonging, the first harvest (masc.), that is, God's basis of sustenance. The following unit (2:4–3:4) alternates between addressing the audience as male Jacob/Israel, and as the female nameless wife. In a direct language invective (2:4–9) using the form of a lawsuit (ריב) YHWH accuses the people and its leaders of forgetting how he cared for them in the formative days of wandering in the wilderness. This accusation is God's basic complaint against his people. It is followed by a sequence of metaphors, all of them exposing the outrageousness of Israel's (masc. + fem.) conduct that has turned every normal attitude upside down, or— with Mary E. Shields—has "overstepped boundaries."[2] No other nation (גוי) has changed its "gods" like "my people" (2:9–13, masc.); Israel has committed himself to slavery, because he has forsaken YHWH (2:14–19, vv. 14–17 masc., 18–19 fem.); she has turned herself into the unimaginable, a wild vine, a restive young camel, and a wild ass in heat, in other words, an unfaithful, libido-driven woman (2:20–25, fem.); Israel is as shamed as a thief because he seeks incapable gods instead of listening to the God who never fails (2:26–32, masc.); she seeks love (אהבה) from strangers and tries to escape YHWH's punishment, but in vain (2:33–37, fem.), and in the end the divorce between God and the people will be final (3:1–4, fem.).

For decades, the average scholarly commentator would adhere to the understanding of God in Jer 2–3 as a loving father, broken-hearted by the sins of his people, having to punish them to save them from their wicked ways. Now the picture has changed, and a new understanding has emerged.

The understanding of the imagery (and theology) in Jeremiah as unpleasant and sexist is due primarily, though not only, to feminist exegesis. For the past 25 years, Jer 2–3 have been at the center of feminist readings of the book of Jeremiah. Drorah Setel's reading of female sexual imagery in Hosea as poetic pornography in 1985[3] became a powerful inspiration for writers in the influential *Feminist Companion to the Latter Prophets* (1995). The first, and largest, part of this volume was occupied by "The Case of Hosea," but in part II Athalya Brenner discussed the

---

2. Mary E. Shields, "Circumcision of the Prostitute: Gender, Sexuality, and the Call to Repentance in Jeremiah 3:1–4:4," in *Prophets and Daniel* (ed. A. Brenner; FCB 2/8; Sheffield: Sheffield Academic, 2001), 121–36 (125).

3. T. Drorah Setel, "Poetic Pornography: Female Sexual Imagery in Hosea," in *Feminist Biblical Interpretation* (ed. L. M. Russell; Philadelphia: Westminster, 1985), 86–95.

interaction of propaganda and pornography in Jer 2–3. Through this article Jer 2–3 was once and for all designated as an improper text with an improper message conveyed in even more improper language and imagery, a text with which no decent—female or male—reader of the Bible should consort, except in order to uncover and/or dismantle it. The text poses a danger to its female readers. It is abusive, pornographic, propagating female submission to a male, patriarchal fantasy, almost irresistible even to well-educated, academic readers (such as Brenner) since it is a part of the reader's cultural system.[4]

The denigration was continued by Mary E. Shields in her article on Jer 3:1–4:4 in the 2001 *Feminist Companion*, Second Series.[5] Also Shields must warn her readers against the impact of the text:

> …as a woman, I see this text as arguing for a change of (male) behavior on the religious and political planes, planes defined and governed by males. However, with regard to female behavior, this text, by virtue of its imagery, confines women (and myself as a female reader) to two roles – faithful wife and daughter. Any behavior taking women outside these roles identifies them as prostitutes…. Thus, the entire symbolic world of the discourse operates to marginalize women and women's interests.[6]

A few years later, Shields followed up on feminist Jeremiah scholarship in an article in which she gave a broad, but apt, overview on trends in recent publications, and presented the future questions implicated in those trends.[7] According to Shields, the questions so far had been:

> What is one to do about this imagery? Is it only very powerful rhetoric showing the emasculation of the male power holder? Is it culturally conditioned language that should only be discussed in its own historical context? Is it language that is powerful enough to shape contemporary conceptions of male and female relationships? Should these texts be studied only through a literary or postmodern or ideological lens?[8]

---

4. Athalya Brenner, "On Prophetic Propaganda and the Politics of 'Love': The Case of Jeremiah," in *A Feminist Companion to the Latter Prophets* (ed. A. Brenner; FCB 8; Sheffield: Sheffield Academic, 1995), 256–74 (274).

5. Shields, "Circumcision."

6. Ibid., 132–33.

7. Mary E. Shields, "Impasse or Opportunity or…? Women Reading Jeremiah Reading Women," in *Jeremiah (Dis)Placed: New Directions in Writing/Reading Jeremiah* (ed. A. R. P. Diamond and L. Stulman; LHBOTS 529; London: T&T Clark International, 2011), 290–302; the article is based on a presentation at the SBL Annual Meeting in Boston 2008.

8. Ibid., 291.

Shields regrets that most of this work is done—and read—only by women, but finds it "yet more troubling" that there is "an apparent divide among feminist scholars in their approaches to these texts," and that this divide creates distance between feminist scholars.[9] She presents current feminist work on Jeremiah in two strands, the one within the literary or rhetorical (and ideology critical) turn, the other "new-historical"/socio-historical. Shields presents herself as belonging to the group which focuses on the rhetoric as an active power, trying to "persuade the audience to adopt a certain way of viewing marriage, proper male and female relationships, and so on."[10]

Distancing herself from a more detached, sociohistorical attitude ("This is the way it was in ancient Israel. Our culture is different. End of story."), Shields advocates the point of view that dismantling the abusive imagery and ideology as historical and "no longer a meaningful contribution to the current discourse on marriage nor to the gender relations in general,"[11] is not enough. Rather, feminist scholarship should move beyond binary oppositions, also between methodological approaches, e.g. historical vs. literary/poststructural.[12]

Shields's own focus is on the influence the biblical text may have on people's lives and how biblical readers think.

> So when they [the average Joe and Jane in Christian circles] read, for instance, that God punishes women for having uncontrolled sexuality, they actually believe that it is acceptable to use violence as a way to keep women in check…. There are many people today, especially within strong Judeo-Christian traditions, who look to these texts as a kind of pattern after which they ought to structure their own relationships. And future feminist scholarship must, I submit, address this reality.[13]

Shields's work is a fine example of the ideological-critical feminist approach, and I shall use her article as *exemplum instar omnium*. What makes her considerations so interesting is that she raises the question of what to do and how to cope with a text which pictures God as abusing his wife and emasculating his male audience, while being at the same time an absolute religious authority. Do we have to give up the notion of

---

9. Ibid., 294.

10. Ibid., 296.

11. Ibid., 298, quoting—and disagreeing with—Christl Maier's opinion; cf. Christl M. Maier, *Daughter Zion, Mother Zion: Gender, Space, and the Scared in Ancient Israel* (Minneapolis: Fortress, 2008), 139.

12. Shields, "Impasse," 298.

13. Ibid., 299.

the Bible as the word of God?, she asks.[14] Shields agrees with Gerlinde Baumann that texts with "positive" images of God cannot be used as "equalizers" balancing and neutralizing the "negative" images.[15] But in the end she seems to end up in an epistemological and religious *cul-de-sac*: "There has to be a way to take into account *how* the language was used in its own context *while* still critiquing its constructions of gender, gender roles, and theology…both then and now."[16]

My question is: Have we really reached a *cul-de-sac*, or maybe even a point of no return, where it is no longer enough to analyze texts like Jer 2–3, but where we have to distance ourselves from a prophetic book like Jeremiah? From the outset I do not think so, and in what follows I shall try to find my way through the thicket.

Ways in the Wilderness

History

In light of the influence of the *Feminist Companion to the Latter Prophets*, it is interesting that—to the best of my knowledge—almost nobody seems to reflect on Robert P. Carroll's response in the same volume to Fokkelien van Dijk-Hemmes's article on Ezekiel and Athalya Brenner's on Jeremiah.[17] Knowing that he is "entering a minefield of ideological contentions,"[18] Carroll, who should not be accused of ignorance to ideology[19] or of being a historicist, conservative scholar, opts for a reading that focuses on historical questions: Who wrote these texts and to whom and with which intent were they written?

> The voice I hear and read in Jeremiah 2–3 (and also in 5.7–8) is a voice expressing strong disapproval of the community or nation's past behaviour as wild, uncontrolled and apostate…. The target of the mockery is

14. Ibid., 300.
15. Ibid., 301.
16. Ibid., 302; Shields's italics.
17. Fokkelien van Dijk-Hemmes, "The Metaphorization of Woman in Prophetic Speech: An Analysis of Ezekiel 23," in Brenner, ed., *A Feminist Companion to The Latter Prophets*, 244–55; Brenner, "Prophetic Propaganda."
18. Robert P. Carroll, "Desire Under the Terebinths: On Pornographic Representation in the Prophets—A Response," in Brenner, ed., *A Feminist Companion to the Latter Prophets*, 275–307 (276).
19. See, e.g., his contributions to *Troubling Jeremiah*: Robert P. Carroll, "The Book of J: Intertextuality and Ideological Criticism," 220–43, and "Something Rich and Strange: Imagining a Future for Jeremiah Studies," 423–43, in Diamond et al., eds., *Troubling Jeremiah*.

the male society.... No doubt metaphors can and do carry surplus meaning, but the sheer negativity of the sexual metaphors in the prophets seems
to me to convey the message that the speakers or writers are against all
kinds of activities, including no doubt sexual activity (if the erotic charge
of the metaphors is allowed to leak back into literal descriptions), whether
male or female, outside of their own social norms and values.... Perhaps
it does serve a second temple elite or a group of ideologues in the Persian
or Greco-Roman period.[20]

One of the basic disagreements between Carroll and van Dijk-Hemmes
and Brenner appears to be the understanding of metaphors. Neither
Carroll nor van Dijk-Hemmes or Brenner discuss metaphor theory.
Nevertheless, the question of how the metaphor works is an important
precondition for the discussion. Van Dijk-Hemmes and Brenner seem to
adhere to Max Black's and especially Eva Feder Kittay's understanding
that metaphor produces a new perspective, or a new point of view, on the
topic.[21] Carroll, on the other hand, warns against confusing the topic and
the vehicle (i.e. the imagery illuminating the topic). In response to van
Dijk-Hemmes's reading of Ezek 23 Carroll contends that

> the only women in the chapter are metaphors. The narrative is not about
> women but about cities or the communities represented by those cities....
> Not believing that Ezekiel 23 is about real women I am inclined not to
> read the metaphors as saying anything about actual women in the biblical
> world (of the text).[22]

In expressed discord with van Dijk-Hemmes and Brenner, Carroll states:

> From my point of view the use of metaphors of women for the commu-
> nity, nation, city and land in the prophets may have little to do with the
> representation of women as such, just as the metaphorization of men for
> the community and the nation in the prophets may have little bearing on
> the representation of men as such.[23]

In my opinion, Carroll here presents a too simplistic understanding of the
impact of metaphorical language, not acknowledging the interaction
between tenor/topic and vehicle, as shown by Kittay.[24] A metaphor is by

20. Carroll, "Desire," 288–89.
21. For a recent introduction to metaphor theory, see Benjamin A. Foreman,
Animal Metaphors and the People of Israel in the Book of Jeremiah (FRLANT 238;
Göttingen: Vandenhoeck & Ruprecht, 2011), 4–29.
22. Carroll, "Desire," 277.
23. Ibid., 278.
24. Cf. esp. her perspectival theory of metaphor; Eva Feder Kittay, *Metaphor: Its
Cognitive Force and Linguistic Structure* (Oxford: Clarendon, 1987).

no means "innocent," and the impact of the metaphor on its audience is not to be neglected. In this respect, I do agree with, for example, van Dijk-Hemmes and Brenner. On the other hand, though, Carroll is right when he warns against overemphasizing misogyny and overlooking a possible parallel misandry in the prophetic texts.[25] Taken out of their contexts, some prophetic images are certainly abusive and misogynistic, but read within their societal and literary contexts these texts must be understood as aiming at a primarily male audience, and thus in the end more "misandric" than misogynistic.

Carroll vehemently refuses the understanding that metaphorizing women as a sign for something else is a form of disembodiment of the female subject, as it is urged by, for example, van Dijk-Hemmes.[26] This in turn leads him to discuss the issue of pornography in the prophets. When he himself coined the description "religious pornography" for material in Hosea and Jeremiah in his commentary on Jeremiah he used the phrase metaphorically [and in a historically descriptive way], while van Dijk-Hemmes and Brenner, following Drorah Setel,[27] use it in a modern sense.[28]

Now, what is the rationale behind Carroll's fierce criticism of feminist exegesis, exemplified by van Dijk-Hemmes and Brenner? As stated above, it is not that Carroll should be viewed as a conservative writer, neither academically nor religiously;[29] rather, he was a provocative voice in the Jeremiah guild for decades. His objective was not to "save" the text from criticism; on the contrary, Carroll has a long legacy of criticizing the ideologies of the Bible.[30] What made him criticize van Dijk-Hemmes and Brenner so vehemently is a profound methodological disagreement. He writes:

25. Carroll, "Desire," 288.

26. Van Dijk-Hemmes, "Metaphorization," 244.

27. And thus, according to Carroll, also following Andrea Dworkin's radical feminist position which lies behind Setel's, and thus behind van Dijk-Hemmes's and Brenner's understanding of pornography; Carroll, "Desire," 294–95.

28. Ibid., 286.

29. See also the reference to Carroll's position that "an ideological/theological discussion of the book of Jeremiah must begin 'where *we are now*'" in Diamond's and Stulman's introduction to *Jeremiah (Dis)Placed*, 30.

30. See also Robert P. Carroll, *Wolf in the Sheepfold* (London: SPCK, 1991); American edition under the more "domesticated" title *The Bible as a Problem for Christianity* (Philadelphia: Trinity Press International, 1991).

> I do not think that texts should be subjected entirely to a one-sided
> imposition of meaning by the modern reader. There should be some room
> in every reading for the text to resist the imposed meaning of the reader. I
> remain loyal to my roots in the historical-critical methodology for reading
> the Bible—at least to the extent that I wish to avoid the modern tendency
> to practice an aggravated anachronistic approach to ancient texts.[31]

Carroll's lengthy discussion of the concepts of pornography vs. sexual
fantasy and erotica would definitely deserve a more thorough treatment
than is possible in this connection. What strikes me as important in the
quote above is his insistence on the text's right to "resist the imposed
meaning of the reader." He continues by negating "modern ideologies
which impose their own meaning on texts" and prefers "to see texts as
polysemous and therefore as being capable of resisting single-meaning
readings."[32] This attitude is what definitely delimits his reading strategy
from typical historical criticism on the one hand, and an ideological
reading strategy on the other. The intention of Carroll's reading is to hear
the message of the text as clearly as possible, given the distance in time,
space, and culture between the texts and its current reader[33]—and then to
criticize its ideology.

Socio-history—Disaster—Trauma
Robert Carroll's *Ideologiekritik* approach has found many followers
in Jeremiah scholarship. Under the auspices of the Society of Biblical
Literature, a group of younger scholars, inspired by Carroll's thoughts,
organized *The Composition of the Book of Jeremiah Group* in the 1990s.[34]
Twelve years later the group (now seniors!) was revitalized in the SBL
Writing/Reading Jeremiah Group, reflecting the important renewal of
Jeremiah studies which has emerged on both sides of the Atlantic. One of
the influential approaches represented in this framework has been that of
trauma as a sociohistorical backdrop for the ideology/theology and thus
the imagery of the book of Jeremiah.

   This approach is presented by one of the group's original founding
mothers, Kathleen M. O'Connor, in her 2011 book, *Jeremiah: Pain and
Promise*. O'Connor's point of departure was a growing unhappiness with

---

31. Carroll, "Desire," 293.
32. Ibid.
33. Cf. ibid., 305.
34. The discussions in this group were collected in Diamond et al., eds.,
Troubling Jeremiah.

the book of Jeremiah during her professional and personal life, due to its "portrait of a violent, angry God and the book's entry and reentry into violent images, metaphors, and relationships."[35] As a recurring contributor to feminist work on Jeremiah, O'Connor is well aware of the challenges of Jer 2–3.[36] However, through the lenses of trauma experience and the need of coping with trauma for the generations after the fall of Jerusalem, she finds a background for *understanding* the unpleasant discourse.[37]

Trauma and its offspring, Post Traumatic Stress Disorder (PTSD), is the result of meeting overwhelming disaster. But according to disaster studies "…'disasters' only become 'disastrous' when the events exceed the ability of the group to cope, to redefine and reconstruct."[38] What is important, then, is precisely the coping strategy. Seeing the book of Jeremiah as a product of disaster and trauma, O'Connor scrutinizes its coping strategies through lamentation, explanation, and re-creation.

> Studies of trauma and disaster…explain Jeremiah's massive attention to collapse as well as the book's preservation as sacred literature. They show how the words ascribed to the prophet contribute to the moral rebuilding of the shattered community. The book of Jeremiah is a story of disaster, love, and rebirth. Hidden beneath its harsh turbulence, indeed, because of its very turbulence, Jeremiah offers readers a process both for coping and for building hope.[39]

Unlike Brenner and Shields, O'Connor is not focusing on the female imagery, although she acknowledges the abuse implied. Rather, she views Jer 2:1–3:5; 3:6–4:4 as a discourse to a broken nation, men and women, describing it as a drama about a broken family, about how "a family comes undone." O'Connor shows how the family drama, through the meaning-productive powers of metaphor, makes the world understandable to the audience so that they are not blinded by the horrors:

---

35. O'Connor, *Jeremiah: Pain and Promise*, ix.

36. See the close reading of the pericope in her joint article with A. R. P. Diamond, "Unfaithful Passions: Coding Women Coding Men in Jeremiah 2–3 (4.2)," in Diamond et al., eds., *Troubling Jeremiah*, 123–45; cf. also O'Connor, *Jeremiah: Pain and Promise*.

37. This approach was already touched upon in her commentary on Lamentations; see Kathleen M. O'Connor, *Lamentations and the Tears of the World* (Maryknoll: Orbis, 2003).

38. Daniel L. Smith-Christopher, *A Biblical Theology of Exile* (OBT; Minneapolis: Fortress, 2002), 79.

39. O'Connor, *Jeremiah: Pain and Promise*, 27.

"Rather than confronting matters head on, Jeremiah tells and retells the catastrophe indirectly, metaphorically, in unforgettable poetic ways"—at a slant.[40]

> ...the family drama is actually showing Jeremiah's audience their own world, interpreting how their relationship with God teeters on the edge of extinction. It sets their overwhelmingly painful lives into a domestic realm, onto a small stage. In this family feud, they can see their reality and recover language to talk indirectly about what happened to them. The drama tells the truth "slant" in the symbolic world of poetry, without rehearsing the literal horrors of their past and traumatizing them anew.[41]

In O'Connor's reading the family drama ends in a reunion ceremony where the children, in the stylized language of liturgy, announce their desire to return, thereby offering a way of return to the implied audience, the descendants of the first victims. Liturgical language is action language that coaxes people reduced to passivity by traumatic disruptions to move back together in a common effort, reassembling them to make meaning in the present, drawing them back to one another from isolating pain, and serving as an antidote to victimhood and helplessness. "Yet in these chapters, the children's ritual language does not enact reconciliation because God fails to respond."[42]

This assessment notwithstanding, O'Connor still discusses the appropriateness of Jer 2–3 for a modern reader. With reference to feminist criticism she condenses the picture: "the husband is domineering, the wife a nymphomaniac, and relations between them miserable."[43] This is a picture unfit for any modern reader; but O'Connor insists on seeing it from the outset as a product of its culture: "...it would have been a surpassing marvel were it to have escaped limitations regarding relations between men and women."[44]

Moreover, O'Connor is uneasy (to say the least) with the book's "rhetoric of responsibility," that is, the blaming of the victims. Even if this strategy reassures the survivors that God controls and is still in charge of the world, and that, on the other hand, because they are responsible for the disaster, they may be able to prevent similar catastrophes and thereby gain a sense of control, O'Connor finds the rhetoric utterly

---

40. Ibid., 33.
41. Ibid., 36.
42. Ibid., 40–41.
43. Ibid., 43 with reference to Renita Weems and Mary E. Shields.
44. Ibid.

unsatisfactory.[45] But the drama of the broken family, with its blatant sexism and its flawed blaming of the victim, has a certain role in the process of coping with trauma. It speaks to an audience, whose world has already been burned up by the wrath of God. For O'Connor, Jeremiah's poetry is "a potent agent of change. It acts upon the world by creating vital, explosive speech that both reveals and wounds."[46]

Through her trauma-based reading of Jeremiah, O'Connor condones the harsh language of Jer 2–3. She does so in spite of acknowledging its offensiveness to modern readers, male and female alike. As opposed to purely feminist readings like van Dijk-Hemmes's, Brenner's, Shields's, and Baumann's (see below), she focuses on the context of the female metaphors, both textually and societally, and thus broadens the scope of her inquiry. This is even more accurate when the full length of O'Connor's book is taken into consideration.[47]

Otherness and Authority of the Bible

Let us return to Mary E. Shields's challenge, "There has to be a way to take into account *how* the language was used in its own context *while* still critiquing its constructions of gender, gender roles, and theology… both then and now."[48] My immediate reaction is that the problem arises because Shields—and others with her—insist on arriving at the meaning for a modern audience too fast. There is certain impatience in the demand for a balanced understanding, which can be approached by "any Jane or Joe." What is important to remember is *the otherness* of these ancient texts. By judging them by modern standards the reader misses the original message of the text—a message which in turn can be offensive or at least debatable.

When we read, for example, Jer 2:23–24, we must begin with recognizing the text as a text very distant from our own world. If we do not acknowledge the *otherness* of the text, we cannot appreciate it. It is not possible for us to escape our own hermeneutic background, or to align ourselves with the historical audience. But the text has a right to be heard from the outset on its own historical and ideological terms. We must try

45. "Jeremiah's household drama overlooks the aggrandizing greed of Babylon, the economic weakening of Judah, the failure of Judah's leadership, the failure of allies to come to their aid, and many other matters"; see ibid., 44.
46. Ibid.
47. See, e.g., her "Epilogue: A Work of Hope and Resilience," in ibid., 135–37.
48. Shields, "Impasse," 302 (Shields's italics).

to hear it as one voice in a chorus of voices talking about the relationship between God and humankind.

However, this does not mean that the reader should not be open to the possibility that certain parts of the biblical text are offensive. They might even have been meant to be offensive from the beginning. This is no doubt the case with Jer 2–3. The implied—male—audience is supposed to be offended, emasculated by an imagery that turns them into wayward, nymphomaniacal, unfaithful women. This is how the metaphor is supposed to work by the implied author in a patriarchal society, based on honor and shame. The implied—male—audience is supposed to understand the message that God is still in control, but also that their God is a jealous and violent God. *We* might not like this picture—but the picture is there on purpose and we need to be able to understand its message. Put concisely: the abusive message is deliberately abusive.

At the same time, this does not mean that we should delimit our reading to questions about the historical background of the text. Studies in metaphor and gender are of invaluable importance for the understanding of the prophetic texts and their cultural and societal background.[49] We would not be able to realize the force of the abusiveness of Jer 2–3 if we did not ponder the rule of metaphors we live by, or if we were not attentive to the gendering of language (a look into scholarly literature before the 1980s proves me right).

This attentiveness contributes to sharpening our recognition of the strangeness and otherness of the text, thereby helping to alienate us from the text, bringing us onwards to "la seconde naïveté" from where understanding and discussion emanates. This alienation is indispensable both for the academic reader and for "average Jane and Joe," and it is the duty of the academic reader to show this to Jane and Joe. Here, I fully agree with Maier when she writes:

> The use of the sexualized and highly polemic language is due to the social-historical context and the then common language of warfare. Living in a totally different world and culture, modern readers should read these texts critically and challenge their one-sided portrait of God as the violent, victorious master of history and of his people. Furthermore, informed readers today should challenge any attempt to legitimate violence and war by referring to this portrait of the biblical God in current political or religious discourses.[50]

---

49. The same applies to post-colonial studies, which help open the reader's eyes to, for example, power dynamics in the texts.

50. Maier, *Daughter Zion*, 139–40.

It might be that critiquing the constructions of gender, gender roles, and theology in ancient texts as a part of the historical analysis seems to be a bit futile. We cannot change anything. What we can do, however, is be sensitive and open to the critique already present in the texts themselves. Above, I touched on Gerlinde Baumann's dictum, quoted by Shields, about using biblical texts with positive images about God as a counterpart to the unpleasant presentation in, for example, Jer 2–3:

> Images of God as the rapist or abuser of his daughter cannot be "neutralized" even by the most positive "counter-images." Their scandalousness cannot and should not be softened by counter-texts. Only permanent outrage is an adequate response to an outrageous image of God. There is no biblical "medicine" that can help the story of God as the abusive husband of his "wife" Israel to come to a happier end.[51]

I respectfully disagree. No text is an island; to claim that is to disregard the con-textuality and inter-textuality of the Bible. The enlightened challenge to old-school conservative, literal understandings of biblical texts is the recognition that the texts are mutually at odds, and that they do contradict each other. This holds true, not least for the Old Testament. Not only do the texts openly discuss theological matters; they virtually fight over theology, that is, how to understand God and the relationship between God and humanity. The book of Jeremiah is a very vivid example of an intra-textual discussion.[52] As Bible scholars and Bible readers we are part of this ongoing discussion. This means that the authority of the Bible is not an authority of permanence, but an authority of dialogue. If we refuse to participate in this discussion, because we find the interlocutor offensive, we have basically relegated ourselves to a position of powerlessness as regards influencing how the Bible is read in society, academy, and churches.

In other words: as a text, written by humans for humans about God, the Bible is as fallible as any other book. It is also as culturally embedded as any other book, reflecting a society in which gender and authority, honor and shame, domination and subordination, war and peace, were comprehended differently from now. It is important to take this cultural

---

51. Gerlinde Baumann, *Love and Violence: Marriage as Metaphor for the Relationship Between YHWH and Israel in the Prophetic Books* (Collegeville: Liturgical, 2003), 236.

52. Jer 36 thematizes the textual development in the narrative of the king's destruction of Jeremiah's scroll, and especially the importance of God's repetition of his words to Jeremiah (Jer 36:27–32).

limitation into consideration in order to be able to go behind the wording
and enter the theological discussion. The biblical text is also a haunting
text,[53] and so the reader should not expect the reading to be easy or
comforting or reassuring. What could and should be expected is a textual
demand of engagement from the reader, since this text is by no means
trivial.[54]

This type of engagement with the text might pose a special challenge
to the Protestant reader, taking into consideration Luther's concept
of *sola scriptura*. For my part, I find myself in line with O'Connor's
(explicitly Roman Catholic) statement: "Interpretation of biblical texts is
always a conversation, not a one-way set of blueprints for life. That
means that the biblical text is only one theological source in naming,
approaching, and living with God."[55] However, even Luther did not
demand reading the Bible uncritically or a-historically, even if his understanding of history is pre-modern. Moreover, the principle of *sola scriptura* cannot (and should not) prevent us from addressing the texts from a
contemporary perspective, including our hermeneutical awareness. It is
from this position that we enter the biblical conversation or discussion, a
discussion that reflects the temporal continuity from the earliest bits of
narrative and poetry to the latest scholarly addenda to the text.

We have the right heartily to agree with some kinds of the God-talk
in the Bible and vehemently to disagree with others. Yet, as biblical
scholars we do not have the right to refuse to listen to the biblical voices
with which we disagree. Maybe it will not change our own perception of
the matter, but for "average Jane and Joe," sharing our skills as critical
readers is of ultimate significance.[56]

---

53. I owe the phrasing to Walter Brueggemann, *Like Fire in the Bones: Listening
for the Prophetic Word in Jeremiah* (Minneapolis: Fortress, 2006), 139–40, although
I disagree with his understanding of how to respond to the haunting.

54. O'Connor's struggle with the books of Jeremiah and Lamentations is an
instructive example of this engagement with the text; see especially O'Connor,
Lamentations, 110–22.

55. Ibid., 121.

56. From another field of research, film theorist Linda Williams acknowledges
that "'film feminisms' have indeed become a more heterogeneous, dynamic, and
contested set of concepts and practices" and discusses her reservations toward a too
isolationistic feminist approach to her subject; see Linda Williams, "Why I Did Not
Want to Write This Essay," *Signs* 30 (2004): 1264–71 (1270). In my opinion lots of
Williams's considerations cover the field of feminist biblical studies, as well, and
might be taken as an answer to Mary Shields's questions; cf. above, 103.

Post-script about Current Cultural Contexts

Mary Shields's concern about the impact of gendered God-talk on the "average Jane and Joe," though, might look different from a Northern European, more precisely Danish, perspective than from a North American one. The question is how important the biblical imagery is in everyday life in a part of the world where religion and politics are far more separated than in the United States.[57] Religion is of almost no consequence in the life of "average Hanne and Hans in Denmark," and texts like Jer 2–4 are basically unknown to them, and as such without any importance. Should Hanne or Hans happen to hear about it, they might take offense, but then they would dismiss this text as untimely and old-fashioned. This does not mean that they do not consider themselves Christians—almost 80% of all Danes are members of the Evangelical-Lutheran Church of Denmark. People in general have their newborns baptized, 50% of all marriages are celebrated in the church, and almost all members will be buried by their local churches. But Hanne and Hans insist on creating their personal, individual understanding of Christianity and spirituality and pick and choose from the offerings of the church.[58]

The German professor of the Study of Religion, Bernhard Lang, labels this "postmodern" type of religious faith "personal piety," and proffers a current example from Germany. On the question "In which God do you believe," the actress Susanne L. (born 1960) answers:

> I do respect that people believe in God, because it gives them stability to understand life. I myself, though, am too intelligent for that; I cannot. I believe that a human being needs God to elucidate stuff and, not least, to stop worrying. If destiny hits me severely, I might even turn to God and start praying. I do light a candle in church, so I am not without reverence. I could put it this way: I believe in the God who protects my family and me but I do not know if he exists.[59]

---

57. This holds true, even if religion and state are separated by the constitution in the United States, while there is some overlap between state and church in Denmark and Norway (and historically also in Sweden and Northern Germany). Section 4 of the *Danish Constitutional Act* reads: "The Evangelical-Lutheran Church of Denmark (Folkekirken) is the established Church of Denmark and, as such, is supported by the State."

58. For an American sociologist's representation of Scandinavian religiosity, see Phil Zuckerman, *Society Without God* (New York: New York University Press, 2008).

59. Bernhard Lang, "Persönliche Frömmigkeit: Vier Zugänge zu einer elementaren Form des religiösen Lebens," *Hephaistos: Kritische Zeitschrift zu Theorie und*

The abusive, sexist theology of Jer 2–4 might offend Susanne L. as well as Danish Hanne and Hans, if they heard about it; but ultimately they would not feel haunted by the God of the book of Jeremiah. I could add that in my experience only a few (Danish) students of theology take immediate offense, as opposed to Kathleen O'Connor's (American) students.[60] The perception of the authority of the Bible by the average student of theology in Denmark (and Scandinavia and Northern Germany as well) is so influenced by a critical approach that only a few will feel haunted by Jeremiah's God—and those few, being uncharacteristically close to American evangelicalism, would hardly ever question the will of God and the righteousness of his judgment.

Praxis der Archäologie und angrenzender Gebiete 28 (2011): 19–36 (31) (author's translation from German).

    60. See O'Connor, *Jeremiah: Pain and Promise*, 1–2, 4–5.

"LIKE A WOMAN IN LABOR":
GENDER, POSTCOLONIAL, QUEER, AND TRAUMA PERSPECTIVES ON THE BOOK OF JEREMIAH

L. Juliana Claassens

Introduction

In recent years, a number of non-traditional methodologies have been used to read the intriguing collection of oracles contained in the book of Jeremiah. Angela Bauer's *Gender in the Book of Jeremiah*,[1] Steed Vernyl Davidson's postcolonial exploration of Jeremiah, *Empire and Exile*,[2] Stuart Macwilliam's essay on "Queering Jeremiah,"[3] and Kathleen O'Connor's recent book, *Jeremiah: Pain and Promise*,[4] which employs trauma and disaster studies as reading lens, all have offered valuable perspectives on the book of Jeremiah and, as a result, definitively changed the face of Jeremiah scholarship.

However, quite often these alternative methods stand in a contentious relationship to one another. So queer theorists accuse feminist theologians of falling victim to essentialist binary categories of male and female,[5] while feminist writers bemoan postcolonial theorists' lack of attention to

---

1. Angela Bauer, *Gender in the Book of Jeremiah: A Feminist Literary Reading* (New York: Lang, 1999).

2. Steed Vernyl Davidson, *Empire and Exile: Postcolonial Readings of the Book of Jeremiah* (LHBOTS 542; London: T&T Clark International, 2011).

3. Stuart Macwilliam, "Queering Jeremiah," *BibInt* 10 (2002): 384–404.

4. Kathleen O'Connor, *Jeremiah: Pain and Promise* (Minneapolis: Fortress, 2011).

5. Macwilliam, "Queering Jeremiah," 390. See also Deryn Guest, who argues that most feminist interpreters "appear to read from a relentless two-sex paradigm that does not recognize all gender as performative"; cf. eadem, "From Gender Reversal to Genderfuck: Reading Jael Through a Lesbian Lens," in *Bible Trouble: Queer Reading at the Boundaries of Biblical Scholarship* (ed. T. J. Hornsby and K. Stone; SBLSS 67; Atlanta: Society of Biblical Literature, 2011), 9–43 (20).

the gendered reality of the texts they are studying.[6] Despite the distinct differences in approach, these methods nevertheless have much in common, sharing key features and overall goals. For example, Jeremy Punt explores the intersections between queer theory and postcolonial criticism, arguing for a shared interest in identity and social location.[7] And postcolonial feminist interpreters such as Kwok Pui-lan, Musa Dube, Katharine Sakenfeld, and Judith McKinlay have reminded us that gender oppression does not only pertain to male–female relations, but consists of "an interlocking system of oppression because of racism, classism, colonialism, and sexism."[8]

Personally, as a feminist biblical theologian who lives in a South African context that has to come to terms with its colonial past, and who moreover is sensitive to the issues important to the LBGTI community, I do not want to choose between methods. In my own work, I have found that these methods complement one another and that a multidimensional approach helps to expand what one sees in the text.

In this essay, I will demonstrate the intersections between feminist, postcolonial, queer, and trauma interpretation by focusing on one particular metaphor that is used in the book of Jeremiah. The metaphor of a woman in labor is employed nine times throughout the book in order to describe Judah's experience in coming to terms with the devastating effects of the Babylonian invasion and its aftermath. For instance, in Jer 4:31, the metaphor is used to express the feelings of absolute helplessness in the face of the conquering army (cf. also 6:24; 22:23; 30:6). In 13:21, it is significant that this metaphor occurs in a context of sexual violence. And in the second half of the book, this metaphor is picked up

---

6. Kwok Pui-lan, "Making the Connections: Postcolonial Studies and Feminist Biblical Interpretation," in *The Postcolonial Biblical Reader* (ed. R. S. Sugirtharajah; Malden, Mass.: Wiley-Blackwell, 2006), 45–63 (46–47).

7. Jeremy Punt, "Queer Theory, Postcolonial Theory, and Biblical Interpretation: A Preliminary Exploration of Some Intersections," in Hornsby and Stone, eds., *Bible Trouble*, 321–41 (322). Punt proposes that one can find common ground between queer and postcolonial theory in at least six areas: "epistemological and hermeneutical considerations; notions of difference; center and margins, or marginality and exclusion; agency; mimicry, and its avoidance; and prophetic vision for inclusivity or a new world" (329).

8. Kwok Pui-lan, "Making the Connections," 52. Cf. also Musa W. Dube, "Rahab Says Hello to Judith: A Decolonizing Feminist Reading," in Sugirtharajah, ed., *The Postcolonial Biblical Reader*, 142–58 (142); Katharine D. Sakenfeld, "Whose Text Is It?," *JBL* 127 (2008): 5–17; Judith E. McKinlay, *Reframing Her: Biblical Women in Postcolonial Focus* (Sheffield: Sheffield Phoenix, 2004).

once again in a continued attempt to make sense of the trauma that had befallen Judah; this metaphor is applied to Moab, Edom, Damascus, and even the Babylonians in the oracles against the nations (48:41; 49:22, 24; 50:43). Finally, in the Book of Consolation, the metaphor of a woman in labor is used in 31:8 to very different effect as a source of hope. By contemplating this particular metaphor in its various manifestations from gendered, postcolonial, queer, and trauma perspectives, I propose that not only the rhetorical function of the woman-in-labor metaphor is illuminated, but also our understanding of the book of Jeremiah as a whole.

Disaster Overtakes Disaster

A first perspective that is helpful in considering the rhetorical significance of the woman-in-labor metaphor regards the context of disaster and trauma associated with the colonization, conquest, and exile of Israel by the hand of the Babylonian invaders in the early sixth century into which this metaphor is introduced. For instance, the first occurrence of the woman-in-labor metaphor in Jer 4:31 is preceded by the dramatic exclamation by the prophet in vv. 19–20:

> My anguish, my anguish! I writhe in pain!
> Oh, the walls of my heart! My heart is beating wildly;
> I cannot keep silent; for I hear the sound of the trumpet, the alarm of war.
> Disaster overtakes disaster, the whole land is laid waste.
> Suddenly my tents are destroyed, my curtains in a moment.

This description of anguish and despair is followed by a haunting portrayal of the undoing of creation. In an almost slow-motion return to the Hebrew תהו ובהו of pre-creation chaos, the prophet offers a first-person account of the devastation of war: the cities destroyed, the people like the birds vanishing in thin air. Within these desperate circumstances, the anguished cries of the people are likened to those of a woman in labor (v. 31):

> For I heard a cry as of a woman in labor, anguish as of one bringing forth
> her first child, the cry of daughter Zion gasping for breath, stretching out
> her hands, "Woe is me! I am fainting before killers!"

Also the occurrence of the woman-in-labor metaphor in Jer 6 appears in a context of disaster. References to war abound as terror is said to be all around (v. 25)—the cruel enemy coming from the north whose "sound is like the roaring sea" (vv. 22–23) leaving the people to respond as follows in v. 24: "We have heard news of them, our hands fall helpless; anguish has taken hold of us, pain as of a woman in labor."

Kathleen O'Connor has compellingly demonstrated how disaster and trauma studies offer new ways to make sense of the often perplexing oracles found in Jeremiah. She defines the goal of trauma and disaster studies as seeking "to gain further understanding of the life-destroying effects of violence upon people and ultimately to find processes that help people to endure, survive, and perhaps eventually thrive."[9]

According to O'Connor, trauma quite often leaves its victims numb, without language. Stuck in a "kind of half-life," trauma victims find themselves "unable to move toward recovery or to flourish as vital human beings."[10] Seen within this context, the oracles found in Jeremiah constitute an attempt to break through the silence. The words, images, metaphors, and stories used by the prophet in these oracles play an important role in the process of finding language again. O'Connor writes how these metaphors, which very well could be applied to the woman-in-labor metaphor that is the subject of this essay, evoke "associations, feelings, and ideas that lure us into the imagery and show us what we had not seen before."[11]

By using metaphors such as the woman-in-labor metaphor in order to narrate the traumatic events, the people are thus helped by the prophet to face the trauma that had befallen them, so moving through the pain and eventually beyond it. This process of making sense of the senseless, integrating the memories of violence into an interpretative framework that reframes the traumatic events, gives some sense of coherence to the chaos brought about by the trauma.[12]

Considering Gender

In terms of a gendered reading of the woman-in-labor metaphor, Angela Bauer has offered an insightful analysis regarding the way gender functions in the book of Jeremiah. One could define a feminist approach by lifting up the number of rhetorical questions Bauer poses in the conclusion to her book, *Gender in the Book of Jeremiah*. She asks for instance:

---

9. O'Connor, *Jeremiah*, 2.

10. Ibid., 3–4.

11. Ibid., 35.

12. Ibid., 47. O'Connor points out that this recovery is a slow process that "does not occur in chronological order nor in any order at all." As she argues, "Victims have to come to terms over and over again with catastrophe, to find language for the terrors, to re-enter and face fragmented memories, to overcome numbness, to grieve deeply, to find stories to guide them through the void" (45).

Whose voices do we hear in the book of Jeremiah? In what way is women's experience employed to promote a male agenda? And what are the gender dynamics inscribed within the rhetorical strategies employed by Jeremiah's writers?[13]

In response to these questions that are central to a gendered reading of Jeremiah, Bauer points out that we hear chiefly the male voices of the prophet [Jeremiah]/the scribe Baruch/the narrator/the Deuteronomistic editor(s) who are employing female imagery to address a primarily male audience. The female imagery utilized by these male authors constitutes a male construction of female experience of women's pain and suffering, which, as Bauer contemplates, conceivably may be "used to promote the male discourse on war and destruction, theologized as judgment."[14] Moreover, these rhetorical strategies build upon the gendered power dynamics of the time, which according to Bauer include "male fear of female sexuality, fear of loss of control over possessions/wives, fantasies of sexualized violence with the stated intention of making the male audience turn around/repent."[15]

These points are helpful in discerning the rhetorical effects of the distinctly gendered woman-in-labor metaphor in Jeremiah: First, it is significant that the overtly female experience of the pain in childbirth is employed to describe people's fear and anguish in the face of the Babylonian invasion. For instance in Jer 4:31 we find that a woman giving birth to her firstborn is trapped in labor without end—her anguished cries merging with the terror-filled cries of people facing destruction by the hand of the enemy.[16] However, the focus of this metaphor is not on the birth of the child that lies at the end of the laboring process. Bauer notes that this metaphor "introduces a moment of death into the struggle for

13. Bauer, *Gender*, 160–61.
14. Ibid., 161.
15. Ibid.
16. Typically, the woman-in-labor metaphor in the biblical traditions is interpreted to denote a sign of weakness, expressing feelings of profound vulnerability and helplessness. Katheryn Pfisterer Darr argues that the "travailing woman simile" is regularly used in biblical texts such as Isa 13:6–8; 21:1–11; Jer 6:23–24; Ps 48:5–6 to describe people's feelings of helplessness and despair in the face of enemy attacks; cf. "Two Unifying Female Images in the Book of Isaiah," in *Uncovering Ancient Stones: Essays in Memory of H. Neil Richardson* (ed. L. M. Hopfe; Winona Lake: Eisenbrauns, 1994), 17–30 (25). Cf. also my exposition on this metaphor in Isa 42 in L. Juliana Claassens, *Mourner, Mother, Midwife: Reimaging God's Liberating Presence in the Old Testament* (Louisville: Westminster John Knox, 2012), 49–62.

new life. The woman is indeed struggling…she stretches out her hands. The struggle to give birth has become a struggle to survive herself."[17]

By reducing the woman-in-labor metaphor to the pain of childbirth and the threat of death, a whole range of associations regarding the joy and the promise of new life that comes with the birth of a child is obscured.[18] In terms of a gendered reading, one could argue that this is a largely male construction of the birthing process—the female experience of giving birth co-opted to describe the effects of war. So the miracle of giving birth is couched in a negative light—reducing the woman to a vulnerable, despairing entity. Granted, childbirth was considered a dangerous enterprise; many women died in childbirth. Throughout the ages, though, women also have experienced the powerful life-giving nature of giving birth—connotations that seem largely lost in the prophet's application of this metaphor. However, as we will see later in this essay, in at least one instance, the connotations of new life related to childbirth will feature as a source of resistance (Jer 31).[19]

Second, it is important to consider the gender dynamics at work within this manifestation of the woman-in-labor metaphor. According to Bauer, the emphasis on death rather than new life is evidence of the common perception that "the pain of childbirth represents 'women's punishment for disobedience' (cf. Gen 3:16)."[20] This association of labor pain as retribution is reinforced by the link to female promiscuity associated with yet another female image introduced just before the woman-in-labor metaphor in Jer 4:31. In v. 30, one reads of a woman dressed in crimson, decorated with gold ornaments and make-up. Bauer argues that this woman "dressed to (be) kill(ed)," which is reminiscent of Jezebel who in the history of reception has become an icon for the sexually alluring but dangerous *femme fatale*, is "the promiscuous woman familiar to the reader from the first cycle of oracles (2:20, 25, 33; 3:1–5)."[21] These two metaphors work together further to convey the association of labor pain as punishment, rooted in the (male) perception of woman as the source of evil who deserves to be punished.

---

17. Bauer, *Gender*, 71.

18. Ibid., 162.

19. Elsewhere I have argued that the woman-in-labor metaphor functions in Isa 42 as a symbol of new life, denoting a different understanding of power in the midst of vulnerability; see Claassens, *Mourner, Mother, Midwife*, 57–59.

20. Bauer, *Gender*, 162.

21. Ibid., 69.

Third, in Jer 13, the metaphor of a woman in labor is introduced in a context of sexual violence that further enforces this overtly negative interpretation of labor pain. We read in vv. 21–22:

> What will you say when they set as head over you those whom you have trained to be your allies? Will not pangs take hold of you, like those of a woman in labor? And if you say in your heart, "Why have these things come upon me?" it is for the greatness of your iniquity that your skirts are lifted up, and you are violated.

The reference "your skirts are lifted up" is euphemistic speech for sexual assault, which, in conjunction with the Hebrew term חמס ("to suffer violence"), denotes rape. In this juxtaposition of metaphors, the pain experienced in labor and the pain of being sexually assaulted are brought together in order to express the people's feelings of being violated by the Babylonian empire. The woman-in-labor metaphor as symbol of the people's vulnerability is thus framed by an image of a woman being sexually violated because of "the greatness of [her] iniquity" (v. 22). Reading the woman-in-labor metaphor in terms of sexual violence imposes a very different meaning upon this metaphor—the focus being on the violated and exposed female body rather than on the productive nature of labor pain in bringing about the birth of a child. Moreover, instead of being intimately involved in the birthing process (cf. e.g. the metaphor of God as midwife in Pss 22:9–10; 71:6), God is depicted as being responsible for the violation; as O'Connor boldly asserts, God is imaged in this text as Zion's rapist.[22]

Feminist scholars have strongly critiqued the violent imagery that not only employs the violation of a female body to portray the nation's fall but also deems sexual assault a suitable punishment by an angry deity-husband.[23] It remains a question, though, what to do with these troubling texts. I propose that a gendered critique of this disturbing portrayal is greatly enhanced by two of the other approaches considered in this essay,

---

22. O'Connor, *Jeremiah*, 54.

23. Cf. e.g. the various contributions to the *Women's Bible Commentary* (ed. C. A. Newsom and S. H. Ringe; Louisville: Westminster John Knox, 1998), in which feminist authors like Susan Ackerman (Isaiah), Gale Yee (Hosea), Kathleen O'Connor (Jeremiah), Katheryn Pfisterer Darr (Ezekiel), and Judith Sanderson (Nahum) all struggle to make sense of the prophetic texts that employ violence against women as rhetorical strategy. Cf. also Cheryl Exum, "The Ethics of Biblical Violence Against Women," in *The Bible in Ethics: The Second Sheffield Colloquium* (ed. J. W. Rogerson and M. D. Carroll R.; Sheffield: Sheffield Academic, 1995), 248–71.

particularly when it comes to making sense of the rape language that is used in conjunction with the woman-in-labor metaphor. For instance, in terms of trauma and disaster theory, Kathleen O'Connor has argued that the shocking nature of these images is imperative in understanding this oracle. She writes: "The fact that God's rape of Zion is outrageous, unbearable, and unspeakable is surely the point of the imagery. To be invaded by another country, to be victims of attack, occupation, and dislocation *is* outrageous, unbearable, and unspeakable."[24]

A trauma-centered approach helps one see that the rape language used in this text in conjunction with the woman-in-labor metaphor is an attempt to voice the trauma experienced by the people. O'Connor rightly suggests that the language of "God's rape of Jerusalem expresses the horrors Judah experienced as a society. It reveals aspects of the nation's destruction, now reduced to an attack on one vulnerable figure who embraces the whole. Rape is what happened to them."[25] In this way, the rape language, like the woman-in-labor metaphor preceding it, forms part of Jeremiah's attempt to find new language speaking about events for which there are no words.

Moreover, employing postcolonial criticism with an eye to trauma theory, Gale Yee, in an exposition of a similar metaphor of sexual violence in Ezekiel, argues that the pornographic representation of gender violence should be understood in light of the effects of empire on the defenseless Judean people. One could likewise argue that Jeremiah's portrayal of sexual violence as retribution, which refers back to the metaphor of the male deity-husband punishing his unfaithful wife in Jer 2–3, is to be understood in terms of the humiliation the victorious colonizer afflicted upon the group of disgraced Judean males.[26] The

24. O'Connor, *Jeremiah*, 55.

25. Ibid. In the ancient Near East, rape language can often be found in descriptions of the effects of war. The violent acts of the enemy forces invading the land and destroying the property and the people in it are couched in terms of sexualized violence and rape, reminiscent of the real acts of violence that accompany war. Cf. Brad E. Kelle, "Wartime Rhetoric: Prophetic Metaphorization of Cities as Female," in *Writing and Reading War: Rhetoric, Gender, and Ethics in Biblical and Modern Contexts* (ed. B. E. Kelle and F. R. Ames; SBLSymS 42; Leiden: Brill, 2008), 95–112. Kelle argues that, "[c]ertainly the violation of women as a metaphor fits the destruction of capital cities, for the stripping, penetration, exposure and humiliation of the women is analogous to siege warfare, with its breaching of the wall, entrance through the gate, and so forth" (104).

26. Gale Yee, *Poor Banished Children of Eve: Woman as Evil in the Hebrew Bible* (Minneapolis: Augsburg Fortress, 2003), 112–15 (118).

prophet portrays Judah as a female because after the humiliating attacks by the Babylonian invaders the Judahite survivors feel quite similar to a violated woman—as Yee argues with regard to Ezekiel, and one could also say Jeremiah, transposing "the political dealings of the Judean male elite with foreign nations onto the fractured, beaten, and sexually ravaged body of a woman."[27] Together with the woman-in-labor metaphor, the violent image of sexual violation further emphasizes the vulnerability and helplessness Israel felt in the face of the conquering army, having lost any sense of agency or control over their fate.

Even though trauma and disaster theory and postcolonial interpretation are helpful in better understanding the woman-in-labor metaphor, which has been juxtaposed with a metaphor of sexual violence, a gendered reading of the text is nevertheless important, seeing that feminist inter-preters are concerned about the impact of these metaphors on the bodies of real women.[28] As with queer interpretation, which will be the subject of the next section, inherent to a feminist interpretation is a strong sense of advocacy, calling upon readers to resist texts whose interpretations may contribute to normalizing unequal gender relations that, in their most extreme form, may culminate in the eruption of violence.

The Value of Queering

At the heart of the woman-in-labor metaphor one finds an act of gender reversal, also called genderswitch or genderfuck,[29] in which men are forced to identify with a female figure. As in the case of the sexual violence metaphor, this gender reversal has the purpose of expressing the male experience of humiliation and shame in the face of the violence experienced at the hand of their captors.[30] This act of gender reversal, which is central for understanding the way the woman-in-labor meta-phor functions in Jeremiah, is illuminated by applying insights from queer theory, defined as follows by Deryn Guest: "The confrontational,

27. Ibid., 132–34.

28. Exum, "The Ethics of Biblical Violence Against Women," 254–55; Bauer, *Gender*, 4–7.

29. Guest prefers to use the term "genderfuck," which shows how masculine and feminine gender codes are mixed in order to subvert the dominant gendered norms, rather than the term "gender reversal," which according to Guest reinforces "the two-sex, two-gender binary of male/female and masculine/feminine." See Guest, "From Gender Reversal to Genderfuck," 9.

30. Bauer, *Gender*, 161.

uncompromising stance of queer theory is one of resistance to such [male/female and masculine/feminine] binaries: subverting, undoing, deconstructing the normalcy of sex/gender regimes, cracking them open, focusing on the fissures that expose their constructedness."[31] In his article, "Queering Jeremiah," Stuart Macwilliam identifies the following queer insights with regard to the marriage metaphor in Jer 2–3, which can well be applied to the woman-in-labor metaphor in Jeremiah. He argues that "if queer theory views sexual identity, and indeed gender itself, as not innate but the product of continual re-enactment," then the fact that the text confuses "the male element of the tenor (male citizenry and faithfulness/apostasy) and the female element of the vehicle (the wife and her loyalty/adultery)" qualifies as a queer insight.[32] Thus, the fact that the woman-in-labor metaphor requires the male reader, who feels extremely vulnerable in the face of disaster, to associate himself with the role of a woman in a way that undermines the cultural expectations of the day is an example of the purposeful confusion of generally fixed gender categories and the questioning of neatly defined notions of sexual and gender identity.[33]

Actually, Bauer's gendered reading of the woman-in-labor metaphor already contains what can be called a queer insight when she argues for a broader category of gender. For instance, she identifies yet another occurrence of the woman-in-labor metaphor in Jer 4:19 when she translates the verse as: "My belly! My belly! I writhe in labor!" Within this translation, she follows—together with the LXX and the Vulgate—the *kethib* reading, that is, the cohortative of חיל, "let me writhe in labor," instead of the *qere* Hiphil cohortative of יחל, "let me wail."[34] Bauer argues that quite dramatically, Jeremiah in first-person speech is speaking in a female voice, employing an image of the torment of

---

31. Guest, "From Gender Reversal to Genderfuck," 9. Queer reading of the Bible is defined by Ken Stone as "a diverse set of approaches to biblical interpretation that take as their point of departure a critical interrogation, or active contestation, of the ways in which the Bible is read to support heteronormative and normalizing configurations of sexual and gender practices and sexual and gender identities." See Ken Stone, "Queer Reading Between Bible and Film: *Paris Is Burning* and the 'Legendary Houses' of David and Saul," in Hornsby and Stone, eds., *Bible Trouble*, 75–98 (94).

32. Macwilliam, "Queering Jeremiah," 396–97, and 400.

33. Ibid., 400. Cf. also Deborah F. Sawyer's exposition of the blurring of gender roles in Jer 30:6, "Gender-Play and Sacred Text: A Scene from Jeremiah," *JSOT* 83 (1999): 99–111 (104–5)

34. Bauer, *Gender*, 63.

labor pain in order to express the suffering of female Jerusalem.[35] Once again, the cries of Daughter Zion in response to the invading army are encapsulated in the mournful cries of a woman in labor, but this time it is the prophet to whom the female metaphor is applied. The rhetorical function of this gender reversal is to show how the prophet, by embracing the female experience of labor, so closely identifies with the plight of the people who throughout the first chapters of Jeremiah are imaged in female terms that he takes on a female persona.

The value of such a queer reading of the text is that it resists traditional gender roles, helping the reader to grasp something of the notion of gender as performative, that is, that gender is never static but is a product of continual enactment.[36] In the process, the reader may realize that gender categories are more fluid than previously believed, so moving beyond narrow gender stereotypes. Even though such an interpretation probably is not intended by the text, the act of breaking open fixed gender categories may give readers many centuries later the opportunity to imagine otherwise—which has the effect, as Sean Burke so eloquently argues, "to make it possible for more bodies to matter—for more bodies to be recognized as fully human."[37]

The Effects of Empire

A final perspective that may be helpful in illuminating our understanding of the woman-in-labor metaphor comes from the work done by postcolonial interpreters. Postcolonial interpretation is defined by Davidson as "a method of literary enquiry about geo-political power and its implications in everyday life."[38] With regard to a text such as Jeremiah, postcolonial interpretation holds that biblical texts created in the shadow of the empire show signs of dealing with the effects of colonization.

35. Ibid., 64. Cf. also Barbara Bakke Kaiser, who argues that Jeremiah adopts the female persona of Daughter Zion, acting as a "female impersonator." See her "Poet as 'Female Impersonator': The Image of Daughter Zion as Speaker in Biblical Poems of Suffering," *JR* 67, no. 2 (1987): 164–82 (171–74).

36. Cf. Macwilliam's application of Judith Butler's work; he argues that Butler calls "for critical strategies, subversive tactics, that reveal the constructedness of gender, that…denaturalize it" (cf. "Queering Jeremiah," 385).

37. Sean D. Burke, "Queering Early Christian Discourse: The Ethiopian Eunuch," in Hornsby and Stone, eds., *Bible Trouble*, 175–89 (176).

38. Davidson, *Empire and Exile*, 38.

However, one also finds instances in the biblical text in which imperial power is subverted and resisted.[39]

A first postcolonial perspective regards the way "the other" is construed in the "contact zone," namely, that space in which an encounter between nations transpires. A key aspect of postcolonial criticism is to consider, as Fernando Segovia asks: "what images and representations of the other-world arise from either side?" and "how is 'the other' regarded and represented?"[40]

With regard to Jeremiah, "the other" is most visibly present in the Oracles against the Nations which, in the last part of the book (Jer 46–51), strongly revile the neighboring nations, ending with a sharp critique against Babylon. In these oracles, we repeatedly encounter the metaphor of a woman in labor, which in the first part of Jeremiah was used to capture Judah's experience of extreme vulnerability in response to the enemy attacks. In the Oracles against the Nations, this metaphor is applied to the neighboring nations of Moab, Edom, and Damascus, as well as the assailant Babylon, in order to predict the demise of these nations. For example, in Jer 48 one reads how God will bring an end to Moab, whose towns shall be captured and whose inhabitants will experience the disgrace of having their hair shaved and their beards cut off. Within this context of disaster, "the hearts of the warriors of Moab" are said to be "like the heart of a woman in labor" (v. 41). And in Jer 49 it will be Edom who will be the object of horror, whose city will be overthrown like Sodom and Gomorrah (vv. 17–18) and whose warriors are described in terms of the woman-in-labor metaphor (v. 22; cf. also the application of this metaphor to Damascus in v. 24). Finally, in Jer 50 the metaphor of woman in labor is used to describe the downfall of the king of Babylon, whose hands, faced with the threat of the enigmatic enemy of the north "fell helpless; anguish seized him, pain like that of a woman in labor" (v. 43).

In terms of postcolonial criticism it is significant to consider how these foreign nations are depicted. In what may constitute wishful thinking on the part of Judah, one finds, on the one hand, that Judah revels in the downfall of their archenemies Moab and Edom, with whom they shared a long history of antagonism. By using the woman-in-labor metaphor to describe these mighty nations, the author of the Oracles against

---

39. Ibid., 42.

40. Fernando F. Segovia, "Biblical Criticism and Postcolonial Studies: Toward a Postcolonial Optic," in Sugirtharajah, ed., *The Postcolonial Biblical Reader*, 33–44 (38).

the Nations lessens the hold these powerful nations once had over Judah as Moab, Edom, Damascus, and even the mighty Babylon are represented as helpless entities. On the other hand, one finds a glimpse of sympathy when the speaker is said to wail and mourn for the people of Moab (v. 31; cf. also the image in v. 36 when the prophet's heart is moaning for Moab like a flute). It may be that this reference is ironic in nature; however, it nevertheless seems that these oracles reveal a keen understanding of the effects of empire on defenseless nations—an acknowledgment that imperial power crushes everyone in its way. The fact that the metaphor of a woman in labor is used to describe the anguish both Judah and her neighbors are experiencing attests to a common vulnerability in the face of the enemy attacks, as well as some sense of solidarity between neighboring nations.

Judah's relationship to the other nations is also illuminated from a trauma perspective, when O'Connor argues that the oracles that predict Babylon's downfall in terms of a woman-in-labor metaphor reflect the people's deep desire for justice, that is, that their oppressors will receive their just deserts for the terrible harm they had inflicted upon Judah. As she argues, "They [these oracles] express yearnings for a future where God will return to Judah's side and vindicate the nation. These desires are momentarily realized and enacted in the world of symbolic poetry; they create a form of literary justice."[41] O'Connor proposes that this "poetry of revenge" forms a healthy part of the recovery process as it carves out a "space for hatred, fury, and outrage."[42] Instead of acting upon these longings, the people transmit their yearning for revenge upon God whom they expect to execute justice.

A second postcolonial perspective relates to those instances in the biblical text in which the empire's hold is resisted. In his postcolonial exploration of Jeremiah, Davidson not only describes the effects of the empire on Judah reflected in the book of Jeremiah, but also considers instances in which the empire's hold is resisted. For instance, with regard to the oracle envisioning the downfall of Babylon, Davidson argues that this sharp critique of Babylon shows some subtle signs of resistance to the empire.[43] Moreover, regarding Jer 40, Davidson argues that "in the face of imperial aggression that threatens the dispossession of the land, this text employs a form of resistance that preserves the subjectivity of

41. O'Connor, *Jeremiah*, 117.
42. Ibid., 119.
43. Davidson, *Empire and Exile*, 47.

the people and keeps a place for them in the world."[44] In his reading of
Jer 40, Davidson employs bell hooks's notion of "homeplace"—a concept from her African American experience—to articulate the notion of
a space in which the colonized can develop a "counter-language" that is
not controlled by the colonizer and that may serve as "a language of
resistance, a language of refusal, the speech of the margins" that challenges the hegemony of the dominant power.[45]

With regard to the woman-in-labor metaphor, it is significant that in
the Book of Consolation in Jer 30–31, the woman-in-labor metaphor
functions in quite a different way so as to qualify as a counter-language
that resists the dominant discourse. Actually, in Jer 30:6 the woman-
in-labor metaphor occurs in the now-familiar expression of denoting
extreme vulnerability in the face of disaster when it is asked why strong
men have become like women bearing children. However, in the next
chapter in Jer 31:7–9, the same metaphor is used to quite a different
effect:

> For thus says the LORD: Sing aloud with gladness for Jacob, and raise
> shouts for the chief of the nations; proclaim, give praise, and say, "Save,
> O LORD, your people, the remnant of Israel." See, I am going to bring
> them from the land of the north, and gather them from the farthest parts
> of the earth, among them the blind and the lame, those with child and
> those in labor, together; a great company, they shall return here.

In this text, the woman-in-labor metaphor is introduced in a context of
restoration. Together with a group of mothers and disabled people, those
in labor are included in a parade of seemingly vulnerable people called
by God to lead the procession back home, serving as evidence of God's
restorative action.

The fact that mothers are included with the women in labor evokes
some very different connotations for this image than what we have seen
thus far, denoting an alternative reality that is suggestive of the counter-
language referenced above. It reminds the reader of the ultimate goal of
labor, i.e., to bring new life into the world, which stands in contrast to the
application elsewhere in Jeremiah where the labor without end appeared
futile. So even though this group may appear vulnerable, the mothers and
the soon-to-be mothers hold the future in their hands. In contrast to the
terror enforced by the empire and the anguish and panic caused by the

---

44. Ibid., 87.
45. Ibid., 104; bell hooks, *Yearning: Race, Gender, and Cultural Politics*
(Boston: South End, 1990), 44–45.

brute enforcement of imperial rule, this text is one of hope and belief in the possibility of new life. Used in this way, the woman-in-labor metaphor in Jer 31 conceivably may serve as an example of resistance that shows how the colonized within the dominant power survived by imagining an alternative reality.

This emphasis on resistance within a postcolonial interpretation is shared by feminist interpreters. For instance, Rita Nakashima Brock argues that one sees in Jer 31 an alternative view of power. Focusing on the complex image of a female surrounding the warrior in Jer 31:22, which is used to describe God's restorative action in an oracle following the woman-in-labor image, Brock argues that "surrounding" is suggestive of a new form of power that resists violence and death and overcomes pain and suffering.[46] Also Deborah Sawyer sees a radically different view regarding gender roles in this text, with the female becoming the subject, taking an active role in transforming the nature of the relationship between male and female. So the act of surrounding (סבב) is to be understood in terms of active protection and care in contrast with the hierarchical rule (משל) that is the dominant view in Gen 3:16.[47] Viewed in this fashion, the woman-in-labor metaphor featured in this text (Jer 31:9) may be understood as an example of female agency, pointing to a hopeful future that transforms the conventional understanding of helplessness and vulnerability associated with this metaphor.

Conclusion

In this essay, we explored the woman-in-labor metaphor from gender, queer, postcolonial, and trauma-centered perspectives. From this exposition, it is evident that the woman-in-labor metaphor is a rich metaphor with multiple applications throughout the book of Jeremiah when viewed in terms of these methods. We have, moreover, seen numerous instances in which gender, queer, postcolonial, and trauma-centered approaches were found to complement one another. I propose that it is important to identify common ground between these methods, as a multidimensional

---

46. Rita Nakashima Brock, "A New Thing in the Land: The Female Surrounds the Warrior," in *Power, Powerlessness, and the Divine: New Inquiries in Bible and Theology* (ed. C. L. Rigby; Atlanta: Scholars Press, 1997), 158. For an in-depth exposition of the various interpretative possibilities regarding this ambiguous reference of the female surrounding the warrior, cf. also Bauer, *Gender*, 139–45.

47. Sawyer, "Gender-Play and Sacred Text," 109–10.

approach is better able to do justice to the varied shades of meaning associated with this metaphor. For instance, these methods share a commitment to move beyond mere description of the rhetorical effect of these metaphors, to also lift up the counter-voices in the text that imagine an alternative reality. As Davidson formulates this approach: "[to] listen… to the voices that write back from the margins to the center, [to] search… for the echoes of protest in imitations,…[to] detect…a distinct sound in multivocal reverberations."[48] With this task in mind, the woman-in-labor metaphor manages to speak in more than one voice—capturing Judah's anguish and experience of vulnerability in the face of disaster; defining Judah's relationship to its neighbors but also serving as a means to imagine an alternative reality of a life beyond the pain.

It is important to note that the woman-in-labor metaphor forms part of an act of interpretation that, as O'Connor has argued, is essential to the survival of the people. As she argues: "If the world is ever again to be trustworthy, victims need interpretation. For their lives to rest on the most minimal order, they must have meaning, interpretation, explanation, even if the explanation is ephemeral, inadequate, partial, or outright wrong. Explanation puts order back in the world."[49]

In the woman-in-labor metaphor we see such an act of explanation that gives structure to Judah's world by repeatedly employing formulaic language. As we have seen in this essay, it is important, though, critically to engage this interpretation, especially when it comes to its association with gender violence. This act of critical engagement is shared by gender, queer, postcolonial, and trauma-centered interpretation rooted in a stubborn belief in the possibility of a transformed society.

48. Davidson, *Empire and Exile*, 53.
49. O'Connor, *Jeremiah*, 43.

God's Cruelty and Jeremiah's Treason: Jeremiah 21:1–10 in Postcolonial Perspective

Christl M. Maier

The book of Jeremiah narrates the struggle of the Judean people during the time of political coercion by the neo-Babylonian empire, the Babylonian conquest of Jerusalem, and the aftermath of destruction and exile. This empire, like its neo-Assyrian predecessor, sought to drive the small states on the Levantine coast into political subjugation, if not by treaties then by military force. Postcolonial theory has analyzed the power structures, oppressive attitudes, and effects of imperialist regimes. According to Edward W. Said, "[I]mperialism is the practice, the theory, and the attitudes of a dominating metropolitan centre ruling a distant territory. Colonialism, which is almost always a consequence of imperialism, is the implantation of settlements on distant territory."[1] Due to the brevity of neo-Babylonian rule, the Babylonians did not found settlements in Judah or any other Levantine state. Yet, their policies of domination and coercion in the case of political resistance suffice for scholars to call the neo-Babylonian rule an imperialist regime and its practice an attempt to colonize the Judeans. Because of this political-historical context, the perspective of postcolonial theory has received some attention from Jeremiah scholars, as some recent volumes on the book of Jeremiah[2]

---

1. Edward W. Said, *Culture and Imperialism* (London: Chatto & Windus, 1993), 8; similarly Fernando F. Segovia, "Mapping the Postcolonial Optic in Biblical Criticism: Meaning and Scope," in *Postcolonial Biblical Criticism: Interdisciplinary Intersections* (ed. S. D. Moore and F. F. Segovia; New York: T&T Clark International, 2005), 23–78 (40).

2. The shift from historical-critical interpretations of Jeremiah to deconstructive and reader-oriented ones is mirrored in the anthology *Troubling Jeremiah* (ed. A. R. P. Diamond et al.; JSOTSup 260; Sheffield: Sheffield Academic, 1999). This volume includes 24 essays on new perspectives, none of which explicitly uses postcolonial theory. Twelve years later, however, another anthology authored and edited by a similar group of scholars includes 22 articles, five of which engage postcolonial theory or aspects of postcolonial thinking; see the contributions of Carolyn J. Sharp,

and also this volume demonstrate. Being a German Jeremiah scholar grounded in European historical-critical methodology yet with a critical feminist perspective, I am interested in probing a postcolonial reading of passages in Jeremiah primarily because of the political-historical setting of the book's narrative. Although Germany must be counted among the European colonizer nations, I have to admit that my life and scholarship have not been influenced by this history to any significant extent of which I am aware. Only through overlaps and similarities between feminist and postcolonial critique was my interest in the latter ignited. I know that with regard to my own socio-political background I would rather be counted as a member of the hegemonic and imperialist culture than among the marginalized and colonized. Yet, I believe that everybody interested in ideological criticism should be able and allowed to use any de-centered perspective, be it feminist, postcolonial, queer, and so on, as a heuristic tool in his/her approach to biblical texts. My foray into a postcolonial reading of Jer 21:1–10 is greatly indebted to discussions in sessions organized by the Writing/Reading Jeremiah group at SBL annual meetings from 2007 to 2011, and especially to Steed Vernyl Davidson's postcolonial readings of Jeremiah that are now available in his monograph *Empire and Exile*.[3]

This essay offers an interpretation of Jer 21:1–10 through a postcolonial lens with a focus on the characterizations of God and Jeremiah. Whereas God seems to be extremely cruel and uncompromising, Jeremiah is depicted as a traitor to the Judean cause. My thesis is that a postcolonial perspective facilitates modern readers' comprehension of the portrayal of YHWH and Jeremiah as fighting against Judah and of the historical situation from which these characterizations evolved. In this essay, I will combine a traditional redaction-critical approach and a postcolonial reading. First, I will introduce the text and its main literary features with regard to a redaction-critical assessment while at the same time transgressing the boundaries of what is regularly considered redaction criticism. My goal is then to demonstrate that the dating of this passage to a certain period in Judah's history greatly influences the

Daniel Smith-Christopher, Else K. Holt, Steed Vernyl Davidson, and Alice Ogden Bellis in *Jeremiah (Dis)placed: New Directions in Writing/Reading Jeremiah* (ed. A. R. P. Diamond and L. Stulman; LHBOTS 529; New York: T&T Clark International, 2011). For a fuller assessment of postcolonial theory, see the work of Steed Davidson, mentioned in the next note.

3. See Steed Vernyl Davidson, *Empire and Exile: Postcolonial Readings of the Book of Jeremiah* (LHBOTS 542; New York: T&T Clark International, 2011).

evaluation of God's character. A third section will introduce aspects of Homi K. Bhabha's thesis on the relation between the colonizer and the colonized and explore the "ambivalence" of God's character in Jer 21:1–10. Finally, I will discuss the status and role of so-called "subalterns" in Jer 21:8–10 using the definition and thesis of the postcolonial thinker Gayatri Chakravorty Spivak.

1. *Jeremiah 21:1–10—Text and Context*

Jeremiah 21:1–10 introduces the cycle of words addressed to the kings (21:1–23:8), a collection of oracles of doom against the last Judean rulers that ends by announcing the amazing emergence of a righteous branch of the Davidic line (23:5–8). Since the first oracle mentions the last Judean king Zedekiah as a representative of the mistaken politics of Judah, the beginning already hints at the disreputable end, namely the fall of the Davidic monarchy. Some other literary features underline that this cycle has been heavily reworked by the exilic and postexilic editors of the book: The chronological order of kings is disturbed;[4] some passages do not name the ruler (22:1–5, 10, 13–17, 18aβ–19), yet prose introductions or announcements of doom identify some kings (22:11, 18aα); other sayings address the royal palace (22:6–7) or an unnamed personified city (22:20–23); and two announcements concerning the fate of a specific king differ from records about the same person in other sources.[5]

Jeremiah 21:1–3 situates the following in the time of the siege of Jerusalem by Nebuchadrezzar,[6] recounting that king Zedekiah sends

4. Cf. Robert P. Carroll, *Jeremiah: A Commentary* (OTL; London: SCM, 1986), 404.

5. For the variations in Jehoiakim's fate in Jer 22:19 and 2 Kgs 24:6 see Carroll, *Jeremiah: A Commentary*, 432–34; Christopher T. Begg, "The End of King Jehoiakim: The Afterlife of a Problem," *JSem* 8 (1996): 12–20; for the fate of Coniah (Jer 22:24–27, 28–30) alias Jehoiachin (2 Kgs 25:27) see Carroll, *Jeremiah: A Commentary*, 436–43.

6. This spelling of the name is confirmed in the Babylonian Chronicle (BM 21946 obv.; cf. Donald J. Wiseman, *The Vassal Treaties of Esarhaddon* [London: The British School of Archeology in Iraq, 1958], 66–67), which mentions the Akkadian name *Nabū-kudurri-uṣur* "Nabu, protect the (eldest) son." While Ezekiel also uses Nebuchadrezzar (Ezek 26:7; 29:18–19; 30:10), Jer 27–29 name the king "Nebuchadnezzar" eight times (Jer 27:6, 8, 20; 28:3, 11, 14; 29:1, 3; cf. also Daniel). Adrianus van Selms ("The Name Nebuchadnezzar," in *Travels in the World of the Old Testament* [ed. M. S. H. G. Heerma van Voss et al.; Assen: Van Gorcum, 1974], 223–29), considers the spelling with "n" to be a pejorative name, since Akkadian *kūdanu(m)*, *kudannu* means "mule, hinny."

his officials Pashhur and Zephaniah to Jeremiah in order to entreat the prophet that he may communicate with YHWH. The wording of the king's request demonstrates that he still hopes for divine rescue in a situation of severe military threat. Marked by introductory formulas, 21:1–10 present three different divine oracles that Jeremiah is called to deliver. The first two respond to Zedekiah's delegation (vv. 4–6 and 7), the third addresses the people apprehended in Jerusalem (vv. 8–10).[7] Verses 1–7 read:

> This is the word that came to Jeremiah from YHWH, when King Zedekiah sent to him Pashhur son of Malchiah and the priest Zephaniah son of Maaseiah, saying, "Please inquire of YHWH on our behalf, for King Nebuchadrezzar of Babylon is attacking us; perhaps YHWH will act for our sake in accordance with all his wonders, so that Nebuchadrezzar will withdraw from us."
>
> Then Jeremiah said to them: "Thus says YHWH, the God of Israel: I am going to turn the weapons of war that are in your hands and with which you are fighting against the king of Babylon and against the Chaldeans who are besieging you from outside the walls, and I will assemble them[8] in the center of this city. I myself will fight against you with outstretched hand and mighty arm, in anger, in fury, and in great wrath. And I will strike down the inhabitants of this city, both human beings and animals; they shall die of a great pestilence."
>
> "Afterwards," says YHWH, "I will give King Zedekiah of Judah, his servants, and the people in this city—those who survive the pestilence, sword, and famine—into the hands of King Nebuchadrezzar of Babylon, into the hands of their enemies, into the hands of those who seek their lives. He shall strike them down with the edge of the sword; he shall not pity them, or spare them, or have compassion."

7. Due to the different introductory formulas and contradictory oracles, the chapter is commonly perceived as an editorial assemblage of sayings; cf. William McKane, "The Construction of Chapter Jeremiah XXI," *VT* 32 (1982): 59–72.

8. Due to the nature of the Hebrew phrasing, the referent of the accusative pronoun may be the weapons or the enemies. The Old Greek has a shorter and clearly structured sentence, in which the weapons are redirected from outside the walls into the midst of the city. The Greek version is most probably the older text that has been expanded in the typically pre-Masoretic manner; cf. Hermann-Josef Stipp, *Das masoretische und alexandrinische Sondergut des Jeremiabuches* (OBO 136; Freiburg: Universitätsverlag; Göttingen: Vandenhoeck & Ruprecht, 1994), 101–3. That the phrase מחוץ לחומה "from outside the wall" does not belong to the second relative clause but to the main action of turning the weapons is also argued by William L. Holladay, *Jeremiah 1: A Commentary on the Book of the Prophet Jeremiah, Chapters 1–25* (Hermeneia; Philadelphia: Fortress, 1986), 571.

In contrast to the king's hope that YHWH will save the city of Jerusalem as he formerly did, the divine response in vv. 4–6 announces death to all inhabitants of the city including the animals. The answer is utterly cruel since YHWH characterizes himself as a warrior who fights against his own people and thus seems to aggravate the fate of death by smashing those who turned to him asking for rescue from the Babylonian army.

Against this clear announcement of total annihilation, the second word of YHWH in v. 7 begins from the assumption that some have survived the conquest of the city. The oracle proclaims that all survivors, including King Zedekiah and his entourage, will nevertheless be handed over to their enemies and killed by their sword.

As if this response would not be enough to swallow, v. 8 abruptly announces a third word to Jeremiah to be delivered "to this people," an addressee who according to the introduction in vv. 1–3 is not present at all. Verses 8–10 read:

> And to this people you shall say: "Thus says YHWH: See, I am setting before you the way of life and the way of death. Those who stay in this city shall die by the sword, by famine, and by pestilence; but those who go out and surrender to the Chaldeans who are besieging you shall live and shall have their lives as booty.[9] For I have set my face against this city for evil and not for good," says YHWH. "It will be given into the hands of the king of Babylon, and he will burn it with fire."

The divine statements in vv. 4–6, 7, and 8–10 contradict each other with regard to the fate of the people. Verse 6 includes the inhabitants of the city among those facing death and v. 7 counts the survivors among those who will die at the hands of the Babylonians.

Verse 9, however, argues that surrendering oneself to the enemy will be the only way to survive. One solution to resolve the strong tension between vv. 4–7 and 8–10 is to assume that the latter announcement would be valid only for individuals or a small group of people while the majority of Jerusalem's inhabitants would face death. Yet, with regard to the introduction in vv. 1–3 and the terminology used, it is obvious that the three oracles forward mixed messages despite their common setting and thus do not form a coherent literary text.

---

9. The word "booty" brings in an ironical note since booty is sought in war, yet normally as material gain of the soldiers who plunder the enemies after defeating them. See Carroll, *Jeremiah: A Commentary*, 411; Kathleen M. O'Connor, *Jeremiah: Pain and Promise* (Minneapolis: Fortress, 2011), 74.

The formulaic introduction in Jer 21:1 consists of typical Deutero-Jeremianic prose.[10] This feature, the passage's function as introduction of the cycle of words to the kings, and the fact that Zedekiah is mentioned out of sequence emphasize that Jer 21:1–10 is a passage placed by the book's editors. With regard to terminology and contents, both responses to the delegation in vv. 4–6, 7 and the announcement to the people in vv. 8–10 parallel other verses in the book and even allude to texts beyond Jeremiah. With regard to traditional redaction-critical criteria, Jer 21:1–10 are late, that is, exilic or post-exilic rewordings of other material in Jeremiah, as I will demonstrate in the following.[11]

> Zedekiah's sending of a delegation has a parallel in Jer 37:3 but with slight differences: In Jer 21, among the royal emissaries Pashhur is mentioned instead of Jehucal, as in Jer 37. The purpose of the delegation also changes: while the characters in Jer 21:2 ask Jeremiah to "inquire on our behalf" (דרש־נא בעדנו),[12] those in 37:3 request that Jeremiah "pray" to God in the sense of prophetic intercession (התפלל־נא בעדנו).[13] The phrase "with an outstretched hand and with a strong arm" (Jer 21:5a) alludes to God's

10.   "Deutero-Jeremianic prose" names the style that was formerly known as Deuteronomistic prose. For this new wording see Hermann-Josef Stipp, *Deuterjeremianische Konkordanz* (ATSAT 63; St. Otilien: Eos, 1998), 2–3; Stipp lists all occurrences of phrases in this particular prose style as well as their parallels in the Deuteronomistic History. For the debate about whether it is Jeremiah's wording or the style of the book's editors, see the research review in Christl Maier, *Jeremia als Lehrer der Tora: Soziale Gebote des Deuteronomiums in Fortschreibungen des Jeremiabuches* (FRLANT 196; Göttingen: Vandenhoeck & Ruprecht, 2002), 14–33. Many recent studies of Jeremiah follow Stipp's terminological suggestions and his assumption that it is the redactors' style.

11.   Christof Hardmeier names Jer 21:1–23:2 a "geschichtstheologische[r] Traktat über die Schuld und das Versagen des nachjoschijanischen Königtums"; see Christof Hardmeier, "Zur schriftgestützten Expertentätigkeit Jeremias im Milieu der Jerusalemer Führungseliten (Jeremia 36): Prophetische Literaturbildung und die Neuinterpretation älterer Expertisen in Jeremia 21–23*," in *Die Textualisierung der Religion* (ed. J. Schaper; FAT 62; Tübingen: Mohr Siebeck, 2009), 105–49 (133).

12.   This phrase is also used by a delegation sent out by King Josiah in 2 Kgs 22:13.

13.   Many scholars consider Jer 21:1–10 a Deuteronomistic adaptation of the record of events in ch. 37; see Wilhelm Rudolph, *Jeremia* (HAT 12; Tübingen: J. C. B. Mohr, 1947), 117; Winfried Thiel, *Die deuteronomistische Redaktion von Jeremia 1–25* (WMANT 41; Neukirchen–Vluyn: Neukirchener, 1973), 230–37 (although he argues that the redactor reworked two probably authentic sayings of Jeremiah in vv. 3–7 and 8–10); Gunther Wanke, *Jeremia. Teilband 1: Jeremia 1,1–25,14* (ZBKAT 20/1; Zurich: Theologischer Verlag, 1995), 190; Carroll, *Jeremiah: A Commentary*, 407.

fighting for Israel in the Exodus story "with a strong hand" (Exod 3:19; 6:2) and "with an outstretched arm" (Exod 6:6).[14] The interchange of adjectives may indicate a reversal of the direction of God's fighting: it is no longer the enemy but God's people who are the target of the divine assault. The phrase "in anger, in fury, and in great wrath" (21:5b) also occurs in Deut 29:27, a verse that looks back to the exile. The listing of "pestilence, sword, and famine" in vv. 7 and 9 is typical for Deutero-Jeremianic prose (Jer 14:14; 24:10; 32:36; 24:17[15]). Having the people choose between the "way of life" and the "way of death" in 21:8 alludes to the covenant ceremony in Deut 30:15, 19.[16] Jeremiah 21:10 refers to Jeremiah's oracle against those who fled to Egypt in Jer 44:11, since both passages use the expression "to set one's face against somebody" (שים פנים +ב) in describing God's wrath. The wording "for evil, not for good" (לרעה ולא לטובה) in 21:10b also occurs in Jer 39:16 and 44:27.

Moreover, the oracle in 21:8–10 has several parallels in the narrative chapters of the book, which record events during the Babylonian siege of Jerusalem. The announcement in Jer 21:9 is almost identical to Jer 38:2, yet the verb נפל "to surrender, to desert" is used only in 21:9. In the narrative context of the latter, Jeremiah's call to "all the people" to save their bare lives by "going out to the Chaldeans" results in his persecution by some royal officials, among them Pashhur. These officials argue that Jeremiah's speech ruins the morale of both the warriors and the people enclosed in the city. King Zedekiah, who is characterized as a weak and unstable ruler,[17] gives Jeremiah into their hands and Jeremiah is thrown into an empty cistern. Ebed-melech, the eunuch and master of the king's house, however, rescues Jeremiah from the muddy pit. After the fall of Jerusalem recorded in 39:1–3, Jeremiah announces to Ebed-melech and to Baruch, his scribe—in words similar to 21:9b—"you will have your own life as booty" (Jer 39:18; 45:5). According to Jer 38:17–18 Jeremiah even addresses his call to surrender to the Babylonians to Zedekiah and promises that his life and the city would be spared. However, the king fears that he will be killed by those of his own people who have already deserted to the Babylonians and does not follow Jeremiah's advice.

14. The phrases are also taken up in Deuteronomy and the Deuteronomistic History, cf. "with a strong hand" (Deut 5:15; 6:21 etc.) and "with outstretched arm" (Deut 4:34; 2 Kgs 17:36).

15. For a complete list of references and their variations in the Deuteronomistic History, see Stipp, *Konkordanz*, 49–50.

16. While Deut 30:15, 19 only mention "life or death," the wording "way of life" in Jer 21:8 concurs with 15 references to 'way and deed' (מעלל דרך) in Jer 4:18; 7:3, 5; 17:10; 25:5; 26:13; cf. Stipp, *Konkordanz*, 40.

17. For an intriguing assessment of Zedekiah's character, cf. John Applegate, "The Fate of Zedekiah: Redactional Debate in the Book of Jeremiah," *VT* 48 (1998): 301–8.

My thesis that Jer 21:1–10 quotes these other passages and not vice versa is grounded in the observations that the oracles in ch. 21 (a) offer a florilegium of words and phrases taken from other passages, (b) are set in the prose style of the book's editors, and (c) are not in sequence with the context. While this is a traditional redaction-critical assessment of the text, the question remains when and why the authors/editors of 21:1–10 placed this cruel image of God and the characterization of Jeremiah's call to defect to the enemy at the beginning of the cycle of words to the kings. There is no doubt that this introduction to the cycle makes the critique against the kings fade and invalidates the following calls to repent and thus strongly affects a reader's perception of the other passages. As Carolyn Sharp has brilliantly demonstrated with regard to the complex redaction history of Jeremiah, "Redacted texts reveal differences in their aporias and unexpected shifts of emphasis."[18] Sharp rightly argues that redactions react or respond to given texts by scribes of later generations; they may interpret them faithfully or destroy them. While their rewriting is often key to preserve the tradition, it may also weave in foreign elements. In the following, I will further explore how the dating of Jer 21:1–10 affects the oracles' interpretation.

2. Dating the Text Affects Interpretation

In my view, it is crucial for interpretation that the harsh divine response to Zedekiah's request for rescue was written after the fall of Jerusalem despite its current narrative frame. Before the fall, the image of God fighting against his own people would have been perceived as utterly sarcastic. A prophet who delivered such a message would have been useless as an intermediary between the Judeans and their deity. Jeremiah's oracles collected in chs. 2–6—some may include authentic material—deliver a similarly harsh message, yet God's role in bringing evil is only implied and not elaborated in phrases like: "I am going to bring upon you a nation from far away" (5:15); "Take warning, O Jerusalem, or I shall turn from you in disgust, and make you a desolation, an uninhabited land" (6:8); "for I will stretch out my hand against the inhabitants of the land" (6:12); "Hear, O earth; I am going to bring disaster on this people, the fruit of their schemes" (6:19); "See, I am

18. Carolyn J. Sharp, "Jeremiah in the Land of Aporia: Reconfiguring Redaction Criticism as Witness to Foreignness," in Diamond and Stulman, eds., *Jeremiah (Dis)placed*, 35–46 (37).

laying before this people stumbling blocks against which they shall stumble" (6:21).[19]

Given the poetic sections of the book, I agree with Walter Brueggemann that the prophetic speech is "almost completely lacking in specific sociopolitical references" and that the poetry "avoids specifically political commentary or even recommendation."[20] In Jer 2–6, the identity of Judah's enemy is veiled by the image of an "enemy from the north" and God is not explicitly characterized as fighting against Judah.[21] Similarly, in Jer 2–6 Jeremiah does not explicitly mention the Babylonians or specific political constellations.

After 586 B.C.E., however, the Judeans who survived had to accept that Jerusalem had not been spared from conquest and ruin as in the year 701. They had to realize that Jeremiah's message of doom had come true. The narratives of Jer 27–29 and 33–44 then characterize Jeremiah as a political spokesman who summons his audience to surrender to the Babylonians.[22] Whether or not Jeremiah actually uttered a call to desert to the Babylonians, when their army was on the brink of breaching Jerusalem's walls, can hardly be proven. The authors of Jer 38 state this and have Jeremiah urge not only the ordinary people (38:1–2) but also the king (38:17) to comply. When Jer 21:8–10 repeats and reinforces this call apart from its original narrative context, however, it gains rhetorical force and strengthens Jeremiah's portrayal as a pro-Babylonian partisan and traitor to the Judean cause.

---

19. Jer 2–3 presents accusations to the people of Jerusalem and Judah as well as calls to repent; in Jer 4–6 the enemy from the north is in the foreground while not being named, yet portrayed as a wild beast (Jer 5:6) or a storm (4:11–12).

20. Walter Brueggemann, "The 'Baruch Connection': Reflections on Jeremiah 43.1–7*," in Diamond et al., eds., *Troubling Jeremiah*, 367–86 (374). Brueggemann further argues that it is the figure of Baruch who is involved in quarrels about policy and utilizes Jeremiah's prophecy for a pro-Babylonian position.

21. That Jer 21:1–10 stand out with regard to explicitness and 'historical' setting among the oracles in chs. 1–25 is also noticed by Louis Stulman, *Jeremiah* (AOTC; Nashville: Abingdon, 2005), 207.

22. Similarly Stipp argues that Jer 26, 36–43, 45* form a tendentious narrative of a pro-Babylonian group of Judean officials who try to recommend themselves for positions under Babylonian rule by arguing that their political position accords with the "true" prophet Jeremiah. See Hermann-Josef Stipp, *Jeremia im Parteienstreit: Studien zur Textentwicklung von Jer 26, 36–43 und 45 als Beitrag zur Geschichte Jeremias, seines Buches und judäischer Parteien im 6. Jahrhundert* (BBB 82; Frankfurt a. M.: Hain, 1992).

For modern commentators, Jeremiah's role in the politics of his time obviously requires an explanation whereas God's wrath and punishment seem so familiar that they do not need any justification. Thus, many exegetes who comment on Jer 21:8–10 try to vindicate Jeremiah against the assessment that he is a traitor—assuming that the 'historical' prophet called the people to desert—yet they do not take issue with this cruel image of God presented in vv. 4–7.[23] With regard to vv. 8–10, Wilhelm Rudolph, Artur Weiser, and Georg Fischer argue that Jeremiah's call to desert to the enemy is not 'unpatriotic' but guided by his knowledge about God's love for the people.[24] William Holladay poses the question "is Jrm [i.e. Jeremiah] simply a traitor?" without answering it.[25] Regarding Jer 21:4–7, he asserts that this oracle basically includes the same message that the prophet had delivered in the years before. Yet his last comment on the passage reveals Holladay's own reluctance: "What is it like for a prophet to extinguish all hope in his hearers?"[26] Jack Lundbom names the divine warrior's fighting against his own people "a terrible fit of rage"[27] and analyzes the use of metaphors of holy war in the passage. Only Ronald Clements anticipates concerns of modern readers emerging from this characterization of God and tries to explain the intricacies of the political situation under the last kings of Judah that may have led Jeremiah to assume such an uncompromising political position.[28] He also argues that Zedekiah's hope that God would rescue the city as he did in 701 B.C.E. was false and misinterpreted the character of the Israelite deity.[29] Finally, Clements sides with God and with Jeremiah's position and holds the people of Judah and their kings responsible for their own demise.

---

23.   Stulman (*Jeremiah*, 220–21) sees in Jer 21–24 a perspective at work, which favors the Babylonian *golah*; thus he endorses the total destruction of state and city as necessary for "the inauguration of the new workings of God" (220).

24.   Rudolph, *Jeremia*, 117; Artur Weiser, *Das Buch des Propheten Jeremia Kapitel 1–25,14* (8th ed.; ATD 20; Göttingen: Vandenhoeck & Ruprecht, 1981), 180; Georg Fischer, *Jeremia 1–25* (HTKAT; Freiburg: Herder, 2005), 645: "Jer 21 ist fern davon, Gott einen 'Seitenwechsel' zu unterstellen, im Gegenteil: Es weist *seine Treue im vollen Engagement* (V. 5) *für Recht und Leben* auf… Darin liegt Gott mit seinem bisherigen Tun auf einer Linie" (italics in original).

25.   Holladay, *Jeremiah 1*, 574.

26.   Ibid., 572.

27.   Jack R. Lundbom, *Jeremiah 21–36: A New Translation with Introduction and Commentary* (AB 21B; New York: Doubleday, 2004), 94–107 (107).

28.   Ronald E. Clements, *Jeremiah* (IBC; Atlanta: John Knox, 1988), 127–28.

29.   Ibid., 129–30.

In sum, most commentaries argue against the text's wording, that God is not cruel but simply reacting to Judah's vices and apostasy and that Jeremiah is no traitor but instructed by God. Yet, these comments do not solve the problem that this passage heavily overshadows God's love with his wrath. Only in recent years have Jeremiah scholars begun to voice the worries and bewilderment of modern readers who face such a cruel characterization of God. For example, Angela Bauer analyzes the function of the negative female imagery used to denote the people's behavior and argues that modern readers search for fluidity in gender and transgression of traditional gender roles.[30] Kathleen O'Connor reads the book through the lens of recent disaster studies and trauma theory.[31] In my view, Jer 21:1–10 formulates a strategy of those who survived the Babylonian conquest of Jerusalem to legitimate both their own survival and their submission to Babylonian rule. In their eyes, God has to be always in control and Jeremiah is on their side. This interpretation is informed by postcolonial theory, as the next section will demonstrate.

3. *"Ambivalence" in God's Role*

Although Jer 21:2, 4 explicitly names the Babylonian army as invaders of Jerusalem, the whole passage discusses the power and authority of YHWH.[32] Presented as a direct address to the leaders of Judah, the Israelite deity takes the role of subduing Jerusalem and Judah to Babylonian domination by directly fighting against the people (21:4–6). In this oracle, God is far removed from being a liberating deity, in which King Zedekiah and his court set their hope. Yet, Jer 21:8–10 delivers a less violent portrayal of YHWH insofar as this oracle discloses a chance of survival. In contrast to vv. 4–6, God's role is less directly stated in the three subsequent phrases of v. 10, which transfer the liability for the

---

30. Angela Bauer, "Dressed to Be Killed: Jeremiah 4.29–31 as an Example for the Functions of Female Imagery in Jeremiah," in Diamond et al., eds., *Troubling Jeremiah*, 293–305.

31. Kathleen M. O'Connor, "Reclaiming Jeremiah's Violence" in *The Aesthetics of Violence in the Prophets* (ed. C. Franke and J. M. O'Brien; LHBOTS 517; New York: T&T Clark International, 2010), 37–49; eadem, *Jeremiah: Pain and Promise*, esp. 19–27. O'Connor refers to Daniel Smith-Christopher whose studies on motifs of war and trauma in the prophets, esp. in Ezekiel, have been seminal for a new approach to the divine violence in prophetic texts. Cf. Daniel L. Smith-Christopher, *A Biblical Theology of Exile* (OBT; Minneapolis: Fortress, 2002).

32. The references to YHWH's speaking are numerous; cf. Jer 21:4, 7, 8, and 10.

city's destruction from God to the Babylonians: Whereas the first phrase names God as the subject ("I have set my face against the city for evil"), the passive formulation in the second one conceals the agent: "the city *will be given* into the hands of the king of Babylon." The third sentence refers to the king of Babylon: "he will burn it [i.e. the city] with fire." Therefore, the different oracles in Jer 21:1–10 are rather ambiguous in characterizing God's role in relation to the siege and conquest of Jerusalem. As Steed Davidson has plausibly argued in a recent study, the temple sermon in Jer 7 reflects a similar level of ambiguity or "ambivalence" in its announcement of the destruction of Jerusalem's temple.[33]

The term "ambivalence" was introduced into postcolonial theory by Homi K. Bhabha in order to describe the complex mix of attraction and repulsion that characterizes the relationship between the colonizer and the colonized.[34] Drawing from Freud's definition of the term and its application to the colonial context by Frantz Fanon,[35] Bhabha argues that ambivalence pertains both to the authority of the colonizer and to the self-perception of the colonized. The colonizer seeks to impose his attitudes, values and habits upon the colonized; he establishes structures of control that simultaneously teach the colonized to resemble colonial society, but never to replicate it fully, since replication would threaten colonial authority.[36] With regard to the colonized, Bhabha observes a similar ambivalence in their attempt to "narrate" their nation,[37] that is, to

33. Steed V. Davidson, "Ambivalence and Temple Destruction: Reading the Book of Jeremiah with Homi Bhabha," in Diamond and Stulman, eds., *Jeremiah (Dis)placed*, 162–71.

34. Homi K. Bhabha, *The Location of Culture* (London: Routledge, 1994), 121–31, 153–56. For a summary see Bill Ashcroft et al., *Post-Colonial Studies: The Key Concepts* (London: Routledge, 2000), 12–14.

35. Born in Martinique, Frantz Fanon worked as a psychiatrist in Algeria during the struggle for independence from France. He supported the independence movement and analyzed the issues of the anti-colonial resistance in his writings, among them *The Wretched of the Earth* (trans. C. Farrington; New York: Grove, 1963); and *Black Skin, White Masks* (trans. C. L. Markmann; New York: Grove, 1967).

36. See Bhabha, *The Location of Culture*, 122–25. Bhabha names the attempt of the colonized to adjust to colonial society "mimicry," yet argues that the colonized will be "almost the same, *but not quite*" (123; italics in original).

37. Homi K. Bhabha, ed., *Nation and Narration* (London: Routledge, 1990), esp. 1–7; the introduction written by Bhabha is entitled "Narrating the Nation" (1). His essay "DissemiNation: Time, Narrative, and the Margins of the Modern Nation," 291–322, appears as Chapter 8 in his book *The Location of Culture*, 199–244; references to this chapter are taken from the latter.

establish their narrative of community-building in a situation of colonial command.[38]

Bhabha regards the concept of nation as "a narrative strategy" and "an apparatus of symbolic power"[39] for the colonized. Focusing on the temporality of the nation rather than on its horizontal location, Bhabha argues that the people living at the margins of the empire require "a kind of 'doubleness' in writing."[40] Writing their own nationhood within a colonial or postcolonial context leads to a de-centered logic and dispersed cultural formations; such ambivalence, while not necessarily being intentional, is potentially subversive to the dominant discourse.

Since the book of Jeremiah narrates the end of Judah as a state and the destruction of Jerusalem including the history that led to these events and the struggle of the survivors who live under foreign rule, it seems appropriate to apply some aspects of Bhabha's reflection on "ambivalence" and the "nation" to the texts in Jeremiah. From a postcolonial perspective, the book of Jeremiah forms a narrative that explains why Judah had to surrender to the Babylonian regime. Yet, within this narrative, there are different assessments of God's and Jeremiah's role, since the book's narrative is a complex redacted text that includes many voices. For the survivors of the catastrophe, who added Jer 21:1–10, it is important to state that their God is not as powerless as it seems in facing Babylon's victory. They perceive their subjugation to the Babylonian empire as a last resort willed by YHWH and their survival as granted by God. In stating that God turned the weapons against his own people, they assure themselves that he has always been in control and that the Babylonians are only tools of divine wrath, not agents in their own right. Viewed diachronically, the exilic redactors' expansion of the narrative reinforces God's agency in history in order to weaken the power of the Babylonian empire. By having Jeremiah command that they desert to the enemy for the sake of their lives, those who survived Jerusalem's fall "narrate" their fate as willed by God. From their perspective, having gained their lives

---

38. I here follow Steed Davidson's assumption that Bhabha's concept of "nation" is "fluid enough to apply it to the pre-modern context of the ancient Near East"; see Davidson, "Ambivalence and Temple Destruction," 163 n. 6. Cf. Bhabha, *The Location of Culture*, 201: "What I am attempting to formulate…are the complex strategies of cultural identification and discursive address that function in the name of 'the people' or 'the nation' and make them the immanent subjects of a range of social and literary narratives."

39. Bhabha, *The Location of Culture*, 201.

40. Ibid., 202.

as "booty" of war, their own survival now signifies the nation's survival and God's protection of his people—albeit decimated and under foreign rule. Yet, who are these survivors who in retrospect write their nation's history including God's and Jeremiah's characterization? Because the prophet in 21:8–10 addresses the ordinary people, one wonders whether to find here the 'voice' of the subaltern whose ability to speak and act has been discussed in postcolonial theory.

4. *The Ruling Class and the Subalterns in the Book of Jeremiah*

Gayatri Chakravorty Spivak's famous article "Can the Subaltern Speak?" offers a philosophical and political analysis of the agency of colonized people of India who do not belong to the local elites.[41] The term "subaltern" means "of inferior rank" and was used by the Italian Marxist Antonio Gramsci to refer to those groups in society who are subject to the hegemony of the ruling classes, for example peasants, workers, and—as Spivak claims—many women in India.[42] Spivak argues that, in defining the colonized subject as "the other," Western philosophical discourse exerts epistemic violence and prevents the subaltern groups from raising their voice and exerting agency for survival. As an example, Spivak cites the *satī* (in English: *suttee*), the death of a woman on her husband's funeral pyre or on a separate pyre soon afterwards.

> The practice was common only among Bengali families during the eighteenth and early nineteenth centuries and was perceived to turn the widow into a *satī*, "a good woman," who was highly praised.[43] In 1826, the British banned the practice since they found it outrageous and oppressive to women. Nevertheless, during the colonial period in India, many women followed this self-sacrifice in order to revolt against the British Empire. For Spivak, *satī* or suttee demonstrates the disappearance of the female subject between Indian patriarchy and British imperialism into a

41. Gayatri C. Spivak, "Can the Subaltern Speak?," in *Marxism and the Interpretation of Culture* (ed. C. Nelson and L. Grossberg; Urbana: University of Illinois Press, 1988), 271–313. A German translation by A. Joskowicz und S. Nowotny of the original English version was published as: Gayatri C. Spivak, *Can the Subaltern Speak? Postkolonialität und Subalterne Artikulation* (Vienna: Tura & Kant, 2008).

42. For a definition of the term and its use in postcolonial studies, see Ashcroft et al., *Post-Colonial Studies*, 215–19.

43. See also Julia Leslie, "Sati," in *Encyclopedia of Religion*, vol. 12 (2d ed.; Detroit: Macmillan Reference USA, 2005), 8129–31.

dialectical movement that persists in a deferred figuration of the "Third-world woman" imprisoned between tradition and modernism.[44] Thus, in her view, the subaltern cannot speak and simultaneously survive colonial rule.

In what follows I will apply Spivak's idea that the colonized subaltern groups cannot speak or can only speak through the sacrifice of their lives to my interpretation of Jer 21:8–10. Searching for the "subaltern" in the book of Jeremiah, one can bracket out the king and his officials as well as Jeremiah and his supporters in the Shaphan family, since both groups clearly belonged to the local elites. However, there certainly were ordinary Judeans, men and women, afflicted by the politics of the day but not responsible for it. Some of them survived the catastrophe only to find themselves impoverished and still deprived of any political power. Their "booty" of war was, indeed, only bare life and much grief over the loss of family members. To this group Jer 38:2 and 21:8–10 deliver the message that they will save their lives if they surrender to the Babylonians. In retrospect, the population in Jerusalem under siege had only two options: They could either "voice" their patriotism and resistance to the imperialist regime by defending their city until their own death—a situation that Spivak envisions with regard to Indian women under British dominion—or they could defect to the enemy and save their lives. Even after the fall of Jerusalem, these options were applicable, as the story of Gedaliah's reign in Mizpah and his murder by Ishmael (40:7–42:6) illustrates. In this narrative, resistance to the Babylonians and their local collaborators leads only to further disruption. The ordinary people are described as pawns in the power-play of leaders: many refugees gather in Mizpah seeking protection from Gedaliah (40:12); many are murdered or taken captive by Ishmael (41:3, 10), but later turn to Johanan (41:13–14), who nevertheless escorts them to Egypt (41:16–18) in fear of Babylonian retaliation after their governor's assassination. Both options may not be perceived as agency toward stabilizing identity or securing survival. Yet, those who outlived the fall of Jerusalem saw surrender to the Babylonians as necessary for them to exist and to maintain any sort of agency.

Like Jer 21:4–7, the function of vv. 8–10 is to justify survival by stating that their deity offered this option through Jeremiah calling them to leave the city and desert to the Babylonians. While I would not argue that the survivors were necessarily all "subaltern," the different oracles in

---

44. Spivak, "Can the Subaltern Speak?," 306 (English version); 110 (German version).

Jer 21 hint at a diversification of groups among the survivors. I suggest
that the authors of Jer 21:8–10 are former Judean officials with a pro-
Babylonian political agenda. They had reason to justify not only their
own surrender and endurance but also the survival of ordinary Judeans,
whom they perceived as inferior to themselves, elites under Babylonian
hegemony. Thus, I would argue that it is not the subalterns—the ordinary
Judeans—who actually "speak" in Jer 21:8–10; instead, one hears the
voice of those who seek to represent and "speak for" them.

5. *Conclusion: God's Cruelty and Jeremiah's Treason as Narration Under Babylonian Hegemony*

Postcolonial theory, I argued, is helpful to dismantle hierarchies of
power in the book of Jeremiah and to explain the overall strategy of a
narrative with which a group of survivors of the catastrophe reclaim their
past and ground their identity at the margins of the Babylonian empire.
Assessing the attempt of Jeremiah and those who further transmitted his
message "to narrate the nation," one can discern a discourse that hinged
upon the roles of God and the Babylonian army, as well as the positions
of Jeremiah and Judah's population before and after the destruction of
Jerusalem. After the conquest of the capital, the failure of King Zedekiah
and his officials' policy became obvious. Although the role of the Babylonian army in subjugating the Judeans was evident, the exilic redactors
who placed Jer 21:1–10 as introduction to the cycle of words against the
kings explicitly emphasized God's role in handing the city to the enemy.
In retrospect, the statement that not the Babylonians but YHWH himself
defeated them serves to diminish the power of Babylon as an imperialist
regime. Jeremiah 21 thus argues against the obvious assumption that
YHWH may be a powerless deity unable to control the events. In this line,
Jeremiah is presented as more concerned with the survival of the people
than with the fate of Jerusalem. When 21:1–10 is read synchronically
and in comparison to chs. 1–6, the variety of characterizations of God
generates "ambivalence" with regard to God's authority and Babylon's
power. The ambiguities of both characterizations signal that there is no
easy and clear-cut answer to the question of responsibility. As a multi-
layered and multi-voiced narrative about the end of Judah as a state and
the destruction of its capital city, the book of Jeremiah provides answers
for those who live under Babylonian imperial rule without ignoring the
questions that Jeremiah and his contemporaries pondered. For the survivors, both elite groups and the common people, it is crucial that God has

been in control and Jeremiah is on their side. They narrate their own history as the nation's story in a new light. Although one may still not hear the voice of the subalterns in 21:8–10, there are people in exilic and post-exilic Judah who try to speak for them and to legitimate their survival and life under Babylonian rule. The statement that after Gedaliah's assassination all the rest of the people fled to Egypt (41:16–18) is another voice added to this complex narration that presents a pro-Golah perspective. What postcolonial theory can add to the discourse on Jeremiah is to distinguish these different perspectives and to explain them with regard to the varied interests of ancient authors/redactors and their audiences. Finding a rationale for characterizations of both God and Jeremiah, which are hard to digest for modern readers, also means to introduce new perspectives on an ancient text. While this text tells a nation's story, it offers surprising insights into the ways people are able to survive traumatic events and to live under imperialist regimes—even if this means that at first sight God seems to be cruel and Jeremiah a traitor.

BUYING LAND IN THE TEXT OF JEREMIAH: FEMINIST COMMENTARY, THE KRISTEVAN ABJECT, AND JEREMIAH 32

Carolyn J. Sharp

From the perspective of the feminist commentator, the landscape of the book of Jeremiah constitutes challenging terrain for a number of reasons. First among those is the fact that viable subjectivity within the book is encoded as male. The male prophet speaks to a God gendered as male both linguistically and socio-culturally; all of the significant actors in the plot are male. The female characters who speak and act in the text are presented by the narrator as appallingly unfaithful, for if we bracket the voice of Daughter Zion and the voice of matriarch Rachel as tropes more than "characters" as such, that leaves us with only the distorted voices and actions of the vilified worshippers of the Queen of Heaven (7:18; 44:15–19). The feminized and shamed social body of Judah is troped as a devoted bride who has gone astray, sprawling under every green tree and playing the whore (2:2, 20) and "committing adultery with stone and tree" (3:8). Judah is imaged as a wild she-ass in heat and insatiably lustful (2:23–24); as a wicked woman whose skirts are stained by the blood of the innocent poor (2:33–34); as a feminized city whose urban "body" is made repugnant by its hosting of oppression, wickedness, violence, destruction, sickness, and wounds (6:6–7); and as the rebellious community of those diaspora women in Egypt, worthy only of extermination by sword and famine. This is a difficult text indeed. It presents challenges not only for the feminist interpreter but for any reader who seeks to explore Jeremiah as a historical representation of an ancient community under siege, or as a tumultuous work of ancient literary art, or as a sacred text speaking an authoritative word of witness for contemporary believers.

At the heart of the feminist endeavor lies the honoring of the lived experience and wisdom of those who do not identify as patriarchy's faux-normative male subject. Second-wave feminism has made a strong claim for honoring women's lived experience. I certainly affirm that, but I insist that the lived experience of genderqueer folks and non-normative males be privileged as well, within a larger feminist paradigm of deep respect for all living creatures. Because I decline to give credence to biologically or culturally essentialist constructions of "woman"[1] and because I am committed to ending the marginalization of transgender and alternatively gendered expressions of identity, I do not foreground women's experience alone. As a biblical commentator, I locate myself in an interpretive space energized not only by resistance to the life-distorting ways of patriarchy but also by generative tension with the focus in second-wave feminist biblical studies on women characters in the Bible, the "feminine side" of God, and so on. That is a rich stream of interpretive tradition that has yielded important results, to be sure. But the underlying conceptual and political limitations of such engagement are significant, for wherever biblical traditions signify about women or the feminine, men or the masculine, power relations, and conceptions of the good and the illegitimate in communal life, the distortions of the male gaze are inevitable. This is to say nothing of the myriad biblical texts that offer little or nothing regarding women in particular. Reading Jeremiah, the

---

1. A number of essays in the important anthology *Feminist Frontiers* (ed. V. Taylor et al.; 9th ed.; New York: McGraw–Hill, 2012) work to destabilize essentialist paradigms of gender, sex, and race. For recovery of the history of transgender activism as essential to feminist critique, see Susan Stryker, "Transgender Feminism: Queering the Woman Question," in Taylor et al., eds., *Feminist Frontiers*, 63–69; Stryker writes, "Transgender studies offers us one critical methodology for thinking through the diverse particularities of our embodied lives, as well as for thinking through the commonalities we share through our mutual enmeshment in more global systems" (68). For a feminist piece that theorizes the intersection of literal and figurative borderlands, ethnic identity, and migration politics, see, in the same volume, Denise A. Segura and Patricia Zavella, "Gender in the Borderlands," 75–86. They urge feminists to engage "borderlands theory" to "[craft] a tapestry of voices and resistance to nativist politics and silencing discourse as well as traditional gendered expectations. By exploring multiple sites of gendered control and contestation, borderlands research reveals the complex representations, experiences and identities that women construct within the context of globalization and transnational migration" (83), an observation that surely has value for scholars of the ancient diaspora and post-diaspora contexts within which the book of Jeremiah was formed. For a foundational work that moved North American feminism decisively toward deconstructing essentialist paradigms of gender, see Judith Butler, *Gender Trouble: Feminism and the Subversion of Identity* (2d ed.; New York: Routledge, 1999).

feminist commentator may find relatively little traction for constructive work when considering the androcentric character of the plot, the regular use of misogynist metaphorization, and phallocentric constructions of subjectivity in the book.

In important ways, then, the second-wave feminist project of recuperation of "the female" labors under a set of implicit assumptions about gender ontology that are fatally flawed. Judith Butler can help here. She offers the following series of rhetorical questions toward rendering a critical history of queer theory. For my purposes here, I choose to understand Butler's questions as indicating the inescapable limitations of feminist work that seeks to rehabilitate positive valences for essentialist views of women:

> How is it that the apparently injurious effects of discourse become the painful resources by which a resignifying practice is wrought? Here it is not only a question of how discourse injures bodies, but how certain injuries establish certain bodies at the limits of available ontologies, available schemes of intelligibility. And further, how is it that those who are abjected come to make their claim through and against the discourses that have sought their repudiation?[2]

How indeed? It is a formidable challenge. While I honor the fruitful work that has been done to revise and re-vision "woman" in the Hebrew Scriptures, I maintain that critical interrogation of essentialist gender constructions is absolutely vital for feminist biblical studies.

The feminist commentator on Jeremiah is confronted by far more than the androcentrism of the ancient text. A second challenge has to do with the rhetorical dynamics of shaming and disenfranchisement that pervade Jeremiah. Punitive voicing dominates the Deutero-Jeremianic prose traditions, constructing as despicable and worthy of extermination those Judeans who remained in the land after the fall of Jerusalem and the Judeans who fled to Egypt (see especially Jer 24 and 44). In the oracles against foreign nations, too, the reader finds virulent language of military despoliation and the sexualized shaming of enemies. The cultural violence of this rhetoric must be named. The final form of Jeremiah works hard to dehumanize political adversaries, and this constitutes a serious stumbling block for all interpreters who want to take the witness of the ancient Other seriously while utilizing biblical interpretation as a resource for the construction of ethically just communities. If feminist critique

---

2. Judith Butler, *Bodies That Matter: On the Discursive Limits of "Sex"* (London: Routledge, 1993), 170.

positions itself in opposition to relations of exploitation and domination—as I believe it must—then Jeremianic and Deutero-Jeremianic
language of shaming, rejection, and extermination presents a major
obstacle for feminist readers even when it is not overtly gendered.

Consider a third challenge: for scholars working within institutions
influenced by North American and German biblical scholarship, powerful indeed are the theoretical constraints that are cued and reinforced
within guild culture concerning feminist analysis. If feminist questions
are hosted at all (and there are many theological schools that do not
welcome such inquiry), feminist criticism is often treated as a "special
topic" to be pursued on the margins of historical scholarship. Vast areas
of scholarly inquiry continue to be engaged and particular topics pursued
without anything resembling what Annette Kolodny has called "an acute
and impassioned attentiveness" to gendered constructions of power.[3]
Within Pentateuchal criticism and work on the Deuteronomistic History,
to name two sprawling research areas, it is mainly the (few) scholars who
identify as feminist, womanist, or queer who do sophisticated work with
those materials' gendered figuring of power and powerlessness, representations of sexual violence, and related subjects.[4] Feminist attentiveness to hierarchies and dynamics of power, as those are encoded and
enacted through ancient texts, contextual research, and scholarly hermeneutical methods, should not be considered a "special topic." Rather,
feminist critique presses a robust challenge to fundamental epistemological assumptions and normative frameworks upon which many branches

---

3. Kolodny writes, "What unites and repeatedly invigorates feminist literary
criticism…is neither dogma nor method but…an acute and impassioned *attentiveness* to the ways in which primarily male structures of power are inscribed (or
encoded) within out literary inheritance"; see Annette Kolodny, "Dancing Through
the Minefield: Some Observations on the Theory, Practice, and Politics of a Feminist
Literary Criticism," *Feminist Studies* 6 (1980): 1–25 (20); emphasis in original.

4. Still relatively few in number are monographs that present sustained and
well-theorized engagement of gender or sexuality in the Pentateuch and the Deuteronomistic History. Article-length treatments and collections of essays on feminist
method are more numerous, of course. Worthy of mention are the Feminist Companion commentary series edited by Athalya Brenner and Luise Schottroff, Silvia
Schroer, and Marie-Theres Wacker, *Feminist Interpretation: The Bible in Women's
Perspective* (trans. M. and B. Rumscheidt; Minneapolis: Fortress, 1998). Two excellent book-length treatments are Ken Stone, *Sex, Honor, and Power in the Deuteronomistic History* (Sheffield: Sheffield Academic, 1996), and Sarah Shectman,
Women in the Pentateuch: A Feminist and Source-Critical Analysis (Sheffield:
Sheffield Phoenix, 2009).

of biblical studies have relied in the modern history of the discipline and within which androcentrism and misogyny continue to silence and oppress women and others.

As a commentator who desires to honor the ancient voices of those speaking through the Jeremiah traditions, I find myself in a difficult position. With Emmanuel Lévinas, I believe that a generous response to the face of the Other is necessary.[5] The ethical mandate is authoritative, for me, not only in the urgent sense of engaging difference as that is embodied in material ways and persons in our lived experience, but also in terms of honoring the voices of authors from across the centuries. From this commitment follows the necessity of generously hosting polyphony, in hermeneutical terms. The texts of ancient Other are to be respected even when the implications of that ancient Other's discourses may be critiqued or resisted. The discursive practices of the Deutero-Jeremianic prose remain, in some key dimensions, deeply problematic for me. Yet as a member of a believing community that cherishes Scripture as sacred, I do not take it as an option for myself, personally or as an ordained leader within my Episcopal Church tradition, simply to dismiss offensive or disturbing biblical texts as some feminist critics feel free to do.[6] Hence, well-theorized and carefully designed hermeneutical strategies are needed for the feminist who wishes to work productively with these texts.

5. In *Alterity and Transcendence* (trans. M. B. Smith; New York: Columbia University Press, 1999), Lévinas writes, "I have attempted to carry out a phenomenology of sociality, starting out from the face of the other man, reading, before all mimicry, in its facial directness, a defenseless exposure to the mysterious forlornness of death, and hearing, before all verbal expression, from the bottom of that weakness, a voice that commands, an order issued to me not to remain indifferent to that death, not to let the other die alone, i.e., to answer for the life of the other man, at the risk of becoming the accomplice of that death" (29).

6. For example, Athalya Brenner writes of pornographic texts in the biblical prophetic corpus, "I do not share in the hope or assessment that biblical texts like the pornoprophetic passages are redeemable for readers like me. On the balance, I fail to see how the texts' unsavoury properties can be neutralized and separated from their religious message. But then, I too am a conditioned and subjective reader—exactly like those readers who operate on other premises and who do wish to continue using such disturbing texts as instruction within their religions and cultural traditions"; see Athalya Brenner, *The Intercourse of Knowledge: On Gendering Desire and "Sexuality" in the Hebrew Bible* (Leiden: Brill, 1997), 174.

A Strategy for Commentary-Writing on Jeremiah

In the collaborative writing process with Christl Maier that will yield our feminist and postcolonial commentary on Jeremiah,[7] I will construct a feminist interpretive framework for Jer 26–52 that privileges dialectical engagements of lament and transgression. In this model, I define "lament" as sociopolitical protest that names woundedness and loss, making visible the vulnerability of cultural systems of meaning-making and declining to be complicit in the erasure of pain and brokenness from communal memory.[8] I define "transgression" as the privileging of creative interventions, ancient and contemporary, that resist or reframe destructive social norms. The feminist commentator may identify "transgressive" moves on the part of ancient traditionists who, working with the words and persona of the historical Jeremiah, sought to reconfigure communal theopolitical norms; she may explore creative moments of resistance and new vision within the history of interpretation; and finally, the interpreter may enact her own transgressive critical interventions. In my dialectical engagements, I will deploy Jeremiah's powerful figure of Rachel weeping for her children (31:15) and the fascinating interpretive crux of 31:22, נקבה תסובב גבר ("the female surrounds/encompasses/ the warrior-male"),[9] as two semantic resources by means of which to interrogate other Jeremiah texts.

One can argue for such a hermeneutical decision on a variety of methodological grounds. On redaction-critical grounds, the likely late date at which the Book of Consolation came into the book of Jeremiah allows the diachronically oriented reader to privilege that material as an ancient redirection of earlier Jeremiah traditions. On structural and thematic grounds, as some have argued,[10] the centrality of the Book of

---

7. The collaborative commentary will be produced by Christl M. Maier (Jer 1–25) and myself (Jer 26–52) for Kohlhammer's series entitled International Exegetical Commentary on the Old Testament/Internationaler Exegetischer Kommentar zum Alten Testament.

8. Important essays on the book of Lamentations and lament in the ancient Near East may be found in Nancy C. Lee and Carleen Mandolfo, eds., *Lamentations in Ancient and Contemporary Cultural Contexts* (SBLSymS 43; Atlanta: Society of Biblical Literature, 2008). See also Scott Ellington, *Risking Truth: Reshaping the World Through Prayers of Lament* (Eugene: Wipf & Stock, 2008); Nancy C. Lee, *Lyrics of Lament: From Tragedy to Transformation* (Minneapolis: Fortress, 2010).

9. So Angela Bauer, *Gender in the Book of Jeremiah: A Feminist-Literary Reading* (New York: Lang, 1999), 132.

10. On the importance of Jer 30–31 for the book of Jeremiah, see, for example, two essays in Martin Kessler, ed., *Reading the Book of Jeremiah: A Search for*

Consolation in the literary structure of Jeremiah gives the promise material a unique visibility. On reader-response and *wirkungsgeschicht-liche* grounds, one can argue that the image of Rachel weeping has enjoyed deep traction in the history of interpretation.[11] Similarly, the mysterious crux of 31:22 has compelled the attention of interpreters for many centuries. The diversity of suggestions in recent commentaries hints at the wide range of semantic possibilities: Robert P. Carroll has "a woman protects a man"; William McKane gives it as, "a woman is turned into a man"; Gerald L. Keown, Pamela J. Scalise, and Thomas G. Smothers suggest "female encircles he-man"; Louis Stulman translates it theologically as "faithful daughter Israel...at last embraces or 'encompasses' her God"; Leslie C. Allen offers "a female courts a man."[12]

Coherence (Winona Lake: Eisenbrauns, 2004): Ronald Clements, "Jeremiah's Message of Hope: Public Faith and Private Anguish," 135–47, and Bob Becking, "Divine Reliability and the Conceptual Coherence of the Book of Consolation (Jeremiah 30–31)," 163–79.

11. See Christine Ritter, *Rachels Klage im antiken Judentum und frühen Christentum: Eine auslegungsgeschichtliche Studie* (AGJU 52; Leiden: Brill, 2003). The figure of Rachel weeping is important to the interpretation of Herod's slaughter of the Holy Innocents in the Gospel of Matthew (Matt 2:18), in visual art such as a seventeenth-century woodcut by Christoffel van Sichem II and an eighteenth-century oil painting by Charles Willson Peale, and in literature. Linda Beamer writes, "In English literature, Rachel the mourning mother is alluded to with considerable frequency. In Chaucer's *Prioress's Tale* (7.627), the slain boy's mother is a 'newer Rachel' as she swoons by his bier. Melville's *Moby-Dick* describes the captain of the *Rachel* hunting for a lost son, weeping for children who are not. Charles Lamb ('In Praise of Chimney Sweepers') describes many noble Rachels weeping for their children, referring to the Victorian practice of abduction of boys for the sweep trade. In T. S. Eliot's *The Waste Land*, a 'murmur of maternal lamentation' (367) recalls Rachel's inconsolable grief"; see Lamb, "Rachel," in *A Dictionary of Biblical Tradition in English Literature* (ed. D. L. Jeffrey; Grand Rapids: Eerdmans, 1992), 652. An award-winning contemporary bronze sculpture, "Rachel Weeping for Her Children" by Sondra L. Jonson, enjoys permanent installation at St. Germanus Parish in Arapahoe, Nebraska.

12. See Robert P. Carroll, *Jeremiah* (OTL; Philadelphia: Westminster, 1986), 601; William McKane, *A Critical and Exegetical Commentary on Jeremiah, Volume 2: XXVI–LII* (ICC; Edinburgh: T. & T. Clark, 1996), 806; Gerald L. Keown, Pamela J. Scalise, and Thomas G. Smothers, *Jeremiah 26–52* (WBC; Nashville: Thomas Nelson, 2000), 117; Louis Stulman, *Jeremiah* (AOTC; Nashville: Abingdon, 2005), 270; Leslie C. Allen, *Jeremiah* (OTL; Louisville: Westminster John Knox, 2008), 343. Gunther Wanke (*Jeremia. Teilband 2: Jeremia 25,15–52,34* [ZBKAT 20/2; Zurich: Theologischer Verlag, 2003) translates the phrase as, "Weibliches umgibt den Mann" (286), and says that this clause "dieses Neue als einen Umschwung vom

Michael L. Brown's helpful summary regarding other options may be cited here in the interests of concision:

> Of the recent major commentaries, suggestions include: "the female shall be the initiator in sexual relations" (Holladay), and the warriors, taunted as though women, will be victorious (also Holladay, citing Calvin); "the women must protect the (fighting) man" (because of his weakness [Lundbom]); "virgin Israel shall arise, something of an Amazon, and do exploits" (Thompson); "a woman is changed into a man," focusing on Yahweh's new regime, which will institute such radical change as to turn the world upside down (McKane); compare also Malbim, who sees the woman as Israel and the man as the Lord, who brings them back to the land in a different way from before (i.e., without battle and conquest).[13]

The play of ambiguous and contestatory possibilities in and about נקבה תסובב גבר makes this syntagm an excellent locus for the interpretive efforts of a feminist commentary on Jeremiah.

In the case of נקבה תסובב גבר, I also plan to explore the polyvalence of the verb סבב more generally. Among a variety of possibilities, the root סבב may be used of encircling, turning in a new direction, turning aside so as to evade, and surrounding or hemming in a house or city with hostile intent.[14] I would contend that the presence of סבב constitutes a major semantic "event" in the text of Jeremiah, given that the city of Jerusalem itself is under siege. In the commentary, I will consider the powerful negative nuance of a similar formulation that functions as a catchword in Jeremiah, מגור מסביב ("terror all around"), which is applied to the besieging enemy with sword in hand (6:25), to Jerusalem's dire straits (20:10), to Pashhur the priest as an adversary of Jeremiah (20:3), and to the horror facing Egypt and Kedar at their defeat by the Babylonian army (46:5; 49:29). And in a move influenced by the hermeneutical praxis Elisabeth Schüssler Fiorenza has articulated, viz.,

---

Unheil zum Heil versteht: Wie im einleitenden Jakobspruch (30,6) das Unheil damit umschrieben wird, daß sich Männer wie gebärende Frauen aufführen, so könnte hier die Umkehrung der Verhältnisse bildlich durch die 'Dominanz' der Frau gegenüber dem Mann beschrieben sein" (289).

13. Michael L. Brown, *Jeremiah* (rev. ed.; Expositor's Bible Commentary 7; Grand Rapids: Zondervan, 2010), 392.

14. On סבב with the sense of surrounding with hostile intent, see, for example, Gen 19:4 (the men of the city of Sodom encircling the house in which Lot is staying), Josh 6 (of the Israelites' cultic encircling of Jericho before battle), Josh 7:9 (of Joshua's anxiety that the Canaanites will surround Israel and obliterate it), Judg 16:2 (of the Gazites lying in wait for Samson), and 1 Kgs 5:17 (of enemies of King David surrounding him with warfare on every side).

feminist critical interpretation for liberation,[15] I will work with 31:22 writ
larger as a signifier connecting witness for newness—a "new thing on
the earth," חדשה בארץ—to the "new covenant" material in 31:31–34
(ברית חדשה).

It is important to theorize well the ways in which Jeremiah's discursive strategies render abject (a part of) the Judean "body." Exploration of
the literary and ideological dynamics of abjection will equip the reader to
analyze the power of the rhetoric here and to evaluate the choices made
by interpreting communities who appropriate the text. In what follows, I
will briefly sketch dimensions of the notion of abjection articulated by
psychoanalyst and literary theorist Julia Kristeva. Then I will offer some
exegetical soundings in Jer 32, using this text as a site to illustrate the
relevance of Kristeva's theory for constructions of the subjectivity of
Judah, God, and Jeremiah.

The Kristevan Abject

Kristeva has analyzed ways in which a cultural system may mark as
horrifying, decadent, or repulsive those dimensions of embodied living that are perceived to threaten that system's internal coherence. In a
wide variety of ways, cultural representations seek to displace impurity,
foreignness, illness, offal, and death from the boundaries of the (constructed) viable subject. Ironically, though, in its focus on the expelling,
forbidding, destroying, or refusal of that which threatens, a cultural
system in fact ensures that the threat remains present, for revulsion can
come only from the continued (implied) presence of that which is compelling disgust. Kristeva says that abjection

> does not radically cut off the subject from what threatens it—on the
> contrary, abjection acknowledges it [*that is, the subject*] to be in perpetual
> danger.... [B]raided, woven, ambivalent, a heterogeneous flux marks out
> a territory that I can call my own because the Other, having dwelt in me
> as *alter ego*, points it out to me through loathing.[16]

15. On the critical practice of biblical interpretation in service of liberation, see
Elisabeth Schüssler Fiorenza, *Bread Not Stone: The Challenge of Feminist Biblical
Interpretation* (anniversary ed.; Boston: Beacon, 1995), and *Wisdom Ways: Intro-
ducing Feminist Biblical Interpretation* (Maryknoll: Orbis, 2001).
16. Julia Kristeva, *Powers of Horror: An Essay in Abjection* (trans. L. S.
Roudiez; New York: Columbia University Press, 1982), 9–10.

For Kristeva, the displacement of the drive toward violence means that abjected death becomes an inescapable part of the being of the subject. The subject contains within the self, the "I," both purity and impurity in a heterogeneous mixture in which abomination, or at least the threat of abomination, is always present.[17]

Biblical scholars may note a profound ambivalence in ancient Israel's anxious and violent refusal of the foreign, the loathsome, and the monstrous. As Butler has said, reflecting on the Kristevan abject,

> The "abject" designates that which has been expelled from the body, discharged as excrement, literally rendered "Other." This appears as an expulsion of alien elements, but the alien is effectively established through this expulsion.... [T]he operation of repulsion can consolidate "identities" founded on the instituting of the "Other" or a set of Others through exclusion and domination.[18]

Many Hebrew Bible texts reflect ancient cultural economies that render abject the impure, the outsider, the diseased, the female, and the dangerous. Priestly traditions and Deuteronomistic traditions, in particular, seem fearful about that which threatens to render the boundaries of the androcentric plural subject, Israel's communal "body," porous or vulnerable. In the obliteration of Jericho, Rahab the Canaanite prostitute is allowed to survive and is said to live in Israel "to this day" (עד היום הזה, Josh 6:25); but she is also put "outside the camp of Israel" (מחוץ למחנה ישראל, 6:23), where the unclean had to await purification, where unusable parts of sacrifices were burned, and where those who had been executed were buried. The holy-war ideology of Joshua requires the extermination of indigenous groups living nearby; when the Gibeonites trick Joshua into letting them live, their reward is perpetual subjugation. In Ezra–Nehemiah, the expulsion of foreign wives and children is tantamount to the banishing of that which is potentially condemnable within Israel itself—not just in its relationships but in its cultural psyche and bloodlines. What is sought, overtly, is a purified and well-guarded Judean social body. But the traces of disease (as it were) in this ethnically "cleansed" body cannot be erased, and Israelite scribes' dis-ease regarding foreignness cannot finally be cured either. Ezra–Nehemiah's vivid narration of the casting out of those women and children has

---

17. Ibid., 112.

18. Butler, *Gender Trouble*, 169–70. Pursuant to my rejection of essentialism earlier in this essay, I would note that Butler is among those who have critiqued Kristeva for essentialism in her psychoanalytic constructions of the maternal body (see, e.g., ibid., 101–19).

ensured that their presence has been secured in the literary traditions of ancient Israel. The unacceptable dimensions of communal life are robustly subjugated in the literature of ancient Israel—through ritual praxis, through martial rhetoric, through sublimation. But through that very subjugation, they come to be permanently inscribed in the formational texts of the ancient culture and remain perpetually threatening.

Consider the hyperbolic obliteration of Achan in Josh 7 for his theft of holy-war spoils, which he had buried underneath his tent in a move that should surely delight psychoanalysts of later centuries. This chilling story has been read by Lori Rowlett as seeking to suppress dissent from (internal) rebels against the Josianic monarchy and its program.[19] That which has been abjected—the disobedient Achan and those associated with him, all of whom were cast out, burned, crushed, and buried under a heap of stones—indeed continues within the "body" of Israel. If it were otherwise, there would be no need for the story of Achan.

In Jeremiah, we may consider the metaphorization of Israel as a camel in heat in Jer 2:23–25.[20] The sexual drive of the animal is mapped, of course, onto implicit values regarding human behavior. Here a complex of assumptions is at work concerning males' guarding of female bodies and female sexual desire, communal accountability regarding Israelite norms of cultic fidelity, and the illegitimacy of international political alliances. Metaphors work to organize cognitive and affective responses of the implied audience according to implicit value systems. Far from being merely secondary stylistic reflexes or only semantically decorative, metaphors are powerful tools for creating and reifying certain codes of meaning-making within cultural systems. The social response of abjection is cued by Jeremiah's hyperbolic metaphor for Israel as an animal in heat. Concerning this trope, Athalya Brenner rightly uses the term "dehumanization," noting that

> the metaphorized 'wild she-ass' is both more and less than a merely natural animal: whoever heard of an animal who is constantly [in] heat, forever lustful? Such an animal would not qualify as natural. She/it is fabulous, mythic. Thus, the animalization of woman argues that "she" posits "herself" outside the human, social order by being (a) wild and (b) always [in] heat…. Let us remember: this fantasy of womanliness must

19. See Lori K. Rowlett, "Inclusion, Exclusion, and Marginality in the Book of Joshua," *JSOT* 55 (1992): 15–23 and *Joshua and the Rhetoric of Violence: A New Historicist Analysis* (Sheffield: Sheffield Academic, 1996).

20. See the essay in this volume by Else K. Holt, "'The Stain of Your Guilt is Still Before Me' (Jeremiah 2:22): (Feminist) Approaches to Jeremiah 2 and the Problem of Normativity."

correspond to a similar fantasy of the target audience in order for the propaganda to be effective. Disgust and shame will not be produced unless the listeners recognize the validity of the description for female sexual behaviour in general.... The dehumanization of the metaphorical woman is the analogy chosen to reflect the condemned, inhuman conduct of the extra-metaphorical referent, the addressed community.[21]

Similarly designed to cue a response of abjection and similarly directed against the internal Other are the diatribes in Jer 24 and 42–44, hurled at Judeans who remained in the land after the fall of Jerusalem and Judeans in the Egyptian diaspora. Many other texts within Jeremiah are implicated in ancient strategies of abjection as well. At this point, we may profitably turn our attention to dynamics of abjection in Jer 32.

Jeremiah 32

Jeremiah 32 presents an extended sign-act: the redemption of a plot of land by Jeremiah during the Babylonian siege of Jerusalem. Narrated with notable attention to the pragmatic details of the transaction, the sign-act proper is followed by a theologized interpretation whose prolixity and sustained focus on the identity of God mark it as unique among sign-act interpretations in Jeremiah. The narratological context of Jer 32 is important: the words and actions of Jeremiah and God are situated in a crucial liminal moment during the siege of Jerusalem, underlining the high stakes for the characters in the plot and heightening the anxiety of the implied audience immersed in this drama. Some readers have seen this text as crucially important for the larger purposes of the heavily redacted and tumultuous book of Jeremiah. Of 32:28–35, Jack Lundbom writes, "In this oracle and the one following, which are the last recorded judgment oracles given to a Jerusalem audience, we have what sounds like an aged Jeremiah compressing into single oracles the preaching of 35 years, a florilegium, if you will, of quotations or main points contained in earlier oracles."[22] Chapter 32 is notable as the resumption of prose narration immediately following the mostly poetic diction of hope of the Book of Consolation (chs. 30–31). That luminous promise

---

21. Athalya Brenner, "On Prophetic Propaganda and the Politics of 'Love': The Case of Jeremiah," in *A Feminist Companion to the Latter Prophets* (ed. A. Brenner; FCB 8; Sheffield: Sheffield Academic, 1995; repr. New York: T&T Clark International, 2004), 256–74 (263).

22. Jack R. Lundbom, *Jeremiah 21–36* (AB 21B; New York: Doubleday, 2004), 515.

material might well be expected to unsettle an implied audience used to relentless oracles of shame and doom in Jeremiah heretofore.

How does Jer 32 relate to all of the material that precedes it? Scholars and non-academic readers alike have tended to see in Jer 32 a sign of hope similar to the hope expressed in the Book of Consolation: Jerusalem may be under siege, but restoration awaits in a future radiant with promise. But I suggest that the positioning of Jer 32 on the "seam" where prose joins the poetry of the Book of Consolation may highlight a more ambiguous relationship to that foregoing promise material. A few scholars have explored the possibility of complex and darker implications of Jer 32. Among those is Steed Davidson, who views the chapter through a postcolonial lens. Davidson probes political tensions inherent in the ways in which the redemption of patrimonial land is made to signify in earlier and later layers of text. (For our purposes here, the terms "earlier" and "later" may be understood redactionally or as simple literary terms, with earlier material coming first as the chapter unfolds.) Davidson finds that Jer 32 betrays "tensions between the urban elite dwellers and their counterparts in the villages": the foregrounding of ancestral kinship ties to the land in vv. 6–15 emphasizes the importance of the land for tribal identity, but the focus on the economic transaction in the latter part of the chapter underlines the importance of land as commodity for those in positions of privilege in urban centers.[23] Davidson notes the liminal position of the prophet in this volatile mix of cultural significances. The prophet is accountable both to Babylon and to local Judeans in power, and civic leaders at Anathoth have already shown him strong opposition (see 11:21–23). Davidson writes,

> As a subject, Jeremiah operates as the immediate focus of both the local governing authorities and the imperial power. This doubled gaze emphasizes the ambiguous nature of the position of the prophet.... [T]he prophet's potentially conflicting and dual loyalties rhetorically engage in the same activity.... [T]he symbolic action suffices to give voice to marginal positionalities.[24]

Jeremiah seeks to secure a future for his people that cannot be undone by siege, by Babylon's ongoing expressions of imperial will, or by his own deportation. He cannot risk (further) alienating leaders among his own

---

23. See Steed V. Davidson, *Empire and Exile: Postcolonial Readings of the Book of Jeremiah* (LHBOTS 542; New York: T&T Clark International, 2011), 81–82.

24. Ibid., 83.

people, either—he must be subtle. Laying claim to territory in an economic transaction internal to the colonized community is strategically savvy, for overt rebellion would be punished severely by Babylon. Davidson sees the redemption of the field as a way to signal resistance to Judeans without heightening the already intense threat posed by Babylon. As Davidson puts it, Jeremiah

> enacts in symbolic fashion the claims of the pre-imperial past of the people in the face of the impending imperial enterprise…. [T]hrough the staging of the past the colonized interrogates the contemporary ventures of empire…. In the face of imperial aggression that threatens the dispossession of the land, this text employs a form of resistance that preserves the subjectivity of the people and keeps a place for them in the world. [25]

I agree that securing the claim to patrimonial land does constitute a strong signal regarding the promise of future endurance and *shalom*. This sign-act is brilliant in hermeneutical terms as well, from the meta-narratological standpoint of the redaction critic. The legacy of the prophet is arguably under threat within the history of composition of the book, for the Deutero-Jeremianic scribes responsible for the "submit to Babylon and live" political platform did not welcome overt political rebellion either. To purchase land for an undefined future allows room for contestatory visions of Judah's liberation to inhabit the same textual space.

But at what cost does the prophet stake his claim in this fraught moment of crisis, with the enemy at the gates? Conflict surges just beneath the surface of this text, for there is tremendous loss for Jeremiah and for God in this narrative's theologizing of the horrific experience of Judah's subjugation. Close attention to key terms, tone, and other rhetorical features of Jer 32:16–44 reveals trajectories of ferocious prophetic resistance, divine rage, and the abjection of all involved. These trajectories are worked in a subtle but thoroughgoing way into this material. Readings that underline only the theological hope here are missing a significant dimension of what is at stake, both for the prophet and for the deity. In what follows, rhetorical-critical attention to three distinct moves in Jer 32:16–44 will demonstrate that this material makes visible Jeremiah's hyperbolic rejection of his people, his fierce resistance to the standard (Deuteronomistic or Deutero-Jeremianic) theology on offer, and God's enraged response.

---

25. Ibid., 78 and 87.

The Abjection of Judah: Verses 23 + 29–35

In Jeremiah's prayer and God's first response, Judah is rendered as an unthinkably corrupt, despicable Other. The prophet says that when the people were brought out of slavery and given the Promised Land, they did not obey God's law. God showed signs and wonders in Egypt during Israel's captivity and has continued to show wondrous proof of the divine power to redeem, "to this day in Israel and among all humankind" (v. 20), yet Israel has been heedless of the mighty and glorious deeds of God. Even though the people took possession of the land of Canaan and enjoyed its beneficence as a land "flowing with milk and honey" (v. 22), they were unwilling to honor the God who had so richly blessed them. In a rhetorical flourish reminiscent of the brutal anti-"salvation history" in Ezek 20, Jeremiah adds that the people neither listened to God's voice nor comported themselves in accordance with God's law, and in fact would do nothing of all God commanded (את כל־אשר צויתה לעשות לא עשו, v. 23). According to this prophetic diatribe, there are no terms on which Israel could dare to ask for recognition of its subject status as God's people. The faithless Judah has been cast out, expunged from any subject identification among those who enjoyed covenant with God.

God continues the ruthless abjection of Israel, pressing charges in vv. 30–35 with a sweeping expansiveness against "the people of Israel and Judah" construed as disobedient from their youth (מנעריהם). God includes the kings and officials, priests and prophets, citizens of Judah and residents of Jerusalem—all the segments of Judean society—and levels a blistering indictment: Jerusalem has been evil "from the day it was built until this day." The deity thunders to a conclusion that shames Judah beyond recovery, charging that Judeans set up abominations in the Temple itself and sacrificed children to Molech. Rhetorically speaking, this is virulent abjection of every aspect of identity of God's people. Heedless and disobedient from earliest history, worshipping in a temple that is a locus of moral abomination and evil, engaging in the most abhorrent practices: no vested member of Judean culture is left unshamed. Judah has been inscribed as a defiled and repulsive thing, a "jettisoned object"[26] that can no longer lay claim to relationship with God on any meaningful terms. In a chapter entitled "Semiotics of Biblical Abomination" in her book *Powers of Horror*, Kristeva writes,

---

26. See Kristeva, *Powers of Horror*, 73.

The pure/impure mechanism…carries…the brunt of the struggle each
subject must wage during the entire length of his personal history in order
to become separate, that is to say, to become a speaking subject and/or
subject to Law…. [T]he "material" semes of the pure/impure opposition
that mark out the biblical text…are responses of symbolic Law, in the
sphere of subjective economy and the genesis of speaking identity.[27]

In Jer 32, the narrated history of Judah's illegitimate cultic and moral
antagonism toward God's power and God's law means, for Jeremiah and
for God, that Judah is no longer a covenant subject. The abjected Judah
dare not speak.

The Abjection of God: Verses 16–25

Perhaps more radical than this thoroughgoing abjection of the people is
the prophet's confrontation of God regarding the incomprehensibility
of the divine promise to restore. In vv. 16–22, Jeremiah gives himself
over to effusive praise of God: "It is you who made the heavens and the
earth by your great power and by your outstretched arm! Nothing is too
hard for you…. O great and mighty God…great in counsel and mighty in
deed, whose eyes are open to all the ways of mortals…." This hyperbolic
praise is unlike any other diction in the book of Jeremiah, and as such
may be seen as excessive—not false, but true in a markedly heightened
way that will be used toward ironic purposes later in Jeremiah's prayer.
Jeremiah's praise builds toward a fierce challenge near the end of his
prayer that is reminiscent of the prophet's bitterest lament (Jer 20:7–
18). In this dramatic moment when Babylonian siege ramps have been
cast up against the city, the prophet notes acerbically that all God had
spoken (that is, judgment) has come to pass, "as you yourself can see"—
והנך ראה (v. 24b), a phrase missing from the Septuagint. "An odd
remark" is what William McKane calls this moment in Jeremiah's
speech.[28] "Rude" might be more to the point.[29] Jeremiah's effusive

---

27. Ibid., 94.

28. McKane, *Jeremiah II*, 845.

29. Andrew G. Shead's treatment of this LXX minus (*The Open Book and the
Sealed Book: Jeremiah 32 in Its Hebrew and Greek Recensions* [JSOTSup 347;
Sheffield: Sheffield Academic, 2002]) is worth quoting here: "Tg provides
supporting evidence of ancient reservations about this expression. On the other hand,
Bogaert…regards the plus as an example of M's concern with the effectiveness of
the divine word…. In my judgment, the clause does not have the character of a
'natural accretion' (Streane 1896: 223), and since haplography in G is relatively rare,
Zlotowitz's appeal to it is somewhat strained (1981: 63). Though Zlotowitz is right

emphasis on God's power and omniscience in the earlier verses of the prayer ironically renders God's own authority in the present moment fragile, if not indeed risible. God's command to Jeremiah to purchase the field makes no sense. This God who has been incomparably mighty to redeem Israel throughout the nation's history has given Israel over to subjugation and death. The prophet, while technically obedient in the real-estate transaction, hurls a theological challenge with a subtle but extremely sharp point. Here, again, we should remember that this is a prophet who has accused God of betrayal using a metaphor with undertones of sexual violation (20:7). With carefully controlled fury, Jeremiah has used ostentatiously courteous rhetoric to show his cognizance of the power relations of the situation, but in this phrase in v. 24b, he finally thrusts the spear. With והנך ראה, Jeremiah in essence calls God's ways incomprehensible, and not in the awe-inspiring sense of that term. With breathtaking audacity veiled in hyper-polite circumlocutions, the prophet implies that God is impotent. Given the way in which Jeremiah has just narrated Israel's prior *Heilsgeschichte* with God, the prophet's discourse threatens to cast God himself out of the history of salvation. The deity faces the possibility of divine abjection and must respond.

The Abjection of Jeremiah: Verses 36–44

In vv. 36–44, the deity clearly has understood the insolent challenge that the prophet has pressed. God's retort renders Jeremiah, as speaking subject, unreliable for the way in which he has robustly proclaimed God's decree of punishment against his people. Jeremiah is not portrayed as having prophesied falsely—his depiction of the dire circumstances of the people constitutes the witness of a "true prophet." The narrator's careful noting of the siege context (32:2) serves to confirm this; further, the orthodox Jeremianic viewpoint in 28:8 has been clear enough on that score more generally: "The prophets who preceded you and me from ancient times prophesied war, famine, and pestilence against many countries and great kingdoms. As for the prophet who prophesies peace, when the word of that prophet comes true [*and only then; construed as an entirely unlikely scenario*], then it will be known that the Lord has truly sent the prophet." But here, Jeremiah's powerful articulation of the plight of his people is revoiced and corrected by the Lord in a way that shames the prophet. Jeremiah, commissioned by God from the womb,

---

to claim that G tolerates anthropomorphisms, this statement could be taken to imply divine ignorance, so that the theologically motivated abridgement seems the most likely cause" (140–41).

valiant in suffering alone under the burden of the prophetic vocation, one for whom God's purposes have burned like a fire in his bones, a man threatened, beaten, and imprisoned for his fidelity to the divine message: this mighty prophet must watch as God derisively puts his words in the mouths of the faithless people.

The singular prophetic speaker becomes the second plural of the stubborn, rebellious people in vv. 36 and 43. God characterizes as inadequate the perspective that Jerusalem has been given into the power of the king of Babylon by means of sword, famine, and pestilence *and* the perspective that the land is a desolation, with neither human inhabitant nor animal, given into the power of the Chaldeans. The markers of disputation are undeniably there: "*you* [plural] say"—אתם אמרים—and God's perspective clearly contradicts what has been said.[30] In this way the prophet Jeremiah, whose true prophecy has aptly named the divine wrath falling upon his people, is reduced to one whose view of the present and future is limited, inadequate, incomplete. If Jeremiah felt violated and betrayed before (20:7–18), how much more must the prophet feel humiliated by this rhetorical move of the Lord whom he serves!

Thus, submerged beneath the surface of the dialogue in 32:16–44 are trajectories that render abject the people of Judah, God, and Jeremiah. Jeremiah's redemption of the field at Anathoth offers a narrative site of forceful contestation between the prophet and his God, the drama unfolding before an implied audience—the people of Judah—that has itself been made an object of horror. These trajectories of thoroughgoing and multifarious abjection may be argued to yield a number of important implications for interpretation of the book of Jeremiah. Here are three.

First, the ancient implied audience is coerced to stand over against its own history of sin and the abjected Judean identity implicated there. That is to say, the ancient audience is divided against itself—the "version" of itself that has been rendered so despicable—and is forced to choose

---

30. See Dalit Rom-Shiloni, "The Prophecy for 'Everlasting Covenant' (Jeremiah xxxii 36–41): An Exilic Addition or a Deuteronomistic Redaction?," *VT* 53 (2003): 201–23, for the perspective that the disputation here is late in the redactional history of Jer 32 and reflects "polemics between the exiles [in Babylon] and the remnant" (205). On the blurring of speaker identity between Jeremiah and the people, which I am suggesting is an intentional rhetorical move, Rom-Shiloni offers an interesting comment on the text-critical variation here between the MT and the LXX: "…the phrases in v. 36 emerge as an anonymous citation, whereas in all the other occurrences they appear as the words of God or the prophet. Accordingly, the Septuagint presents the singular: σὺ λέγεις, referring to the prophet as the speaker" (208).

reformation. The language of Judah's abjection is all-encompassing in geopolitical and diachronic terms ("the people of Israel and the people of Judah have done nothing but evil in my sight from their youth," 32:30) and thus cannot be easily mapped onto the partisan polemics launched by the diaspora Judeans in Babylon against those Judeans who remained in the land or who fled to Egypt (see Jer 24 and 42). The sweeping promise language in Jer 32 would seem, rather, to emphasize restoration apart from those intra-Judean disputes. The history and Judean identity of the past have been rendered completely untenable, worthy of mockery, and thus unavailable to those who would rebuild Judean culture along partisan lines after the exile. The abjection of the "old" Judah invites— indeed, virtually forces—the implied audience to embrace the potentiality of the reformed Judah as a unified, God-fearing new subject.

Second, the challenge flung by the prophet Jeremiah against a (potentially) abjected deity in 32:16–25 constitutes a powerful theological resource for an ancient community that suffered devastating military predation, colonization, and diaspora. Against any facile theologizing that God had always been in control, Jer 32 presses a potent claim: the God of the ancient covenant is vulnerable in relationship. God must respond to God's shattered people or face derision, charges of impotence, and ejection from the history of salvation. If God does not act to redeem, God will be unrecognizable as God and will undergo the erasure of divine subjectivity from future installments in the narrative of redemption. Daring? Absolutely, but then, Jeremiah has always been the most courageous of the biblical prophets. His challenge invites the ancient audience to know that they may claim the covenant tradition even now— not on the basis of their own merit, to be sure, but on the basis of the power and agency of the God who called them into identity as a people in the first place.

Third, the abjection of Jeremiah himself as prophet makes visible the cost of prophetic engagement with a deity who is, finally, God and no mortal (Hos 11:9). Even Jeremiah, the paradigmatic true prophet whose word has always been entirely reliable, will be rendered false if he insists only on what he knows—doom and destruction: war, famine, and pestilence (28:8)—because God is always capable of doing a new thing. God will create שלום even where peace and flourishing might have seemed unthinkable. This is a deeply poignant rebuke to the prophet. Jeremiah has been valiant in speaking dangerous words of truth, in giving himself over to the agony of prophetic judgment burning like fire in his bones, in facing down brutal opposition from locals in Anathoth and priests and monarchs in Jerusalem. And now, in his very faithfulness to the terrible word of doom, Jeremiah risks abjection, because God will not be bound—not even by God's own word. The promise made to Judah at this desperate moment of siege (narratologically speaking, 32:2) becomes a liturgy of hope that sacrifices the prophet on the altar of God's untrammeled power to do good.

Conclusion

This essay has identified two ways for the feminist commentator to "occupy" the land of Jeremiah in a new way. First, we may hear the mysterious clause in 31:22, נקבה תסובב גבר ("the female surrounds/ encompasses/the warrior-male"), as authorizing a visionary commitment to שלום requiring the besieging of *all* citadels, including the over-compensatory towers of patriarchy and the crumbling fortresses of xenophobic militarism. Second, we may reconfigure אתם אמרים as authorizing disputation, a prophetic mode of engagement that can ironize the death-dealing discursive practices of patriarchy and invite the silenced into voice.[31] Our exploration of dynamics of abjection in Jer 32 has sought to illustrate the power of such new vision for שלום and the urgency of courageous disputation. Further, Jer 32 has shown us that all vested subjects are vulnerable in the mutuality of covenant. Community, God, and prophet must be willing to suffer their own fragility while claiming their particular truths fiercely. Vulnerability and courage are both essential for the living of authentic covenantal relationship. This is not an easy truth, but it is vital for the feminist commentator who offers critique and works for newness in communities of conviction, whether those be academic, ecclesial, political, or other.

What horizons lie before us, methodologically speaking? Feminist commentary should be adept at meta-narratological analysis and micro-analysis on a wide variety of issues. Feminist interpreters should engage in historical contextualization with a sophisticated eye to the manifold ways in which historiographical practices from ancient to modern times have distorted the vibrancy and fragility of human community by focusing

---

31. Among the feminist texts that seek to give voice to silenced female char-acters in the Bible, see Phyllis Trible, *Texts of Terror: Literary-Feminist Readings of Biblical Narratives* (Philadelphia: Fortress, 1984); Anita Diamant, *The Red Tent* (New York: Picador, 1998); Jacqueline E. Lapsley, *Whispering the Word: Hearing Women's Stories in the Old Testament* (Louisville: Westminster John Knox, 2005); Athalya Brenner, *I Am… Biblical Women Tell Their Own Stories* (Minneapolis: Fortress, 2005).

fetishistically on wars, power struggles among male political, military, and religious elites, and monumental building projects. Feminist interpreters will want to mine the insights of cultural anthropology in ways that critique and resist any politics of Othering, naming misogyny, homophobia, violence, and other forms of oppression in the practices of ritualization[32] and communal identity formation that they research with regard to the Bible. Feminists will need to engage philology and semantics, staying alert to the inevitable biases and distortions encoded in language, metaphorization, and narrativization, and seeking en route to expose interpreters' assumptions about the limitations and possibilities of signifying. Feminist genre criticism will want to take account of ways in which ancient writers deploy genres to promote, reinforce, decline, or subvert particular cultural norms that may be helpful or inimical to the feminist project. Redaction criticism will remain crucial for those interested in understanding the genetics of the book of Jeremiah and for those—including literary critics more broadly—who seek to honor polyphony and Otherness as features of textual signification.[33] Feminist interpreters will need to design and engage sophisticated modes of cultural analysis concerning the preserving and altering of textual witnesses, something crucial for the sub-fields of philology, redaction criticism, and text criticism, as well as for the study of *Fortschreibung* and inner-biblical intertextuality.

32.   Important here is the work of Catherine Bell. See her treatment of ritual oppositions and hierarchies in "The Ritual Body," in *Ritual Theory, Ritual Practice* (New York: Oxford University Press, 1992), 94–117, where Bell explores implications of the fact that ritual systems are often built on "asymmetrical relations of dominance and subordination" (102). As Bell notes in *Ritual: Perspectives and Dimensions* (New York: Oxford University Press, 1997), "ritual practices and traditions have been critical to the establishment and naturalization of cultural hierarchies based on age and gender" (89). Also relevant: Nancy Jay, *Throughout Your Generations Forever: Sacrifice, Religion, and Paternity* (Chicago: University of Chicago Press, 1992); Jonathan Klawans, *Impurity and Sin in Ancient Judaism* (Oxford: Oxford University Press, 2000), esp. 38–41; and many contributions by Howard Eilberg-Schwartz, including his "The Problem of the Body for the People of the Book," in *People of the Body: Jews and Judaism from an Embodied Perspective* (ed. H. Eilberg-Schwartz; Albany: State University of New York Press, 1992), 17–46.

33.   On this, see my "Jeremiah in the Land of Aporia: Reconfiguring Redaction Criticism as Witness to Foreignness," in *Jeremiah (Dis)placed: New Directions in Writing/Reading Jeremiah* (ed. A. R. P. Diamond and L. Stulman; LHBOTS 529; New York: T&T Clark International, 2011), 35–46.

The most excellent feminist commentaries will interweave macro-structural and social critique with local insights on each biblical text, addressing not only the representations of women and female bodies but also men and male bodies, imperialism, economic exploitation, and other dynamics of oppression and marginalization. Feminist commentary should catalyze reader engagement by promoting a vigorous politics of transformation. Feminist analysis will offer invitations and challenges that are expressly configured over against gendered and other systems of oppression, whether those be identified in the biblical text, in the history of reception, or in contemporary guild practices that authorize certain interpretive postures while implicitly silencing or ignoring others.

Feminist commentators can help to illuminate the past as theorized in Homi Bhabha's work on the hybridity of the postcolonial subject,[34] and they can work to construct the future adumbrated in Gloria Anzaldúa's prophetic vision of "the new *mestiza*," one who declines abjection and turns ambiguity into a fruitful "new thing on the earth" (Jer 31:22). Anzaldúa writes,

> The new *mestiza* copes by developing a tolerance for contradictions, a tolerance for ambiguity. She learns to be an Indian in Mexican culture, to be Mexican from an Anglo point of view. She learns to juggle cultures. She has a plural personality, she operates in a pluralistic mode—nothing is thrust out, the good, the bad and the ugly, nothing rejected, nothing abandoned. Not only does she sustain contradictions, she turns the ambivalence into something else.... *En unas pocas centurias,* the future will belong to the *mestiza.* Because the future depends on the breaking down of paradigms, it depends on the straddling of two or more cultures. By creating a new mythos—that is, a change in the way we perceive reality, the way we see ourselves and the ways we behave—*la mestiza* creates a new consciousness.[35]

Thus the work of feminist commentary must be sustained by the daily courage of communities of justice that refuse abjection for themselves and for the perceived Other, instead working creatively to change oppressive paradigms. The "acute and impassioned attentiveness" each interpreter can bring to her own research and writing on issues of power and justice will help to create a "new consciousness" in which meaning-making is not constrained by prejudice, hatred, or fear. Such a feminist

---

34. See Homi K. Bhabha, *The Location of Culture* (London: Routledge, 1994).
35. See Gloria Anzaldúa, *Borderlands/La Frontera: The New Mestiza* (3d ed.; San Francisco: Aunt Lute, 2007), 101–2.

hermeneutic will have as one of its chief goals the realization of a hermeneutically ethical world in which no interpreting subject is cast out. On that day, the rich contradictions, ambiguities, and hybridities of text and reader alike will be celebrated, and a new thing will have been wrought indeed.

THE PROPHET AND HIS PATSY: GENDER PERFORMATIVITY IN JEREMIAH*

Stuart Macwilliam

I

If the book of Jeremiah has not been the prime battleground in the gender and sexuality wars that have swirled around the biblical texts in recent decades, it has nevertheless witnessed sporadic guerrilla attacks from feminist scholars and their successors. As one of those successors (and debtors), what I should like to do in this chapter is to pursue the fate of Jeremiah's masculinity. In the language of queer theory, how does Jeremiah fare on the treadmill of performativity? And perhaps, more generally, what does it mean for a prophet to be a man in ancient Israel/Judah?

I should like to begin with the scholarly struggle that has centered round the prophet's outburst in 20:7:

> O LORD, you have enticed me
> and I was enticed;
> you have overpowered me,
> and you have prevailed.
> I have become a laughing-stock all day long;
> everyone mocks me.

The evolving discussion about this verse may be seen as a microcosm of a larger debate. The key point has been the meaning of the verb פתיתני. A glance at a Hebrew dictionary will show that פתה in the Piel has a semantic range from "persuade" via "deceive" to "seduce," but of what is the prophet accusing (if it is indeed an accusation) YHWH in this verse? The suggestion that divine deception is involved has disturbed

* I gratefully acknowledge the encouragement and help of Francesca Stavrako-poulou in the writing of this paper; it is dedicated to her and to our friend Geoff Urwin.

commentators from at least the time of Calvin; in William Holladay's words, "the language here, if this understanding is correct, raises grave theological issues."[1] But what makes this suggestion of an untrustworthy deity even stranger is the implication of sexual seduction. Since Abraham Heschel argued for that interpretation of the verb in this verse,[2] a number of scholars have taken the same line (for instance, John Bright and John Berridge).[3] It is hard to decide whether it is discomfort with the theological implications and sexual language or just "dispassionate" scholarship that led David Clines and David Gunn to dispute these contentious interpretations of פתה. They did so in robust terms, arguing that simply because the verb has sexual connotations in some instances such an interpretation could not automatically be assumed elsewhere; to do so would be "to commit the error of 'illegitimate totality transfer',"[4] a phrase taken from James Barr.[5] Their conclusion, that YHWH is being described as "attempting to persuade" Jeremiah is convincingly dismissed by Holladay,[6] who himself argued that it is justifiable to read sexual innuendo here; he cites 15:16 in support, and could well have pointed, as others have, to Hos 2:16, where the language of sexual persuasion is used, in a positive context, to describe YHWH's consolatory promise to Judah. When I first read Jack Lundbom's translation of this verse, I myself committed the error of illegitimate totality transfer: "You enticed me, Yahweh, and I was enticed. You laid hold of me, and you overcame."[7] Was it over-eagerness to prove my point or merely sex-obsession that led me immediately to assume that Lundbom saw sexual connotations in this verse? My assumption was quickly disproved by Lundbom's later comment that "the verbs...have nothing to do with seduction and rape" and his conclusion that what YHWH did "was to act

1.   William L. Holladay, *Jeremiah 1: A Commentary on the Book of the Prophet Jeremiah, Chapters 1–25* (Hermeneia; Philadelphia: Fortress, 1986), 552.

2.   Abraham Heschel, *The Prophets* (New York: Harper & Row, 1962; repr. 2001), 113–14.

3.   John Bright, *Jeremiah: Introduction, Translation and Notes* (AB 21; Garden City: Doubleday, 1965), 132; John Berridge, *Prophet, People and the Word of Yahweh* (Zurich: EVZ, 1970), 151–55.

4.   David J. A. Clines and David M. Gunn, "'You Tried to Persuade Me' and 'Violence! Outrage!' in Jeremiah XX 7–8," *VT* 28 (1978): 20–27 (21).

5.   James Barr, *The Semantics of Biblical Language* (London: Oxford University Press, 1961), 218.

6.   Holladay, *Jeremiah 1*, 552–53.

7.   Jack R. Lundbom, *Jeremiah 1–20: A New Translation with Introduction and Commentary* (AB 21A; New York: Doubleday), 851.

in a heavy-handed manner with the young Jeremiah."[8] Yet, although the verb "entice" does not necessarily carry sexual connotations,[9] there nevertheless remains that suspicion about it in Lundbom's translation (what *was* YHWH's heavy hand doing, exactly?), in a way that parallels the original Hebrew verbs.

But it is perhaps at this stage in the debate that we should pinpoint a change in the terms of engagement. So far, even those scholars who accepted the possibility of a sexual interpretation of פתה in 20:7 seem to have shied away from contemplating its implications. So, Robert Carroll typifies this avoidance; he concedes that sexual imagery may be present, but finds it "grotesque."[10] It is feminist scholars, of course, who have spearheaded a revolution that has challenged a millennium and more of self-assured masculine assumptions about gender roles in the Hebrew Bible. Their assault upon Jeremiah has tended to focus on the "marriage metaphor,"[11] but 20:7 has not escaped their attention. Angela Bauer emphasizes the implication of physical force in not only the verb פתה, but also its parallel verb חזק, and in doing so moves the terms of the story from seduction to rape.[12] This ploy may be seen as a wider challenge to the moral authority of the biblical text in its treatment of gender relations.

Bauer's observations are interesting to a queer theorist. They may be characterized as qualified essentialism: Jeremiah is a male, he remains a male, and it is as a "female impersonator" that he protests against "sexual violation by the deity."[13] He is, one must surmise, only pretending to be a woman. Yet even this assumption of a female persona casts some doubt upon his status as a man. His pretence is rather too convincing. My own brief comments on this verse in a previous publication take a different

---

8. Ibid., 855.

9. The Oxford English Dictionary defines the verb "entice" as "[t]o allure, attract by the offer of pleasure or advantage; *esp.* to allure insidiously or adroitly," n.p. [cited 8 November 2012]. Online: http://www.oed.com.

10. Robert P. Carroll, *Jeremiah: A Commentary* (OTL; London: SCM, 1986), 398–99.

11. "Marriage metaphor" is used here as a conceptual shorthand for the sexual imagery used in the description of the relationship between YHWH and Judah/Israel in Jer 2–3, Hos 1–3, and Ezek 16 and 23.

12. To be sure, some element of forceful seduction is hinted at by Berridge (*Prophet, People,* 151–55) and others, but they do not argue the case with Bauer's zest, nor explore the implications.

13. Angela Bauer, *Gender in the Book of Jeremiah: A Feminist-Literary Reading* (New York: Lang, 1999), 116.

line: I have suggested that "we may have here an example of a semi- or faux-reluctant desire on the part of one man to be sexually overwhelmed by a stronger man."[14] But in its own way this interpretation of Jeremiah as a gay bottom[15] is every bit as essentialist as Bauer's female impersonator, and if I were to set out to review my opinion, I might take a more nuanced approach. Whatever the case, those interpretations of 20:7 that invoke some sexual nuance have in common a view of Jeremiah's masculinity as compromised—in the language of queer theory a "necessary failure," a breakdown in the regulatory system of gender performativity.[16]

I feel that I must linger a little longer on this picture of gender breakdown. The notion that YHWH could *deceive* Jeremiah is startling enough,[17] but that it is YHWH who is pictured as the underminer of Jeremiah's masculinity, the key determinant of his identity, is even more powerful. YHWH, the engineer of this necessary failure, is here very far from being the creator of the "natural" gender order offered to us in Gen 2 and 3. Moreover, Jer 20:7 is not the only possible contributor to the notion that the relationship between YHWH and the prophet has sexual overtones. It has already been mentioned that Holladay sees marriage imagery in Jer 15:16.[18]

> Your words were found, and I ate them,
> and your words became to me a joy and the delight of my heart;
> for I am called by your name,
> O LORD God of hosts.

14. Stuart Macwilliam, *Queer Theory and the Prophetic Marriage Metaphor in the Hebrew Bible* (BibleWorld; Sheffield: Equinox, 2011), 38.

15. An explanation may be helpful to those not familiar with this term, one that I have always found amusingly ambiguous: a bottom is someone who takes the so-called passive role in same-sex intercourse.

16. For an explanation of these terms, see Macwilliam, *Queer Theory*, 18–22. "Failure" and "success" in gender performativity are measured in terms of the maintenance of heteronormativity. I should, I suppose, put such terms in quotation marks, since a breakdown of heteronormativity, a "failure," may be welcomed by many.

17. It is interesting how divided the English versions are on the translation of פתה in 20:7. Most opt for "deceive" (e.g. NIV, GNT) or such synonyms as "misled" (NLT) or "tricked" (CEV); one or two prefer theological caution à la Clines and Gunn, such as "you persuaded me" (ASV) or "you pushed me into this" (TM); I found three that allowed a possibly sexual flavor: "seduced" (NJB) and "enticed" (NRSV and NJPS).

18. Holladay, *Jeremiah 1*, 552–53.

His comment focuses on the paired words שָׂשׂוֹן and שִׂמְחָה, "joy" and "delight." He argues that they are associated with wedding imagery at Jer 7:34 and 16:9; he does not spell out the implications, which seem to be that interaction between the prophet and YHWH was in some way a joyful marriage.[19] It has to be conceded that the echoes of nuptial language here may seem fainter than the sexual imagery of Jer 20:7. The association of the paired words שָׂשׂוֹן and שִׂמְחָה with marriage is not found outside Jeremiah,[20] but Holladay could have cited a third place where the association does occur in Jeremiah (35:11). Furthermore, the image of Jeremiah bearing the name of YHWH in Jer 15:16 makes Holladay's case a little stronger (he argues that this is what wives did in ancient Israel/Judah and cites Isa 4:1), but what is even more striking is the contrast that links 15:16 and 20:7–8: the words of YHWH are a delight and joy to Jeremiah in the earlier verse, but have become a disgrace to him in 20:8. This transition from a joyful wedding to a failed marriage that Holladay presents has not been taken up by subsequent commentators, as far as I have discovered. Even Bauer does not mention Jer 15:16—perhaps the implication of a joyful wedding may not at first sight bolster the case for subsequent violence, but it could equally be argued that the two texts taken together paint a convincing scenario of early bliss leading on to disillusionment.

Sandwiched between these two pictures of a marriage is what could be cited as further damage to Jeremiah's masculinity on the part of YHWH. In Jer 16:2, Jeremiah is forbidden to take a wife or have children. Now, a traditionalist view would point to the following verses to make clear that this veto is a measure of the desperate straits in which the people of Judah find themselves. But a more radical view would emphasize that such a veto goes against all societal norms that contribute to the definition of manhood. In other words, Jeremiah is unmanned here by YHWH just as he is in ch. 20. It is interesting that these three passages display between them an increasing disillusionment on the part of Jeremiah about YHWH's dealings with him: the first celebrates their relationship, the second announces an enforced celibacy, and the third makes accusations of rape. We shall see a parallel crescendo in Baruch's relationship with Jeremiah.

19. This is an idea previously put forward by Heschel, *Prophets*, 136–37.

20. The pairing of שָׂשׂוֹן and שִׂמְחָה occurs in, for example, Ps 51:8 (EV 10) and in three places in Isaiah (35:10; 51:3, 11) without any overtones of marriage.

II

I have argued elsewhere that in the book of Jeremiah, as in the books of Hosea and Ezekiel, the men of Israel/Judah are unmanned through the operation of the marriage metaphor.[21] They are the collective wife of YHWH who, treacherously unfaithful to him, is eventually promised ultimate forgiveness. Against this background of unsuccessful performativity, is it possible to trace patterns and consequences of this failure in Jeremiah's own career? This is a challenge, given the uncertain and at times chaotic structure of the text overall and the difficulty of establishing any biographical information about the prophet himself. And after all, how should we picture a prophet in ancient Israel/Judah performing masculinity successfully? It is important to stress at this stage that queer theory need not confine its operations to questions of sexual desire or behavior. Simply because a slippage in Jeremiah's masculinity has expressed itself in terms of same-sex behavior, an answer to the question of successful performativity of masculinity need not lie only in the evidence of hearty heterosexuality. Masculinity, along with femininity, has to be patrolled, has to retain the *appearance* of spontaneous naturalness; the boundaries have to be clear, and clues to this clarity lie in behaviors that are not primarily sexual.[22] Ken Stone amply demonstrated long ago that gender performativity can be assessed outside the bedroom.[23]

One candidate for the title of Top He-Man of the Hebrew Prophets might be Elijah. If reliability is one criterion of masculinity,[24] then Elijah certainly chalks up a high score on his very first appearance in the Hebrew Bible, when he successfully predicts a country-wide drought (1 Kgs 17:1, 7). We hear nothing of his domestic circumstances, but instead we are treated to a picture of him as a considerate and heroic

21. Macwilliam, *Queer Theory*, 84–96; see also A. R. Pete Diamond and Kathleen M. O'Connor, "Unfaithful Passions: Coding Women Coding Men in Jeremiah 2–3 (4:2)," *BibInt* 4 (1996): 288–310.

22. For more on naturalness and boundary patrol, see Macwilliam, *Queer Theory*, 9–26.

23. Ken Stone, "Lovers and Raisin Cakes: Food, Sex and Divine Insecurity in Hosea," in *Queer Commentary and the Hebrew Bible* (ed. K. Stone; London: Sheffield Academic, 2001), 116–39. Stone explores codes of masculine honor in terms of a man's ability to provide adequate supplies of food for his family.

24. By this, I mean that in biblical times, at least, a man was expected to be a steadfast provider of, among other things, security for his family circle (cf. previous note).

guest, who saves the life of his hostess's son (1 Kgs 17:10–24), and earns her affirmation of his *bona fide* prophetic status.[25] To this virtue we may add resolute courage displayed in standing up to a king (1 Kgs 18:6–18) and in issuing him a bold challenge; this is not his first confrontation with Ahab (1 Kgs 17:1) nor his last (1 Kgs 21:20–24). But for his most manly act the achievements on Mount Carmel (1 Kgs 18:20–40) must win the gold medal: he is in control throughout, one man against 850; he derides their incompetence, insists on making his own task as difficult as possible; with apparent insouciance brings about an immediate and dramatic result; then ruthlessly slaughters his opponents. And is anyone really surprised at his final whirlwind-driven ascent into heaven (2 Kgs 2:11)? True, this partial account has neglected to mention his panic-stricken flight from Jezebel (from a woman!),[26] not to mention YHWH's less-than-patient reaction to his prophet's fretful complaints (1 Kgs 2:3–18). Yet these seem relatively minor blemishes on the prophet's manly brow. Overall, he performs his masculinity very well indeed.

III

How does Elijah's performance compare to Jeremiah's? It is clear that Jeremiah certainly fulfils one or two of the criteria so masterfully ticked off by Elijah. Occasional courage, for instance, is not lacking: among other passages, one could point to his open defiance of Pashhur (Jer 20:1–7), or his bold proclamation to "all the people of Judah and to all the inhabitants of Jerusalem" (Jer 25:2–14). And it could be argued that even as late as ch. 37, during the crisis of Jerusalem's fall, Jeremiah emulates Elijah's defiance of Ahab in his confrontation with Zedekiah, though with a distinctly less favorable outcome. But to highlight a different side to Jeremiah's masculinity, I should like to explore his

25. In a telling reversal of the usual duties of care that host bears towards guest, Elijah explicitly mentions his own status as a guest when he prays for the child's recovery (1 Kgs 17:20); he may be a guest, but as a man he owes a duty of care towards a woman and child in whose house he is staying.

26. That such a man as Elijah could show fear was evidently too much for the Masoretes who pointed the verb וירא so as to mean "and he saw" rather than "and he feared" (the more reliable reading is reflected in the LXX, the Vulgate, and some Hebrew manuscripts). Perhaps, after all, this reluctance was unnecessary, since it could be argued that Elijah's reaction to Jezebel illustrates not so much his lack of manliness as Jezebel's monstrous failure in *her* performativity as a woman; indeed Ahab's poor showing as a man also serves to emphasize her unnaturalness.

relationship with Baruch. This is not an easy undertaking. Baruch makes an appearance in only four passages in the book, and at some length only in one (ch. 36; the other passages are 32:4–25; 43:1–7, and ch. 45); apart from ch. 36, Carroll remarks, he "is a very shadowy figure in the book."[27] And in a sense he has become an even more obscure figure because of the weight that both ancient tradition and modern Western scholarship have placed on his insubstantial shoulders. He plays a major role in apocryphal and pseudepigraphical literature, and enormous energy has been expended on assessing his supposed contribution to the formation of the book of Jeremiah itself. Of his historical place, if any, in the fraught politics of his time and in the professional and religious institutions of Judah we have some tantalizing glimpses, enlivened by the debate on his supposed bulla that was discovered in the 1980s.[28] But historical considerations aside, can the texts show us anything about masculinity, worked out in the relationship between Jeremiah and Baruch, or rather— since this will be a key element of the discussion—between YHWH, Jeremiah, and Baruch? If the discussion is confined to what is in the text, one obvious preliminary consideration is the state of that text. The arrangement of the book of Jeremiah in general is perplexing, and no less so when one looks at the four Baruch passages. Why is Baruch's first appearance in ch. 32 dated in the tenth year of Zedekiah (32:1), whereas the second is dated several years earlier in the fourth year of Jehoiachim? Chronologically the third episode (43:1–7) is less puzzling: it occurs just after the fall of Jerusalem, but the fourth (ch. 45) is wildly out of place chronologically: it is dated the fourth year of Jehoiachim, that is, the same as the second episode, the earliest of the four. Of course, the explanation for this apparent jumble may be simple accident: this is how the scraps of text emerged from the scribal pouch or memory.[29] But as far as the Baruch texts are concerned, what emerges from the arrangement as preserved for us, whether an accident or not, is a gradual crescendo of surprise and complexity that would have been denied us in a more strictly linear narrative.[30] And as a further comment on the arrangement of the

27. Robert P. Carroll, *Jeremiah* (Sheffield: Sheffield Academic, 1989), 37.

28. For a short discussion and bibliography of the bulla, see William L. Holladay, *Jeremiah 2: A Commentary on the Book of the Prophet Jeremiah, Chapters 26–52* (Hermeneia; Philadelphia: Fortress, 1989), 215–16.

29. See further Karel van der Toorn, *Scribal Culture and the Making of the Hebrew Bible* (Cambridge, Mass.: Harvard University Press, 2007).

30. Such a literary development has already been noted in the three marriage-to-rape narratives, discussed earlier.

texts, it is worth observing the place of these four episodes in the overall structure of the book. The most significant point is that the appearance of Baruch comes after the three passages that allude to Jeremiah's unmanning by YHWH discussed earlier, and I shall argue that this sequence produces a particular narrative effect. A further significant point about the place of the Baruch passages is that they follow on from passages in which Jeremiah is depicted as being in considerable danger (chs. 20–26, culminating in his rescue by Ahikam from death threats; cf. 26:24). What emerges is a sequence Abused lover → Danger → Baruch. The significance of this sequence may become clear after some discussion of the four Baruch episodes.

Chapter 32:6–25

On the face of it, the first Baruch episode marks merely the appearance of the man and very little more, unless one counts the mention of Baruch's grandfather, as well as of his father, as significant.[31] More significant are the contents of vv. 13–16. The process of carrying out the symbolic act of buying land in Anathoth involves the use of Baruch as some sort of agent for Jeremiah. At this stage, I make two observations: first, that Baruch seems to have accepted the commission without demur (that seems to be the implication of v. 16); secondly, Jeremiah's commission to Baruch is introduced by a prophetic formula (v. 14), and he charges Baruch using the verb צוה. This verb is a favorite in the book of Jeremiah,[32] and is most often used with YHWH (occasionally, Elohim) as subject (in Jeremiah this is the case in 24 of the 39 occurrences). Elsewhere in Jeremiah, it is used of kings five times and of Jonadab six times. Jeremiah uses the verb twice more in addressing Baruch (36:5 and 8). This is a high tone for Jeremiah to take. Either it is a measure of a marked superiority in his status *vis-à-vis* his addressee, or he is, in effect, speaking as YHWH. This is a point to which I shall return, but it is worth adding at this point that the last occurrence of צוה in the book is at 51:59, where the prophet addresses Baruch's brother Seraiah, and that episode too is something that will be revisited presently.

---

31. Baruch's genealogy may not strike the modern reader as particularly significant, although Holladay (*Jeremiah 2*, 215–16) uses the mention of Baruch's grandfather as one indicator of his grandson's high status.

32. According to Félix García López ("צוה," *TDOT* 12:277) "more than half of all occurrences in the prophetic books are concentrated in the book of Jeremiah."

Chapter 36

We thus come to ch. 36, which features Baruch's most substantial appearance in the book of Jeremiah, with the beginnings of a pattern emerging in the relationship between the two men, or rather between the two men and YHWH. Commentators have long reflected on the historical implications of this chapter, particularly with regard to the composition of the book as a whole, and Baruch's own role in that.[33] Others have seen editorial embroideries evidenced by parallels with ch. 26 and with 2 Kgs 22. Carroll indeed rejects historicity altogether in a story "created to legitimate the role of the scribe in the creation and transmission of the Jeremiah tradition."[34] He may also be right to argue that the focus of the chapter is the "brilliant story of conflict between the prophet and the king,"[35] and elsewhere maintains that "to focus on Baruch in 36 is to miss the point of the story."[36] But by ignoring authorial intentions (at least as Carroll sees them) and by exploring some byways in this complicated narrative, without regard to the historical debate, we may be able to uncover another story from the nods and winks of the text.

Baruch's role *vis-à-vis* Jeremiah may be a good place to begin. Carroll wryly comments that "Baruch...has been regarded on the strength of these few references to have been Jeremiah's companion, secretary, confidant, and amanuensis,"[37] but in ch. 36, Baruch performs two clear functions: scribe (vv. 2–4, 27, 32) and public reader (vv. 5–17). The word scribe presents an immediate difficulty: it covers the secretarial function described in ch. 36, whereby he writes at Jeremiah's dictation; but it may also suggest membership of a particular professional group, whose functions varied from village letter writer to senior administrative official. Baruch is described in v. 32 as ספר, a term which seems both to describe what he has been doing on Jeremiah's behalf and also to link him in some way with the officials in vv. 11–13, although it is worth pointing out that this is the only instance in the biblical texts in which he is so designated, and that the equivalent Greek word (γραμματεύς) is missing in the LXX (= 43:32). Nobody knows whether the suggestion that Baruch was a professional scribe reflects historical reality, editorial

33. For one such discussion based on the date of ch. 36, see Holladay, *Jeremiah 2*, 16–21; for a brief bibliography, see ibid., 250.

34. Robert P. Carroll, *From Chaos to Covenant: Uses of Prophecy in the Book of Jeremiah* (London: SCM, 1981), 15.

35. Ibid., 152.

36. Carroll, *Jeremiah: A Commentary*, 666.

37. Carroll, *Jeremiah*, 36.

invention, or interpretative fantasy, but what is more pertinent is to ask why Jeremiah needs or uses a scribe.[38] Elsewhere he is reported as perfectly capable of doing his own writing (29:1; 30:2; 51:60), so his use of a scribe here, in Carroll's words, is "unusual and necessitates interpretation."[39] Carroll's own tentative answer is Deuteronomistic self-promotion, but perhaps one can find here a further step to discerning the pattern of the relationship between YHWH, Jeremiah, and Baruch. It is portentous, if not pretentious, of Jeremiah to summon (קרא) Baruch to take dictation; it recalls YHWH's dictation of the words of the covenant to Moses (Exod 34:27–28),[40] and it looks even more as though there is some identity confusion here. Jeremiah's dealings with Baruch seem to mirror those between YHWH and Jeremiah. This impression of confusion continues in the account of Baruch's public reading (vv. 5–32). The passage begins with Jeremiah's instruction to Baruch to go and read the scroll within the temple. But "instruction" hardly captures the tone of the verb, which is another occurrence of צוה, the lordly word we met in ch. 32. And whose words is Baruch to read? In v. 6 they are דברי יהוה, as they are in v. 8, which refers back to the instruction (and again uses the verb צוה), but when it comes to the actual reading, what Baruch reads are דברי ירמיהו. By v. 11 they have become once more דברי יהוה. Holladay remarks that "there is no obvious implication of these shifts."[41] Leslie Allen comments on v. 10 that "Yahweh's messages…are now called 'Jeremiah's messages' inasmuch as Jeremiah received them (vv. 2, 4),"[42] yet if this explains anything at all, it certainly does not shed light upon the reversion to דברי יהוה in the next verse. All that we can say is that from Baruch's point of view—for the shift occurs during his reading of the words—there seems to be a confusion between YHWH and Jeremiah. What does this odd confusion amount to? While I read and re-read these verses I was continually reminded of a certain management practice observable in some U.K. public institutions in recent years: a

---

38. On the question of oral and written prophecy, see Philip R. Davies, "Pen of Iron, Point of Diamond," in *Writings and Speech in Israelite and Ancient Near Eastern Prophecy* (ed. E. Ben Zvi and M. H. Floyd; Atlanta: Society of Biblical Literature, 2000), 65–81.

39. Carroll, *Jeremiah*, 37.

40. Of course, this was the second edition of the commandments; the first (31:18; 32:15–16) was written by God himself, as was the version in Deut 5 (see v. 22).

41. Holladay, *Jeremiah 2*, 256.

42. Leslie C. Allen, *Jeremiah: A Commentary* (Louisville: Westminster John Knox, 2008), 397.

fairly remote top executive manages his[43] senior staff by intimidating instructions; the response of the senior staff is to mirror the top man's actions and pass the instructions down the line to a hapless junior. And as we carry on reading ch. 36, along with the remaining two episodes in which Baruch plays a part, there are some unpleasant accompanying circumstances and consequences that bear out what seemed at first a rather fanciful association. The first rule of this management practice is that you do not take a risk; you must pass it down to the one next in line below you. Jeremiah has already in the past paid the price of risky endeavors,[44] but now delegates the risk to Baruch. That it is a substantial risk can be gauged by the public nature of the reading that Baruch is made to undertake: he is told to read "on a fast day in the hearing of the people in the LORD's house…also in the hearing of all the people of Judah who come up from their towns" (36:6); this universality is repeated in the description of the fast at which Baruch carries out the instruction (36:9), and again in v. 10 ("all the people"). It is dramatically confirmed by the effect: the climactic nature of the three readings (vv. 10, 15, and 21), the fearful reaction of the שׂרים (v. 16), the advice to Baruch and Jeremiah to go into hiding (v. 19), and the king's instruction to have them arrested (v. 32). In view of this grave risk, what are we to make of Jeremiah's instruction to Baruch? In v. 5 he tells Baruch that he is עצור and thus unable to come to the temple himself. The force of the word here is unclear: William McKane remarks that "the sense of v. 5 has been widely discussed, but an assured conclusion is difficult to reach."[45] "In hiding" (NJPS), "restricted" (Holladay), "excluded" (McKane), or "prevented" (NRSV) are not as strong translations as the LXX's φυλάσσο-μαι; and yet a translation such as "under guard" or "imprisoned," which is what the Greek implies, is at odds with v. 19: as Allen puts it, "he [i.e. Jeremiah] was free enough to hide."[46] Now commentators may speculate all they like in order to account for עצור. Indeed one may sympathize with those who abandon the integrity of the narrative and conclude that this is an editorial device created either to provide "the motive for

---

43. Gender specificity here is very slowly becoming less applicable, at least in the institutions I have observed, although the management practices remain the same.

44. For instance, Pashhur's punishment of him for prophesying in the temple (20:1–4); his narrow escape from death after another temple appearance (ch. 26).

45. William McKane, *A Critical and Exegetical Commentary on Jeremiah, Volume 2: XXVI–LII* (ICC; Edinburgh: T. & T. Clark, 1996), 901.

46. Allen, *Jeremiah*, 397.

writing the prophecies down,"[47] or to give Baruch a role.[48] But if we trust the narrative and take it on its own terms, we can ask, "Why is Jeremiah עצור?" And the answer is that no reason is given, because there is no reason—Jeremiah is simply making an excuse: it is part and parcel of the procedure of risk delegation. He sends Baruch off to take his risk for him.[49] Chapter 36, then, continues the confusion between YHWH and Jeremiah and Jeremiah and Baruch that made its first appearance in ch. 32, and from this confusion a chain of imposition emerges: YHWH unmans Jeremiah; in response Jeremiah arranges for Baruch to be scape-goated, as it were, on his behalf. Consequences are explored in chs. 43 and 45.

Chapter 43:1–7

The setting for this brief reappearance of Baruch is the aftermath of the destruction of Jerusalem. In the confusion and slaughter, a group of survivors asks Jeremiah's advice. He tries to persuade them to stay in Judah and not to go to Egypt. His advice is angrily rejected and during the argument Jeremiah is accused of lying (שקר), and Baruch of inciting Jeremiah against the survivors (מסית). We last hear of Baruch as being taken to Egypt with Jeremiah and the rest of the survivors (v. 9). The significance of Baruch's reappearance in ch. 43 has aroused scholarly interest. Some see it as "a source beginning to develop the figure of Baruch in his own right,"[50] and this is somehow linked to the tradition that he was the editor of chs. 37–44. McKane reports an innuendo, favored by some older scholars, that Jeremiah, "in his old age, was losing his grip and that Baruch was exercising undue influence on him."[51] Others try to situate him in the pro-Chaldean vs. pro-Egyptian political camps in Judah.[52] In a skilful navigation through the choppy waters of

47. Holladay, *Jeremiah 2*, 255.
48. Carroll, *Jeremiah: A Commentary*, 665.
49. To return briefly to the analogy of management practices, the reason often given by senior staff for delegating difficult work that they themselves should be expected to do is that they themselves are excluded from such work by the burden of strategic thinking.
50. Carroll, *Chaos*, 239; cf. Holladay, *Jeremiah 2*, 300.
51. McKane, *Jeremiah, Volume 2*, 1052.
52. Holladay and Carroll could be cited as recent opposite poles in the historicity debate; for a useful summary see Walter Brueggemann, "The 'Baruch Connection': Reflections on Jer 43:1–7," *JBL* 113 (1994): 405–20 (405, 407–8). For a defender of the maximalist position, though not specifically concerned with Jer 43, see J. Andrew Dearman, "My Servants the Scribes: Composition and Context in Jeremiah 36," *JBL* 109 (1990): 403–21.

the fiction/historicity debate, Walter Brueggemann situates Baruch as a
representative figure (whether fictional or historical) in the canonical
process.[53] But the one clear fact that emerges from the narrative itself
is that Azariah and his friends, in Allen's words, "finger Baruch as the
'eminence grise' responsible for Jeremiah's negative message.... The
community projects the content of its own underlying fear in 41:18 and
42:10 onto Baruch in self-justification and derogatory blame."[54] Blame is
the key point here, and although it is voiced by Azariah and the others, as
far as the text is concerned it has been engineered by Jeremiah. Risk
delegation is blame deflection. In the one word מסית it is made clear in
ch. 43 that Baruch has become, in that telling U.S. expression, Jeremiah's
patsy.

Chapter 45

And how does Baruch react to this? On the face of it, ch. 36 gives the
impression that there was no demur on his part. In v. 8 it is related that
he acted "in accordance with all that Jeremiah commanded him." But
perhaps in the next verse there is some hint of a different tale. The dating
formula of v. 9 informs us that Baruch's public reading took place a year
after Jeremiah's command.[55] No reason is given for the delay; perhaps
we are to suppose that Baruch was waiting for the next suitable public
occasion on which to carry out Jeremiah's order. But perhaps the narrative is suggesting some reluctance on Baruch's part. Certainly less than
total compliance is confirmed by the brief contents of ch. 45, the events
in which are related as being contemporary with those of ch. 36. If the
chapter is chronologically odd,[56] as narrative it makes dramatic sense,
since at last we are presented with a complete picture of the testosterone-
induced angst of the YHWH–Jeremiah–Baruch entanglement, and a more
rounded picture of Baruch, the man at the bottom of the hierarchy. In v. 3
we hear of Baruch's grief, compounded by YHWH himself: "You said,
'Woe is me! The LORD has added sorrow to my pain....'" The lament is
a familiar form in the Hebrew Bible, but Baruch's version particularly
recalls those of Jeremiah himself earlier in the book, and indeed it is not

53. Brueggemann, *Baruch*.

54. Allen, *Jeremiah*, 438.

55. The gap is even longer according to the LXX, which has ἐν τῷ ἔτει τῷ ὀγδόῳ
for the Masoretic בשנה החמשית.

56. The apparent anomaly between the chronology of ch. 45 and its overall place
in the book of Jeremiah has persuaded some commentators to reject v. 1 as a
Deuteronomistic addition; for the details, see Holladay, *Jeremiah 2*, 308.

surprising that one or two commentators have suggested that the chapter originally followed 20:18 and point to the references to יגון in v. 3 and 20:18.[57] But this identity with Jeremiah and with Jeremiah's complaints against YHWH is emphasized by the terms in which the lament is delivered. It is not uncommon, for instance, for grammatical subjects in Hebrew to change without notice to the reader, and this is very much the case here: the "you" in v. 3 refers to Baruch, in v. 4 to Jeremiah and in v. 5 back to Baruch. The effect in these verses is to confuse the identities of the two men. Moreover, Baruch's lament is not expressed at first hand; instead, it is reported back to him by YHWH speaking through Jeremiah. This confusion makes us wonder to whom Baruch addressed his lament in the first place. To YHWH? To Jeremiah? The picture here is of a Baruch who obeyed but did not do so with any enthusiasm. His complaint is thrown back at him by Jeremiah, speaking on behalf of YHWH (or is it Jeremiah using YHWH as an excuse, a common management technique?). And finally, there are those minatory verses, 4–5. Baruch has had the temerity to seek for גדלות. There is no information about the focus of his hopes. Perhaps we are expected to interpret them as hubristic personal ambition from the viewpoint of YHWH/Jeremiah, in which case Baruch is being told that he is lucky to escape with his life; or else that the ambition, though unrealizable, is sufficiently meritorious to earn him his bare escape from death. However we view the גדלות, Baruch recedes from our sight, his complaints brushed aside and his hopes quashed.

IV

Baruch is to Jeremiah as Jeremiah is to YHWH. Indeed, as I have argued, in some places in these episodes it is difficult to tell one from the other. Jeremiah is unable to carry on the process of performing his own masculinity effectively since he has been unmanned by a man higher in the hierarchy. And in some sort of compensatory procedure he retaliates vicariously by unmanning the feebly protesting Baruch. But it does not end there. Performing gender is a constant effort. Judith Butler famously argued that gender is "a set of repeated acts within a highly rigid regulatory frame."[58] Her dictum may come to mind when by the end of the book of Jeremiah the prophet's struggle to perform *his* masculinity seems

---

57. For a brief discussion of this point, see ibid., 309.
58. Judith Butler, *Gender Trouble: Feminism and the Subversion of Identity* (2d ed.; London: Routledge, 1999), 43.

to have no end. In his very last reported appearance (51:59–64), we catch sight of him with Seraiah, Baruch's brother, just before Seraiah sets off as part of an embassy to Babylon. Jeremiah is instructing (that word צוה again!) him to read in the Babylonians' own heartland a prophecy that predicts their utter destruction. Jeremiah himself is staying behind; of course (is he עצור perhaps?). What a man!

"Exoticizing the Otter":
The Curious Case of the Rechabites in Jeremiah 35

Steed Vernyl Davidson

The episode "Food Fight" of the webcomic *Cat and Girl* pokes fun at the term "exoticizing the other."[1] The comic features a conversation between the girl and the cat on the economics of the new food morality in the developed world. While the girl expresses her objections to the hubris associated with changes in food culture, the cat makes tangential comments. As the cat observes that his "professors had such bad handwriting," he realizes that for the past decade he was "exoticizing the otter." The phrase "exoticizing the otter" may well be the result of bad handwriting, but equally could result from mishearing, misconceiving, or even misappropriating an intellectual catch phrase. The cat's declaration sits in the middle of the comic and draws no response from the girl. Yet, the phrase's central place gives it the kind of visibility that in the norms of popular culture results in the production of T-shirts and other memorabilia. Clearly, "exoticizing the otter" has nothing to do with aquatic mammals and everything to do with humans marginalized by dominant cultures that ironically benefit even when the spotlight is shone on the marginalized.

The crucial concepts of exoticism and otherness in the phrase point to their frequency in much recent academic discourse. Obviously, the cat's realization of his confused academic jargon stands as a ridicule of "word dropping" to prove one's intellectual prowess. That exoticism and otherness gets reduced to the obscurity of otters suggests a number of things about academic discourse, but the more troubling aspect of the phrase lies in the ease with which otherness or difference may easily be obscured by otters. Twenty-first-century cultural norms reflect familiarity with the practice of exoticization as deployed in colonial discourse.[2] The

1. Online: http://catandgirl.com/?p=2377. N.p. Cited 17 August 2012.
2. For example, pop singer Rihanna adopts a "tribal" look in her video "Where Have You Been?" and takes on the guise of a geisha in "Princess of China." See the

confusion of otherness with otters exposes the success of exoticization that intends not meaningful relationships or knowledge but rather the masking of the full identity of the subject of study.

Exoticization proves ambiguous in postcolonial studies. On the one hand, postcolonialism identifies the deployment of the trope of the exotic in colonial discourse as a mechanism of control and domestication.[3] Exoticization of the best kind is seen as patronizing. Yet the articulation of postcoloniality performs some of the functions of exoticization, except with different actors. If the exotic appears as different, strange, or odd particularly viewed from Western eyes, then the postcolonial willingly offers up its difference for a Western readership's gaze. Graham Huggan warns that postcoloniality easily becomes the academic exotic captured by the commodifying tendencies of late capitalism.[4] He, instead, advocates a "strategic exoticism" that subverts the "exoticist codes of representation" as the means of revealing a different set of power relations.[5] The absurdist phrase, "exoticizing the otter," takes us in the direction of that "strategic exoticism" that promises a focus on the representation of a particular subject, in the case of the comic a marginalized other, but instead reveals something else, the otter.

This essay engages in an act of "strategic exoticism" through its exploration of the representation of the Rechabites in Jer 35. The otherwise unknown group appears to be a fiction of the book of Jeremiah[6] deployed for the purpose of shaming the Judeans. The rhetoric of the chapter mirrors several of the exoticist codes of representation common to modern European colonial discourse. The success of this representation appears in the subsequent appropriation of the Rechabites in later

---

blog "Pop Culture and the Third World" and its treatment of the rise of orientalism in music videos from Rihanna, Gwen Stefani, and Nicki Minaj. N.p. Cited 28 August 2012. Online: http://popthirdworld.tumblr.com/post /16524881655/asian-culture-and-the-pop-music-world.

3. Graham Huggan, *The Postcolonial Exotic: Marketing the Margins* (London: Routledge, 2001), 14.

4. Ibid., 23.

5. Ibid., 32.

6. Carroll's conclusions that ch. 35 "should be treated as a fabricated story rather than a historical account" holds merit; see Robert P. Carroll, *Jeremiah II* (Sheffield: Sheffield Phoenix, 2006), 656. Knights's position that "the singular, unique—even bizarre—nature of the events" proves their historicity remains unconvincing since much in the book of Jeremiah can be so described; see Chris H. Knights, "The Structure of Jeremiah 35," *ExpTim* 106 (1995): 142–44 (144).

traditions as a proto-ascetic group that defines the renunciation of urban and civilized life. This characterization of the Rechabites persists in the history of interpretation and influences the scholarship relating to the history of the group as well as the interpretation of this chapter. Consequently, an exotic genealogy, of sorts, in relation to the Rechabites exists that presents an easy target for a postcolonial project. Narrating the construction of the genealogy of the postcolonial exotic, the Rechabites, obviously serves as the primary focus of this essay. While this narration forms the early portion of this essay, the essay subverts the exoticist codes by presenting the Rechabites in an alternative power relationship.

The Representation of the Exotic

Colonial expansions brought Europeans in contact with non-Western peoples and cultures. Through mostly travelogues and venues such as zoos, the exotic non-Western appeared, constructed from the vantage point of the European gaze. By deploying devices such as essentializing, stereotyping, infantilization, eroticization, debasement, idealization, and self-affirmation,[7] non-Western cultures and people are not only produced for European consumption but, as Dibyesh Anand puts it, "render[ed]... disciplined."[8] This disciplined representation while it appears to provide knowledge of peoples and cultures ironically presents them as unknowable, or as Homi Bhabha observes "'other' and yet entirely knowable and visible."[9]

The production of the exotic emphasizes its strangeness and difference from the normative culture. Ashcroft, Griffiths, and Tiffin point out that as early as 1599 the term exotic implied "alien, introduced from abroad, not indigenous."[10] They indicate that by 1651 the *Oxford English Dictionary* offers the meaning as "a foreigner" or "a foreign plant not acclimatized."[11] Further, Tzvetan Todorov indicates that in France at the start of the twentieth century, exoticism tended to focus on certain external

7. Dibyesh Anand, "Western Colonial Representations of the Other: The Case of Exotica Tibet," *New Political Science* 29 (2007): 23–42 (23).

8. Ibid., 31.

9. Homi K. Bhabha, *The Location of Culture* (New York: Routledge, 1994), 70. Huggan (*The Postcolonial Exotic*, 13) describes exoticization as "a kind of semiotic circuit that oscillates between the opposite poles of strangeness and familiarity."

10. Bill Ashcroft et al., *Key Concepts in Post-Colonial Studies* (London: Routledge, 1989), 94.

11. Ibid.

subjects to the extent that it morphs into what he describes as "tropical-ism."[12] This focus on otherness and difference of the exotic as present within European society rather than spatially separate reflects what Bhabha sees as the conflicted representation of the colonial subject in colonial discourse. This discourse draws attention to the colonial subject as racially and sexually different, but in so doing the discourse expresses its desire for that subject. Bhabha notes that this conflict occurs because the body appears "in both the economy of pleasure and desire and the economy of discourse, domination and power."[13] Ultimately, the glossy pictures of the exotic functions as forms of power that Huggan offers contain the potential to control even though falling short of full domi-nation.[14]

Exoticization achieves its desired outcomes in terms of the exertion of power primarily due to the unequal relationship between the seer and the seen, the colonizer and the colonized. Since the target audience to which representations of the exotic are advertised remains precisely Western culture, exoticization already guarantees an advantage in what Edward Said, in referring to the construction of the orient by Western culture, views as "flexible *positional* superiority."[15] The flexibility to which Said refers not only confers proximity on the observer of the exotic but also, as Huggan points out, "the objects of its gaze are not supposed to look back."[16] The extent of the power afforded the Western observer produc-ing the exotic appears in the reality that Todorov describes, that exoti-cism focuses on cultures "defined exclusively by their relation to the observer."[17] Defining the exotic occurs by deploying various forms of power, among which, Said offers, are political, intellectual, cultural, and moral.[18] The exotic, therefore, becomes not simply that which is different but that which is rendered different for the purpose of controlling and domesticating it.

---

12. Tzvetan Todorov, *On Human Diversity: Nationalism, Racism, and Exoticism in French Thought* (trans. C. Porter; Cambridge, MA: Harvard University Press, 1993), 323.

13. Bhabha, *The Location of Culture*, 67.

14. Huggan, *The Postcolonial Exotic*, 14.

15. Edward W. Said, *Orientalism* (New York: Vintage, 1978), 7 (italics in original).

16. Huggan, *The Postcolonial Exotic*, 14.

17. Todorov, *On Human Diversity*, 264.

18. Said, *Orientalism*, 12.

Unlike other forms of alterity, exoticization produces difference for the praise and imitation of the observer. The production of the exotic other avoids the negation that results in the emptying of the undesirable other that needs to be shunned. As Anand notes, the process of debasing evacuates the non-Western other of language, agency, and history and the process of negation rewrites the image of the indigene with that of the colonial image. Processes like idealization on which exoticization is based merely form the reverse side of the same coin.[19] Exoticization makes the otherwise undesirable other into an object of desire. In the words of Todorov, "otherness is systematically preferred to likeness."[20] Contrary to all appearances, the exotic other still remains other with all the oppressive connotations that alterity implies. The desirability of the exotic emerges not for its own sake nor because it proves to be an asset for the exotic other, and not even because as a result of these desirable attributes the exotic other gains ascendancy over the colonial observer. Exoticization of the non-Western serves the interests of the West. Huggan speaks of exoticization as "self-empowering, self-referential,"[21] and Said views orientalism as more concerned with "the culture that produced it than…its putative object."[22]

As a rhetorical strategy in colonial discourse, exoticization repeats the colonial subject in various guises. Since biblical texts offered ready justification for the execution of modern European colonialism,[23] finding the exotic in texts like Jer 35 offers little surprise. The power relationships constructed between the Rechabites and the Judeans by the observer Jeremiah appear surprising in this narrative, given the presence of the Babylonian empire that should disrupt smooth binary relationships. Additionally, since the Babylonians have rendered the Judeans as other, the ease with which the besieged and beleaguered Judeans presuppose ascendancy over the Rechabites in the midst of the imperial action requires scrutiny. We shall now examine how Jeremiah's discourse constructs the Rechabites as the exotic for the Judeans.

---

19. Anand, "Western Colonial Representations," 33.
20. Todorov, *On Human Diversity*, 264.
21. Huggan, *The Postcolonial Exotic*, 14.
22. Said, *Orientalism*, 22.
23. R. S. Sugirtharajah, *The Bible and the Third World: Precolonial, Colonial and Postcolonial Encounters* (Cambridge: Cambridge University Press, 2001), 1.

Exoticizing the Rechabites

The Rechabites simply appear out of nothing in Jer 35. Sandwiched between two chapters that feature narratives focused on kings, ch. 35 with the Rechabites in the starring role appears both unpredictable and illogical.[24] Given that a clearly defined central logic eludes most readers of the book of Jeremiah, the unusual nature of the chapter and its featured actors should not seem that strange. Yet, interpreters view the Rechabites and this particular chapter as a curiosity, precisely since the narrative constructs them in this way. Elena Di Pede shows how the passive Rechabites of the Old Greek text become more active agents in the Masoretic text. She notes, for instance, the switch from the third person address in the Old Greek to the second person address in the MT where Jeremiah speaks the divine word directly to them (v. 18). In the MT the string of active verbs (תעשׂו, ותשׁמרו, שׁמעתם v. 18) represents the Rechabites as more than the passive recipients of an ancestral command.[25] Similarly, McKane notes the MT's expansion in v. 17b offering again the justification to destroy Jerusalem for disobedience as necessary for an exilic audience.[26] This expansion sharpens the contrast between the Rechabites and the Judeans and in so doing focuses attention on the Rechabites as exceptional. The MT version of the narrative shapes a unique picture of the Rechabites.

The opening verses of the chapter presume knowledge of the Rechabites by the lack of details of the group and the presentation of Jeremiah's actions as normal. The text delays any details about the Rechabites until v. 6 and notably leaves until v. 10 the clarification that Jonadab and not Rechab serves as their ancestral figure.[27] The refusal of wine voiced by the entire community (beginning at v. 6 and continuing through to v. 11), describing their commitment to vows that reject certain living practices, forms the first indication of the unusual nature of the group. Shaping the

---

24. Commentators note the oddity of the chapter: William McKane, *A Critical and Exegetical Commentary on Jeremiah, Volume 2: XXVI–LII* (ICC; Edinburgh: T. & T. Clark, 1996), 896: "[vv. 2–11 is] a bizarre accumulation of detail which one reads with mounting incredulity"; Carroll, *Jeremiah II*, 653: "a strange tale."

25. Elena Di Pede, "Un oracle pour les Récabites (Jr 35,18-19) ou à leur propos (42,18–19 LXX)?," *SJOT* 20 (2006): 96–109 (101).

26. William McKane, "Jeremiah and the Rechabites," *ZAW* 100 (1988): 106–23 (112).

27. Leah Bronner, "The Rechabites, a Sect in Biblical Times," in *De Fructu Oris Sui: Essays in Honour of Adrianus Van Selms* (ed. I. H. Eyberts et al.; Leiden: Brill, 1971), 6–16 (7).

narrative with the divine instructions to Jeremiah to go, imitating the imperative forms used in 7:1 (cf. 26:2; 13:1; 18:1–2), creates the expectation that not even Jeremiah possesses knowledge of the group or the direction his encounter with them may take.[28] Framing the Rechabites as falling outside the boundaries of conventional knowledge, in this case the knowledge of Jeremiah, and having that knowledge filled in by them, the text constructs the Rechabites as unusual and strange while trying to make them familiar. The travel itinerary that includes Jeremiah leading the Rechabites from their house (v. 2) to the temple (v. 4), the center of community life where they are put on display for the city, adds to the processes of exoticization that emphasize the difference of the Rechabites.[29]

The Rechabites lack any context in the book of Jeremiah. This decontextualized appearance forms the basis of their exoticization in the chapter as an unknown group that becomes knowable but still remains mysterious. The text takes a curious path to providing knowledge of the group. Rather than have Jeremiah or the narrator present the details about the Rechabites, this information comes directly from the Rechabites. No single speaker provides this information, even though the narrative already identifies Jaazaniah (v. 3) as a possible group leader. The reported speech in vv. 6–11 comes from the entire community speaking as one ("but they replied," ויאמרו, v. 6). Making the Rechabites an undifferentiated group even to the point of not having a spokesperson indicates that the narrative provides only a veneer of knowledge about the group.[30] Further, while at first it appears that this information comes

28. McKane (*Jeremiah, Volume 2*, 896) insists that should the encounter be a test of the Rechabites' fidelity then it represents "a coarse-grained and insensitive piece of behaviour" because Jeremiah would have known the outcome and merely stages the event to "make an impression on the Jerusalem community." So too Walter Brueggemann, *To Build, to Plant: A Commentary on Jeremiah 25–52* (Grand Rapids: Eerdmans, 1991), 112. For similar reasons Holladay does not classify this as symbolic action, unlike Carroll; see William L. Holladay, *Jeremiah 2: A Commentary on the Book of the Prophet Jeremiah Chapters 26–52* (Hermeneia; Minneapolis: Fortress, 1989), 246; Carroll, *Jeremiah II*, 654.

29. McKane (*Jeremiah, Volume 2*, 897) notes that the obvious reading of this text puts all of Jerusalem following this parade led by Jeremiah to a public place "with a mixture of disdain and curiosity," where Jeremiah unmasks the display he intended.

30. Gamberoni calls attention to the number of times the Rechabites mention their ancestor when they introduce themselves without offering any data that help determine his identity. He also points to the unusual lack of ethical motivation in

directly from the Rechabites and should therefore be seen as authentic, the passage is framed as a first-person account from Jeremiah. In effect, vv. 6–11 stand as the words of Jeremiah, the observer representing knowledge of the Rechabites.[31] This scant knowledge builds the exotic character of the Rechabites as knowable and therefore able to be characterized, controlled, and domesticated. The brief details given offer enough information of their lifestyle to mark them as different. The catalogue of practices that they eschew (vv. 6–7) paints them as outside the mainstream of civilized culture without ever explaining the basis for their choices. Rather than the knowledge presented here making the group more transparent, it renders them more opaque, more mysterious, exotic. As Anand observes when it comes to the exotic other a paradox exists: "the project of rendering the Other knowable and the image of it as primitive and simple went had (*sic*) in hand with the recognition that there are elements of inscrutability and mystery that eluded complete understanding of the Other."[32]

The text indicates how the Rechabites narrate their sincere obedience to a lifestyle laid out for them by an eponymous ancestor's son Jonadab (v. 6). Locating the origins of the Rechabites' practices in an ancient era builds the case of their difference from a contemporary audience. When it becomes clear that they reject advances in what can be seen as civilization, such as living in houses or planting vineyards,[33] then the picture of the Rechabites as quaint fully emerges. For the purposes of the narrative, the Rechabites serve as what Todorov calls the "primitive exoticism" that eventually leads to the figure of the noble savage.[34] Todorov offers that a "certain minimalism" defines the figure of the "noble savage," indicating that this figure can exist without most of the things

the prohibitions. See Johann Gamberoni, "'Jonadab, unser Vater, hat uns geboten' (Jer 35,6): Die Rechabiter—am Rand und in der Mitte," in *Schrift und Tradition: Festschrift für Josef Ernst zum 70. Geburtstag* (ed. K. Backhaus and F. G. Untergassmair; Paderborn: Schöningh, 1996), 19–31 (21).

31.   Migsch points to several syntactic shifts in the narrative between I-statements representing Jeremiah's words and reported speech that do not always easily indicate that Jeremiah is the one speaking. He notes that these subtle shifts achieve a measure of coherence in the reading. See Herbert Migsch, "Die vorbildlichen Rechabiter: Zur Redestruktur von Jeremia XXXV," *VT* 47 (1997): 316–28 (317).

32.   Anand, "Western Colonial Representations," 31.

33.   These activities are associated with "establishing a settlement" in Deuteronomy. See Adele Berlin, "Jeremiah 29:5–7: A Deuteronomic Allusion," *HAR* 8 (1984): 3–11 (3).

34.   Todorov, *On Human Diversity*, 266.

required by advanced civilizations.[35] He further indicates that the "noble savage" is deployed to promote "the critique of one's own society."[36] Given the minimalism reflected in the description of the Rechabites' lifestyle and Jeremiah's invocation of their example of obedience to inveigh against the failures of the Judeans (vv. 13–16), the representation of the Rechabites fills out the position of the exotic other, the noble savage.

The representation of the Rechabites as the exotic other emphasizes their enviable devotion to their vows. The narrative goes beyond merely stating the extent of their obedience regarding the avoidance of wine. In an encounter that starts out as a seeming test of their teetotalism, the focus expands to other prohibitions. Jonadab, an ancestral figure whose identity and precise socio-religious functions remain hidden in the narrative, orders all these prohibitions. The absence of the religious infrastructure of temple, priesthood, or prophets, in addition to the lack of a centralized monarchy among the Rechabites, draws a sharp contrast with the Judeans, who possess all these aids but lack the level of devotion displayed by the Rechabites, especially given the events reported in chs. 34 and 36. This stark contrast calls attention to their obedience but does so after making a point about the simplicity of their life practices. Jeremiah's praise for the Rechabites focuses on their obedience. In fact, it singles out their fidelity to Jonadab's order only with regard to the avoidance of wine (v. 14), making no mention of the other prohibitions. The diminishing attention to the range and nature of the prohibitions the Rechabites observe reveals that no serious engagement takes place between the Rechabites and Jeremiah and those present at the encounter.[37] Rather, the narrative trots out the Rechabites and their quaint life practices in order to call attention to the Judeans' lack of fidelity to their promises and their unresponsiveness to numerous divine calls for repentance (v. 15). As the exotic other, the Rechabites function as foils for the Judeans in Jeremiah's rhetoric.

The exoticization of the Rechabites thrives upon their idealization as the exemplars of obedience. Their quaint lifestyle, with its rejection of the markers of settled living, frames them as natural and more original,

---

35. Ibid., 274.

36. Ibid., 271.

37. Allen sees that Jeremiah "while making use of the group, holds them at arm's length"; see Leslie C. Allen, *Jeremiah: A Commentary* (Louisville: Westminster John Knox, 2008), 392.

reflecting an aboriginal past long since dead but still desirable. The innocence of that idealized past represents that which is desired. Invoking that past in the figure of the exotic makes no call to undo progress and civilization to return to a more "natural" way of life. While the figure of the exotic is domesticated enough to exist in the dominant culture, it cannot be so subversive as to change that culture. As the exotic other, the Rechabites find a place in the consciousness of Judean society only as a result of their unusual devotion and obedience. The bold reward offered to the Rechabites for their obedience of a perpetual place in the divine economy (vv. 18–19) represents the ultimate domestication of the Rechabites: their marginal status gets drawn into the center and absorbed by the center. As Jon Levenson shows, the comparison of the promises offered to the Rechabites should properly be made with promises to David (33:17–18) and the Levites (33:17–26) in the book of Jeremiah rather than with those given to Baruch (ch. 45) and Ebed-melech (39:15–18). The similarity, Levenson observes, lies in the fact that the "language of covenant" occurs in the case of the Rechabites, David, and the Levites.[38] Should the divine rewards of vv. 18–19 take effect, then the Rechabites' life practices will cease to exist as they did before. Of course, the Rechabites as a model of obedience would be incorporated into the Judean society as an artifact to Judean devotion or the lack thereof. All other possible potentials to transform Judean society, particularly the subversive lifestyle of stateless living, remain muted in Jeremiah's rhetoric.

Jeremiah's rhetoric in ch. 35 renders the Rechabites exotic. The otherness of the Rechabites stands behind the effusive praise the text heaps upon them. For such praise, Jeremiah asks only that the Judeans learn the mode of the Rechabites' obedience (v. 13). That the rhetoric of judgment persists in Jeremiah's word to the Judeans (vv. 14–16) indicates that nothing has changed among the Judeans. The Rechabites' presence does not alter Judean society, given that in this case the Rechabites enter as the exoticized other. As Huggan observes, the relationship with the exotic is far from mutual and far from a relationship: "Exoticism posits the lure of difference while protecting its practitioners from close involvement."[39]

---

38. Jon D. Levenson, "On the Promise to the Rechabites," *CBQ* 38 (1976): 508–14 (509–10).
39. Huggan, *The Postcolonial Exotic*, 22.

The Curious Case of Tradition and Scholarship

Having constructed the Rechabites as the exotic in this reading, the book of Jeremiah helps shape the view of the Rechabites. With no other mention of the Rechabites as a social group outside of this chapter, later biblical tradition fills out the exoticization of the Rechabites that begins in Jeremiah. Doing so requires adding sufficient knowledge about the Rechabites while still maintaining the perspective of the group as mysterious and outside the mainstream of society. Ronit Nikolsky shows how the Rechabites emerge as a pious group of converts in Midrash. Among the developments she notes are the establishment of a lineage between the Rechabites and Jethro based upon 1 Chr 2:55.[40] Since the Jethroites are regarded as an emblem of pious converts, this connection passes that trait on to the Rechabites. Additionally, she points to the Midrash, *Mekhilta de-Rabbi Shimon ben Yochai*,[41] which equates Jethro as a lover of Torah with the Rechabites' obedience as narrated in Jer 35:14.[42] Equally striking, she notes that the same Midrash shows the Rechabites offering an explanation to Jeremiah regarding their abstinence from wine. According to *Mekhilta* the Rechabites tell Jeremiah: "Our father commanded us not to drink wine as long as this house is destroyed."[43] This Midrash tries to sort out the historical discrepancies between the command to mourn for a destroyed temple and the fact that the temple is standing during the putative time of the Rechabites by indicating that the Rechabites' ancestor orders a proleptic mourning practice. In the process of clearing up the historical discrepancies, the Midrash establishes a connection between the Rechabites' abstinence and mourning customs. The emphasis on asceticism suggests that the Rechabites should be seen as other groups that follow ascetic customs, such as Nazirites (Num 6:3), priests (Lev 10:9), and mysterious prophetic figures like Elisha.[44]

---

40. Knights argues that the genealogical link between the Kenites and the Rechabites in Chronicles should properly be seen as a geographic link and believes that no reference to the Rechabites exists in the verse. See Chris H. Knights, "Kenites = Rechabites? 1 Chronicles II 55 Reconsidered," *VT* 43 (1993): 10–18 (17).

41. A text from the Tannaitic period of early Judaism, between 70–200 C.E.; see W. David Nelson, *Mekhilta de-Rabbi Shimon Bar Yohai* (Philadelphia: Jewish Publication Society, 2006), xi.

42. Ronit Nikolsky, "The *History of the Rechabites* and the Jeremiah Literature," *JSP* 13 (2002): 185–207 (189).

43. Ibid., 190.

44. Ibid., 191. For similarities between the Rechabites and Elisha see J. T. Cummings, "The House of the Sons of the Prophets and the Tents of the Rechabites,"

The "independent apocryphal composition" the *History of the Rechabites*, which forms part of what Nikolsky regards as a fourth-century Byzantine Palestinian text, *Journey of Zosimos*, provides further elaboration of the exoticization of the Rechabites.[45] In *Journey of Zosimos* the Rechabites live in an Edenic state and are known as the "the Blessed Ones." *History of the Rechabites* serves as the back-story for the Rechabites, characterizing them as a devout group responding to Jeremiah's preaching and engaging in acts of repentance in order to forestall the destruction of Jerusalem. This action presumably takes place during the Babylonian siege of 597 B.C.E., given that God does not destroy Jerusalem. The action at that time involves ascetic practices such as shedding clothes and refraining from wine. In the aftermath of the near destruction of Jerusalem, a new king emerges who demands that the Rechabites integrate into normal life. Upon their refusal, they are imprisoned. This imprisonment sets the stage for a miraculous release and relocation to the Edenic paradise.[46]

History of the Rechabites constructs the Rechabites as a decidedly ascetic group, although not given to extremes such as celibacy, which stands by its vow but this time in the face of threat. While specific elements of the Rechabites' piety such as praying are not present in the Jeremiah text,[47] the apocryphon expands upon their characterization in the Jeremiah text as an overly pious group. The demonstration of resistance to the lure of settled existence in this apocryphon utilizes the same exoticizing trope as Jer 35, viz., of deploying the life practices of the Rechabites to critique contemporary society. The Rechabites' steadfastness in the face of threats to their life as well as their miraculous rescue adds to the mystery about the group. These techniques of exoticization will commend the Rechabites in Christian literature as the ideal ascetic types. Nikolsky lists eleven authors of Christian texts from the third to the seventh century who mention the Rechabites, with eight of these authors writing between the fourth and fifth centuries, a time of heightened Christian asceticism. She notes that all these instances, though

in *Studia biblica 1978: Sixth International Congress on Biblical Studies, Oxford 3–7 April 1978*. Vol. 1, *Papers on Old Testament and Related Themes* (ed. E. A. Livingstone; JSOTSup 11; Sheffield: University of Sheffield, 1979), 119–26 (122).

45. Nikolsky, "The *History of the Rechabites*," 186.

46. Ibid., 187.

47. Chris H. Knights, "The *History of the Rechabites*: An Initial Commentary," *JSJ* 28 (1997): 413–36 (423).

brief, praise the obedience of the Rechabites and situate them as "proto-ascetics."[48] While the representation of the Rechabites in these texts as ascetics offers some evidence of exoticization, these texts draw upon earlier exoticized representations to situate the Rechabites as socially marginal figures posing a mysterious fascination and challenge to mainstream culture.

The arc of exoticization of the Rechabites feeds back into contemporary scholarship on the group. Since the various guises within which the Rechabites have been represented show them as marginal figures rejecting the lure of civilization in preference for a more "primitive" form of living, contemporary scholarship goes in search of histories to confirm this portrayal. Theories about the Rechabites as nomads,[49] metal-workers,[50] an early ascetic group like the Essenes,[51] or an overzealous group of Yahwists[52] derive from the desire to locate the group on the fringes of society and to build out knowledge of the group based upon knowledge of other groups that intentionally self-locate on the margins. The genealogical link that the Chronicler establishes between the Rechabites and the Kenites, as well as the establishment of the family relation of a shared sense of devotion between the Kenites and the Rechabites in Midrash, opens the space in modern scholarship to recontextualize the Rechabites.[53] The representation of the Rechabites in Jer 35 decontextualizes them as part of the framing of the Rechabites as

48. Nikolsky, "The *History of the Rechabites*," 202.

49. Bronner, "The Rechabites," 7.

50. Frick places the Rechabites as "social outcasts among nomads and pas-toralists" as a result of their work as craftsmen makes participation in settled life impossible; see Frank S. Frick, "The Rechabites Reconsidered," *JBL* 90 (1971): 279–87 (285). McNutt ties the Rechabites with the Kenites and Midianites as metal-workers destined to be "socially marginal" but still viewed as "mysterious and magical"; see Paula M. McNutt, "The Kenites, the Midianites, and the Rechabites as Marginal Mediators in Ancient Israelite Tradition," *Semeia* 67 (1995): 109–32 (118).

51. Knights debunks the notion that the Rechabites serve as influence for the Essenes; see Chris H. Knights, "The Rechabites of Jeremiah 35: Forerunners of the Essenes?," *JSP* 10 (1992): 81–87 (86).

52. Thompson calls them "an unusual reactionary group" whose Yahwism "had fossilized at the nomadic stage"; see John A. Thompson, *The Book of Jeremiah* (NICOT; Grand Rapids: Eerdmans, 1980), 616–17.

53. Frick ("The Rechabites Reconsidered," 281) points to 2 Kgs 10:15–17 as a foundation legend about the Rechabites that feeds "an eisegetical contention" of their nomadic lifestyle. So too Gamberoni, "Jonadab, unser Vater," 30.

the exotic other.[54] This decontextualization shapes the Rechabites as culturally dislocated with no connections to ancestors known to Judeans and no intersecting histories with the culture in which they are being displayed. Modern scholarship, on the other hand, attempts to supply details about the Rechabites' history that, among other things, names their ancestry, narrates a possible history, and offers them an identity and vocation. Yet while this recontextualization culturally locates the Rechabites, it places them firmly in the outer margins of society as an esoteric group, mysterious, and out of step with the mainstream culture; exotic yet again.

The exoticization loop in which the Rechabites are located also feeds into the interpretation of Jer 35. Commentators find it necessary to use the requisite word "curious" to describe the Rechabites.[55] In the narrative, Jeremiah essentially invites the group to perform its life practices, which may be seen to be similar to the performance displays of exotic people taken to Europe during the colonial period. The divine command sets up the performance (v. 1) with Jeremiah as the theatrical producer who may or may not know the outcome of the invitation. Nonetheless, in the narrative the Rechabites are expected to play to the stereotype of the exotic in order for the performance to be of benefit to the audience. In this case the Judean audience needs to marvel at their quaint practices and in the process be reminded of their lack of devotion. Di Pede's observation that the MT shapes the reward notice (v. 18) as a second-person plural address to the Rechabites may indicate a more human representation than the Old Greek, where they are spoken about.[56] However, this is undercut by presenting the reward to Jonadab in the MT (v. 19) unlike his descendants in the Old Greek (υιου Ρηχαβ). The MT feeds this performance motif by masking a reward to an absent figure as given to the gathered group.

Given that the narrative reveals how the Rechabites play to the exotic stereotype in their refusal to drink wine (v. 6), interpreters go further to stage the performance of the Rechabites to fill out other aspects of their

---

54. Anand ("Western Colonial Representations," 33) notes that the twin processes of decontextualization and othering form part of the idealization that occurs in the representation of the exotic. Similarly, Huggan (*The Postcolonial Exotic*, 16) names decontextualization as one element that connects ancient and modern forms of exoticization.

55. See, e.g., Brueggemann, *Jeremiah 25–52*, 113: "a religious curiosity"; Levenson, "On the Promise to the Rechabites," 508: "a curious group."

56. Di Pede, "Un oracle pour les Récabites," 100.

life, in particular the command to live in tents. By presuming the Rech-abites as a nomadic group that stands under the tyranny of the commands of an ancestral figure that force them to live in tents, either within or outside the city limits, exegetes reinscribe the command to perform the exotic role.

Breaking the Exoticist Code

The postcolonial turn in reading this chapter requires stepping back from the exoticist code that renders the Rechabites mere fodder for the book of Jeremiah's theo-political arguments and moving forward by revealing a different set of power relations in the narrative. While the fanciful depiction of the Rechabites in this narrative may make them appear as real as the otter of the webcomic, the narrative as narrative within the book of Jeremiah offers the presence of another group that confronts the implications of the Babylonian empire. Breaking the exoticist code enables the text to reveal a group of persons also caught in the maelstrom of empire but one that constructs a different relationship with empire.

The Hebrew text of Jer 35 reads ambiguously about the Rechabites' presence in Jerusalem. The designation, "the house of the Rechabites" (הלוך אל־בית הרכבים, v. 2), in the divine instruction to Jeremiah, need not be read as a physical structure as several English translations imply,[57] given that Jeremiah reports taking named individuals and "the whole house of the Rechabites" (כל־בית הרכבים, v. 3) to the temple. Clearly in v. 3 בית properly translates as "community" and should equally hold the same valence in v. 2. Placing the emphasis on the Rechabites as a "community" not only provides a humanized portrait in place of the hard institutionalized one that "house" communicates, but it points to them as a social group negotiating its way among alternative social organizations. The general characterization of the Rechabites as a hapless group of refugees caught in the crossfire of war and seeking shelter in Jerusalem focuses attention on their vulnerability rather than on the success of their social organization. The passage may give the impression of a cult living in deference to an ancestor. However, the passage also provides hints that the Rechabites' social organization may not be simply the result of a

---

57. KJV, ASV, NASB, and NRSV render v. 2 as "the house of the Rechabites," while NIV and CEV offer alternatives such as "family of the Rechabites" or "the Rechabite clan." For other alternative translations see Allen, *Jeremiah*, 388; McKane, *Jeremiah, Volume 2*, 885; Thompson, *Book of Jeremiah*, 614.

personality cult. The discrepancy regarding the leading role between Jonadab and Rechab suggests what Karel van der Toorn sees as a social group already given to these life practices as "part of their ancestral lore."[58] Van der Toorn offers that Jonadab in the text adopts a traditional custom as a rule in order to honor that tradition instead of the creation of a new practice.[59] The relational terms of "father" (אב, vv. 6, 8, 10) and "brother" (אח, v. 3) that appear in the passage may suggest a cultish organization[60] but in fact should resonate more strongly with other forms of social organization such as those envisaged in the book of Deuteronomy, the apprenticeship relationships between older and younger prophet, or even relationships in scribal groups as implied by Proverbs. While the neat modern distinctions between religious and social organization obviously disappear in conversations about the ancient world, to characterize the Rechabites simply as cultish and therefore to dismiss them as quaint would be to dismiss several aspects that form the fabric of Judean social life. The striking similarities between what Brueggemann styles as a Pentalogue (vv. 6–7) and the Moses-defined Decalogue[61] points to elements in the Rechabites' organization that resemble those of Israel's social organization.

The debate over whether the Rechabites live in tents or houses while in Jerusalem remains an important one.[62] In some regards, though, it distracts from the fact that the model of statelessness the Rechabites employ offers them an advantage in negotiating imperial power. Unlike the Judeans, involved in the city-state organization that puts them in

58.   Karel van der Toorn, "Ritual Resistance and Self-Assertion: The Rechabites in Early Israelite Religion," in *Pluralism and Identity: Studies in Ritual Behaviour* (ed. J. Platvoet and K. van der Toorn; Leiden: Brill, 1995), 229–59 (235).

59.   Ibid., 236.

60.   Gamberoni ("Jonadab, unser Vater," 29) points out that "father" (אב) is the subject of verbs in vv. 6, 10, 14, 16, 18 and appears with suffixes in vv. 14, 16, 18, suggesting a form of absolutism.

61.   Brueggemann (*Jeremiah 25–52*, 113) offers that this list "seems designed to warn against accommodation to the values of the dominant society." Arguably, the framing of the Mosaic law intends a similar outcome.

62.   Migsch offers a compelling argument that the Rechabites do live in houses in Jerusalem given the verb form in v. 11 and notes the difference between their stays outside of Jerusalem and inside of Jerusalem. He believes that v. 11 starts with a description of their time outside Jerusalem that enables them to keep their vow, but at the end of v. 11 the description of their stay in Jerusalem indicates that they break the vow. See Herbert Migsch, "Wohnten die Rechabiter in Jerusalem in Häusern oder in Zelten? Die Verbformationen in Jer 35,8–11," *Bib* 79 (1998): 242–57 (254).

competition with the Babylonian empire, the Rechabites are not the targets of imperial aggression. Further, they lack the things that either interest or threaten imperial power. Organized around an identity either originally shaped as a social critique or one that evolves into a form of social resistance,[63] the Rechabites' rejection of settled existence enables them to live counter-imperially. In so doing they define themselves not so much as a nation but more as a community. Adopting the reductionist definition of a nation that Benedict Anderson offers, "an imagined political community...both inherently limited and sovereign"[64] with the emphasis on limited referring to physical and other boundaries and sovereignty applying to claims to territory, the Rechabites do not present themselves as a nation. Anderson's third element of community representing "deep, horizontal comradeship" exemplifies the Rechabites' mode of organization.[65] Characterizing the Rechabites as community more than nation is not an anachronism since their life practices lack several features of social organization that the book of Jeremiah places upon the Judeans and the Babylonians, such as monarchy or temple.

The usual contrast of the Rechabites' landlessness vs. the sedentary life practices of the Judeans misses the resistance that landlessness poses to empire. Landlessness or nomadism stands not simply as a rejection of sedentary cultures, but rather as a rejection of the accumulative actions of empire. That the Rechabites appear comfortable with their decision to seek refuge in Jerusalem and that the description of their sojourn there as curious occurs more at the level of interpretation than the text reveal that the Rechabites in their life practices pose a challenge to empire more than they do to the monarchal city-state of Jerusalem. John Noyes's views of nomadism as the Hegelian negative of empire and "a technological negation of both physical space and solar time"[66] help to describe the triadic relationship of this chapter. This relationship reveals the Babylonians in an aggressive posture towards Jerusalem with the nomadic Rechabites as offering the alternative to empire. Rather than the Rechabites being the weakest link, they represent for the Judeans an enviable commitment to an anti-imperial way of being. Their devotion

63. Van der Toorn, "Ritual Resistance and Self-Assertion," 250.
64. Benedict Anderson, *Imagined Communities: Reflections on the Origin and Spread of Nationalism* (London: Verso, 1991), 6.
65. Ibid., 7.
66. John K. Noyes, "Nomadism, Nomadology, Postcolonialism: By Way of Introduction," *Interventions* 6 (2004): 159–68 (160–61).

to a lifestyle that Noyes describes as "a social (dis)arrangement and a subjective (dis)order on the fringes of empire"[67] models for the Judeans an alternative form of resistance to the Babylon empire.

The landless Rechabites occupy the margins of society as a subversive move against empire. Their withdrawal from constructing houses and vineyards represents in essence a departure from the tributary mode of production that formed the basis of the ancient economy in service to empire.[68] Michael Hardt and Antonio Negri characterize withdrawal from concentrations of power that mark nomadism as "a corporeal exodus."[69] Much of the discourse about the Rechabites positions them as a nomadic group with the tendency to view the nomadic lifestyle as resulting from lack of land. However, the narrative indicates a deliberate choice by the Rechabites to forego relationships with land such as those chosen by the Judeans. In this case landlessness speaks more of the mobility to transgress what Hardt and Negri view as "the walls of nation, ethnicity, race, people, and the like."[70] Unhinged from land, the Rechabites appear, not as a homogenous ethnic group, but rather as a fluid social organization that admits entrants based upon their embrace of this lifestyle.[71] Given that "father" (אב) as a term of respect could mean more than mere biological relation,[72] the Rechabites as a social unit intentionally embrace difference, or, as Hardt and Negri put it, "being-against,"[73] as the means of destabilizing dominant power. The mobility of the Rechabites admits that the reach of imperial power reduces the spaces that exist beyond its control and that "being-against" becomes a transhistorical way of life, a message the Rechabites firmly deliver while in Jerusalem.

---

67. Ibid., 160. Noyes does point out that not all forms of nomadism resist empire since warlike nomadic forces can serve the interests of empire.

68. Norman K. Gottwald, "Sociology of Ancient Israel," *ABD* 6:79–89 (84).

69. Michael Hardt and Antonio Negri, *Empire* (Cambridge, Mass.: Harvard University Press, 2000), 364.

70. Ibid., 362.

71. Keukens adopts the position on the fluidity of the group's membership based upon the use of, literally "sons of the house of the Rechabites" (בני בית־הרכבים, v. 5) as similar to Gen 15:2 and Qoh 2:7 that indicate the acquisition of slaves. Karlheinz H. Keukens, "Die rekabitischen Haussklaven in Jeremia 35," *BZ* 27 (1983): 228–35 (230).

72. Keukens (ibid.) offers that "father" should be seen not as the founder of a guild but as a patron of house-born slaves.

73. Hardt and Negri, *Empire*, 211.

Conclusion

For most of the book of Jeremiah only the Babylonians interact with the Judeans, until the Rechabites enter the narrative in ch. 35. With this entrance comes another group that the dominant voice of the book can use as a foil for the recalcitrant Judeans. The placement of this narrative alongside Zedekiah's failed covenantal arrangements in ch. 34 shows the editorial manipulation of the Rechabites and their story. In addition, the narrative itself reveals a lack of serious interaction with this group, an emphasis on the Rechabites' obscure origins, a display of their unusual devotion to an ancestral vow, and a penchant for living outside of the mainstream. By these means, ch. 35 already stands as an example of exoticization, making it quite easy for interpretation, exegesis, and scholarship regarding the Rechabites to continue the trend of exoticizing the group.

Colonial discourse creates the exotic and in the process creates distances between cultures and peoples new to the Western gaze. Intentionally producing difference and otherness serves to create a different set of power relations. The persistence of the colonial discourse that results in exoticization, rather than revealing the discovery of new types of difference that can be labeled exotic, instead demonstrates how difference and otherness may be deployed as mechanisms of control. This mechanism of control ultimately reproduces the exotic as the obscure other, or perhaps as (un)knowable as the otter. The Rechabites' narrative proves untroubling for the book of Jeremiah, precisely because at various levels, whether in the construction of the MT text, exegesis, or historical recovery, they are the insignificant exoticized otter/other.

The postcolonial turn in reading the story of the Rechabites offers more than simply observing the construction of their difference in the narrative. Rather, the postcolonial perspective draws attention to how the difference and otherness of the Rechabites pose a challenge to imperial power. The subversive ploy of embracing difference as a mode of resistance to dominant power increasingly marks social discourse and social action. Examples of social trends like rental vs. ownership, couch surfing vs. all-inclusive resorts, and leaderless movements vs. structured institutions present new sites from which to read the narrative of the Rechabites.

THE SILENT GODDESS AND THE GENDERING
OF DIVINE SPEECH IN JEREMIAH 44

James E. Harding

In Jer 44:1–30, the reader is confronted with a multi-voiced text that represents a conflict between Jeremiah, claiming to speak for YHWH and presumably—though not certainly—aligned ideologically with the voice of the narrator, and a group representing a shadowy, unnamed deity, the Queen of Heaven.[1] YHWH's voice is mediated through that of Jeremiah, which in turn is mediated through that of the narrator. While the devotees of the Queen of Heaven are granted a voice by the narrator, their patroness remains silent.

What is going on here? On one level, this passage represents the possibility of contesting, in the aftermath of the destruction of Jerusalem in 586 B.C.E. and the exile of the majority of its inhabitants, the theodic claim that in these catastrophic events, YHWH was executing his justice, sanctioned by the terms of his covenant with Israel, against a refractory people. This theodicy now dominates Deuteronomy and the work we have come to call the Deuteronomistic History, and is aligned with the

---

1. There are textual difficulties with "Queen of Heaven" wherever the phrase appears in Jeremiah. The consonantal text of the Aleppo and St Petersburg codices would have us read מְלֶכֶת השמים, "the queen of the heavens," which is reflected in Aquila, Symmachus, and Theodotion at Jer 7:18 and the LXX at 51:17, 18, 19, 25 (ἡ βασιλίσσα τοῦ οὐρανοῦ), the Vulgate at 7:18; 44:17, 18, 19, 25 (*Regina caeli*), and the Peshitta at 44:19 (ܡܠܟܬ ܫܡܝܐ). On the other hand, an alternate reading, one supported by the consonantal text of many other MSS (incl. Codex Reuchlinianus), would have us read מְלָאכֶת השמים, "the work (?) of the heavens" (cf. Pesh. ܦܘܠܚܢ ܫܡܝܐ at 7:18; 44:17, 18, 25). In 7:18 the LXX has ἡ στρατία τοῦ οὐρανοῦ, "the army of heaven." The Targum has כוכבת השמיא, "the star of the heavens," presumably indicating Venus (cf. Robert Hayward, *The Targum of Jeremiah: Translated, with a Critical Introduction, Apparatus, and Notes* [The Aramaic Bible 12; Wilmington, Del.: Michael Glazier, 1987], 71 n. 8). Probably מלכת, "queen" is original, the vocalized text reflecting an ancient attempt to remove an embarrassing echo of Judah's polytheistic past. That it is a *female* deity who is occluded is most significant for the gendering of the divine in the transmission of the Jeremiah tradition.

dominant, though by no means the only, voice in the complex and often messy book of Jeremiah. The claim of the devotees of the Queen of Heaven represents one possible response to that theodicy; the book of Lamentations,[2] and arguably the book of Job,[3] represent others.

There is, however, more to this passage. First of all, when read in its surrounding context, Jer 44:1–30 also appears to be concerned with the question of discernment, and should thus be read in relation to passages earlier in Jeremiah that deal directly with the question of who is, and is not, speaking what is שֶׁקֶר, "falsehood," on YHWH's behalf. The fact that Walter Moberly ignores, or overlooks, this passage in his monograph *Prophecy and Discernment* (2006)[4] suggests that the relation between Jer 44:1–30 and that theme needs to be unpacked. Second, there is the question of the extent to which devotion to the Queen of Heaven is compatible with the worship of YHWH. This issue has come to the fore in an article by Teresa Ann Ellis,[5] which explores the tension between two discursive streams in this part of Jeremiah, the rhetorically dominant "JerGod" (Jeremiah/God) stream that is hostile to devotion to the Queen of Heaven, and the rhetorically subdominant "SoH" (Sovereign of Heaven) stream, which is favorable to the worship of the Queen of Heaven and does not see it as incompatible with the worship of YHWH. Ellis convincingly shows how the JerGod stream is unstable and fails, perhaps deliberately, to unseat its rival. Third, there is the issue of how these two discursive streams are gendered, and what effect this gendering has on how the written representation of divine speech, and the distinction within the text between the masculine and the feminine, relate to each other. Although he does not deal with Jer 44:1–30, Roland Boer has recently explored the way prophetic masculinity is constructed in relation to writing in the Latter Prophets.[6] This, however, leaves open the

---

2. For an exceptionally thorough treatment of the theodic and antitheodic aspects of the book of Lamentations and the works of its modern interpreters, see now Miriam J. Bier, "'Perhaps There Is Hope': Reading Lamentations as a Polyphony of Pain, Penitence, and Hope" (Ph.D. diss., University of Otago, 2012).

3. For Job as a deep critique of the possibility of integrity within the framework of the Deuteronomic covenant, see Susannah Ticciati, *Job and the Disruption of Identity: Reading Beyond Barth* (London: T&T Clark International, 2005), 59–65.

4. Walter Moberly, *Prophecy and Discernment* (Cambridge Studies in Christian Doctrine 14; Cambridge: Cambridge University Press, 2006).

5. Teresa Ann Ellis, "Jeremiah 44: What if 'the Queen of Heaven' Is Yhwh?," *JSOT* 33 (2009): 265–88.

6. Roland Boer, "Too Many Dicks at the Writing Desk, or How to Organize a Prophetic Sausage-Fest," *Theology & Sexuality* 16 (2010): 95–108.

question of how prophetic masculinity is constructed in relation to the *written* representation of divine *speech*.

The purpose of this essay is to explore how these three strands in recent research converge on Jer 44:1–30. I am not concerned with the purely historical question of the identity of the Queen of Heaven, though I do lean in the direction of identifying her with Asherah as YHWH's consort rather than with, say, Astarte or Ishtar or some syncretistic combination thereof;[7] nor am I concerned with unraveling the tradition history of the book of Jeremiah, and the place of Jer 44:1–30 in that complex process of textual development. I am, rather, concerned with the effect of how the text of Jer 44:1–30 has been crafted on the inter-relationship between gender, orality, writing, prophecy, divine speech, and the representation of truth and falsehood.

Jeremiah 44:1–30 and the Discernment of True (and False) Prophecy

Jeremiah 44:1–30 may not look like a text concerned directly with the discernment of true prophecy, which is such an explicit issue elsewhere in Jeremiah. Yet in 44:28 Jeremiah, claiming to channel the voice of YHWH, predicts a disaster about to befall the Judahites in exile in Egypt that will make clear for the remnant of Judah that came to Egypt whose word will be established: Jeremiah's, or theirs. Jeremiah announces a sign that will confirm the truth of his words: Pharaoh Hophra will be delivered into the hand of his enemies, just as Zedekiah had been (44:30).

This is part of an ongoing theme in this section of the book: in Jer 43:2 Johanan ben Kareah had accused Jeremiah of speaking falsehood when he claimed that YHWH had promised to bless them if they stayed in Judah rather than seeking refuge in Egypt after the assassination of Gedaliah. Johanan's claim was that it was *Baruch* rather than YHWH who was the

---

7. Contrast Susan Ackerman, *Under Every Green Tree: Popular Religion in Sixth-Century Judah* (HSM 46; Atlanta: Scholars Press, 1992), 5–35, who identifies the Queen of Heaven as "a syncretistic deity whose character incorporates aspects of west Semitic Astarte and east Semitic Ištar" (34). Ackerman also, however, identifies the סמל הקנאה in Ezek 8:3, 5 with an image of Asherah, and holds the view that in some quarters of the problematically termed "popular" religion of early sixth-century B.C.E. Judah Asherah was identified as the consort of YHWH (55–66). It seems plausible to me to see that idea behind Jer 7:1–8:3 and 44:1–30, albeit that the picture of devotion to Asherah we find there may itself be profoundly stamped by traditions connected with Astarte and Ishtar.

decisive influence on Jeremiah, causing him to speak falsehood with the intent of enticing Johanan and the other Judahite exiles to remain in Judah to face death or exile at the hands of the Babylonians. The language of "falsehood" (שקר) picks up on Jeremiah's earlier attack on the prophets, and on his conflict with Hananiah. It is also one of several points connecting Jeremiah's conflict with the Judahite exiles in Egypt with his temple sermon in Jer 7:1–8:3 (esp. 7:4).

It is perhaps surprising, then, that in his important study of Jeremiah in *Prophecy and Discernment*, Walter Moberly does not address how Jer 44:1–30 contributes to the theme of prophetic conflict in Jeremiah. This may be partly because of the distinction he makes between texts concerned explicitly with discernment as such, chiefly 23:9–22, and texts concerned with prophetic conflict, in which category he places both the conflict between Jeremiah and Hananiah in 28:1–17, and the conflict between Micaiah and his prophetic opponents in 1 Kgs 22:1–38.[8] Yet this distinction is surely over-subtle: to a Judahite confronted with competing claims on behalf of YHWH in the case of the conflict between Jeremiah and Hananiah, or with competing claims on behalf of YHWH and the Queen of Heaven in the case of Jer 44:1–30, the problem would have been precisely one of *discernment*.

On the surface, Jer 44:1–30 might not appear to be directly connected with texts such as 23:9–22 or 28:1–17. It is not, strictly speaking, an account of a *prophetic* conflict, since the two parties in conflict are not both making predictions in the name of YHWH, nor, indeed, do they even seem to be speaking on behalf of the same god. Jeremiah is speaking on behalf of YHWH against exiles from Judah who are speaking on behalf of the Queen of Heaven, who does not herself speak, and are defending their ongoing devotion to her. It is true that in terms of the tradition history of the book, it is by no means clear that 28:1–17 and 44:1–30 originally had anything directly to do with each other; but they are now associated with each other within the enormously intricate literary complex we have received as the book of Jeremiah. They both contribute to the way the book constructs its truth claims, and, on closer examination, a number of important connections emerge.

To begin with, both Jeremiah's response to Hananiah and his response to the devotees of the Queen of Heaven are related in some way to the temple sermon in 7:1–8:3. In 28:1–17, Jeremiah accuses Hananiah of making the people trust in a lie (28:15). For Moberly, this suggests that

---

8. See Moberly, "Does God Lie to His Prophets? The Story of Micaiah ben Imlah as a Test Case," *HTR* 96 (2003): 1–23; *Prophecy and Discernment*, 109–29.

Hananiah is himself an example of the position against which Jeremiah warned in 7:4: "Do not trust in the lying words, 'temple of Yhwh, temple of Yhwh, temple of Yhwh'" (אל תבטחו לכם אל דברי השקר לאמר היכל יהוה היכל יהוה היכל יהוה המה).[9] This is not explicit in 28:1–17 itself, though the conflict between Hananiah and Jeremiah does take place in the temple (28:1), and is placed shortly after Jeremiah's trial for sedition, in the wake of his temple sermon, in 26:1–19, a passage that is also concerned with discernment. In the context of the book as a redacted whole, Hananiah is credited with grounding his conviction that the end of Babylonian domination was imminent in a fundamental trust in the unconditional inviolability of the Jerusalem temple, which Jeremiah seems to regard as trust in a form of cheap grace.[10] The connection between 44:1–30 and 7:1–8:3 is more direct. In both, Jeremiah charges devotees of the Queen of Heaven with responsibility for the calamity that befell Jerusalem. The moral theology of Jeremiah, according to his temple sermon, makes no distinction between the obligations to act justly and not to oppress one's neighbor on the one hand, and the prohibition against worshipping gods other than Yhwh on the other (7:5–6).[11]

---

9. Moberly, *Prophecy and Discernment*, 108. Cf. Jer 7:8, 14. As Moberly notes, in 28:15 Jeremiah's charge that Hananiah has "made this people trust in a lie" (הבטחת את העם הזה על שקר) is not said to have been communicated to Jeremiah by Yhwh. For Moberly, there would have been no point, for Jeremiah would never have been in any doubt that this was Yhwh's view; yet this rather obvious point circumvents what is really troubling about this verse, which is that a crack has opened up here in the text's presentation of the unity of Jeremiah's voice with Yhwh's. A reader persuaded by the final form of the text to identify the two may well either ignore or downplay the fact that Jeremiah is attacking Hananiah as a false prophet without being said to be mediating the word of Yhwh. There is a gap in the text that confronts the reader with a problem: can we trust the text's broader association of Jeremiah's words with Yhwh's, or not? Verses 16–17 are apparently intended to suggest that we *are* to trust them, but how far is the reader being manipulated by a willful narrator into trusting a Jeremiah whose veracity would once have been much harder to discern? The fact that the LXX in 35:1 replaces the neutral הנביא, "the prophet," with the decidedly negative ὁ ψευδοπροφήτης, "the *false* prophet," highlights the textual manipulation already present in other parts of the *Vorlage* by intensifying it further in translation.

10. The division between Hananiah and Jeremiah here may well hinge around differences in appropriating the Isaiah tradition, as Marvin Sweeney has suggested in "The Truth in True and False Prophecy," in *Truth: Interdisciplinary Dialogues in a Pluralist Age* (ed. C. Helmer and K. De Troyer; Studies in Philosophical Theology 22; Leuven: Peeters, 2003), 9–26.

11. Cf. Jer 7:8–10.

Within this moral theology, then, false prophecy cannot be distinguished, in terms of moral status, from devotion to gods other than YHWH, since both are forms of disobedience within the moral framework of the Deuteronomic covenant. Thus the book of Jeremiah, at least in its final form, is at one with the laws of Deuteronomy, where a non-YHWH prophet who speaks a word that comes true (Deut 13:2–6) is just as guilty of opposing YHWH's will as a YHWH prophet who speaks what does not come true (Deut 18:9–22). Consequently, the fact that the conflict between Hananiah and Jeremiah is between prophets who both speak for YHWH, rather than between spokespersons for different gods, is of little or no significance.

The connection between 44:1–30 and 7:1–8:3 is obvious. In 7:1–8:3, Jeremiah speaks out in YHWH's name against transgressions that are taking place in the open in Jerusalem and Judah (ובערי יהודה ובחצות ירושלם),[12] announcing that these transgressions will provoke YHWH's destructive wrath. Among the transgressions singled out by Jeremiah are various acts of devotion towards gods other than YHWH, including in particular baking cakes for the Queen of Heaven (לעשות כונים למלכת השמים)[13] and offering libations to other gods (והסך נסכים לאלהים אחרים).[14] At this point Jeremiah's speech would seem to be not merely prediction, but warning, seeking a response of repentance. In 44:1–30, Jeremiah looks back at the fulfillment—cf. Deut 18:15–22—of his earlier warnings, by which his position appears to be vindicated, at least in the context of the final shape of Jeremiah. In particular, he announced in Jer 7:20 that YHWH's anger would be poured out upon the temple, and would be unleashed indiscriminately against everything and everyone in its path. In a terse summary, the fulfillment of this warning is announced by Jeremiah in 44:6. The implication is that Jeremiah's audience should have heeded his warning, did not, and suffered the just reward for their disobedience.

To a significant extent, 44:1–30, taken together with 7:1–8:3, functions as a vindication of Jeremiah as a true spokesperson for YHWH. It shares this function with 28:1–17, and, like 28:1–17, is a narrative about the opposition a true spokesperson for YHWH can expect to face. Both narratives include a sign announced by Jeremiah that is intended to denote that his words are truly those of YHWH. In 28:15–17, the juxtaposition of Jeremiah's announcement of Hananiah's death sentence with

12. Jer 7:17; 44:6, 17, 21.
13. Jer 7:18; cf. 44:19.
14. Jer 7:18; cf. 7:9; 44:3, 5, 8, 17, 18, 19, 25.

the narrator's announcement of Hananiah's death seems to be intended to vindicate Jeremiah's truth claims, even if the cause of Hananiah's death may not have been as supernatural as the book of Jeremiah may imply.[15] In 44:29–30 Jeremiah announces the impending death of Pharaoh Hophra, but in contrast with 28:15–17, there is no suggestion that Hophra's assassination is just punishment for wrongdoing. It has no other purpose in the text than to vindicate Jeremiah's truth claims. Also in contrast with 28:1–17, the reader must supply the sequel: either this text was written before Hophra's assassination, with the intended reader meant to expect Hophra's death at some indeterminate point in the future, or it was written in full knowledge that Hophra had been assassinated, with the intended reader meant to draw on extratextual knowledge to supply the fulfillment of Jeremiah's prediction. In neither case is Jeremiah's announcement an attempt to seek a response from the victim to be. In Hananiah's case, his death is a *fait accompli*, it can no longer be escaped, and it will come about regardless of Hananiah's response; in the case of Pharaoh Hophra, the announcement of his impending assassination is intended for others, and is apparently meant to move the Judahite exiles to repent.

Both 28:1–17 and 44:1–30 reflect a particular attitude to tradition. In 28:8–9, Jeremiah identifies both himself and Hananiah as standing in a tradition of prophecy—perhaps incorporating some form of the Isaiah tradition?[16]—stretching back to ancient times.[17] He uses his knowledge of, and identification with, this tradition to suggest a framework within which contemporary prophetic truth claims might be tested: since prophets have tended truthfully to predict disaster, a prophet who predicts שלום is more likely than not to be speaking untruthfully, and perhaps with self-serving motives. By associating both himself and Hananiah with the same prophetic tradition, he is presumably intending either to persuade Hananiah to change his position, or to persuade the audience in

---

15.　J. Maxwell Miller and John H. Hayes, *A History of Ancient Israel and Judah* (2d ed.; London: SCM, 2006), 410. In fact, Jer 28:17 is teasingly laconic: "And Hananiah died" (וימת חנניה) leaves a significant gap (contrast, e.g., 44:12), opening the way for the reader to speculate how and under what circumstances Hananiah met his end, as if—as also in the case of 28:15 (cf. n. 9 above)—the reader is being *deliberately* drawn into questioning the gaps in the text, and into confronting the instability of the text's specious ideological coherence.

16.　Cf. the work of Marvin Sweeney (n. 10 above).

17.　Jeremiah refers to "the prophets who were before both me and you from ancient times" (הנביאים אשר היו לפני ולפניך מן העולם) in Jer 28:8.

the temple that this prophetic tradition does not support Hananiah.[18] In 44:4, Jeremiah, speaking in the name of YHWH, defends his god on the grounds that he had persistently sent his servants the prophets to warn the people to turn back from their wicked ways or face the punishment warranted by their disobedience. Prophetic tradition is referred to in a similar way earlier in the book, in Jer 25:3–7, and also in the narratorial summaries in 2 Kings.[19] The response-seeking, warning speech of the prophets, with whose mission Jeremiah identifies himself, has failed in its objective on account of the obstinacy of the people, and the people have been confronted with the just recompense for their obstinacy.

Two things are noteworthy about these references to a prophetic tradition. First, they have a theodic purpose: they are a means of bolstering Jeremiah's defense of YHWH's moral integrity. Since "true" prophets have continually warned the people that YHWH will enact the curses of the covenant if they continue to transgress his commandments, YHWH and his prophets—among whom this book counts the Elide priest Jeremiah—are vindicated. Second, Jeremiah is identified as a faithful representative of a coherent, trustworthy, ancient tradition, while Hananiah and the devotees of the Queen of Heaven are not. Hananiah is presented in 28:8–9 as an unfaithful representative of the same prophetic tradition to which Jeremiah appeals. The devotees of the Queen of Heaven appeal in their defense to the devotion of their ancestors to this goddess, but Jeremiah—and the narrator?—regard this as supporting *their* position, since these ancestors were engaged in the very transgressions that the destruction of Jerusalem was intended to punish.

In his turn, Jeremiah became the focus for an extensive tradition of his own. This cannot be said of the devotees of the Queen of Heaven, whose voices now exist solely in the writings of an apparently unsympathetic narrator, and cannot be said of Hananiah either, though there are certainly traditions in the Tanakh—the Zion psalms, for example, and the book of Nahum—with which he would doubtless have had much sympathy.[20] All this is significant because, in the socio-religious contexts implied by 28:1–17 and 44:1–30, all three parties—Hananiah, the devotees of the Queen of Heaven, and Jeremiah—appear to have

18. In Jer 28:7 Jeremiah speaks to both Hananiah (באזנך) and all the people (באזני כל העם).

19. 2 Kgs 17:13, 23; 21:10; 24:2. Cf. Jer 7:25; 25:4; 26:5; 29:19; 35:15; 44:4; Ezek 38:17; Amos 3:7; Zech 1:6; Dan 9:6, 10; Ezra 9:11.

20. And, of course, a certain understanding of the Isaiah tradition, if Marvin Sweeney's work is followed (n. 10 above).

believed they were speaking from a position of moral and religious integrity. Even if these narratives are nothing more than literary fictions, they imply at least the *possibility* that contexts *could have existed* in which these competing parties disagreed with one another in good faith, not with random claims, but with deep conviction, rooted in rich, living traditions. The difference between them is simply that for a variety of complex, ideologically determined reasons, Jeremiah's position was the one that helped to shape the moral-theological framework within which exegetes such as Moberly would later be able to explore questions of discernment. It is the weight and authority of this tradition more than the intrinsic worth of Jeremiah's claims that creates the impression, or illusion, that Jeremiah had got it right.

The literary presentation of Jeremiah's position is, in any case, by no means watertight. Noteworthy with respect to the coherence of Jeremiah on the issue of discernment is the claim made by Azariah ben Hoshaiah, Johanan ben Kareah, and "all the insolent men" (כל האנשים הזדים) in 43:2–3 that Jeremiah himself is speaking a lie (שקר אתה מדבר) and YHWH has not sent him (לא שלחך יהוה), the very charges leveled by Jeremiah against Hananiah. The fact that Jeremiah makes a prediction shortly after his altercation with Azariah, Johanan, and their putatively insolent companions that apparently never came true (43:7–13)[21] does nothing to cement his authority in the conflict that follows in 44:1–30.[22] To some extent, the charge of falsehood against Jeremiah in 43:2 is outweighed in the context of the Jeremiah tradition by Jeremiah's more numerous charges of falsehood against his opponents, yet this says nothing about the intrinsic truth value of Jeremiah's charges, merely about the way the ideology of the Jeremiah tradition has been con-structed and reinforced. The charge leveled against Jeremiah by his opponents cannot be meaningfully answered on moral grounds, because the description of Jeremiah's opponents as אנשים זדים may be no more than negative labeling on the part of the narrator, designed to manipulate the reader into siding with Jeremiah. We have, of course, no evidence outside the Jeremiah tradition that would enable us to assess the veracity

21. See also the apparently unfulfilled prophecy in Jer 34:9.

22. On the puzzling presence of Johanan ben Kareah's countervoice in this section of Jeremiah, and on the less than approbatory references to Baruch in chs. 43 and 45, see Ellis, "Jeremiah 44," 475–77. They point to the instability of the rhetori-cally dominant discursive stream in Jeremiah: why should the reader side with Jeremiah—or the narrator—rather than with the devotees of the Queen of Heaven or, for that matter, Hananiah?

or otherwise of the charges of immorality leveled by both the narrator and Jeremiah against their opponents.

The Silent Goddess and the Gendering of Divine Speech

The link between 44:1–30 and the issue of discernment is only part of the story. This passage is heavily coded in terms of gender. The dominant discursive stream in 44:1–30 aligns truth with the voice of a male god (YHWH), mediated through a male prophet (Jeremiah). It aligns false-hood with *female and possibly male* worshippers of a *female* deity. While male devotees of the Queen of Heaven are given a voice in the final form of the MT, the goddess herself is not, and it is clear neither whether the voice of *female* devotees is represented in 44:19—the text of the MT is problematic—nor whether we are dealing with the genuine voice of the devotees of the goddess, rather than with a voice invented by the narrator.

The debate between Jeremiah and the devotees of the Queen of Heaven is framed by the narrator, who places the scene among Judahite exiles in Egypt (44:1). Within this framing, Jeremiah speaks, quoting what he claims are the words of the male god, YHWH (44:2–6, 7–10, 11–14, 25, 26–30, 31).[23] Within the words claimed by Jeremiah—and implicitly by the narrator?—to be from YHWH, attention is drawn with the authority of YHWH's voice to the wrongdoing of the kings of Judah *and their women* (following Pesh. and *BHS* n.), and to the wrong-doing of Jeremiah's (male?)[24] addressees *and their women* (44:9). The sins that have cried out to heaven for vengeance are thus explicitly gendered, and the focus drawn to the relationship between men and women in provoking YHWH to anger. This is complicated further in 44:15, where a response is reported, by the narrator, to have been given to Jeremiah by "all the men who knew their women had been offering burnt grain offerings to other gods" (כל האנשים הידעים כי מקטרות נשיהם לאלהים אחרים), implying that it was *their women* whose wor-ship was considered illegitimate, but that *the men* were also culpable for not stopping them. This verse is ambiguous, however, since the subject

---

23. Note that in Jer 44:20–23 Jeremiah does not explicitly attribute his words to YHWH, leaving the same kind of gap we found in 28:15.

24. The suffix in "your wicked acts" (רעתכם) is second person masculine plural. The phrase "evil deeds of your fathers" (רעות אבותיכם), the first set of sins men-tioned here, includes no explicit female counterpart to the addressees' (fore)fathers.

of the verb also seems to include "all the women who were standing, a great assembly" (וכל הנשים העמדות קהל גדול). This group contests the veracity of the words Jeremiah had spoken to them "in the name of YHWH" (בשם יהוה), associating their current plight with their failure to maintain devotion to the Queen of Heaven (Jer 44:18), presumably an allusion to the reforms attributed in 2 Kgs 23:1–25 to King Josiah.[25]

This group thus does not associate devotion to the Queen of Heaven with illegitimate worship. They may believe they have been worshipping the Queen of Heaven legitimately in contradistinction to the worship of YHWH; but on the other hand they may, as Ellis argues, be detaching devotion to the Queen of Heaven from Jeremiah's charge of offering burnt grain offerings to "other gods." In this scenario, devotion to the Queen of Heaven would be assumed to be compatible with legitimate YHWH worship,[26] perhaps because from their perspective, the worship of both YHWH *and his consort*—if the Queen of Heaven is to be associated with Asherah—could not be considered apostasy, and could not on that account provoke divine retribution. That devotion to the Queen of Heaven need not be separate from devotion to YHWH is strongly suggested by Jer 44:26, where those who will suffer YHWH's wrath are those who have previously made vows in YHWH's name.[27]

25. *Pace* e.g. Bernhard Duhm, *Das Buch Jeremia* (KHC 11; Tübingen: J. C. B. Mohr, 1901), 331, who thought it unlikely that the women among the Judahite exiles in the mid-580s B.C.E. would be alluding to an event several decades earlier.

26. Thus also William McKane, "Worship of the Queen of Heaven (Jer 44)," in *"Wer ist wie du, Herr, unter den Göttern?" Studien zur Religionsgeschichte Israels für Otto Kaiser zum 70. Geburtstag* (ed. I. Kottsieper; Göttingen: Vandenhoeck & Ruprecht, 1994), 318–24 (319). The problem for the women is not that the worship of YHWH *per se* was problematic, but that the *exclusive* worship of YHWH represented by Jeremiah—and perhaps by Josiah's reform—was problematic because it had entailed the suppression of the cult of the Queen of Heaven: cf. McKane, *A Critical and Exegetical Commentary on Jeremiah, Volume 2: XXVI–LII* (ICC; Edinburgh: T. & T. Clark, 1996), 1087–89. It is not necessary to infer that there was a division of labor between the Queen of Heaven, concerned with household matters of interest to women, and YHWH, concerned with the state, war, politics, and justice, matters of more concern to men: this suggestion of Duhm (*Das Buch Jeremia*, 331) might say at least as much about perceptions of, and assumptions about, the roles of men and women in Duhm's world as it does about the realities of the Judahite cult in the early sixth century B.C.E. Duhm's picture of the scene confronting Jeremiah is of bossy women speaking out not only on their own behalf, but on behalf of their indecisive, somewhat embarrassed husbands, in defense of the cult of the Queen of Heaven.

27. That no contradiction was perceived, in at least some quarters, to exist between devotion to YHWH and that to Asherah is clear not only from inscriptions

The situation is complicated further in 44:19, in part because of textual uncertainty over who exactly is, and has been, speaking. In 44:19b it is the women alone who are speaking, but in the MT they speak without introduction, raising the question whether in an earlier version of the text they had been speaking *throughout* 44:15–19,[28] their voices later to be subsumed beneath those of their men. In the Peshitta, 44:19a begins, "And all the women answered and said..." (ܐܡܪ̈ܝܢ ܗܘ̈ܝ ܠܗܝܢ ܢܫ̈ܐ ܟܠܗܝܢ ܘܥܢܝ), a reading shared by the Lucianic recension of the LXX (καὶ αἱ γυναῖκες εἶπον), and by a marginal Syro-Hexaplar reading.[29] These variants can be read as explanatory glosses introduced to make sense of an awkward Hebrew text that is undoubtedly *lectio difficilior*,[30] yet this cannot rule out the possibility that the more difficult reading itself arose due to an incomplete process of editing out the voices of the women. Here textual criticism and feminist/ideological criticisms meet: the process of resolving the textual difficulties of 44:15–19 draws attention to the way the gendering of the text shifts and alters during the process of transmission. That is to say, the most plausible scenario for the evolution of this text—following Duhm and McKane, *inter alia*—is that there

from Kuntillet 'Ajrûd and Khirbet el-Qôm, but from Deut 16:21, where the possibility of erecting an image to Asherah—lit. "an *asherah*," a cultic pillar associated with the goddess—beside a YHWH altar is in mind, and, from a Deuteronomic perspective, prohibited (לא תטע לך אשרה כל עץ אצל מזבח יהוה אלהיך). See Diana V. Edelman, "Huldah the Prophet—of Yahweh or Asherah?," in *A Feminist Companion to Samuel and Kings* (ed. A. Brenner; FCB 5; Sheffield: Sheffield Academic, 1994), 245.

28. Thus, e.g., Duhm, *Das Buch Jeremia*, 331–33; McKane, "Worship of the Queen of Heaven," 323–24; *Jeremiah, Volume 2*, 1076–77. On the basis that the women would have had no need to mention the men's complicity if these same men had already acknowledged they had offered worship to the Queen of Heaven (Jer 44:16–18), McKane argues, largely following Duhm, that the word-string כל־האנשים ... אחרים ו in Jer 44:15 is an expansion in the MT of a *Vorlage* in which the women alone spoke.

29. Frederick Field, ed., *Origenis Hexaplorum quae supersunt; sive Veterum interpretum Graecorum in totum Vetus Testamentum fragmenta*, vol. 2 (Oxford: Clarendon, 1875), 703 n. 53; Joseph Ziegler, ed., *Ieremias, Baruch, Threni, Epistula Ieremiae* (2d ed.; SVTG 15; Göttingen: Vandenhoeck & Ruprecht, 1976), 438.

30. The difficulties in the MT (v. 19) are the phrase "We will continue to make burnt grain offerings to the Queen of Heaven" (אנחנו מקטרים למלכת השמים), where the participle מקטרים is *masculine* plural, and the phrase "Did we make cakes for her without our men?" (המבלעדי אנשינו עשינו לה כונים), where the speakers are obviously women. These Greek and Syriac variants can be explained as primarily attempting to explain the latter phrase.

existed a Hebrew text in which *women alone* responded to Jeremiah. This was subsequently overlaid by a redactional layer, in which *male* voices were introduced, but which failed to remove the women's voices entirely from 44:19b. Descendants of this now uneven text were subsequently worked over in Greek and Syriac to resolve a textual difficulty, so that the marginalized women were able to creep back into half a verse.

When Jeremiah responds, according to the narrator it is to "all the people who answered him," both "the men" (הגברים) and "the women" (הנשים; cf. 44:20). At first he speaks in his own voice (44:22–23) before claiming to channel YHWH (44:25). In 44:25 (MT) the distribution of feminine gendered verbs and masculine gendered suffixes is very confusing. As it stands in the MT, it is unclear whether a text originally addressed to women (cf. the LXX) has been imperfectly masculinized (cf. vv. 15–19), or whether the suffixes are correct and, as Ellis suggests, function as a gendered taunt against the men. This depends on reading verbs that could be construed as either second person feminine plural or third person feminine plural as unequivocally the latter.[31] The LXX, notably, has Jeremiah addressing the women directly (ὑμεῖς γυναῖκες), which makes the women primarily responsible for devotion to the Queen of Heaven. Claiming to channel the voice of YHWH, Jeremiah quotes the women as committing themselves to fulfill their vows to the Queen of Heaven. Is this their genuine voice, or a parody focalized in terms of the perspective of Jeremiah's YHWH? That is, do we hear the *genuine* voice of devotees of the Queen of Heaven, or a parody constructed by whoever was responsible for the JerGod discursive stream?

---

31. The MT of Jer 44:25 reads as follows:

כה אמר יהוה צבאות אלהי ישראל לאמר אתם (2m.pl. pronoun)
ונשיכם (2m.pl. suffix) ותדברנה (3f.pl./2f.pl.) בפיכם (2m.pl. suffix)
ובידיכם (2m.pl. suffix) מלאתם (2m.pl.) לאמר עשה נעשה
את נדרינו אשר נדרנו לקטר למלכת השמים ולהסך לה נסכים הקים
תקימנה (3f.pl./2f.pl.) את נדריכם ועשה תעשינה (3f.pl./2f.pl.)
את נדריכם (2m.pl. suffix)

Ellis's interpretation yields the following translation: "Thus says YHWH of Hosts, the God of Israel, saying: *You and your wives—they have spoken with your mouths and with your hands you have fulfilled*, saying, 'Surely we shall perform our vows that we have vowed—to burn grain-offerings to the Sovereign of Heaven and to pour out libations to her.' *Surely they shall confirm your vows and surely they shall perform your vows!*" ("Jeremiah 44," 181). That is, the women have ordered their men, and the men have obliged, which would chime rather nicely, in fact, with Duhm's reconstruction of the goings-on in 44:15–19 (see n. 26 above).

What is clear here is that the voice of authority lies with Jeremiah and YHWH, and this voice marginalizes—perhaps even caricatures—the voices of women devoted to the Queen of Heaven, and silences the voice of the goddess herself. It is impossible to know whether the *unmediated* voice of the goddess's devotees could at one time have been heard challenging that of Jeremiah and his male god, or even whether the goddess's own voice could at one time have been heard either in concert with, or in conflict with, that of YHWH. By marginalizing the devotees of the goddess and silencing the goddess herself, this text in its various versions genders the voice of the divine—and his prophetic mediator—as unequivocally male.

Prophetic Masculinity and the Written Representation of Divine Speech

The way the voice of the divine is gendered in Jer 44:1–30 has an effect on how the gender of the *prophet* is constructed, which brings us to a recent consideration of prophetic masculinity by Roland Boer. In a characteristically provocative paper—whose title was too much for those responsible for the 2010 SBL program, who, with considerable prudish embarrassment, begged its author to call it something less revealing of male genitals[32]—Boer examines the way texts such as Isa 8:1, Ezek 9:2–3, 11, and Jer 36:1–32 illustrate the deep interrelationship between power, writing, masculinity, and the identity of the prophet.

I will not rehearse the whole of Boer's argument, which I only find partially convincing, but I do wish to revisit a couple of the texts on which he touches, one from Isaiah, the other from Jeremiah. Isaiah 8:1, in particular, is significant both for its focus on writing *per se*, and for its focus on the connection between writing and male sexuality. In Isa 8:1, the prophet is commanded to write on a large sheet of some sort

---

32. This is ironic, in view of Boer's argument, which criticizes the way commentators tend to be "all too ready to espy in *hapax legomena* [in Ezek 16 and 23] references to women's genitals," while failing to consider that a rare word such as קסת in the phrase וקסת הספר במתניו (Ezek 9:2; cf. vv. 3, 11) might have anything to do with male genitals (Boer, "Too Many Dicks," 95–96). Boer's article responds with "an explicit attempt to sexualize, objectify and thereby disempower textual male bodies" (ibid., 96). Boer blogged through the controversy, and eventually delivered his paper with the original title; see Boer, "SBL censorship: 'Sausage-fests' are unacceptable," n.p. [cited 31 August 2012]. Online: http://stalinsmoustache. wordpress.com/2010/10/23/sbl-censorship-sausage-fests-are-unacceptable. In order to access the full discussion, click on the tag "sausage-fest."

(גליון גדול) with "a man's stylus" (חרט אנוש) the name מהר שלל חש בז.
Immediately thereafter, Isaiah inscribes the same in a woman's body,
naming the woman's child at YHWH's command. The trustworthiness of
Isaiah's words is somehow at issue, so the prophet must call upon
"trustworthy witnesses" (עדים נאמנים) to validate his words in some way
(Isa 8:2).[33] In Jer 31:33, YHWH promises to write the words of the new
covenant on the hearts of his people so that he might be their god and
they his people. This is connected with the prophetic marriage metaphor,
both through the use of the verb בעל in Jer 31:32 to refer to the former
relationship between YHWH and Israel,[34] and through the possible echo in
Jer 31:33 of Hos 1:9.[35] If writing is connected with the maleness and
fecundity of the prophet in Isa 8:1, writing is connected with the
maleness of the prophet's god in Jer 31:33.

Writing functions as an expression of power, and in the case of
Jeremiah it is significant that while the words of Jeremiah and his various
opponents are presented as being delivered orally, not only do they come
to us solely through the medium of writing, but that writing both presents
Jeremiah's prophetic voice as dominant, and reflects self-consciously on
the process of writing itself. Centered on the figure of Baruch, Jeremiah's
amanuensis and the one Johanan ben Kareah regards as responsible for
Jeremiah's falsehood, the writtenness of the book of Jeremiah places us
at several steps removed from whatever oral exchanges may lie behind
it, controlling our access—and our lack of it—to them, and creating the
paradoxical situation of an authoritative *written* text whose authority
rests on the trustworthiness and immediacy of an *orally* delivered word
from YHWH. This is part of the process by which scribe and prophet,
originally understood to be independent figures, came eventually to be
elided by the time of 1 and 2 Chronicles,[36] the prophet-as-scribe controlling the written text and its truth claims and determining its authority.

33. Cf. Isa 34:8–11. For further references to the inscribing of the divine word,
both law and prophecy, see Exod 34:1, 27; Isa 4:3; Jer 17:1, 13; 22:30; 25:13; 31:33;
Ezek 24:2; 43:11; cf. Nah 1:1; 1 Chr 29:29; 2 Chr 9:29.

34. The verb בעל can mean "rule over" or "marry" (*HALOT* 1:142b), but given
the patriarchal structure of ancient Israelite marriage it is hard to see that a clear
difference between the two could be maintained. The verb is used for YHWH's
relationship with Israel in Isa 54:5 (cf. Isa 26:13) and Jer 3:14, shortly after the
northern kingdom of Israel has been said to have been presented with a bill of
divorce (Jer 3:8; cf. Deut 24:1–2), and it is used elsewhere with clear reference to
a man's ownership of his woman (Deut 21:13; 24:1; Isa 62:5; Mal 2:11; perhaps
1 Chr 4:22; cf. Gen 20:3; Deut 22:22; Isa 54:1).

35. Cf. Jer 30:22.

36. 1 Chr 29:29; 2 Chr 9:29. See Boer, "Too Many Dicks," 103.

Writing, and the figure of Baruch, book-end the conflict between Jeremiah and the devotees of the Queen of Heaven. Johanan ben Kareah accuses Jeremiah of succumbing to Baruch's influence rather than YHWH's in Jer 43:2, then in 45:1 we read of Baruch *writing down* (בכתבו) on a *scroll* (ספר) the *word* (דבר) that Jeremiah *spoke* (דבר) in the name of his god, YHWH, whom Jeremiah claims has *said* what he is about to relate (כה אמר יהוה, 45:2).[37] Authority resides in the *spoken* word, but our only access is through the *written* words of Baruch, whose words are gendered as those of a male god channeled through a male prophet and a male scribe, but whose trustworthiness is in doubt on account both of their distance from their source and their having been tainted with the charge of falsehood.

Conclusion

A number of conclusions may be drawn. First, in the final form of Jeremiah, Jer 44:1–30 cannot meaningfully be separated from texts earlier in the book concerned with the discernment of prophecy and the conflict between prophets: all are part of the complex construction of truth in the book. Second, the way the language of 44:1–30 is gendered in Hebrew, but also in Greek and Syriac, points to a process by which the dominant discursive strand in the text marginalizes women devoted to the Queen of Heaven, and confines the goddess herself to silence, leading to a gendering of the truth claims associated with the voice of Jeremiah—and thereby with the voice of YHWH—as singular and male. This serves to reinforce the profoundly gendered portrayal of the relationship between YHWH and Israel elsewhere in the book, and elsewhere in the Latter Prophets. Third, the gendering of truthful divine speech as male in the dominant discursive stream contributes to the construction of prophetic masculinity in Jeremiah, and indirectly to the gendering of prophecy, and of divine speech generally, as masculine across the Tanakh.[38]

37. Cf. Jer 25:13; 30:2. For another assessment of Baruch's role see the article of Stuart Macwilliam, "The Prophet and His Patsy: Gender Performativity in Jeremiah," in this volume.

38. Lest Huldah been seen without further ado as an exception, a plausible case can be made for Huldah as originally a prophet of *Asherah*, turned into a prophet of YHWH by those responsible for the present form of 2 Kgs 22:14–20; see Edelman, "Huldah the Prophet."

A RESPONSE BY WALTER BRUEGGEMANN

I should no doubt begin with a disclaimer: I am old, white, male, tenured, and schooled in historical criticism. The inevitable result of that social locus is that there is likely a lot in this collection that I do not quite get, as I am always playing catch-up. As a consequence, this wondrous collection of essays has come at me like a tsunami, filled with threat, embarrassment, instruction, and invitation. It amounts to a threat for me because it calls into question not only many of my governing assumptions, but also the arts whereby I have been able to do interpretation at all. It constitutes an embarrassment for me because readings of text are offered about which I should have long since known and did not. It is a huge instruction for me, both concerning new learnings and concerning unlearnings that are now required. It is an invitation to me to take up new work, to pay attention to new paradigms, and to engage younger scholars who know more and other than I do. So I begin with an expression of my gratitude to this impressive company of scholars of the next generation, and the next one after that.

I take that long to locate myself vis-à-vis this collection because I suspect that this response is not peculiarly and singularly my response. There are a lot of us in the discipline…old, white, male, tenured, schooled in historical criticism…who are engaged in unlearning and catching up. That no doubt is the intent of our scholarly enterprise in general and surely the intent of this collection. This volume surely has the purpose of inviting many readers into fresh perspectives, and I am glad to be among those summoned and invited. In making my response, I have eschewed the dreary convention of commenting *ad seriatim* on each essay. Instead, I have opted for the freedom to state what it is that this collection has caused me to think that I would not have thought without it. I will mention several essays specifically, but this is not to say less about the ones I have not mentioned. I believe the force of these essays is cumulative, and I have tried to take all of them seriously in making a response. The essays have done their work for me in inviting and summoning me well beyond where I was in a prior moment.

These several essays follow a fairly regular pattern. They state the theoretical basis for interpretation that is commonly shared by these writers, a collection of feminist and post-colonial readers; they then take up specific texts as embodiments and performances of that theoretical perspective. It is inescapable that there will be some repetition in the statement of theoretical matters, but these foundational matters cannot be repeated too often, important and fresh as they are.

Christl Maier declares the end of the "One-Man Show."[1] By this she means the singular isolated interpreter, for example a tenured, old, white male schooled in historical criticism. Her advocacy is that commentary must be multi-voiced to reflect the multi-voiced richness of the text, and so must benefit from more than one author. That point is well taken.

But before any of the current commentators who have been "one-man shows," there was an originary, paradigmatic "one-man show," that of René Descartes. His name is not much mentioned here, but his footprints are all over the history of interpretation in our discipline and behind this volume. It was Descartes who put our thinking, reading, interpretation, and believing on the new footing of single-voiced "objectivity." Descartes intended, at the break of the modern world, to provide a new basis not only for science but for faith. He was, however, compelled to defend the possibility of faith on grounds that in fact contradicted that very possibility.[2] He bequeathed to us a legacy of "objectivity" that was able to identify one meaning from one voice in the text, and that by mostly the pursuit of the genetic. Thus our Cartesian legacy has taken the form of historical criticism, a collage of methods that has served to explain away almost everything interesting or difficult in the text, including of course the vexed, vexing character of God. The result is that "God" can be managed with certitude and with reasonableness. Whatever does not fit that required reasonableness must be explained away.

I have wondered why it is that in recent decades it has been old, white tenured males who continue to champion historical criticism while newer methods (as those practiced here) have come largely from those outside of that monopoly. Now I get it! What we have termed "reasonable" is in fact the force of empire, the often unacknowledged service of dominant reason that could be taken as objective, even though it has obviously and readily served vested interests. We have been slow to recognize, I think,

---

1. Note the title of Maier's essay, "After the 'One-Man Show': Multi-Authored and Multi-Voiced Commentary Writing," 72–85, in this volume.

2. See Michael J. Buckley, *At the Origins of Modern Atheism* (New Haven: Yale University Press, 1987).

that such methods in fact served imperial interests, practiced by "urban elites" (like us) who have participated in the benefits of empire.

I have of late been pondering the work of Tomoko Masuzawa and her probe of the emergence of "World Religions" as a subject of study and formulation as an academic discipline.[3] Her thesis is that the inventory of "world religions" in the nineteenth century (the high season of historical criticism) was a project to assess world religions and then to establish the superiority of Christianity and the European Enlightenment culture that supported it. That project, she shows, was particularly acute in identifying Semitic faiths (Judaism and Islam) as primitive and inferior. The argument was in part based originally on the notion that Semitic verbs could not be adequately inflected. It was the assumption of superiority in the service of so-called objectivity with which our historical criticism has colluded, all in the practice of mono-voiced interpretation that was of course top-down.

This entire program of Cartesian mono-voice found one of its great critical respondents in Martin Buber, who explicitly sets out his "dialogic" perspective as a counter and alternative to the mono perspective of Cartesianism. Most famously in *I–Thou*, but everywhere in his work, Buber insisted that reality is at bottom interactive and dialogic, even though in his theological idealism he assumed the priority of the "Thou" of God over the "I" of the human person.[4] It surely cannot be accidental or incidental that Buber was nurtured and situated in Jewish tradition and Jewish texts that the rabbis understood, from the outset, to be dialogic and multi-voiced.

Indeed, it is that same multi-voiced reality of tension, ambiguity, hyperbole, and dispute of a peculiarly Jewish kind that lies behind Freud's great insight about the human self. It turns out that the text is as conflicted, complicated, and multi-layered as is the human self; and conversely, the human self is as conflicted, complicated, and multi-layered

3. Tomoko Masuzawa, *The Invention of World Religions: Or, How European Universalism Was Preserved in the Language of Pluralism* (Chicago: University of Chicago Press, 2005). As her argument relates to our discipline, see Walter Brueggemann and Davis Hankins, "The Invention and Persistence of Wellhausen's World," *CBQ* 75 (2013): 15–31

4. Martin Buber, *I and Thou* (trans. R. G. Smith; New York: Charles Scribner's Sons, 1937); idem, "The History of the Dialogical Principle," in *Between Man and Man* (trans. R. G. Smith; New York: Macmillan, 1965), 209–24. More broadly, see Shmuel Hugo Bergman, *Dialogical Philosophy from Kierkegaard to Buber* (Albany: State University of New York Press, 1991).

as is the Jewish text.[5] The modern practice of thinning the human self or the text to one voice is a contemporary practice that besets our discipline even as it besets our culture.

The legacy of Buber, moreover, is taken up by Emmanuel Lévinas in his insistence that the "face of the other" is the ground of ethical serious-ness.[6] Thus Lévinas pushes beyond Buber's mystical idealism. It is the existence of the other in textual reading that requires us to take seriously the denseness and thickness of interaction in the text and among human selves. From that I note that Martha Nussbaum, in her sturdy response to Samuel Huntington, has observed that the capacity to host the other or to refuse the other is the key question of ethics and finally of social justice and world peace:

> The clash between proponents of ethnoreligious homogeneity and propo-
> nents of a more inclusive and pluralistic type of citizenship is a clash
> between two types of people within a single society. At the same time, this
> clash expresses tendencies that are present, at some level, within most
> human beings: the tendency to seek domination as a form of self-protec-
> tion, versus the ability to respect others who are different, and to see in
> difference as a nation's richness rather than a threat to purity.... The real
> "clash of civilizations" is not "out there," between admirable Westerners
> and Muslim zealots. It is here, within each person, as we oscillate uneasily
> between self-protective aggression and the ability to live in the world with
> others.[7]

If I read rightly, the import of this collection is to move us from an "objective" world, from the Cartesian world of mono-logic reasonable-ness that is top-down, to a multi-voiced alternative that is richly indeter-minate. That move entails not only a challenge to the conventional practices of our discipline, but a deeper challenge to the epistemological assumptions of our culture with our sense of superiority. Thus as evi-denced in dozens of specific texts, the program of the collection is to make clear that the "constructed" is not "given."[8] It is constructed! And

5. See Susan A. Handelman, *The Slayers of Moses: The Emergence of Rabbinic Interpretation in Modern Literary Theory* (Albany: State University of New York Press, 1982), Chapter 5.

6. Emmanuel Lévinas, *Totality and Infinity: An Essay on Exteriority* (Pittsburgh: Duquesne University Press, 1969).

7. Martha Nussbaum, *The Clash Within: Democracy, Religious Violence, and India's Future* (Cambridge: Belknap, 2007), 15, 337.

8. Thus Judith McKinlay, "Challenges and Opportunities for Feminist and Post-colonial Biblical Criticism," 19–37, in this volume, can, quoting R. S. Sugirtharajah, speak of a postcolonial lens used here as "an interventionist instrument which

our continued constructive work, funded by these unsettled materials, is at work against every apparent "given."

These essays rather consistently juxtapose the dominant voice in the text in contest with the voice of pain, the voice of the victim, the voice of the vulnerable and excluded. Thus the enterprise is an act of advocacy both about the text and within the text. While I had not seen this clearly, my own suggestion a bit ago, concerning "structure legitimation" and "embrace of pain," was an inchoate attempt to state the same challenge.[9] Once *pain has been embraced* (by act and speech), *the legitimation of structure* cannot be sustained in such an innocent or unilateral way; everything about such legitimation is now vigorously called into question. It is this voice of the silenced victim, here found everywhere in the text, that jeopardizes the claims of the dominant voice.

The move from the "one-man show" to the work of "multi" calls to mind the work of Michael Hardt and Antonia Negri, who in two insistent volumes have written of "empire" and of "multitude."[10] In *Empire*, they traced the way in which hegemonic power is formed and maintained.[11] In *Multitude*, they envision a massive agency from below that challenges empire and that holds open democratic possibility.[12] Thus in some ways I suggest that these essays are a performance of democratic voice against the loud voice of empire with its authoritarian and absolutist tendency, uttered in order to give voice to those at the margins of power.

I must report my most visceral response to these essays was when reading Steed Davidson on the Rechabites.[13] He offers a top-down reading of the Rechabites from the angle of establishment power. From

refuses to take the dominant reading as an uncomplicated representation of the past" (24). And Carolyn Sharp, "Mapping Jeremiah as/in a Feminist Landscape: Negotiating Ancient and Contemporary Terrains," 38–56, in this volume, lists as her first "driving concern" a practice of feminism that "*interrogates and seeks to destabilize ideologies of subjugation* and the oppressive practices to which those ideologies give rise" (43, original emphasis).

    9. See Walter Brueggemann, *Old Testament Theology: Essays on Structure, Theme, and Text* (ed. P. D. Miller; Minneapolis: Fortress, 1992), 1–44.
    10. Steed Davidson, "'Exoticizing the Otter': The Curious Case of the Rechabites in Jeremiah 35," 189–207 (206), in this volume, cites the work of Hardt and Negri.
    11. Michael Hardt and Antonio Negri, *Empire* (Cambridge, Mass.: Harvard University Press, 2000).
    12. Michael Hardt and Antonio Negri, *Multitude: War and Democracy in the Age of Empire* (New York: Penguin, 2004).
    13. See Davidson, "Exoticizing the Otter."

such a perspective, the Rechabites are viewed as "quaint," "curious," "esoteric," "mysterious," and "out of step with the mainstream culture."[14] He judges that they are, in dominant interpretation, treated by "exoticist codes of representation," so that they are seen as odd and different, but not to be taken seriously. I responded to that labeling with some passion, repelled by such a top-down judgment that Davidson takes as typical of imperial thought. I had no trouble understanding that response on my part. I am a child of a German-speaking immigrant peasant community that was vigilant about being portrayed and treated in condescending or dismissive ways by establishment culture all around us. It was an easy move for me to transfer from that characterization of those who were "exoticized" by top-down judgment to my own immigrant peasant community, even though we were nothing like the Rechabites: we drank wine, we shaved, and we did not live in tents. But the reading of Davidson rang true in my own experience.

But then, midway through his analysis, Davidson reverses field by a shift to postcolonial perspective:

> The postcolonial turn in reading this chapter [Jer 35] requires stepping back from the exoticist code that renders the Rechabites mere fodder for the book of Jeremiah's theo-political arguments and moving forward by revealing a different set of power relations in the narrative.... Breaking the exoticist code enables the text to reveal a group of persons also caught in the maelstrom of empire but one that constructs a different relationship with empire.[15]

They are, Davidson says, a "form of social resistance," able to "live counter-imperially," so that their "landlessness" is itself a form of resistance.[16] Davidson offers this as a gain of post-colonialism in which the sub-group is not defined by the dominant group or its text, but is seen in its own intrinsic intentionality. This shrewd double characterization of the sub-community, by empire and its own determination, is readily transferred in our time to the Euro-Western capacity to practice racist dismissiveness of those unlike us, a racist judgment that continues to feed military adventurism in our own day. My appreciation of this gain from Davidson's rereading is existentially immediate for me with reference to my own community of identity and nurture. The dominant voice characteristically misreads those "below."

14. Ibid., 196, 202.
15. Ibid., 203.
16. Ibid., 205–6.

The methods utilized in this collection are rich and suggestive. I am disappointed, however, that the great tilt is toward feminist matters to the modest neglect of postcolonial issues of a broader kind. Claassens acknowledges that there is "an interlocking system of oppression because of racism, classism, colonialism, and sexism."[17] I am disappointed that lines are not extended in this collection in two directions. First, there is, so it seems to me, a curious neglect of economic matters. Since a primary purpose of empires is to extract wealth from the colony, we might have expected much more on that front. But my greater disappointment is that methodologically there is a refusal to engage in serious theological substance. My impression is that references to God (as in the "cruel image of God") remains at a social-scientific level.[18] I am acutely interested in questions of "biblical theology," questions that have been unfortunately slotted in the dismissive category of "Biblical Theology Movement" as though because of the polemical labeling we therefore need no longer to attend to such issues. Because I live in a culture that appeals to these texts as "reliable," a more serious theological engagement is surely in order. I know all about "theological construction," "ideological vested interest," "projection," and so forth. Given all of that, however, we still have to wonder what we are doing when we take these witnesses with theological seriousness or when we readily dismiss their theological claims. Thus I think there is an ethical responsibility not only to raise questions of truth but to raise questions of truth as they were entertained and processed by those who wrote, processed, and took these texts seriously. Thus it matters if we think that Jeremiah or Hananiah or any other voice in the text intended to be thinking and talking about what they appear to think and talk about. What if, in their purview, this is not the construction of a convenient icon of God but is rather a true God? I think that the questions of "multi-voice" need to be "kicked upstairs" to serious substantive theological issues. What we find in the text is that God is a multi-voiced character with a contested internal life that is more than a projection of any single ideology.[19] What if the reason for such a rendering of God is not just because of many competing human voices or

17. L. Juliana Claassens, "'Like a Woman in Labor': Gender, Postcolonial, Queer, and Trauma Perspectives on the Book of Jeremiah," 117–32 (118), in this volume, quoting Kwok Pui-lan.

18. E.g. Christl M. Maier, "God's Cruelty and Jeremiah's Treason: Jeremiah 21:1–10 in Postcolonial Perspective," 133–49 (140), in this volume.

19. See Walter Brueggemann, *An Unsettling God: The Heart of the Hebrew Bible* (Minneapolis: Fortress, 2009).

many distinct traditions, but because that is how God in Israel turned out to be (revealed, constructed, imagined, or whatever)? I think to remain at a social-scientific level is too easy. And I dare to think such a stance is still too "imperial." It is like the arrival of social scientists at a "primitive island" without having read Clifford Geertz. In such company we know, beforehand, better than the "natives" who practice these strange texts. Knowing beforehand is a seduction of empire, and permits, yet again, for the interpreter to be an objective observer who can adjudicate every social reality. But what are we to make of the "Cruel God" in the text who can exhibit pathos with an absolute infinite in 31:20?[20] What shall we make of a God who can rage and weep, sometimes in the same unit of poetry? I am inclined to think that these essays continue to think top-down about a God connected to imperial interests, without recognition of the playful complexity and complicatedness of the character of God. This leaves for the theological interpreter a wonderment if more can be said than a simplistic rejection of the dominant God for the sake of the victim. I do not think we have any business defending this God and I have no interest in doing so. It is, however, a different matter to take seriously the character of this God as given in the imagination of the text, because there is an articulation of God here that is very different from a one-dimensional imperial icon. Thus Rieger and Kwok can judge:

> The deepest problem of our most common images of God, supported by conservatives and liberals alike, is that images of the divine as omnipotent, impassible, and immutable tend to mirror the dominant powers that be, from ancient emperors to modern CEOs. No wonder people talk about God also as the "guy in the sky" or the "man upstairs".... The connection of God and the dominant powers is no mere coincidence, it seems to us.... Calling in question top-down images of God is therefore not just concern for those who refuse to believe in God but also a concern for Jews and Christians who seek to be faithful to the God of their traditions.... The dominant theism of the Roman Empire was closely linked to classical theistic images of God as omnipotent, immutable, and impassible.[21]

But of course that is not the God given (constructed) in the text of Jeremiah. This is rather a God who sounds in the text in many voices, reflective of an internal unsettled complexity. I suggest that if we are

---

20. On the thickness of God in the Jeremiah tradition, see Abraham Heschel, *The Prophets* (New York: Harper & Row, 1962), 221–323, and Kazoh Kitamori, *Theology of the Pain of God* (Eugene: Wipf & Stock, 2005 [1965]).

21. Joerg Rieger and Kwok Pui-lan, *Occupy Religion: Theology of the Multitude* (New York: Rowman & Littlefield, 2012), 88–89.

to move from Descartes to Buber (as it were), then we have to ponder, more than do these essays, the disputed, contested internal life of the character of God voiced in the text. The God attested in this tradition is not a settlement but a problem, a problem to be taken seriously and not dismissed as icon of empire.

Holt movingly ends her essay by a quotation from Susanne L., from the work of Bernhard Lang:

> If destiny hits me severely, I might even turn to God and start praying. I do light a candle in church, so I am not without reverence. I could put it this way: I believe in the God who protects my family and me but I do not know if he exists.[22]

That is about as indeterminate as we can get, but it is serious. It allows for openness, even while being "too intelligent" to give in easily to the question. Holt ends her shrewd essay by contrasting a "critical approach" with that of "American Evangelicalism":

> The perception of the authority of the Bible by the average student of theology in Denmark (and Scandinavia and Northern Germany as well) is so influenced by a critical approach that only a few will feel haunted by Jeremiah's God—and those few, being uncharacteristically close to American evangelicalism, would hardly ever question the will of God and the righteousness of his judgment.[23]

By "critical approach" Holt means *Enlightenment rationality* and by "American evangelicalism" she means *fundamentalism*. Thus we live in a culture that is reduced to one of these two options, as though there were no other way to formulate and engage the issue. I do not think this collection goes very far with the matter, but tends, itself, to an imperial reductionism of a dominant voice of God that is allied with dominant power. That, so it seems to me, is a misreading that does not allow for the disputatious contestation reflected in God in the text. The poetry exhibits a God with stern uncompromising self-regard and pathos for victims, a combination that continues without resolve. In order to engage the matter it is required to move beyond the safe perspective of social science to enter the venturesome poetic force of the text itself that refuses such reductionism. It may be that the persona of Jeremiah, as given us in

---

22. See Else K. Holt, "'The Stain of Your Guilt Is Still Before Me' (Jeremiah 2:22): (Feminist) Approaches to Jeremiah 2 and the Problem of Normativity," 141–62 (115), in this volume.

23. Ibid., 116.

the text, is offered as the lead character who is willing to go into the dangerous place where Enlightenment objectivity and fundamentalism have no compelling say at all. It is perhaps this next step that this cadre of impressive interpreters might take. We are greatly in their debt; we might hope for a sequel that engages the multi-voiced reality that extends even to the agency of holiness.[24]

24. Sharp, "Mapping Jeremiah," 53, comments: "I submit that the death-dealing ways of imperialism are refused, over and over again, by the God of the Hebrew Scriptures."

ON WRITING A FEMINIST-POSTCOLONIAL COMMENTARY: A CRITICAL EVALUATION[*]

Irmtraud Fischer

A biblical scholar who has gained some standing in the academic guild and has placed some notable publications will probably be invited at some point to write a commentary, especially in German-speaking scholarship. In Europe, the genre "commentary" still enjoys great popularity in spite of the fact that secularism is rising and printed theological literature is in decline. Many larger and smaller commentary series that were initiated in the postwar period have been completed only recently[1] or are currently newly issued.[2] Moreover, there are two recent large-scale commentary projects in German biblical scholarship[3] that programmatically demonstrate an ecumenical breadth (including Judaism) and also invite non-German scholars as authors.[4] As a German-speaking exegete

* English translation provided by Christl M. Maier and Carolyn Sharp.

1. From a Roman Catholic perspective, there are "Neue Echter Bibel" (NEchtB 1980–), published by Echter-Verlag, Würzburg, and "Neuer Stuttgarter Kommentar: Altes Testament" (NSKAT 1992–), published by Katholisches Bibelwerk, Stuttgart.

2. Series with a Protestant background are "Biblischer Kommentar: Altes Testament" (BKAT 1955–), published by Neukirchener Verlag, Neukirchen–Vluyn, "Das Alte Testament Deutsch" (ATD 1949–) by Vandenhoeck & Ruprecht, Göttingen, and "Zürcher Bibelkommentare" (ZBK 1960–) by Theologischer Verlag, Zürich. In these series, the biblical books are currently receiving a complete revision so that effectively "second series" emerge.

3. These are "Herders Theologischer Kommentar zum Alten Testament" (HTKAT 1999–), published by Herder Verlag, Freiburg, initiated by Erich Zenger in the 1990s, and the newly projected "International Exegetical Commentary on the Old Testament" (IECOT 2012–), published by Kohlhammer, Stuttgart, and initiated by a group of scholars under the auspices of Walter Dietrich and David Carr. The latter will be published simultaneously in German and English; its first volume has appeared recently: Paul Redditt, *Zechariah 9–14* (IECOT; Stuttgart: Kohlhammer, 2012).

4. Women as authors have been either non-existent or the proverbial exception that proves the rule.

who published a commentary with a feminist perspective,[5] serves as co-editor of the IECOT series, and has been commissioned with two more commentaries,[6] I know both sides of the concept "biblical commentary" as well as the concerns of both editors and authors.

1. *Writing an Old Testament Commentary Today*

The last 150 years have been dominated by two kinds of commentaries determined by their target audience: scholarly commentaries and commentaries for pastoral work, the latter written to provide accessible information for sermons and Bible studies. Both kinds of commentary have, in the main, been given to historical-critical research. Commentaries with a different approach are rare exceptions[7]—in the German-language arena there are hardly any so far.

Although one may think at present that "biblical commentary" as a genre has been generated by historical-critical research, it celebrated its triumphs prior to that, namely in patristic times, when typological, allegorical, and moral interpretations of Scripture had been dominant.

a. *The Commentary Genre: Legitimate and Excessive Claims*

The genre "biblical commentary"[8] differs from other exegetical publications insofar as these works claim to interpret the Bible, or at least one biblical book, as a whole and simultaneously to comment on each chapter and verse. Even if published in fascicles, commentaries are book projects over against the current scholarly trend, which science imposed on the humanities, to publish short articles in—preferably peer-reviewed—journals, which yield much higher scores in a scholar's evaluation. Commentaries are *per se* going against this trend because they do not aim at producing innovative *solitary observations* in response to highly specific questions but instead offer *comprehensive views*, either on the biblical texts or on research dealing with a whole biblical book. It goes without saying that commentaries may be innovative conceptually.

---

5. Irmtraud Fischer, *Rut* (2d ed.; HTKAT; Freiburg: Herder, 2005).

6. My commentary on Gen 12–36 for the HTKAT series is expected to be released in 2017; another one on Jonah for IECOT will be forthcoming in 2014.

7. See, e.g., "The Forms of the Old Testament Literature" series (FOTL 1983–) and Carol A. Newsom and Sharon H. Ringe, eds., *Women's Bible Commentary* (London: SPCK, 1992; exp. ed.; Louisville: Westminster John Knox, 1998).

8. See Christl M. Maier's essay, "After the 'One-Man Show': Multi-Authored and Multi-Voiced Commentary Writing," 72–85, in this volume.

In these ways, the writing of a biblical commentary is always a tightrope walk with regard to method. While no aspect of meticulous exegesis should be left out, it is impossible to comment on every verse within the given page range of a volume. Today, it is no longer sufficient to explore a biblical book through a classical historical-critical approach; authors are expected to be familiar with other methodologies as well, such as narratological or rhetorical criticism and their quite helpful tools. Authors should also be acquainted with the discourse on intertextuality and canonical criticism in order competently to interpret the final form of the text. The commentary series, which I am co-editing and in the context of which the present volume has emerged, pursues an ambitious agenda with regard to methodological and hermeneutical issues. This commentary has to meet the requirements of the historical-critical research tradition while at the same time incorporating synchronic aspects that emerge from reading the Bible as literature as well as from engaging the narrative context of the biblical canon. A volume written in the twenty-first century should therefore also include the contextual perspectives of social history, liberation theology, and gender studies. Moreover, the current trend to explore not only the history of the text's formation but also its later interpretations ought to be reflected in a commentary via mention of certain elements of reception history.[9] Whereas the approach of *Wirkungsgeschichte* focuses hermeneutically on the effects of readings of the Bible as its object, research on reception history centers on the text's recipients as well as on the social and cultural contexts that generate specific forms of interpretation. Christl Maier's essay in this volume offers an excellent overview of contemporary commentaries that focus on reception history.[10] The IECOT series,[11] which by design is bilingual and thus seeks to connect the German-speaking and Anglophone research traditions, delineates an ideal concept. Editors and authors of the single volumes, however, are fully aware that not all aspects mentioned above can be elaborated to the same degree in all volumes. Like most commentaries—whose publishers desire to sell numerous copies—IECOT is designed to be accessible, if not to lay persons, to professionals who need concise information for their preparation of sermons or Bible studies. Therefore, the commentary's scholarly prose has to be leveled out between the often conflicting goals of high legibility and up-to-date academic rigor.

9. See Irmtraud Fischer, "Von der *Vor*geschichte zur *Nach*geschichte: Schriftauslegung in der Schrift—Intertextualität—Rezeption," *ZAW* 125 (2013): 143–60.
10. Maier, "After the 'One-Man Show'," 77–79.
11. For more details, see the websites www.iecot.com and www.iekat.de.

The IECOT has the significant advantage that authors provide their own translations, since the series is not bound to any denominational Bible translation like other commentaries in the German-speaking countries.[12] Thus, the authors' new translations can avoid or deconstruct interpretive stereotypes that are attached to specific Bible translations and fail to do justice to the biblical text. This is not only essential for the objective of providing a gender-sensitive Bible translation but also for unveiling the position of marginalized groups or imperial policies and for deconstructing discriminatory language.[13] The distance from any tradition of denominational Bible translation and the possibility of fresh translations provide an opportunity for authors to choose new hermeneutical approaches that may generate innovative readings relevant to contemporary society. Apart from presenting a bilingual edition of each volume, Kohlhammer's new commentary series also aims at dual authorship. Leaving behind the "one-man show," the commentary on Jeremiah will be the first in German to be authored by women.[14] Although it will maintain a historical-critical approach, the hermeneutics of this commentary will move away from finding the *ipsissima vox* of a charismatic-prophetic individual to an exploration of the manifold voices in the book of Jeremiah.[15] Thereby the commentary clearly rejects a phenomenon that has been reflected rarely (but often caused anti-Jewish sentiments), namely that historical-critical interpretations frequently declare older texts as more authentic or even more valuable than the canonized final text, which sometimes is held to be epigonic.[16]

12. The German commentary series "Neue Echter Bibel" (NEchtB) is bound to the so-called "Einheitsübersetzung" which in the Hebrew Bible is a Roman Catholic translation.

13. The objective to do justice to women and marginalized persons is claimed by the recent German translation entitled *Bibel in gerechter Sprache* (ed. U. Bail et al.; 3d ed.; Gütersloh: Gütersloher, 2007). For this concern, see also Maier, "After the 'One-Man Show'," 84–85.

14. Maier ("After the 'One-Man Show'") reflects on what it means for two feminist theologians to write a Jeremiah commentary that includes post-colonial perspectives in a scholarly context and research tradition, which until the last two decades was dominated by male exegetes (the sole exception being Helga Weippert, *Die Prosareden des Jeremiabuches* [BZAW 132; Berlin: de Gruyter, 1973]).

15. The authors adopt the concept of different textual voices from Athalya Brenner and Fokkelien van Dijk-Hemmes, *On Gendering Texts: Female and Male Voices in the Hebrew Bible* (BIS 1; Leiden: Brill, 1993). The objective is no longer to focus on the prophet's voice but to look for multiple voices in the text.

16. See Yosefa Raz, "Jeremiah 'Before the Womb': On Fathers, Sons, and the Telos of Redaction in Jeremiah 1," 86–100, in this volume.

b. *Biblical Commentaries Between Postulated "Neutrality" and Declared Advocacy*

Whoever seeks to plant new theses needs to advance them with enthusiasm. It is not feasible to weigh every single phrase because the interpretation presented would lose its verve. The genuine academic tradition, however, requires naming the benefits of other solutions as well as weak points of one's own propositions. Within the long-established historical-critical research tradition, one may point to two aspects that should be avoided in new commentaries. On the one hand, the history of research covered by a commentary becomes more and more restricted to the last forty or fifty years probably due to the fact that secondary literature has become unmanageable. On the other hand, there seems to be an unchallenged neutrality of approach. Especially in "classic" biblical commentaries, most authors do not worry about expounding the hermeneutical perspectives of their exegesis. Failing to state one's objectives, however, does not lead to an unbiased "neutral" or "objective" commentary, but demonstrates instead that the author has approached his or her assignment without hermeneutical reflection.

Louis Stulman's essay, "Commentary as Memoir? Reflections on Writing/Reading War and Hegemony in Jeremiah and in Contemporary U.S. Foreign Policy," critically assesses this aspect of commentary writing. He rightly discusses the self-referentiality of commentary writing by refuting a widespread assumption of historical-critical commentaries—that one could look at biblical texts from outside of history. Any interpretation partakes in a reception history that is inevitably connected with its historical context and the circumstances of its production and its interpretation.[17] Reflecting as clearly as possible one's own socio-cultural context therefore does not inscribe an (undesirable) subjectivity into the exegetical process but contributes to its objectivity in that a disclosure of one's own interests marks critical distance from the task. Christl Maier ponders this truth by borrowing terms of narratological criticism: on the one hand, "the commentator becomes the new narrator, the all-knowing controller and focalizer of textual voices";[18] on the other hand, he or she seeks to become aware of marginalized textual voices as voices of the oppressed, the losers, in order to render them audible.[19]

17. See Louis Stulman, "Commentary as Memoir? Reflections on Writing/Reading War and Hegemony in Jeremiah and in Contemporary U.S. Foreign Policy," 57–71 (59–60), in this volume.

18. Maier, "After the 'One-Man Show'," 73.

19. Maier (ibid., 81–85) illustrates this concern in reference to the passages about the Queen of Heaven and her devotees (Jer 7; 44).

This nascent IECOT commentary on Jeremiah explicitly announces its objectives through a clear option: it will be a feminist-postcolonial commentary. In order to discuss both the potential and constraints of such a commentary, the authors, Christl Maier and Carolyn Sharp, have invited scholars who share gender awareness and knowledge about post-colonial approaches. If one understands "feminist-postcolonial" according to Musa Dube's concise definition, this approach enables interpreters to perceive "imperial and patriarchal oppressive structures and ideologies."[20] As the doyen of postcolonial studies, Fernando Segovia, remarks, the "optic" of the postcolonial approach to research starts with realizing "the problematic of domination and subordination."[21] Imperial centers of power seek to subdue distant territories, to proclaim their culture as inferior, and to introduce the imperial culture—even against the will of the dominated—as a desirable innovation. Applying these propositions to the book of Jeremiah, this volume demonstrates that the "Sitz im Leben" of most texts is a hybrid-composite identity of Judah as a colonized people and that the book, due to its indistinct structure, may be recognized as trauma literature. Between these two poles of colonization and trauma, the gender research presented in this volume gives direction to the commentary's work in progress; its authors are aware of being U.S.-American and German middle-class women in academic positions, not members of colonized nations, and thus ethically bound to refuse dynamics of othering.[22]

2. *Facets of Contemporary Jeremiah Studies: Feminist Criticism, Postcolonial Analysis, and Trauma Studies*

Positioning itself in the landscape of contemporary Jeremiah studies,[23] this volume develops new grounds for interpreting Jeremiah by focusing on three hermeneutical approaches: feminist and postcolonial perspectives and trauma studies.

20. Musa W. Dube, *Postcolonial Feminist Interpretation of the Bible* (St. Louis: Chalice, 2000), 121.

21. Fernando F. Segovia, "Mapping the Postcolonial Optic in Biblical Criticism: Meaning and Scope," in *Postcolonial Biblical Criticism: Interdisciplinary Intersections* (ed. S. D. Moore and F. F. Segovia; London: T&T Clark International, 2005), 23–78 (65).

22. For this goal of their commentary, see Carolyn J. Sharp, "Buying Land in the Text of Jeremiah: Feminist Commentary, the Kristevan Abject, and Jeremiah 32," 150–72, in this volume.

23. Maier, "After the 'One-Man Show'," 77, 81.

a. *Feminist Research*

(i) *Feminist Research Within the Context of New Approaches.* From its inception, feminist research has been characterized by interdisciplinarity and pluralism as well as inter-denominational and inter-confessional cooperation among theologians. Feminist biblical hermeneutics has been and still is well aware that not only marginalization with regard to gender but also other forms of discrimination are at issue. Whoever seeks liberation—and aims at accomplishing it even against some canonized texts—cannot and must not disregard the multiple forms of oppression and marginalization that continue to cause harm in the contemporary world. As early as the 1980s, Elisabeth Schüssler Fiorenza had argued that domination and discrimination due to gender constitute only one dimension among many forms of oppression.[24] Patriarchal societies discriminate with regard to persons positively and negatively based on diverse criteria having to do with gender, age, citizenship status, economic power, and so on. These criteria are employed across a wide variety of androcentric and hierarchical structures, although not all criteria are equally influential in all societies. The chart opposite provides an overview of such criteria in light of socio-historical conditions of ancient Near Eastern cultures.[25]

In the last forty years, research on these criteria has led to much differentiation: *intersectionality studies* have analyzed the interplay of multiple discriminations. Emerging from the realm of management, *diversity studies* seek to eschew partisanship and to assess persons according to their competence, or rather what is generally assumed to be their competence, in order to maximize the yield for the company; this has the deplorable effect, however, that stereotypes are not deconstructed but

---

24. See Elisabeth Schüssler Fiorenza, *In Memory of Her: A Feminist Theological Reconstruction of Christian Origins* (New York: Crossroad, 1985), 29.

25. I used and explained this chart in several of my studies, most recently in Irmtraud Fischer, "Inklusion und Exklusion: Biblische Perspektiven," in *"...dass alle eins seien": Im Spannungsfeld von Inklusion und Exklusion* (ed. A. Pithan et al.; Forum für Heil- und Religionspädagogik 7; Münster: Comenius-Institut, 2013), 9–23; Irmtraud Fischer, Jorunn Økland, Mercedes Navarro Puerto and Adriana Valerio, "Frauen, Bibel und Rezeptionsgeschichte: Ein internationales Projekt der Theologie und Genderforschung," in *Tora* (ed. I. Fischer et al.; Die Bibel und die Frauen: Eine exegetisch-kulturgeschichtliche Enzyklopädie 1/1; Stuttgart: Kohlhammer, 2010), 9–35 (17). Unfortunately, the English version of this essay ("Introduction: Women, Bible, and Reception History: An International Project in Theology and Gender Research," in *Torah* [ed. Jorunn Økland; The Bible and Women: An Encyclopedia of Exegesis and Cultural History 1/1; Atlanta: Society of Biblical Literature, 2011], 1–30; [9–10]), presents only a shortened chart and includes a serious translational error ("ecumenical" instead of "economical"!).

rather intensified.[26] *Aging Studies* attend primarily to the criterion "age" and its interdependency with other criteria as it is especially significant whether a person belongs to a propertied family of the country or is an aging welfare recipient in a foreign country. *Queer studies* focus on the social constructions of sexual and gender identities, engaging in critical analysis of binary male/female models of sex, heterosexuality, and other sexual and gender normativities; they challenge heterosexuality as a postulated sexual norm. *Postcolonial studies* highlight the criterion "ethnicity" with its various constructs of strangeness. A common feature of all these distinctions is that they point to a *multi-dimensional reality* as well as to the fact that *social differences are constructs*. All of these criteria, too, are constructs of an actual society; they are ascribed to human beings, appropriated in the process of socialization, and associated with a dichotomous, positive/negative evaluation.

CRITERION	POSITIVE	NEGATIVE
Status of Citizen in the ANE	free	not free (slave)
Gender	masculine	feminine, queer
Age in ANE: free	old	young
Age in ANE: slave	young	old
Economical status	rich	poor
Psycho-physical status	healthy	sick, disabled
Ethnicity	indigenous	foreign
Religion/ideology	dominant	foreign/deviant

Following Judith Butler, one may describe this process, which is applied not only to "sex/gender" but to all these criteria, as "doing."[27] If this basic framework serves as a starting point for feminist research, the critical inquiries that Carolyn Sharp addresses to second-wave feminism can be put aside.[28] With regard to the European research context, her reproach that second-wave feminism was interested only in the reconstruction of women's life or history and in a positive connotation of femaleness and therefore has not overcome a categorical dualistic essentialism applies only to the so-called feminism of difference, but not to

26. For example, the reason for employing female managers at a higher rate is not gender equity but the viewpoint that women allegedly contribute "other" skills to the company through their femaleness (which is often stereotypically used and not defined).

27. Cf. the highly influential study by Judith Butler, *Undoing Gender* (New York: Routledge, 2004).

28. Sharp, "Buying Land," 150–52.

that feminism which has taken up the cause of equality and liberation in regard of all differences and has always considered "gender" as a fluid social construct. With these premises in mind, one may easily follow Sharp's call for "transgression," that is, a "privileging of creative interventions, ancient and contemporary, that resist or reframe destructive social norms."[29]

(ii) *Feminist Studies on Jeremiah*. Being aware that feminist research on the conspicuously androcentric book of Jeremiah could not analyze only passages that explicitly address "women's issues,"[30] Carolyn Sharp defines her objective as follows:

> And so feminist inquiry into Jeremiah must continue to interrogate ideologies of subjugation in the text and in its reception history, decline the ways in which gender, economic class, sexuality, ethnic identity, and able-bodiedness may be essentialized within the text and in scholarship, and provide readings of the text—critical and constructive—that further the work of justice and *shalom*.[31]

Based on historical-critical methods and including newer methodologies of biblical interpretation, a commentary is about to emerge that approaches not only the texts in the book of Jeremiah but also their reception history from a postcolonial-feminist perspective.

Even if postcolonial and queer theories may not be fully subsumed under a feminist analysis, the commentary's authors deliberately argue for this connection because all of these perspectives question differences and their rationale in a given society. Sharp is motivated by a socio-political engagement that seeks to change unjust structures and to establish justice and *shalom* by destabilizing ideologies of oppression and by overcoming the ubiquitous essentialism visible in the criteria mentioned above.

> Essentialism is a crucial component in many ideologies of oppression and must be addressed vigorously, for it allows oppressors, colonizers, and antagonists to limit and dehumanize those against whom they are working.[32]

---

29. Ibid., 155.

30. See Carolyn J. Sharp, "Mapping Jeremiah as/in a Feminist Landscape: Negotiating Ancient and Contemporary Terrains," 38–56 (39) in this volume: "as a feminist, I have always rejected the notion that a text can be meaningful for me only if it talks about 'women's issues'."

31. Ibid., 45.

32. Ibid., 44.

Sharp argues explicitly against historical research in the sense of a history of institutions and pleads for what is known in German scholarship as socio-historical turn, namely, to consider not only the upper class of any society but all individuals. Thereby, and justifiably so, a compensational history that attends to "special topics"[33] becomes, in fact, obsolete because no group will any longer be "special" or even "normal." Based on this line of argumentation, the objectives of queer studies can be included, as Sharp defines:

> Queer theory inquires into ways in which social constructions reinforce certain ideas of what is normative or "natural," including but not limited to notions of sexuality, sexual identity, and gender identity.[34]

Her interpretation of the exemplary passage Jer 30:5–22 reveals the benefit of this approach: although at first sight, the book of Jeremiah has a clear androcentric imprint it can also be traversed as a "queer landscape."

> Thus, Jeremiah's rhetoric of gender fluidity marks the body of "Israel" as hybrid and genderqueer, and Jer 30 becomes a place of queer freedom within the dominant gender discourse of a brutal honor- and shame-based society. Here a breach has been made—an incurable wound, we may say—in the androcentrism of the book of Jeremiah.[35]

L. Juliana Claassens's essay about the metaphorization of war's inevitable adversity through the image of a woman in labor demonstrates how one may connect the perspectives of gender, queer, postcolonial, and trauma studies and render them fruitful for actual texts.[36] If in some Jeremiah passages the connotation of rape is included, this metaphor envisions the situation of a people inferior in military terms and exposed

---

33. Ibid., 45.
34. Ibid., 46.
35. Ibid., 50.
36. L. Juliana Claassens, "'Like a Woman in Labor': Gender, Postcolonial, Queer, and Trauma Perspectives on the Book of Jeremiah," 117–32, in this volume, following Jeremy Punt, "Queer Theory, Postcolonial Theory, and Biblical Interpretation: A Preliminary Exploration of Some Intersections," in *Bible Trouble: Queer Reading at the Boundaries of Biblical Scholarship* (ed. T. J. Hornsby and K. Stone; SBLSS 67; Atlanta: Society of Biblical Literature, 2011), 321–41. Punt lists several similarities between the different theories: "epistemological and hermeneutical considerations; notions of difference; center and margins, or marginality and exclusion; agency; mimicry, and its avoidance; and prophetic vision for inclusivity or a new world" (329).

to a raping and pillaging band of soldiers. The addressees of this message are, according to Claassens, primarily men who, through this metaphor, are forced into a "gender reversal," in other words, to identify with a female figure and thus to breach the ascription of gender.[37] Claassens's queer reading may lead to the conclusion that it is possible to trace here a process of "undoing gender"—yet only if one emphasizes that the recipients of the message are primarily men. I would like to suggest that such a reading runs the risk of defining the implied recipient or reader of Jeremiah's message in terms that are more androcentric than necessary with regard to ancient Israel: gender then is inscribed as *salient* where it probably was *silent*.[38] A parallel to the figure of the woman in labor, which depicts exclusively female biology, may be seen in the warrior figure, which in the ancient Near East is mainly assigned to a man (both metaphors are used jointly in the context of a divine speech; cf. Isa 42:13–14).[39] The interpretive assumption that female metaphors serve to address situations of women's life and a female audience only and that a queer reading would thus enable to the breaking up of gender roles therefore runs the risk of inscribing gender stereotypes into texts that originally did not reflect them.

Another aspect relevant to divine imagery in Jeremiah, about which feminist scholars of the last two decades have raised awareness, is discussed in Else K. Holt's essay, "'The Stain of Your Guilt Is Still Before Me' (Jeremiah 2:22): (Feminist) Approaches to Jeremiah 2 and the Problem of Normativity." The metaphors and terminology in the book of Jeremiah are not only shaped by violence, but also visualize traces of sexual and sexualized violence and even excesses that may be called pornographic. The effects of passages such as Jer 2, in which God violently acts upon the people personified as female, cannot be ameliorated by referring to texts that depict YHWH as salutary actor. The feature that particularly men are threatened with the horrible fate of violent rape

---

37. See Claassens, "Woman in Labor," 125–27.

38. For this distinction, see Hanne Løland, *Silent or Salient Gender: The Interpretation of Gendered God-language in the Hebrew Bible, Exemplified in Isaiah 42, 46, and 49* (FAT II/32; Tübingen: Mohr Siebeck, 2008). Not in all gendered metaphors is gender salient; in metaphors in which other aspects dominate, gender is silent.

39. See Irmtraud Fischer, "Isaiah: The Book of Female Metaphors," in *Feminist Biblical Interpretation: A Compendium of Critical Commentary on the Books of the Bible and Related Literature* (ed. L. Schottroff and M.-T. Wacker; Grand Rapids: Eerdmans, 2012), 303–18 (306).

contributes to distancing the contemporary reader from the text.[40] Yet it cannot be ignored that such texts, which depict female sexuality as both nymphomaniacal and extremely vulnerable, have a considerably more depressing reception history for women than for men. The history of interpretation as well as the history of religious praxis reveals that such representations of female sexual desire and suffering exert a long-term influence on the malleable constructions of sexuality.[41] Because Holt sees the Bible's authority not as permanent but as dialogic, she draws the following conclusion with regard to the perception of the canon: "In other words: as a text, written by humans for humans about God, the Bible is as fallible as any other book."[42] Yet, in following Kathleen O'Connor's statement that not the biblical text but its interpretation can be perceived as "conversation," Holt contradicts not only Luther but perhaps also herself.

In her essay "Buying Land in the Text of Jeremiah: Feminist Commentary, the Kristevan Abject, and Jeremiah 32," Carolyn Sharp provides another example of feminist interpretation that points to the problem of *male-coding* in all its dimensions. While the prophet and God are coded as male, the disloyal and sinful community is depicted as female: "The...social body of Judah is [feminized]";[43] interpretations have often deepened this dichotomy. In the same perspective, Stuart Macwilliam analyzes gender performativity and thus the problematic construct of Jeremiah's masculinity.[44] As in Jer 20:7 the Hebrew root פתה has often been translated with the verb "to seduce" that carries a sexual connotation, or else with "to assault" that connotes violence, Jeremiah would confess here that he has been sexually overwhelmed by a stronger man.[45] The (positive) marriage metaphor used to denote the relationship between the prophet and his God in other passages (e.g.

---

40. Angela Bauer has referred to the notion that in Jeremiah female metaphors are primarily addressing a male audience; see her *Gender in the Book of Jeremiah: A Feminist Literary Reading* (New York: Lang, 1999), 160–61.

41. I explored such gender-specific effects of female metaphors in the book of Isaiah in Fischer, "Isaiah"; Claassens ("Woman in Labor") also emphasizes them.

42. Else K. Holt, "'The Stain of Your Guilt is Still Before Me' (Jeremiah 2:22): (Feminist) Approaches to Jeremiah 2 and the Problem of Normativity," 101–16 (113) in this volume.

43. Sharp, "Buying Land," 150.

44. Stuart Macwilliam, "The Prophet and His Patsy: Gender Performativity in Jeremiah," 173–88, in this volume.

45. For the following see also ibid., 173–76.

Jer 15:16) and the interdiction to marry (16:2) thus point to continuous damage of the book's stereotypes of masculinity, which also includes the figure of Baruch: "Baruch is to Jeremiah as Jeremiah is to YHWH."[46] Macwilliam further points to constructs of masculinity of other great prophetic figures, for example Elijah, who "performs his masculinity very well indeed."[47] The framework of queer theory offers completely new insights insofar as Macwilliam assembles particular observations of traditional commentaries and reinterprets them with regard to gender performativity.

James E. Harding's contribution, "The Silent Goddess and the Gendering of Divine Speech in Jeremiah 44," explores the problem of the representation of the goddess in Jer 44.[48] The goddess is called "Queen of Heaven," yet her identity remains cryptic; she is characterized from different perspectives, as Harding clear-sightedly argues, but is not herself granted direct speech. The text does not explicitly state whether the veneration of the Queen of Heaven was considered irreconcilable with the cult for Israel's god. At least, Jer 7 and 44 see the people's dedication to this goddess as a reason for Judah's breakdown and characterize Jeremiah as a true prophet in Mosaic succession, since his oracles of doom come true. A male prophet announces the message of a god represented as male to primarily female devotees of a female god. The gender coding of this message thus causes a marginalization of "the female" and a centralization of "the male" on different levels at the same time.

In my own research, I have tried to understand prophecy in its twofold canonical shape from the perspective of the Torah and its idea of Mosaic succession.[49] Therefore, I read Yosefa Raz's essay, "Jeremiah 'Before the Womb': On Fathers, Sons, and the Telos of Redaction in Jeremiah 1,"[50] with great interest and much consent. Starting from the call narrative, Raz deconstructs the romantic image of the prophet and seeks to understand Jeremiah in line with the Deuteronomic law on prophets as a true prophet in Mosaic succession.

46. Ibid., 187.

47. Ibid., 179.

48. See James E. Harding, "The Silent Goddess and the Gendering of Divine Speech in Jeremiah 44," 208–23, in this volume. He assumes that the goddess can be identified with YHWH's consort Asherah (210, 218).

49. See e.g., Irmtraud Fischer, *Gotteskünderinnen: Zu einer geschlechterfairen Deutung des Phänomens der Prophetie und der Prophetinnen in der Hebräischen Bibel* (Stuttgart: Kohlhammer, 2002), 32–62.

50. See Raz, "Jeremiah 'Before the Womb'," 86–100, in this volume.

b. *Postcolonial Criticism*

In her introductory essay, "Challenges and Opportunities for Feminist and Postcolonial Biblical Criticism," Judith E. McKinlay launches a hermeneutical discussion that seeks to identify power structures and their effects on oppressors as well as on the oppressed. She further aims at assessing the implications of a "politicized hermeneutic of suspicion,"[51] applying this hermeneutic to texts and especially to the socio-historical and geopolitical situation in the book of Jeremiah. The essay's rather loose structure and a constant alteration between theory and its application to both Jeremiah texts and today's colonized indigenous ethnic groups of her Australian context turn the essay into an innovative and exciting, albeit somewhat arduous introduction that culminates in pleading—typical for contextual theologies—for an awareness of the limitations and shortcomings in one's own research.

In contrast, Sharp defines postcolonial studies not only in terms of an exertion of centralized power but also in terms of various resistant patterns of reaction by the subjugated, reactions that often are—except in the case of an open revolt—not recognized as resistance:

> Postcolonial criticism refuses the claims, overt predations, and oppressive gestures of empire: namely, cultural discourses and pragmatic actions (military, social, political) that seek to establish the "naturalness" and beneficence of imperial rule over against the supposed primitive, immoral, benighted, or ineffective character of indigenous colonized persons and native cultures. Under pressure of colonialism, colonized subjects—subalterns—deploy a variety of strategies to survive, that is, to resist the colonizing distortions, commodifications, and threatened erasure of their indigenous culture and the deformation of their own subjectivity and agency. Those surviving under colonialism use tactics of assimilation, mimicry, parody, and strategic silence as well as outright resistance.[52]

In her essay, "God's Cruelty and Jeremiah's Treason: Jer 21:1–10 in Postcolonial Perspective," Christl Maier combines the traditional methodology of redaction criticism with a postcolonial reading and thus provides an ostensive example of new insights that this projected commentary may offer. In this passage, YHWH's oracle (21:7) announces that not only Nebuchadnezzar but also he himself will fight against the city and therefore all inhabitants are doomed. Another prediction in 21:8–10, however, discloses the view that those who surrender to the Chaldeans

51. Judith McKinlay, "Challenges and Opportunities for Feminist and Postcolonial Biblical Criticism," 19–37 (19), in this volume; cf. also eadem, "Rahab: A Hero/ine?," *BibInt* 7 (1999): 44–57.

52. Sharp, "Mapping Jeremiah," 45.

will survive the siege. In pointing to intertextual links, Maier concludes that the passage is obviously a florilegium and further argues that the postulated dating of the passage effects its interpretation. If these words are dated prior to Jerusalem's fall, they attest to an unpatriotic position and a sarcastic image of God; if they are formulated *post festum*, they reflect the ambivalent voice of those who survived the conquest and surrendered to the Babylonians.[53] Given this interpretation, the text is part of a particular Judean narration that after 586 B.C.E. strengthens the identity- and community-building of the colonized. In attributing to YHWH a will to destroy the people and the land, this narration asserts that the world has not slipped from God's hands and the imperial enemy is not omnipotent. Although this interpretation is not new—it is rather well-known as Deuteronomistic theology—this postcolonial hermeneutics against the background of trauma studies illustrates that these arguments concern not some odd ancient Near Eastern patterns but approved general coping strategies of colonized and traumatized people:

> While this text tells a nation's story, it offers surprising insights into the ways people are able to survive traumatic events and to live under imperialist regimes—even if this means that at first sight God seems to be cruel and Jeremiah a traitor.[54]

In his essay "'Exoticizing the Otter': The Curious Case of the Rechabites in Jeremiah 35," Steed Vernyl Davidson explores strategies of othering with regard to ethnically foreign groups, which in German-speaking biblical studies had their prime time in the context of so-called orientalism of the nineteenth and early twentieth century.[55] Taking the characterization of the Rechabites in Jer 35 as an example "the essay subverts the exoticist codes by presenting the Rechabites in an alternative power relationship."[56] In most instances, exoticizing evaluates foreigners from the perspective of the dominant imperial culture in order to domesticate and control an embarrassing strangeness. In the case of the Rechabites in the book of Jeremiah, the situation is different insofar as Judah as a colonized people applies exoticist codes not to the imperial power, but to a neighboring people that obviously does without any hierarchical social structure and scrupulously follows its forefather's instructions. Davidson

---

53. See Christl M. Maier, "God's Cruelty and Jeremiah's Treason: Jeremiah 21:1–10 in Postcolonial Perspective," 133–49, in this volume.

54. Ibid., 149.

55. Steed Vernyl Davidson, "'Exoticizing the Otter': The Curious Case of the Rechabites in Jeremiah 35," 189–207, in this volume.

56. Ibid., 191.

plausibly underlines that the biblical text's out-of-context description of the Rechabites leads to their exoticizing in interpretation insofar as it underscores the thesis that they are a marginalized group in society. In breaking this exoticist code, however, one may realize that this people, through its refusal of sedentism, succeeds in establishing—seemingly subversive—relations to the imperial power, because as a fluid social group they can escape territorial control.[57]

c. *Trauma Studies as Key to a New Perspective on Jeremiah*

Applying trauma studies to the book of Jeremiah, as most notably Kathleen O'Connor has shown, in my view enables an explanation—as no other hermeneutical approach can do—of the lack of structure and the erratic alteration of topics in this biblical book. Louis Stulman's dictum "the chaos *is* the message"[58] rightly puts this in a nutshell. Based on Albert Hourani's thesis that being defeated digs deeper into the collective memory than being victorious, Stulman reads the book of Jeremiah as survival and disaster literature, as "communal meditation on the horror of war."[59] For traumatized persons, remembrance and commemoration play a central role in the gradual rehabilitation of their experience through verbalizing and re-coding. Liberation theology in the 1970s named this key function of re-interpretive, actualizing remembrance a "dangerous memory."[60] Traumatized, colonized, or marginalized persons come to terms with their history by naming injustice, by freeing victims from silence and oblivion, and by naming the offenders and stigmatizing them permanently. According to Stulman, Jeremiah's "language of violence" can be explained by assuming that this prophetic book emerged as "*literature of the losers.*"[61] As Stephan Wyss had argued as early as the 1980s,[62] "the mighty speech" of the powerless, which laughs at massive

---

57. Cf. ibid., 201–2.

58. Stulman, "Commentary as Memoir?," 68 (his emphasis).

59. Ibid., 62.

60. The expression was coined by the German liberation theologian Johann Baptist Metz. Cf. his essays "Dogma als gefährliche Erinnerung" and "Gefährliche Erinnerung der Freiheit Jesu Christi," both published in *Glaube in Geschichte und Gesellschaft: Studien zu einer praktischen Fundamentaltheologie* (Mainz: Matthias-Grünewald-Verlag, 1977), 77–86 and 176–80; idem (in cooperation with Johann Reikerstorfer), *Memoria Passionis: Ein provozierendes Gedächtnis in pluralistischer Gesellschaft* (Freiburg: Herder, 2006).

61. Stulman, "Commentary as Memoir?," 70 (his emphasis).

62. Stephan Wyss, *Fluchen: Ohnmächtige und mächtige Rede der Ohnmacht: Ein philosophisch-theologischer Essay zu einer Blütenlese* (Fribourg: Exodus, 1984).

claims to power, belongs to the coping strategies of the defeated and subordinated who are able to fight injustice only by words and to leave revenge to God.[63] If the image of the woman in labor in Jer 31:7–9 is used in relation to especially needy persons, it may "serve as an example of resistance that shows how the colonized within the dominant power survived by imagining an alternative reality."[64]

The application of trauma studies to the book of Jeremiah delineates the context of many oracles of Jeremiah: a freezing and falling silent of traumatized people. Sharp prolifically appropriates the psychological phenomenon of abjection discussed by Julia Kristeva in her exegesis, arguing that narrating their abjection permanently preserves the memory of the abjected. She sees Jeremiah's act of buying land in Anathoth (Jer 32) as resistance against the imminent expropriation of the land by the imperial power.[65] The book of Jeremiah retains the entitlement to the land and gives a voice to those who lost their land. Yet, it also spells the abjection at all three levels of the prophetic process of communication because the risk of abjection may strike everybody: the people abjected as covenant partner because of its sinful behavior, the prophet whose message does not prove himself to be a true prophet, and even YHWH who, through his people's defeat, may himself suffer ill repute as a powerless deity.

3. *The Project of a Feminist Postcolonial Commentary to Jeremiah*

Because such an ambitious commentary will not be able to satisfy all demands, genuine preliminary considerations with regard to hermeneutics and methods are required. In this volume, both authors of the Jeremiah commentary in the IECOT series present a thorough reflection on their approach. Readers may look forward to an unconventional commentary that includes many new perspectives, both in detail and in the overall view. In conclusion, I would thus underline Louis Stulman's dictum:

> In fact, the integration of trauma, postcolonial, and feminist perspectives—
> with their focus on pain, power, and the periphery respectively—might
> present a promising interdisciplinary matrix for Jeremiah commentary
> writing in the next decade.[66]

---

63. This last aspect is emphasized by Claassens, "Woman in Labor," 129.
64. Ibid., 131.
65. Sharp, "Buying Land."
66. Stulman, "Commentary as Memoir?," 71.

Apart from the function to prepare a classical biblical commentary, the volume at hand is not only a treasure trove for new perspectives on Jeremiah studies but also for new approaches to biblical texts as a whole. Rarely have I said with utter conviction after reading such a book: "I have, indeed, learned a lot!"

BIBLIOGRAPHY

Ackerman, Susan. *Under Every Green Tree: Popular Religion in Sixth-Century Judah.* HSM 46. Atlanta: Scholars Press, 1992.

Adam, Andrew K. M. *What Is Postmodern Biblical Criticism?* Minneapolis: Fortress, 1995.

Ahmad, Aijaz. *In Theory: Classes, Nations, Literatures.* London: Verso, 1992.

Allen, Leslie C. *Jeremiah: A Commentary.* OTL. Louisville: Westminster John Knox, 2008.

Althaus-Reid, Marcella. *The Queer God.* London: Routledge, 2003.

Anand, Dibyesh. "Western Colonial Representations of the Other: The Case of Exotica Tibet." *New Political Science* 29 (2007): 23–42.

Anderson, Benedict. *Imagined Communities: Reflections on the Origin and Spread of Nationalism.* London: Verso, 1991.

Anderson, Cheryl B. "Roundtable Discussion: Feminist Biblical Studies: Transatlantic Reflections: Contesting the Margins and Transgressing Boundaries in the Age of Aids." *JFSR* 25 (2009): 103–7.

Anderson, John E. Review of Athalya Brenner, Archie Chi Chung Lee, and Gale A. Yee, eds., *Genesis. RBL* (2010). No pages. Online: http://www.bookreviews.org.

Anzaldúa, Gloria. *Borderlands/La Frontera: The New Mestiza.* 3d ed. San Francisco: Aunt Lute Books, 2007.

Applegate, John. "The Fate of Zedekiah: Redactional Debate in the Book of Jeremiah." *VT* 48 (1998): 137–60 and 301–8.

Ashcroft, Bill, Gareth Griffiths, and Helen Tiffin. *Key Concepts in Post-Colonial Studies.* London: Routledge, 1998.

———, eds. *Post-Colonial Studies: The Key Concepts.* London: Routledge, 2000.

Attridge, Harold W. Review of Gail R. O'Day and David L. Petersen, eds., *Theological Bible Commentary. RBL* (2010). No pages. Online: http://www.bookreviews.org.

Avalos, Hector, Sarah J. Melcher, and Jeremy Schipper, eds. *This Abled Body: Rethinking Disabilities in Biblical Studies.* Atlanta: Society of Biblical Literature, 2007.

Bail, Ulrike et al., eds. *Bibel in gerechter Sprache.* 3d ed. Gütersloh: Gütersloher Verlagshaus, 2007.

Bal, Mieke. *Narratology: Introduction to the Theory of Narrative.* 2d ed. Toronto: University of Toronto Press, 1997.

Baltzer, Klaus. "Considerations Regarding the Office and Calling of the Prophet." *HTR* 61 (1968): 567–81.

Barr, James. *The Semantics of Biblical Language.* London: Oxford University Press, 1961.

Barthes, Roland. *The Pleasure of the Text.* Translated by R. Miller. New York: Hill & Wang, 1975.

———. *S/Z.* Translated by R. Miller. Oxford: Blackwell, 1992.

Barthes, Roland, François Bovon, Franz-J. Leenhardt, Robert Martin-Achard, and Jean Starobinski. *Structural Analysis and Biblical Exegesis: Interpretational Essays.* Translated by A. M. Johnson, Jr. Pittsburgh: Pickwick, 1974.

Bauer, Angela. "Dressed to Be Killed: Jeremiah 4.29–31 as an Example for the Functions of Female Imagery in Jeremiah." Pages 293–305 in Diamond et al., *Troubling Jeremiah.*

———. *Gender in the Book of Jeremiah: A Feminist-literary Reading.* New York: Peter Lang, 1999.

———. "Jeremiah as Female Impersonator: Roles of Difference in Gender Perception and Gender Perceptivity." Pages 199–207 in *Escaping Eden: New Feminist Perspectives on the Bible.* Edited by H. C. Washington et al. The Biblical Seminar 65. Sheffield: Sheffield Academic, 1998.

Baumann, Gerlinde. *Love and Violence: Marriage as Metaphor for the Relationship Between YHWH and Israel in the Prophetic Books.* Translated by L. M. Maloney. Collegeville: Liturgical, 2003.

Beamer, Linda. "Rachel." Page 652 in *A Dictionary of Biblical Tradition in English Literature.* Edited by D. L. Jeffrey. Grand Rapids: Eerdmans, 1992.

Beardslee, William A. "Poststructuralist Criticism." Pages 253–67 in McKenzie and Haynes, eds., *To Each Its Own Meaning.*

Beauvoir, Simone de. *The Second Sex.* Translated and edited by H. M. Parshley. New York: Knopf, 1953.

Becking, Bob. "Divine Reliability and the Conceptual Coherence of the Book of Consolation (Jeremiah 30–31)." Pages 163–79 in Kessler, ed., *Reading the Book of Jeremiah.*

Begg, Christopher T. "The End of King Jehoiakim: The Afterlife of a Problem." *JSem* 8 (1996): 12–20.

Bell, Catherine. *Ritual: Perspectives and Dimensions.* New York: Oxford University Press, 1997.

———. *Ritual Theory, Ritual Practice.* New York: Oxford University Press, 1992.

Benhabib, Seyla, Judith Butler, Drucilla Cornell, and Nancy Fraser. *Der Streit um Differenz. Feminismus und Postmoderne in der Gegenwart.* Frankfurt: Fischer, 1993.

Bergman, Shmuel Hugo. *Dialogical Philosophy from Kierkegaard to Buber.* Albany: State University of New York Press, 1991.

Bergmann, Claudia D. "We Have Seen the Enemy, and He Is Only a 'She': The Portrayal of Warriors as Women." Pages 129–42 in Kelle and Ames, eds., *Writing and Reading War.*

Berlin, Adele. "Jeremiah 29:5–7: A Deuteronomic Allusion." *HAR* 8 (1984): 3–11.

Berquist, Jon L. "Postcolonialism and Imperial Motives for Canonization." *Semeia* 75 (1996): 15–35.

Berridge, John. *Prophet, People and the Word of Yahweh.* Zurich: EVZ, 1970.

Bhabha, Homi K. *The Location of Culture.* London: Routledge, 1994.

———, ed. *Nation and Narration.* London: Routledge, 1990.

The Bible and Culture Collective, ed. *The Postmodern Bible.* New Haven: Yale University Press, 1995.

Bier, Miriam J. "'Perhaps There Is Hope': Reading Lamentations as a Polyphony of Pain, Penitence, and Hope." Ph.D. diss., University of Otago, 2012.

Birch, Bruce C. et al. *A Theological Introduction to the Old Testament.* Nashville: Abingdon, 1999.

Bird, Phyllis, ed. *Reading the Bible as Women: Perspectives from Africa, Asia, and Latin America*. Atlanta: Scholars Press, 1997.

Bloom, Harold. *The Anxiety of Influence: A Theory of Poetry*. 2d ed. New York: Oxford University Press, 1997.

Bloom, Harold, and Geoffrey Hartman. "The Poetics of Prophecy: Jeremiah." Pages 205–23 in *The Bible: Edited with an Introduction by Harold Bloom*. New York: Chelsea House, 2000.

Boer, Roland. "Marx, Postcolonialism, and the Bible." Pages 166–83 in Moore and Segovia, eds., *Postcolonial Biblical Criticism*.

———. *Marxist Criticism of the Bible*. London: Sheffield Academic, 2003.

———. "Too Many Dicks at the Writing Desk, or How to Organize a Prophetic Sausage-Fest." *Theology & Sexuality* 16 (2010): 95–108.

Boer, Roland, and Jorunn Økland, eds. *Marxist Feminist Criticism of the Bible*. Sheffield: Sheffield Phoenix, 2008.

Braun, Christina von, and Inge Stephan, eds. *Gender Studien: Eine Einführung*. 2d ed. Stuttgart: Metzler, 2006.

Brenner, Athalya. "Epilogue: Babies and Bathwater on the Road." Pages 333–38 in *Her Master's Tools? Feminist and Postcolonial Engagements with Historical-Critical Discourse*. Edited by C. Vander Stichele and T. Penner. Atlanta: Society of Biblical Literature, 2005.

———. ed. *A Feminist Companion to the Latter Prophets*. FCB 8. Sheffield: Sheffield Academic, 1995.

———. *I Am... Biblical Women Tell Their Own Stories*. Minneapolis: Fortress, 2005.

———. *The Intercourse of Knowledge: On Gendering Desire and 'Sexuality' in the Hebrew Bible*. Leiden: Brill, 1997.

———. "On Prophetic Propaganda and the Politics of 'Love': The Case of Jeremiah." Pages 256–74 in Brenner, ed., *A Feminist Companion to the Latter Prophets*.

Brenner, Athalya, and Fokkelien van Dijk-Hemmes, *On Gendering Texts: Female and Male Voices in the Hebrew Bible*. BIS 1. Leiden: Brill, 1993.

Brenner, Athalya, Archie Chi Chung Lee, and Gale A. Yee, eds. *Genesis: texts@contexts*. Minneapolis: Fortress, 2010.

Bright, John. *Jeremiah: Introduction, Translation, and Notes*. AB 21. Garden City: Doubleday, 1965.

Brock, Rita Nakashima. "A New Thing in the Land: The Female Surrounds the Warrior." Pages 137–59 in *Power, Powerlessness, and the Divine: New Inquiries in Bible and Theology*. Edited by C. L. Rigby. Atlanta: Scholars Press, 1997.

Bronner, Leah. "The Rechabites, a Sect in Biblical Times." Pages 6–16 in *De Fructu Oris Sui: Essays in Honour of Adrianus van Selms*. Edited by I. H. Eybers et al. Leiden: Brill, 1971.

Brown, Michael L. *Jeremiah*. Expositor's Bible Commentary 7. Rev. ed. Grand Rapids: Zondervan, 2010.

Brueggemann, Walter. *A Commentary on Jeremiah: Exile and Homecoming*. Grand Rapids: Eerdmans, 1998.

———. *An Unsettling God: The Heart of the Hebrew Bible*. Minneapolis: Fortress, 2009.

———. "The 'Baruch Connection': Reflections on Jer 43:1–7." *JBL* 113 (1994): 405–20. Repr. pages 367–86 in Diamond et al., *Troubling Jeremiah*.

————. *Disruptive Grace: Reflections on God, Scripture, and the Church.* Edited and introduced by C. J. Sharp. Minneapolis: Fortress, 2011.

————. *Like Fire in the Bones: Listening for the Prophetic Word in Jeremiah.* Minneapolis: Fortress, 2006.

————. "Meditation Upon the Abyss: The Book of Jeremiah." *Word and World* 22 (2002): 340–50.

————. *Old Testament Theology: Essays on Structure, Theme, and Text.* Edited by P. D. Miller. Minneapolis: Fortress, 1992.

————. "Sometime Wave, Sometime Particle." *CBR* 8 (2010): 376–85.

————. *Texts Under Negotiation: The Bible and Postmodern Imagination.* Minneapolis: Fortress, 1993.

————. *Theology of the Old Testament: Testimony, Dispute, Advocacy.* Minneapolis: Fortress, 1997.

————. *To Build, to Plant: A Commentary on Jeremiah 25–52.* Grand Rapids: Eerdmans, 1991.

Brueggemann, Walter and Davis Hankins. "The Invention and Persistence of Wellhausen's World," *CBQ* 75 (2013): 15–31.

Brunotte, Ulrike. "Religion und Kolonialismus." Pages 339–69 in *Europäische Religionsgeschichte: Ein mehrfacher Pluralismus*, vol. 1. Edited by H. G. Kippenberg et al. Göttingen: Vandenhoeck & Ruprecht, 2009.

Bruns, Gerald. "Canon and Power in the Hebrew Scriptures." *Critical Inquiry* 19 (1984): 462–80.

Buber, Martin. "The History of the Dialogical Principle." Pages 209–24 in Martin Buber. *Between Man and Man.* Translated by R. G. Smith. New York: Macmillan, 1965.

————. *I and Thou.* Translated by R. G. Smith. New York: Charles Scribner's Sons, 1937.

Buckley, Michael J. *At the Origins of Modern Atheism.* New Haven: Yale University Press, 1987.

Burke, Sean D. "Queering Early Christian Discourse: The Ethiopian Eunuch." Pages 175–89 in Hornsby and Stone, eds., *Bible Trouble.*

Bußmann, Hadumod, and Renate Hof, eds. *Genus: Zur Geschlechterdifferenz in den Kulturwissenschaften.* Stuttgart: Kröner, 1995.

Butler, Judith. *Bodies That Matter: On the Discursive Limits of "Sex."* New York: Routledge, 1993.

————. *Gender Trouble: Feminism and the Subversion of Identity.* 2d ed. New York: Routledge, 1990, 1999.

————. *Undoing Gender.* New York: Routledge, 2004.

Callaway, Mary Chilton. "Black Fire on White Fire: Historical Context and Literary Subtext in Jeremiah 37–38." Pages 171–78 in Diamond et al., *Troubling Jeremiah.*

————. "Peering Inside Jeremiah: How Early Modern English Culture Still Influences Our Reading of the Prophet." Pages 279–89 in Diamond and Stulman, eds., *Jeremiah (Dis)Placed.*

————. "Reading Jeremiah with Some Help from Gadamer." Pages 266–78 in Diamond and Stulman, eds., *Jeremiah (Dis)Placed.*

Cardenal, Ernesto. *The Gospel in Solentiname.* Translated by D. D. Walsh. 4 vols. Maryknoll: Orbis, 1976–82.

Carroll, Robert P. "The Book of J: Intertextuality and Ideological Criticism," Pages 220–43 in Diamond et al., *Troubling Jeremiah.*

———. "Century's End: Jeremiah Studies at the Beginning of the Third Millennium." Pages 217–31 in Hauser, ed., *Recent Research on the Major Prophets*.

———. "Desire Under the Terebinths: On Pornographic Representation in the Prophets—A Response." Pages 275–307 in Brenner, ed., *A Feminist Companion to the Latter Prophets*.

———. *From Chaos to Covenant: Uses of Prophecy in the Book of Jeremiah*. London: SCM, 1981.

———. *Jeremiah*. Sheffield: JSOT, 1989. Repr. New York: T&T Clark International, 2004.

———. *Jeremiah: A Commentary*. OTL. London: SCM, 1986. Paperback repr. in 2 vols. Sheffield: Sheffield Phoenix, 2006.

———. "Something Rich and Strange: Imagining a Future for Jeremiah Studies." Pages 423–43 in Diamond et al., *Troubling Jeremiah*.

———. *Wolf in the Sheepfold*. London: SPCK, 1991. Repr. as *The Bible as a Problem for Christianity*. Philadelphia: Trinity Press International, 1991.

Carter, Warren. *John and Empire: Initial Explorations*. New York: T&T Clark International, 2008.

Claassens, L. Juliana. *Mourner, Mother, Midwife: Reimaging God's Liberating Presence in the Old Testament*. Louisville: Westminster John Knox, 2012.

Clements, Ronald E. *Jeremiah*. IBC. Atlanta: John Knox, 1988.

———. "Jeremiah's Message of Hope: Public Faith and Private Anguish." Pages 135–47 in Kessler, ed., *Reading the Book of Jeremiah*.

———. *Old Testament Prophecy: From Oracles to Canon*. Louisville: Westminster John Knox, 1996.

Clines, David J. A. *Interested Parties: The Ideology of Writers and Readers of the Hebrew Bible*. JSOTSup 205. Sheffield: Sheffield Academic, 1995.

Clines, David J. A., and David M. Gunn. "'You Tried to Persuade Me' and 'Violence! Outrage!' in Jeremiah XX 7–8." *VT* 28 (1978): 20–27.

Coggins, Richard, and Jin H. Han. *Six Minor Prophets Through the Centuries: Nahum, Habakkuk, Zephaniah, Haggai, Zechariah, and Malachi*. Blackwell Bible Commentaries 29. Malden: Wiley-Blackwell, 2011.

Collier, Gordon. "Introduction." Pages xii–xv in *Us/Them: Translation, Transcription and Identity in Post-Colonial Literary Cultures*. Edited by G. Collier. Atlanta: Rodopi, 1992.

Crenshaw, Kimberlé. "Mapping the Margins: Intersectionality, Identity Politics, and Violence Against Women of Color." *Stanford Law Review* 43 (1991): 1241–99.

Cross, Frank Moore, and Helmut Koester. Foreword to William L. Holladay. *Jeremiah 1: A Commentary on the Book of the Prophet Jeremiah*. Philadelphia: Fortress, 1986.

Crowell, Bradley L. "Postcolonial Studies and the Hebrew Bible." *CBR* 7 (2009): 217–44.

Cummings, J. T. "The House of the Sons of the Prophets and the Tents of the Rechabites." Pages 119–26 in *Studia biblica 1978: Sixth International Congress on Biblical Studies, Oxford, 3–7 April 1978*. Vol. 1, *Papers on Old Testament and Related Themes*. Edited by E. A. Livingstone. JSOTSup 11. Sheffield: University of Sheffield, 1979.

Darr, Katheryn Pfisterer. "Two Unifying Female Images in the Book of Isaiah." Pages 17–30 in *Uncovering Ancient Stones: Essays in Memory of H. Neil Richardson*. Edited by L. M. Hopfe. Winona Lake: Eisenbrauns, 1994.

Davidson, Steed Vernyl. "Ambivalence and Temple Destruction: Reading the Book of Jeremiah with Homi Bhabha." Pages 162–71 in Diamond and Stulman, eds., *Jeremiah (Dis)Placed*.

———. *Empire and Exile: Postcolonial Readings of the Book of Jeremiah*. LHBOTS 542. New York: T&T Clark International, 2011.

Davies, Philip R. "Pen of Iron, Point of Diamond." Pages 65–81 in *Writings and Speech in Israelite and Ancient Near Eastern Prophecy*. Edited by E. Ben Zvi and M. H. Floyd. Atlanta: Society of Biblical Literature, 2000.

De Lauretis, Teresa. *Alice Doesn't: Feminism, Semiotics, Cinema*. Bloomington: Indiana University Press, 1984.

———. *Practice of Love: Lesbian Sexuality and Perverse Desire*. Bloomington: Indiana University Press, 1994.

———. *Technologies of Gender: Essays on Theory, Film, and Fiction*. Bloomington: Indiana University Press, 1987.

Dearman, J. Andrew. "My Servants the Scribes: Composition and Context in Jeremiah 36." *JBL* 109 (1990): 403–21.

Derrida, Jacques. *Margins of Philosophy*. Translated with additional notes by A. Bass. Chicago: University of Chicago Press, 1982.

———. *Of Grammatology*. Translated by G. C. Spivak. Baltimore: The Johns Hopkins University Press, 1976.

Di Pede, Elena. "Un oracle pour les Récabites (Jr 35,18–19) ou à leur propos (42,18–19 LXX)?" *SJOT* 20 (2006): 96–109.

Diamant, Anita. *The Red Tent*. New York: Picador, 1998.

Diamond, A. R. Pete. "The Jeremiah Guild in the Twenty-First Century." Pages 232–48 in Hauser, ed., *Recent Research on the Major Prophets*.

Diamond, A. R. Pete, and Kathleen M. O'Connor. "Unfaithful Passions: Coding Women Coding Men in Jeremiah 2–3 (4:2)." *BibInt* 4 (1996): 288–310. Repr. pages 123–45 in Diamond et al., *Troubling Jeremiah*.

Diamond, A. R. Pete, and Louis Stulman, "Analytical Introduction: Writing and Reading Jeremiah." Pages 1–32 in Diamond and Stulman, eds., *Jeremiah (Dis)Placed*.

Diamond, A. R. Pete, Kathleen M. O'Connor, and Louis Stulman, eds. *Troubling Jeremiah*. JSOTSup 260. Sheffield: Sheffield Academic, 1999.

Diamond, A. R. Pete, and Louis Stulman, eds. *Jeremiah (Dis)placed: New Directions in Writing/Reading Jeremiah*. LHBOTS 529. New York: T&T Clark International, 2011.

Dijk-Hemmes, Fokkelien van. "The Metaphorization of Woman in Prophetic Speech: An Analysis of Ezekiel 23." Pages 244–55 in Brenner, ed., *A Feminist Companion to the Latter Prophets*.

Donaldson, Laura E. "Postcolonialism and Biblical Reading: An Introduction." *Semeia* 75 (1996): 1–14.

Donaldson, Laura E., and Kwok Pui-lan, eds. *Postcolonialism, Feminism, and Religious Discourse*. New York: Routledge, 2002.

Douglas, Kelly Brown. "Marginalized People, Liberating Perspectives: A Womanist Approach to Biblical Interpretation." *ATR* 83 (2001): 41–47.

Dube, Musa W. *Other Ways of Reading: African Women and the Bible*. Atlanta: Society of Biblical Literature, 2001.

———. *Postcolonial Feminist Interpretation of the Bible*. St. Louis: Chalice, 2000.

———. "Rahab Says Hello to Judith: A Decolonizing Feminist Reading." Pages 142–58 in Sugirtharajah, ed., *The Postcolonial Biblical Reader*.

Dube, Musa W., and Jeffrey L. Staley. "Descending from and Ascending into Heaven: A Postcolonial Analysis of Travel, Space and Power in John." Pages 1–10 in *John and Postcolonialism: Travel, Space and Power*. Edited by M. W. Dube and J. L. Staley. London: Sheffield Academic, 2002.

Duhm, Bernhard. *Das Buch Jeremia*. KHC 11. Tübingen: J. C. B. Mohr, 1901.

Eco, Umberto. *A Theory of Semiotics*. Bloomington: Indiana University Press, 1976.

Edelman, Diana V. "Huldah the Prophet—of Yahweh or Asherah?" Pages 231–50 in *A Feminist Companion to Samuel and Kings*. Edited by A. Brenner. FCB 5. Sheffield: Sheffield Academic, 1994.

Eilberg-Schwartz, Howard. "The Problem of the Body for the People of the Book." Pages 17–46 in *People of the Body: Jews and Judaism from an Embodied Perspective*. Edited by H. Eilberg-Schwartz. Albany: State University of New York Press, 1992.

Ellington, Scott. *Risking Truth: Reshaping the World through Prayers of Lament*. Princeton Theological Monograph Series. Eugene: Wipf & Stock, 2008.

Ellis, Teresa Ann. "Jeremiah 44: What if 'the Queen of Heaven' Is YHWH?" *JSOT* 33 (2009): 265–88.

Evans, Patrick. *The Long Forgetting: Post-colonial Literary Culture in New Zealand*. Christchurch: Canterbury University Press, 2007.

Exum, J. Cheryl. "Developing Strategies of Feminist Criticism/Developing Strategies for Commentating The Song of Songs." Pages 206–49 in *Auguries: The Jubilee Volume of the Sheffield Department of Biblical Studies*. Edited by D. J. A. Clines and S. D. Moore. Sheffield: Sheffield Academic, 1998.

———. "The Ethics of Biblical Violence against Women." Pages 248–71 in *The Bible in Ethics: The Second Sheffield Colloquium*. Edited by J. W. Rogerson and M. D. Carroll R. Sheffield: Sheffield Academic, 1995.

Fanon, Frantz. *Black Skin, White Masks*. Translated by C. L. Markmann. New York: Grove, 1967.

———. *The Wretched of the Earth*. Translated by C. Farrington. New York: Grove, 1963.

Farley, Margaret A. *Compassionate Respect: A Feminist Approach to Medical Ethics*. New York: Paulist Press, 2002.

———. *Just Love: A Framework for Christian Sexual Ethics*. New York: Continuum, 2006.

Felder, Cain Hope, ed. *Stony The Road We Trod: African American Biblical Interpretation*. Minneapolis: Fortress, 1991.

Fewell, Danna Nolan. "Reading the Bible Ideologically: Feminist Criticism." Pages 268–82 in McKenzie and Haynes, eds., *To Each Its Own Meaning*.

Field, Frederick, ed. *Origenis Hexaplorum quae supersunt; sive Veterum interpretum Graecorum in totum Vetus Testamentum fragmenta*, vol. 2. Oxford: Clarendon, 1875.

Fischer, Georg. *Der Prophet wie Mose: Studien zum Jeremiabuch*. Wiesbaden: Harrassowitz, 2011.

———. *Jeremia*. 2 vols. HTKAT. Freiburg: Herder, 2005.

———. *Jeremia—der Stand der theologischen Diskussion*. Darmstadt: Wissenschaftliche Buchgesellschaft, 2007.

———. *Trostbüchlein: Text, Komposition und Theologie von Jer 30–31.* Stuttgart: Katholisches Bibelwerk, 1993.

Fischer, Irmtraud. *Gotteskünderinnen: Zu einer geschlechterfairen Deutung des Phänomens der Prophetie und der Prophetinnen in der Hebräischen Bibel.* Stuttgart: Kohlhammer, 2002.

———. "Inklusion und Exklusion: Biblische Perspektiven." Pages 9–23 in '*...dass alle eins seien': Im Spannungsfeld von Inklusion und Exklusion.* Edited by A. Pithan et al. Forum für Heil- und Religionspädagogik 7. Münster: Comenius-Institut, 2013.

———. "Isaiah: The Book of Female Metaphors." Pages 303–18 in Schottroff and Wacker, eds., *Feminist Biblical Interpretation.*

———. *Rut.* HTKAT. 2d ed.: Freiburg: Herder, 2005.

———. "Von der *Vor*geschichte zur *Nach*geschichte: Schriftauslegung in der Schrift–Intertextualität–Rezeption." *ZAW* 125 (2013): 143–60.

Fischer, Irmtraud, Jorunn Økland, Mercedes Navarro Puerto, and Adriana Valerio. "Frauen, Bibel und Rezeptionsgeschichte: Ein internationales Projekt der Theologie und Genderforschung." Pages 9–35 in *Tora.* Edited by I. Fischer et al. Die Bibel und die Frauen: Eine exegetisch-kulturgeschichtliche Enzyklopädie 1.1; Stuttgart: Kohlhammer, 2010. English version: "Introduction: Women, Bible, and Reception History: An International Project in Theology and Gender Research." Pages 1–30 in *Torah.* Edited by Jorunn Økland. The Bible and Women: An Encyclopedia of Exegesis and Cultural History 1.1. Atlanta: Society of Biblical Literature, 2011.

Fish, Stanley E. *Is There a Text in This Class? The Authority of Interpretive Communities.* Cambridge, Mass.: Harvard University Press, 1980.

Fleras, Augie, and Paul Spoonley. *Recalling Aotearoa: Indigenous Politics and Ethnic Relations in New Zealand.* Auckland: Oxford University Press, 1999.

Foreman, Benjamin A. *Animal Metaphors and the People of Israel in the Book of Jeremiah.* FRLANT 238. Göttingen: Vandenhoeck & Ruprecht, 2011.

Franke, Chris, and Julia M. O'Brien, eds. *The Aesthetics of Violence in the Prophets.* LHBOTS 517. New York: T&T Clark International, 2010.

Fraser, Nancy. *Unruly Practices: Power, Discourse, and Gender in Contemporary Social Theory.* Minneapolis: University of Minnesota Press, 1989.

Fretheim, Terence E. *Jeremiah.* Smith & Helwys Bible Commentary. Macon: Smyth & Helwys, 2002.

Frick, Frank S. "The Rechabites Reconsidered." *JBL* 90 (1971): 279–87.

Gadamer, Hans-Georg. *Wahrheit und Methode: Grundzüge einer philosophischen Hermeneutik.* Tübingen: Mohr, 1960. English translation: *Truth and Method.* 2d rev. ed. Translated by J. Weinsheimer and D. G. Marshall. New York: Continuum, 1998.

Gafney, Wilda C. "A Black Feminist Approach to Biblical Studies." *Encounter* 67 (2006): 391–403.

Gamberoni, Johann. "'Jonadab, unser Vater, hat uns geboten' (Jer 35,6): Die Rechabiter – am Rand und in der Mitte." Pages 19–31 in *Schrift und Tradition: Festschrift für Josef Ernst zum 70. Geburtstag.* Edited by K. Backhaus and F. G. Untergassmair. Paderborn: Schöningh, 1996.

Gedalof, Irene. "Taking (a) Place: Female Embodiment and the Re-grounding of Community". Pages 91–112 in *Uprootings/Regroundings: Questions of Home and Migration.* Edited by S. Ahmed et al. Oxford: Berg, 2003.

Gilula, M. "An Egyptian Parallel to Jeremiah I 4–5." *VT* 17 (1967): 114.

Gordon, Pamela, and Harold C. Washington. "Rape as a Military Metaphor in the Hebrew Bible." Pages 308–25 in Brenner, ed., *A Feminist Companion to the Latter Prophets*.

Goss, Robert E. and Mona West, eds. *Take Back the Word: A Queer Reading of the Bible*. Cleveland: Pilgrim, 2000.

Gottwald, Norman K. "Sociology of Ancient Israel." *ABD* 6:79–89.

Green, Barbara. *Mikhail Bakhtin and Biblical Scholarship: An Introduction*. Atlanta: Society of Biblical Literature, 2000.

———. "Mikhail Bakhtin and Biblical Studies." *Perspectives in Religious Studies* 32 (2005): 241–48.

Griffiths, Gareth. "The Myth of Authenticity: Representation, Discourse and Social Practice." Pages 70–85 in *De-Scribing Empire: Post-Colonialism and Textuality*. Edited by C. Tiffin and A. Lawson. London: Routledge, 1994.

Grosz, Elizabeth A. *Volatile Bodies: Toward a Corporeal Feminism*. St. Leonards: Allen & Unwin, 1994.

Guest, Deryn. "From Gender Reversal to Genderfuck: Reading Jael Through a Lesbian Lens." Pages 9–43 in Hornsby and Stone, eds., *Bible Trouble*.

Guest, Deryn, Robert E. Goss, Mona West, and Thomas Bohache, eds. *The Queer Bible Commentary*. London: SCM, 2006.

Gunkel, Hermann. *Water for a Thirsty Land: Israelite Literature and Religion*. Edited by K. C. Hanson. Minneapolis: Fortress, 2001.

Habel, Norman. "The Form and Significance of the Call Narratives." *ZAW* 77 (1965): 297–323.

Handelman, Susan A. *The Slayers of Moses: The Emergence of Rabbinic Interpretation in Modern Literary Theory*. Albany: State University Press of New York, 1982.

Haraway, Donna J. *Primate Visions: Gender, Race, and Nature in the World of Modern Science*. New York: Routledge, 1989.

———. *Simians, Cyborgs, and Women: The Reinvention of Nature*. London: Free Association Books, 1991.

Harding, Sandra. *Whose Science? Whose Knowledge? Thinking from Women's Lives*. Ithaca: Cornell University Press, 1991.

Hardmeier, Christof. "Zur schriftgestützten Expertentätigkeit Jeremias im Milieu der Jerusalemer Führungseliten (Jeremia 36): Prophetische Literaturbildung und die Neuinterpretation älterer Expertisen in Jeremia 21–23*." Pages 105–49 in *Die Textualisierung der Religion*. Edited by J. Schaper. FAT 62. Tübingen: Mohr Siebeck, 2009.

Hardt, Michael, and Antonio Negri. *Empire*. Cambridge, Mass.: Harvard University Press, 2000.

———. *Multitude: War and Democracy in the Age of Empire*. New York: Penguin, 2004.

Hauser, Alan J., ed. *Recent Research on the Major Prophets*. Recent Research in Biblical Studies 1. Sheffield: Sheffield Phoenix, 2008.

Häusl, Maria. *Bilder der Not: Weiblichkeits- und Geschlechtermetaphorik im Buch Jeremia*. HBS 37. Freiburg: Herder, 2003.

Hayward, Robert. *The Targum of Jeremiah: Translated, with a Critical Introduction, Apparatus, and Notes*. The Aramaic Bible 12. Wilmington: Glazier, 1987.

Hens-Piazza, Gina. "Lyotard." Pages 160–66 in *Handbook of Postmodern Biblical Interpretation*. Edited by A. K. M. Adam. St. Louis: Chalice, 2000.

Heschel, Abraham. *The Prophets*. Perennial Classic. New York: Harper & Row, 1962. Repr. 2001.

Holladay, William L. "The Background of Jeremiah's Self-Understanding: Moses, Samuel, and Psalm 22." *JBL* 83 (1964): 153–64.

———. *Jeremiah 1: A Commentary on the Book of the Prophet Jeremiah, Chapters 1–25*. Hermeneia. Philadelphia: Fortress, 1986.

———. *Jeremiah 2: A Commentary on the Book of the Prophet Jeremiah, Chapters 26–52*. Hermeneia. Philadelphia: Fortress, 1989.

———. "Jeremiah and Moses: Further Observations." *JBL* 85 (1966): 17–27.

Holt, Else K. "The Meaning of an Inclusio: A Theological Interpretation of the Book of Jeremiah MT." *SJOT* 17 (2003): 183–205.

hooks, bell. *Yearning: Race, Gender, and Cultural Politics*. Boston: South End, 1990.

Hornsby, Teresa J., and Ken Stone, eds. *Bible Trouble: Queer Reading at the Boundaries of Biblical Scholarship*. Atlanta: Society of Biblical Literature, 2011.

Hourani, Albert. *A History of the Arab Peoples*. New York: Warner, 1991.

Huggan, Graham. *The Postcolonial Exotic: Marketing the Margins*. London: Routledge, 2001.

Irigaray, Luce. *This Sex Which Is Not One*. Translated by C. Porter with C. Burge. Ithaca: Cornell University Press, 1985 (French ed. 1977).

Irwin, John R. *The Lust of Knowledge: The Orientalists and Their Enemies*. London: Penguin, 2006.

Jacoby, Russell. "Marginal Returns." *Lingua Franca* 6 (September/October 1995): 30–37.

Jay, Nancy. *Throughout Your Generations Forever: Sacrifice, Religion, and Paternity*. Chicago: University of Chicago Press, 1992.

Jobling, David. "Very Limited Ideological Options: Marxism and Biblical Studies in Postcolonial Scenes." Pages 184–201 in Moore and Segovia, eds., *Postcolonial Biblical Criticism*.

Jones, Serene. *Trauma and Grace: Theology in a Ruptured World*. Louisville: Westminster John Knox, 2009.

Jost, Renate. *Frauen, Männer und die Himmelskönigin: Exegetische Studien*. Gütersloh: Gütersloher, 1995.

Junior, Nyasha. "Womanist Biblical Interpretation." Pages 37–46 in *Engaging the Bible in a Gendered World: An Introduction to Feminist Biblical Interpretation in Honor of Katharine Doob Sakenfeld*. Edited by L. Day and C. Pressler. Louisville: Westminster John Knox, 2006.

Kaiser, Barbara B. "Poet as 'Female Impersonator': The Image of Daughter Zion as Speaker in Biblical Poems of Suffering." *JR* 67 (1987): 164–82.

Kalmanofsky, Amy. "Roundtable Discussion: Feminist Biblical Studies: Outside Insiders and the Future of Feminist Biblical Studies." *JFSR* 25 (2009): 129–33.

Keefe, Alice. "Rapes of Women/Wars of Men." *Semeia* 61 (1993): 79–97.

Kelle, Brad E. "Wartime Rhetoric: Prophetic Metaphorization of Cities as Female." Pages 95–112 in Kelle and Ames, eds., *Writing and Reading War*.

Kelle, Brad E., and F. R. Ames, eds. *Writing and Reading War: Rhetoric, Gender, and Ethics in Biblical and Modern Contexts*. SBLSymS 42. Atlanta: Society of Biblical Literature, 2008.

Kelsey, Jane. "From Flagpoles to Pine Trees: Tino Rangatiratanga and Treaty Policy Today." Pages 177–201 in *Racism and Ethnic Relations in Aotearoa/New Zealand*. Edited by P. Spoonley et al. Palmerston North: Dunmore, 1996.

Kelso, Julie. *O Mother, Where Art Thou? An Irigarayan Reading of the Book of Chronicles*. London: Equinox, 2007.

Kenik, Helen A. *Design for Kingship: The Deuteronomistic Narrative Techniques in 1 Kings 3:4–15*. Chico: Scholars Press, 1983.

Keown, Gerald L., Pamela J. Scalise, and Thomas G. Smothers. *Jeremiah 26–52*. WBC 27. Nashville: Nelson, 2000.

Kessler, Martin, ed. *Reading the Book of Jeremiah: A Search for Coherence*. Winona Lake: Eisenbrauns, 2004.

Keukens, Karlheinz H. "Die rekabitischen Haussklaven in Jeremia 35." *BZ* 27 (1983): 228–35.

Kitamori, Kazoh. *Theology of the Pain of God*. 1965. Eugene: Wipf & Stock, 2005.

Kittay, Eva Feder. *Metaphor: Its Cognitive Force and Linguistic Structure*. Oxford: Clarendon, 1987.

Klawans, Jonathan. *Impurity and Sin in Ancient Judaism*. Oxford: Oxford University Press, 2000.

Knapp, Gudrun-Axeli. "Race, Class, Gender: Reclaiming Baggage in Fast Travelling Theories." *European Journal of Women's Studies* 12 (2005): 249–65.

Knights, Chris H. "Kenites = Rechabites? 1 Chronicles II 55 Reconsidered." *VT* 43 (1993): 10–18.

———. "The *History of the Rechabites*—An Initial Commentary." *JSJ* 28 (1997): 413–36.

———. "The Rechabites of Jeremiah 35: Forerunners of the Essenes?" *JSP* 10 (1992): 81–87.

———. "The Structure of Jeremiah 35." *ExpTim* 106 (1995): 142–44.

Kolodny, Annette. "Dancing Through the Minefield: Some Observations on the Theory, Practice, and Politics of a Feminist Literary Criticism." *Feminist Studies* 6 (1980): 1–25.

Kristeva, Julia. *Powers of Horror: An Essay on Abjection*. Translated by L. S. Roudiez. New York: Columbia University Press, 1982.

Kugel, James. *In the Valley of the Shadow: On the Foundations of Religious Belief*. New York: Free Press, 2011.

Kwok, Pui-lan. *Discovering the Bible in the Non-biblical World*. Maryknoll: Orbis, 1995.

———. "Making the Connections: Postcolonial Studies and Feminist Biblical Interpretation." Pages 45–63 in Sugirtharajah, ed., *The Postcolonial Biblical Reader*.

Lang, Bernhard. "Persönliche Frömmigkeit: Vier Zugänge zu einer elementaren Form des religiösen Lebens." *Hephaistos: Kritische Zeitschrift zu Theorie und Praxis der Archäologie und angrenzender Gebiete* 28 (2011): 19–36.

Lapsley, Jacqueline E. *Whispering the Word: Hearing Women's Stories in the Old Testament*. Louisville: Westminster John Knox, 2005.

Lawson, Alan. "Comparative Studies, Post-Colonial 'Settler' Cultures." *Australian and Canadian Studies* 10 (1992): 153–59.

———. "Postcolonial Theory and the 'Settler' Subject." Pages 151–64 in *Unhomely States: Theorizing English–Canadian Postcolonialism*. Edited by C. Sugars. Peterborough: Broadview, 2004.

Lee, Nancy C. *Lyrics of Lament: From Tragedy to Transformation.* Minneapolis: Fortress, 2010.

Lee, Nancy C., and Carleen Mandolfo, eds. *Lamentations in Ancient and Contemporary Contexts.* SBLSymS 43. Atlanta: Society of Biblical Literature, 2008.

Leslie, Julia. "Sati." Pages 8129–31 in *Encyclopedia of Religion*, vol. 12. 2d ed. Detroit: Macmillan Reference USA, 2005.

Leuchter, Mark. *The Polemics of Exile in Jeremiah 26–45.* Cambridge: Cambridge University Press, 2008.

Levenson, Jon D. "On the Promise to the Rechabites." *CBQ* 38 (1976): 508–14.

Lévinas, Emmanuel. *Alterity and Transcendence.* Translated by M. B. Smith. New York: Columbia University Press, 1999.

———. *Totality and Infinity: An Essay on Exteriority.* Pittsburgh: Duquesne University Press, 1969.

Lieb, Michael, Emma Mason, and Jonathan Roberts, eds. *The Oxford Handbook of the Reception History of the Bible.* Oxford: Oxford University Press, 2011.

Liew, Tat-siong Benny. "Margins and (Cutting-)Edges: On the (Il)Legitimacy and Intersections of Race, Ethnicity, and (Post)Colonialism." Pages 114–65 in Moore and Segovia, eds., *Postcolonial Biblical Criticism.*

———. ed. *Postcolonial Interventions: Essays in Honor of R. S. Sugirtharajah.* Sheffield: Sheffield Phoenix, 2009.

Løland, Hanne. *Silent or Salient Gender: The Interpretation of Gendered God-language in the Hebrew Bible, Exemplified in Isaiah 42, 46, and 49.* FAT II/32. Tübingen: Mohr Siebeck, 2008.

Lundbom, Jack R. *Jeremiah: A New Translation with Introduction and Commentary.* 2 vols. AB 21. New York: Doubleday, 1999–2004.

Lyotard, Jean-François. *The Postmodern Condition: A Report on Knowledge.* Translated by G. Bennington and B. Massumi. Minneapolis: University of Minnesota Press, 1984.

Macwilliam, Stuart. *Queer Theory and the Prophetic Marriage Metaphor in the Hebrew Bible.* BibleWorld. Sheffield: Equinox, 2011.

———. "Queering Jeremiah." *BibInt* 10 (2002): 384–404.

Maier, Christl M. *Daughter Zion, Mother Zion: Gender, Space, and the Sacred in Ancient Israel.* Minneapolis: Fortress, 2008.

———. "Himmelskönigin." *WiBiLex.* No pages. Cited 9 November 2012. Online: http://www.bibelwissenschaft.de/nc/wibilex.

———. *Jeremia als Lehrer der Tora: Soziale Gebote des Deuteronomiums in Fortschreibungen des Jeremiabuches.* FRLANT 196. Göttingen: Vandenhoeck & Ruprecht, 2002.

Masuzawa, Tomoko. *The Invention of World Religions: Or, How European Universalism Was Preserved in the Language of Pluralism.* Chicago: University of Chicago Press, 2005.

Mbuwayesango, Dora, and Susanne Scholz. "Roundtable Discussion: Feminist Biblical Studies: Dialogical Beginnings: A Conversation on the Future of Feminist Biblical Studies." *JFSR* 25 (2009): 93–103.

McClure, John S. *Other-wise Preaching: A Postmodern Ethic for Homiletics.* St. Louis: Chalice, 2001.

McKane, William. "The Construction of Chapter Jeremiah XXI." *VT* 32 (1982): 59–72.

————. *A Critical and Exegetical Commentary on Jeremiah: Volume I, I–XXV.* ICC. Edinburgh: T. & T. Clark, 1986.

————. *A Critical and Exegetical Commentary on Jeremiah: Volume II, XXVI–LII.* ICC. Edinburgh: T. & T. Clark, 1996.

————. "Jeremiah and the Rechabites." *ZAW* 100 (1988): 106–23.

————. "Worship of the Queen of Heaven (Jer 44)." Pages 318–24 in *"Wer ist wie du, Herr, unter den Göttern?" Studien zur Religionsgeschichte Israels für Otto Kaiser zum 70. Geburtstag.* Edited by I. Kottsieper et al. Göttingen: Vandenhoeck & Ruprecht, 1994.

McKenzie, N. R. *The Gael Fares Forth.* 2d ed. Wellington: Whitcombe & Tombs, 1942.

McKenzie, Steven L., and Stephen R. Haynes, eds. *To Each Its Own Meaning: An Introduction to Biblical Criticisms and Their Application.* Louisville: Westminster John Knox, 1999.

McKinlay, Judith E. "Meeting Achsah on Achsah's Land." *The Bible and Critical Theory* 5.3 (2009): 39.1–39.11.

————. "Rahab: A Hero/ine?" *BibInt* 7 (1999): 44–57.

————. *Reframing Her: Biblical Women in Postcolonial Focus.* Sheffield: Phoenix, 2004.

McNutt, Paula M. "The Kenites, the Midianites, and the Rechabites as Marginal Mediators in Ancient Israelite Tradition." *Semeia* 67 (1995): 109–32.

Migsch, Herbert. "Die vorbildlichen Rechabiter: Zur Redestruktur von Jeremia XXXV." *VT* 47 (1997): 316–28.

————. "Wohnten die Rechabiter in Jerusalem in Häusern oder in Zelten? Die Verbformationen in Jer 35,8–11." *Bib* 79 (1998): 242–57.

Miller, J. Maxwell, and John H. Hayes. *A History of Ancient Israel and Judah.* 2d ed. London: SCM, 1986.

Miller, Patrick D. Foreword to Louis Stulman, *Jeremiah.* AOTC. Nashville: Abingdon, 2005.

Moberly, Walter. "Does God Lie to His Prophets? The Story of Micaiah ben Imlah as a Test Case." *HTR* 96 (2003): 1–23.

————. *Prophecy and Discernment.* Cambridge Studies in Christian Doctrine 14. Cambridge: Cambridge University Press, 2006.

Moore, Stephen D. "A Modest Manifesto for New Testament Literary Criticism: How to Interface with a Literary Studies Field that Is Post-Literary, Post-Theoretical, and Post-Methodological." *BibInt* 15 (2007): 1–25.

————. "Questions of Biblical Ambivalence and Authority Under a Tree Outside Delhi, or, the Postcolonial and the Postmodern." Pages 79–96 in Moore and Segovia, eds., *Postcolonial Biblical Criticism.*

Moore, Stephen D., and Fernando F. Segovia, eds. *Postcolonial Biblical Criticism: Interdisciplinary Intersections.* New York: T&T Clark International, 2005.

Moughtin-Mumby, Sharon. *Sexual and Marital Metaphors in Hosea, Jeremiah, Isaiah, and Ezekiel.* Oxford: Oxford University Press, 2008.

Nelson, W. David. *Mekhilta de-Rabbi Shimon Bar Yohai.* Philadelphia: Jewish Publication Society, 2006.

Newsom, Carol A. *The Book of Job: A Contest of Moral Imaginations.* Oxford: Oxford University Press, 2003.

Newsom, Carol A., and Sharon H. Ringe, eds. *Women's Bible Commentary.* London: SPCK, 1992. Exp. ed. Louisville: Westminster John Knox, 1998.

Nikolsky, Ronit. "The *History of the Rechabites* and the Jeremiah Literature." *JSP* 13 (2002): 185–207.

Noyes, John K. "Nomadism, Nomadology, Postcolonialism: By Way of Introduction." *Interventions* 6 (2004): 159–68.

Nussbaum, Martha. *The Clash Within: Democracy, Religious Violence, and India's Future*. Cambridge: Belknap, 2007.

O'Brien, Julia M. *Challenging Prophetic Metaphor: Theology and Ideology in the Prophets*. Louisville: Westminster John Knox, 2008.

O'Connor, Kathleen M. "Jeremiah." Pages 169–77 in *The Women's Bible Commentary*. Edited by C. A. Newsom and S. H. Ringe. London: SPCK, 1992.

———. *Jeremiah: Pain and Promise*. Minneapolis: Fortress, 2011.

———. *Lamentations and the Tears of the World*. Maryknoll: Orbis, 2002.

———. "Reclaiming Jeremiah's Violence." Pages 37–49 in Franke and O'Brien, eds., *The Aesthetics of Violence in the Prophets*.

Olyan, Saul M. *Disability in the Hebrew Bible: Interpreting Mental and Physical Differences*. Cambridge: Cambridge University Press, 2008.

Page, Hugh R., Jr., ed. *The Africana Bible: Reading Israel's Scriptures from Africa and the African Diaspora*. Minneapolis: Fortress, 2010.

Patte, Daniel. "Critical Biblical Studies from a Semiotics Perspective." *Semeia* 81 (1998): 3–26.

Pohlmann, Karl-Friedrich. *Studien zum Jeremiabuch: Ein Beitrag zur Frage nach der Entstehung des Jeremiabuches*. FRLANT 118. Göttingen: Vandenhoeck & Ruprecht, 1978.

Premnath, D. N. "Margins and Mainstream: An Interview with R. S. Sugirtharajah." Pages 153–65 in *Border Crossings: Cross-Cultural Hermeneutics*. Edited by D. N. Premnath. Maryknoll: Orbis, 2007.

Prestowitz, Clyde. *Rogue Nation: American Unilateralism and the Failure of Good Intentions*. New York: Basic, 2003.

Punt, Jeremy. "Queer Theory, Postcolonial Theory, and Biblical Interpretation: A Preliminary Exploration of Some Intersections." Pages 321–41 in Hornsby and Stone, eds., *Bible Trouble*.

Rad, Gerhard von. *Old Testament Theology*. Vol. 2, *The Theology of Israel's Prophetic Traditions*. Translated by D. M. G. Stalker. New York: Harper, 1962.

Redditt, Paul. *Zechariah 9–14*. IECOT. Stuttgart: Kohlhammer, 2012.

Reed, Randall W. *A Clash of Ideologies: Marxism, Liberation Theology and Apocalypticism in New Testament Studies*. Eugene: Pickwick, 2010.

Reventlow, Henning Graf. *History of Biblical Interpretation*. Translated by L. G. Perdue. 4 vols. Atlanta: Society of Biblical Literature, 2010.

Rieger, Joerg, and Kwok Pui-lan. *Occupy Religion: Theology of the Multitude*. New York: Rowman & Littlefield, 2012.

Ritter, Christine. *Rachels Klage im antiken Judentum und frühen Christentum: Eine auslegungsgeschichtliche Studie*. AGJU 52. Leiden: Brill, 2003.

Rofé, Alexander. "The Strata of the Law About Centralization of Worship in Deuteronomy and the History of the Deuteronomic Movement." Pages 221–26 in *IOSOT Congress Volume, Uppsala 1971*. VTSup 22. Leiden: Brill, 1972.

Rom-Shiloni, Dalit. "The Prophecy for 'Everlasting Covenant' (Jeremiah xxxii 36–41): An Exilic Addition or a Deuteronomistic Redaction?" *VT* 53 (2003): 201–23.

Romero, Oscar. *The Violence of Love*. Compiled and translated by J. R. Brockman. Rifton, N.Y.: Plough Publishing, e-book publication, 2011.

Rowlett, Lori K. "Inclusion, Exclusion, and Marginality in the Book of Joshua." *JSOT* 55 (1992): 15–23.

———. *Joshua and the Rhetoric of Violence: A New Historicist Analysis*. Sheffield: Sheffield Academic, 1996.

Rudolph, Wilhelm. *Jeremia*. HAT 12. Tübingen: J. C. B. Mohr, 1947.

Russell, Letty M. *Church in the Round: Feminist Interpretation of the Church*. Louisville: Westminster John Knox, 1993.

———. *Household of Freedom: Authority in Feminist Theology*. Philadelphia: Westminster, 1987.

———. *Human Liberation in a Feminist Perspective: A Theology*. Philadelphia: Westminster, 1974.

Russell, Letty M., Kwok Pui-Lan, Ada María Isasi-Díaz, Katie Geneva Cannon, eds. *Inheriting our Mothers' Gardens: Feminist Theology in Third World Perspective*. Philadelphia: Westminster, 1988.

Sakenfeld, Katharine D. "Whose Text Is It?" *JBL* 127 (2008): 5–17.

Said, Edward W. *Culture and Imperialism*. London: Chatto & Windsor, 1993.

———. *Orientalism*. New York: Vintage, 1978.

———. "Traveling Theory." Pages 226–47 in E. W. Said, *The World, the Text, and the Critic*. Cambridge, Mass.: Harvard University Press, 1983.

Sawyer Deborah F. "Gender-Play and Sacred Text: A Scene from Jeremiah." *JSOT* 83 (1999): 99–111.

Schipper, Jeremy. *Disability and Isaiah's Suffering Servant*. Oxford: Oxford University Press, 2011.

———. *Disability Studies and the Hebrew Bible: Figuring Mephibosheth in the David Story*. LHBOTS 441. New York: T&T Clark International, 2006.

Schipper, Jeremy, and Candida Moss, eds. *Disability Studies and Biblical Literature*. New York: Palgrave Macmillan, 2011.

Schmid, Konrad. *Buchgestalten des Jeremiabuches: Untersuchungen zur Redaktions- und Rezeptionsgeschichte von Jer 30–33 im Kontext des Buches*. WMANT 72. Neukirchen–Vluyn: Neukirchener, 1996.

Schökel, Luis Alonso. *The Literary Language of the Bible: The Collected Essays of Luis Alonso Schökel*. Edited by T. Holm. Translated by H. Spencer. North Richland Hills, Tex.: D&F Scott, 2001.

Scholz, Susanne. *Introducing the Women's Hebrew Bible*. Introductions in Feminist Theology 13. New York: T&T Clark International, 2007.

Schottroff, Luise, Silvia Schroer, and Marie-Theres Wacker. *Feministische Exegese: Forschungserträge zur Bibel aus der Perspektive von Frauen*. Darmstadt: Wissenschaftliche Buchgesellschaft, 1995. English version: *Feminist Interpretation: The Bible in Women's Perspective*. Translated by M. and B. Rumscheidt. Minneapolis: Fortress, 1998.

Schottroff, Luise, and Marie-Theres Wacker, eds. *Kompendium Feministische Bibelauslegung*. 2d ed. Gütersloh: Gütersloher, 1999. English version: *Feminist Biblical Interpretation: A Compendium of Critical Commentary on the Books of the Bible and Related Literature*. Grand Rapids: Eerdmans, 2012.

Schüssler Fiorenza, Elisabeth. *Bread Not Stone: The Challenge of Feminist Biblical Interpretation*. Boston: Beacon, 1995. Originally published 1985.

————. *But She Said: Feminist Practices of Biblical Interpretation*. Boston: Beacon, 1992.

————. *In Memory of Her: A Feminist Theological Reconstruction of Christian Origins*. New York: Crossroad, 1983.

————. *Wisdom Ways: Introducing Feminist Biblical Interpretation*. Maryknoll: Orbis Books, 2001.

Schweickart, Patrocinio P. "Reading Ourselves: Toward a Feminist Theory of Reading." Pages 31–62 in *Gender and Reading: Essays on Readers, Texts and Contexts*. Edited by E. A. Flynn and P. P. Schweickart. Baltimore: John Hopkins University Press, 1986.

Sebald, Winfried G. *On the Natural History of Destruction*. New York: Random House, 2003.

Segovia, Fernando F. " 'And They Began to Speak in Other Tongues': Competing Modes of Discourse in Contemporary Biblical Criticism." Pages 1–32 in *Reading from This Place*, vol. 1. Edited by F. F. Segovia and M. A. Tolbert. Minneapolis: Fortress, 1995.

————. "Biblical Criticism and Postcolonial Studies: Toward a Postcolonial Optic." Pages 33–44 in Sugirtharajah, ed., *The Postcolonial Biblical Reader*.

————. "Mapping the Postcolonial Optic in Biblical Criticism: Meaning and Scope." Pages 23–78 in Moore and Segovia, eds., *Postcolonial Biblical Criticism*.

Segura, Denise A., and Patricia Zavella. "Gender in the Borderlands." Pages 75–86 in Taylor, Whittier, and Rupp, eds., *Feminist Frontiers*.

Selms, Adrianus van. "The Name Nebuchadnezzar." Pages 223–29 in *Travels in the World of the Old Testament*. Edited by M. S. H. G. Heerma van Voss et al. Assen: Van Gorcum, 1974.

Setel, T. Drorah. "Poetic Pornography: Female Sexual Imagery in Hosea." Pages 86–95 in *Feminist Biblical Interpretation*. Edited by L. M. Russell. Philadelphia: Westminster, 1985.

Sharp, Carolyn J. "Hewn By the Prophet: An Analysis of Violence and Sexual Transgression in Hosea with Reference to the Homiletical Aesthetic of Jeremiah Wright." Pages 50–71 in Franke and O'Brien, eds., *The Aesthetics of Violence in the Prophets*.

————. *Irony and Meaning in the Hebrew Bible*. Bloomington: Indiana University Press, 2009.

————. "Jeremiah in the Land of Aporia: Reconfiguring Redaction Criticism as Witness to Foreignness." Pages 35–46 in Diamond and Stulman, eds., *Jeremiah (Dis)Placed*.

————. *Prophecy and Ideology in Jeremiah: Struggles for Authority in the Deutero-Jeremianic Prose*. London: T. & T. Clark, 2003.

————. Review of Louis Stulman, *Jeremiah*. *RBL* (2005). No pages. Online: http://www.bookreviews.org.

Shead, Andrew G. *The Open Book and the Sealed Book: Jeremiah 32 in Its Hebrew and Greek Recensions*. JSOTSup 347. Sheffield: Sheffield Academic, 2002.

Shectman, Sarah. *Women in the Pentateuch: A Feminist and Source-Critical Analysis*. Sheffield: Sheffield Phoenix, 2009.

Sherman, Philipp M. Review of Athalya Brenner, Archie Chi Chung Lee, and Gale A. Yee, eds., *Genesis*. *RBL* (2011). No pages. Online: http://www.bookreviews.org.

Sherwood, Yvonne M. "Prophetic Scatology: Prophecy and the Art of Sensation." *Semeia* 82 (2000): 183–224.

Shields, Mary E. "Circumcision of the Prostitute: Gender, Sexuality, and the Call to Repentance in Jeremiah 3:1–4:4." Pages 121–36 in *Prophets and Daniel.* Edited by A. Brenner. FCB 2.8. Sheffield: Sheffield Academic, 2001.

———. *Circumscribing the Prostitute: The Rhetorics of Intertextuality, Metaphor, and Gender in Jeremiah 3.1–4.4.* JSOTSup 387. New York: T&T Clark International, 2004.

———. "Impasse or Opportunity or…? Women Reading Jeremiah Reading Women." Pages 290–302 in Diamond and Stulman, eds., *Jeremiah (Dis)Placed.*

Smith, Linda T. *Decolonizing Methodologies: Research and Indigenous Peoples.* London: Zed. Dunedin: University of Otago Press, 1999.

Smith-Christopher, Daniel L. *A Biblical Theology of Exile.* OBT. Minneapolis: Fortress, 2002.

Sobrino, Jon. *No Salvation Outside the Poor: Prophetic-Utopian Essays.* Maryknoll: Orbis, 2008.

Spivak, Gayatri Chakravorty. "Can the Subaltern Speak?" Pages 271–313 in *Marxism and the Interpretation of Culture.* Edited by C. Nelson and L. Grossberg. Urbana: University of Illinois Press, 1988.

———. *The Spivak-Reader: Selected Works of Gayatri Chakravorty Spivak.* Edited by D. Landry and G. MacLean. New York: Routledge, 1996.

Stafford, Jane, and Mark Williams. *Maoriland: New Zealand Literature 1872–1914.* Wellington: Victoria University Press, 2006.

Stephan, Inge. "Gender, Geschlecht und Theorie." Pages 52–90 in *Gender Studien: Eine Einführung.* Edited by C. von Braun and I. Stephan. 2d ed. Stuttgart: Metzler, 2006.

Stipp, Hermann-Josef. *Das masoretische und alexandrinische Sondergut des Jeremiabuches.* OBO 136. Freiburg: Universitätsverlag. Göttingen: Vandenhoeck & Ruprecht, 1994.

———. *Deuterjeremianische Konkordanz.* ATSAT 63. St. Otilien: Eos, 1998.

———. *Jeremia im Parteienstreit: Studien zur Textentwicklung von Jer 26, 36–43 und 45 als Beitrag zur Geschichte Jeremias, seines Buches und judäischer Parteien im 6. Jahrhundert.* BBB 82. Frankfurt a. M.: Anton Hain, 1992.

Stone, Ken. "Lovers and Raisin Cakes: Food, Sex and Divine Insecurity in Hosea." Pages 116–39 in *Queer Commentary and the Hebrew Bible.* Edited by K. Stone. London: Sheffield Academic, 2001.

———. ed. *Queer Commentary and the Hebrew Bible.* Sheffield: Sheffield Academic, 2001.

———. "Queer Reading Between Bible and Film: *Paris is Burning* and the 'Legendary Houses' of David and Saul." Pages 75–98 in Hornsby and Stone, eds., *Bible Trouble.*

———. *Sex, Honor, and Power in the Deuteronomistic History.* Sheffield: Sheffield Academic, 1996.

Stryker, Susan. "Transgender Feminism: Queering the Woman Question." Pages 63–69 in Taylor et al., eds., *Feminist Frontiers.*

Stulman, Louis. "Conflicting Paths of Hope in Jeremiah." Pages 43–57 in *Shaking Heaven and Earth: Essays in Honor of Walter Brueggemann and Charles B. Cousar.* Edited by C. R. Yoder et al. Louisville: Westminster John Knox, 2005.

————. "Here Comes the Reader." Pages 99–103 in Diamond and Stulman, eds., *Jeremiah (Dis)Placed.*

————. *Jeremiah.* AOTC. Nashville: Abingdon, 2005.

————. *Order Amid Chaos: Jeremiah as Symbolic Tapestry.* Sheffield: Sheffield Academic, 1998.

————. "The Prose Sermons as Hermeneutical Guide to Jeremiah 1–25: The Deconstruction of Judah's Symbolic World." Pages 34–63 in Diamond et al., *Troubling Jeremiah.*

Stulman, Louis, and Hyun Chul Paul Kim. *You Are My People: An Introduction to Prophetic Literature.* Nashville: Abingdon, 2010.

Sugirtharajah, R. S. *The Bible and the Third World: Precolonial, Colonial and Postcolonial Configurations.* Cambridge: Cambridge University Press, 2001.

————. *The Bible as Empire: Postcolonial Explorations.* Cambridge: Cambridge University Press, 2005.

————. "Decolonizing Biblical Narratives" (review of Judith E. McKinlay, *Reframing Her: Biblical Women in Postcolonial Focus*). *ExpTim* 118 (2007): 201.

————. *Postcolonial Criticism and Biblical Interpretation.* Oxford: Oxford University Press, 2001.

————. ed. *The Postcolonial Biblical Reader.* Oxford: Blackwell, 2006.

————. "A Postcolonial Exploration of Collusion and Construction in Biblical Interpretation." Pages 91–116 in *The Postcolonial Bible.* Edited by R. S. Sugirtharajah. Sheffield: Sheffield Academic, 1998.

Sweeney, Marvin. "The Truth in True and False Prophecy." Pages 9–26 in *Truth: Interdisciplinary Dialogues in a Pluralist Age.* Edited by C. Helmer and K. de Troyer. Studies in Philosophical Theology 22. Leuven: Peeters, 2003.

Tannenhouse, Leonard. *The Importance of Feeling English: American Literature and the British Diaspora, 1750–1850.* Princeton: Princeton University Press, 2007.

Taylor, Verta, Nancy Whittier, and Leila J. Rupp, eds. *Feminist Frontiers.* 9th ed. New York: McGraw-Hill, 2012.

Thiel, Winfried. *Die deuteronomistische Redaktion von Jeremia 1–25.* WMANT 41. Neukirchen–Vluyn: Neukirchener, 1973.

————. *Die deuteronomistische Redaktion von Jeremia 26–45.* WMANT 52. Neukirchen–Vluyn: Neukirchener, 1981.

Thompson, John A. *The Book of Jeremiah.* NICOT. Grand Rapids: Eerdmans, 1980.

Ticciati, Susannah. *Job and the Disruption of Identity: Reading beyond Barth.* New York: T&T Clark International, 2005.

Todorov, Tzvetan. *On Human Diversity: Nationalism, Racism, and Exoticism in French Thought.* Translated by C. Porter. Cambridge, Mass.: Harvard University Press, 1993.

Toorn, Karel van der. "Ritual Resistance and Self-Assertion: The Rechabites in Early Israelite Religion." Pages 229–59 in *Pluralism and Identity: Studies in Ritual Behaviour.* Edited by J. Platvoet and K. van der Toorn. Leiden: Brill, 1995.

————. *Scribal Culture and the Making of the Hebrew Bible.* Cambridge, Mass.: Harvard University Press, 2007.

Trible, Phyllis. *Texts of Terror: Literary-Feminist Readings of Biblical Narratives.* Philadelphia: Fortress, 1984.

Wacker, Marie-Theres. "Roundtable Discussion: Feminist Biblical Studies: Challenges and Opportunities in Feminist Theology and Biblical Studies in Europe." *JFSR* 25 (2009): 117–21.

Wanke, Gunther. *Jeremia. Teilband 1: Jeremia 1,1–25,14.* ZBKAT 20.1. Zurich: Theologischer Verlag, 1995.

———. *Jeremia. Teilband 2: Jeremia 25,15–52,34.* ZBKAT 20.2. Zurich: Theologischer Verlag, 2003.

Warner, Michael. "What's Colonial About Colonial America?" Pages 49–71 in *Possible Pasts: Becoming Colonial in Early America.* Edited by R. Blair St. George. Ithaca: Cornell University Press, 2000.

Watts, Edward. "Settler Postcolonialism as a Reading Strategy." *American Literary History* 22 (2010): 459–70.

Weed, Elizabeth, ed. *Coming to Terms: Feminism/Theory/Politics.* New York: Routledge, 1989.

Weinfeld, Moshe. *Deuteronomy and the Deuteronomic School.* Oxford: Clarendon, 1972.

Weippert, Helga. *Die Prosareden des Jeremiabuches.* BZAW 132. Berlin: de Gruyter, 1973.

Weiser, Artur. *Das Buch des Propheten Jeremia Kapitel 1–25,14.* 8th ed. ATD 20. Göttingen: Vandenhoeck & Ruprecht, 1981.

Wellhausen, Julius. *Prolegomena to the History of Ancient Israel.* New York: Meridian, 1957.

West, Gerald O., ed. *Reading Other-Wise: Socially Engaged Biblical Scholars Reading with Their Local Communities.* Atlanta: Society of Biblical Literature, 2007.

West, Gerald O., and Musa W. Dube, eds. *The Bible in Africa: Transactions, Trajectories, and Trends.* Boston: Brill, 2000.

Williams, Linda. "Why I Did Not Want to Write This Essay." *Signs* 30 (2004): 1264–71.

Wyss, Stephan. *Fluchen: Ohnmächtige und mächtige Rede der Ohnmacht: Ein philosophisch-theologischer Essay zu einer Blütenlese.* Fribourg: Exodus, 1984.

Yee, Gale A. "By the Hand of a Woman: The Metaphor of the Woman Warrior in Judges 4." *Semeia* 61 (1993): 99–132.

———. *Poor Banished Children of Eve: Woman as Evil in the Hebrew Bible.* Minneapolis: Augsburg Fortress, 2003.

Ziegler, Joseph, ed. *Ieremias, Baruch, Threni, Epistula Ieremiae.* 2d ed. Septuaginta: Vetus Testamentum Graecum 15. Göttingen: Vandenhoeck & Ruprecht, 1976.

Zuckerman, Phil. *Society Without God.* New York: New York University Press, 2008.

INDICES

INDEX OF REFERENCES

INDEX OF AUTHORS

CPSIA information can be obtained
at www.ICGtesting.com
Printed in the USA
LVOW04s2012041016
507380LV00009B/60/P